YOGA-TARAṄGIṆĪ

Also by Swami Veda Bharti

Yoga Sutras of Patanjali
with the Exposition of Vyasa
(Vol. II: Sadhana-Pada)
Translation & Commentary
ISBN : 978-81-208-2069-2

YOGA-TAṚAṄGIṆĪ

A Rare Commentary on *Gorakṣa-śataka*

Sanskrit Text with Romanized Version

Exhaustive Introduction and English Translation of the Sanskrit Text and the Commentary by

JAN K. BRZEZINSKI
(Jagadananda Das)

Inspired by

SWAMI VEDA BHARATI

HIMALAYAN YOGA PUBLICATIONS TRUST
RISHIKESH • UTTARAKHAND (INDIA)
and
MOTILAL BANARSIDASS PUBLISHERS
PRIVATE LIMITED • DELHI (INDIA)

First Edition: Delhi, 2015

ISBN: 978-81-208-3989-2

Published in arrangement with
Himalayan Yoga Publications Trust
Swami Rama Sadhaka Grama
Virpur Khurd, Virbhadra Road, Rishikesh-249203, India
Tel. : +91-135-2453030
E-mail : info@yogapublications.org
Website : www.yogapublications.org

also available at

MOTILAL BANARSIDASS

41 U.A. Bungalow Road, Jawahar Nagar, Delhi 110 007
8 Mahalaxmi Chamber, 22 BD Road, Mumbai 400 026
203 Royapettah High Road, Mylapore, Chennai 600 004
236, 9th Main III Block, Jayanagar, Bengaluru 560 011
8 Camac Street, Kolkata 700 017
Ashok Rajpath, Patna 800 004
Chowk, Varanasi 221 001

MLBD Catalogue-in-Publication Data
Yoga Taraṅgiṇī : A Rare Commantory on *Gorakṣa-śataka*
by Jan K Brzezinski
Includes Introduction, Translation, Sanskrit Text,
Sanskrit Commentary, Bibliography and Index
ISBN : 978-81-208-3989-2
I. Yoga Taraṅgiṇī II. Commentary III. Gorakṣa Śataka IV. Text
V. Brzezinski, Jan K. VI Swami Veda Bharti

Printed in India
by Avantika Printers Private Limited
New Delhi–110065 and published by JP Jain
for Motilal Banarsidass Publishers Private Limited,
41 U.A. Bungalow Road, Jawahar Nagar, Delhi-110007

Table of Contents

PREFACE

गुरोर्योगे बुध्न्यस्याहेः खे सरितं गाधामहे।
स्पन्दयन्तीं तडिन्मेरुं चित्सुतारां तरङ्गिणीम्।।

guror yoge budhnyasyāheḥ khe saritaṁ gādhāmahe
spandayantīṁ taḍin-meruṁ cit-sutārāṁ taraṅgiṇīm

Long before modern scholars started their tremendous tasks of exploring Sanskrit manuscripts, the traditional vidvāns, āchāryas and yogis have known of many texts and manuscripts in their respective fields. They have then passed on that knowledge orally in teaching their disciples. It is thus that my Gurudeva, the late Swami Rama of the Himalayas spoke to us disciples many times about an important text named *Yoga-taraṅgiṇī* (YT). He did not give us an author's name but charged me to edit and publish the text.

It is thus that I began search for this elusive text. I first found an incomplete copy in the then Darbar library (now National Library) of Kathmandu, Nepal. Often the yoga text YT was confused with another ayurveda text of the same name.

Later other more complete manuscripts of this YT were found through the kind efforts of manuscriptologist Dr. Bibekanand Banerjee of Kolkatta who, in his spare time did the preliminary editing.

The work was passed on to my friend Dr. Jan Brzezinski (Jagadananda Das) who spent much diligent effort in meticulous editing and translating it.

It turned out that YT is a commentary on the well known *Gorakṣa-śataka* (GS). The author of the commentary is not known. Maybe some scholar with keen insight will find some internal evidence in the text by which the time period of the work may be approximated. This may be possible by looking closely at the texts quoted in YT. It is obvious that GS itself is some time after *Bhagavad-gītā* portion of *Mahābhārata* as the verse 2.91 is identical to BhG 6.17.

Dr. Brzezinski made a study of the Gorakṣa and related traditions of yoga practices and then wrote his erudite introduction. It is primarily the fruit of his labours that the text is now in the reader's hands.

The text corroborates some of the subtle practices of yoga that were passed on to me by my Guru for practicing. Some parts however can only be understood if explained by some other practicing master of these traditions; mere lexical effort and guesswork will not do. Like the second part of *Haṭha-yoga-pradīpikā*, many verses of YT also seem to be in what the yogis call *sandhā-bhāṣā* or *sandhyā-bhāṣā* (*sandhāya bhāṣyate*), that which is spoken in a concealed manner. The concealed meaning is explained to select disciples. YT suggests this in numerous places, for example, first time in the text, on verse 1.7, YT says

> ... अन्येषां यस्य यस्य यदा यदा अनुष्ठेयत्वं तस्य तस्य तदा तदा गुरुमुखावगम्यत्वस्य चावश्यकतया...

> ... *anyeṣāṁ yasya yasya yadā yadā anuṣṭheyatvam, tasya tasya tadā tadā guru-mukhāvagamyatvasya cāvaśyaktayā*...

> ...Other [*aṅgas* are included] because of the necessity [that] given [practices] may be undertaken respectively as to when they are to be undertaken only after being learnt from the mouth of a guru...

Not only some of these yoga texts use "concealed" language but they also frequently employ existing terminologies of unrelated fields giving them the meaning related to tantric yoga practices. For example, YT quotes on 1.100 Gobhila's *Gṛhya-sūtra* (GGS) an ancient Vedic text of rites for householders where in the original GGS the reading is slightly different from the YT's rendering but essentially the same:

यः परो विप्रकर्षः सूर्याचन्द्रमसोः सा पौर्णमासी
यः परः सन्निकर्षः साऽमावास्या।

yaḥ paro vi-prakarṣaḥ sūryā-candramasoḥ sā paurṇamāsī
yaḥ paraḥ sannikarṣaḥ sā'māvāsyā

The farthest distance between the sun and the moon, that is Full Moon (*paurṇamāsī*);
The closest contact [between the two], that is No-Moon (*amāvāsyā*).

Gobhila's *Gṛhya-sūtra* 1.7

YT follows the Tantric yoga tradition wherein the sun and the moon are imageries internal to a person. In the same tradition the distance or contact between these points of the imagery is referred to respectively as Full Moon and No-Moon nights. YT uses a text on household rituals to define these two terms but in the sense of sun and moon of the internal imagery to which the ritual text makes no reference.

Similarly the term *khecarī* is (e.g. 1.64ff.) used to mean the well known *haṭha-yoga* practice but soon the subject of *khecarī* leads on to the imagery of sun and the moon, the yellowish white and red points (*bindu*) and so forth, concluding that it is called *khecarī*

चित्तं चरति खे यस्मात्

cittaṁ carati khe yasmāt
because the mind moves into [transcendental] space.
GS 1.67

Unless one has undertaken the practices relating to this sun and moon imagery or to concentration on the yellowish white or red points (*bindu*) of light, and experienced these, what is meant by these terms will not become real.

I bow to my Gurudeva for having given me the experience of some of these levels but not many other levels of reality referred to in the texts.

I offer this work to the feet of my Gurudeva as I am sure, wherever he is, he will be pleased to see that his disciple has even belatedly fulfilled one of his wishes.

(Mahamandaleshwar) Swami Veda Bharati
Swami Rama Sadhaka Grama, Rishikesh
ahymsin@gmail.com

INTRODUCTION

vande guroḥ śrī-caraṇāravindam

This book, which is being published under the name *Gorakṣa-śataka*, is a small work of 200 verses written in Sanskrit. It is one of the earliest texts, if not the earliest, from the Nātha-yoga tradition, through which the techniques of *haṭha-yoga* were developed. It thus sheds a light on *haṭha-yoga*'s most basic theories and practices. Its authorship is attributed to the legendary yogi, Gorakṣanātha. Although this book has been translated into English several times, we here have the honor of presenting it along with the text and translation of the heretofore unpublished anonymous Sanskrit commentary, *Yoga-taraṅgiṇī*.

Gorakṣanātha, who lived a more than a millennium ago, is one of the early founders of a particular branch of yoga called *haṭha-yoga*, "the yoga of force." The miraculous powers and adventures of this great yogi and his guru Matsyendranātha are the stuff of legend, which has kept the mythology of yogic siddhis alive throughout the centuries even to the present day.

Following the time of Gorakṣanātha, *haṭha-yoga* developed its spectrum of practices considerably, branching off in numerous directions. Some aspects of this tradition have become popular around the world, particularly those practices related to the realm of physical culture, i.e., dealing with physical postures or *āsanas*. Naturally, those who develop an attraction to that aspect of *haṭha-yoga* eventually learn of its other *aṅgas* and the benefits that accrue from them, which are considerably more than physical health.

Those whose curiosity has developed into more subtle realms would do well to examine the *Gorakṣa-śataka* and attempt to incorporate some of its counsel into their own practice.

Even before the explosion of international communications in the past 200 years, the influence of the Nāthas had already spread throughout the subcontinent, including the wider India that includes Nepal and Tibet and beyond. Although currently the Nātha *sampradāya* as a living and active tradition seems to be much smaller and less influential that it had been in the past, and though it has had little to do with current interest in *haṭha-yoga*, it also seems to be experiencing something of a revival as a positive consequence of globalization.

Haṭha-yoga itself is a development in the *tantra/yoga* tradition. It follows the same inspiration, i.e., that the microcosmic body is itself a universe that contains all that one needs for spiritual culture. The genius of *haṭha-yoga* is that one need never look outside the body itself for inspiration, satisfaction and pleasure, or final beatitude. Indeed, by mastering certain physical practices alone, the *haṭha-yogī* can set into motion energies that are latent in the body and raise them to the cranium where they effectuate the union of soul and Supersoul that is the ultimate meaning of *yoga*. They can thus dispense with much of the external ritual and accoutrements that tend to play an important role in Tantra.

The *Gorakṣa-śataka*, being an early text from this tradition to which later authors made further additions and emendations, has attracted scholarly attention. Concerted attempts have been made to establish its original text, as there are several books that are closely connected, both by name or content, and which yet differ considerably from each other.

Variants of this same work go under a number of other names such as *Gorakṣa-paddhati*, *Gorakṣa-saṁhitā*, *Mukti-sopāna* and *Viveka-mārtaṇḍa* [VM]. Which of these names is original to the work is a subject of debate.

The name *Mukti-sopāna* appears in verses 1.5 and again at 2.98. In the latter verse, the words *mukti-sopāna-saṁjñakam* appear to indicate that this is the name of the book. Our text explicitly names the book *Gorakṣa-śatakaṁ* in 1.4, but some editions there have *Gorakṣa-saṁhitā* instead. The name *Viveka-mārtaṇḍa* is mentioned here and there in external sources, but this name is not found in the book anywhere.

In particular, the same book under the name *Gorakṣa-paddhati* [GP], having been translated into Hindi and published several times from the Venkateshwar Press in Mumbai, has become the dominant version of the text and, indeed, most resembles the *Gorakṣa-śataka* used by our *Yoga-taraṅgiṇī* [YT] author, even though there are a number differences in verse order and reading.

Perhaps the most immediate problem surrounding the name *Gorakṣa-śataka* is the word *śataka* itself. A *śataka* means a "century" or work of a hundred verses, but in this particular version it contains 202 verses, usually divided into two *śatakas.*[1] This seems to indicate that it is not the original text, but has expanded through interpolation and so on from its original hundred verses into a more complete exposition of the *haṭha-yoga* system.

Briggs in his groundbreaking work *Goraksha and the Kanphat Yogis* (1933) thus translated the first hundred verses of the abovementioned *Gorakṣa-paddhati* and called it *Gorakṣa-śataka*, evidently assuming that these verses represented the integral and original text. Of course, since a great portion of the subject matter promised in the early verses of the book does not materialize until the second *śataka*, his solution must be judged unlikely.

---

[1] One verse is repeated (1.29, 2.15) and two other verses are said by the commentator to be interpolated (2.77-78), which could account for the inexact number. Not that this should be a great difficulty, as there are numerous *śatakas* in Sanskrit literature that exceed that number. There is furthermore a tradition in some genres to exclude the *phala-śruti* verse from the official count.

More recently, researchers at the Lonavla Yoga Institute in Pune claimed, after studying a large number of manuscripts, to have solved the mystery of the original *śataka*, and in 1987 published a version of exactly 100 verses that they said was the original work.

We were quite fortunate that while our work was going on we had a visit from Prof. Mark Singleton, who had synchronistically come to India to do some research on manuscripts of the *Viveka-mārtaṇḍa* [VM]. He put me in touch with Prof. James Mallinson, who has also done a great deal of research into early *haṭha-yoga* texts and come up with a conclusion quite different from that of the Lonavla researchers.

Mallinson's position is based primarily on evidence of the earliest manuscript of the text which is named *Viveka-mārtaṇḍa*. The text of this VM, though missing verses at the beginning and end, matches that of our GŚ, while dispensing with any pretense of having a hundred verses or multiple thereof.[1] In Mallinson's estimation, this work was expanded and then distributed under variants of the name *Gorakṣa-śataka*. Later, to compensate for the excess number of verses, abbreviated or *précis* versions such as that of the Lonavla edition were made.

Mallinson's further research into the original GŚ [GŚo] has resulted in uncovering a completely different work from this *Viveka-mārtaṇḍa* group of texts, and bears a greater similarity to the *Yoga-kuṇḍalī Upaniśad*, with which it has some eighty of its hundred verses in common. As the content of the two *Gorakṣa-śatakas* diverges considerably – only one verse (GŚ 1.55, GŚo 3), an oft-cited couplet about controlled diet, being common to both – we have not given too much attention to this GŚo here.

Gorakṣanātha is said to be the author of a number of other works on *haṭha-yoga*, testifying to his prestigious status as a

---

[1] VM has a total of 173 verses. The manuscript in question from the Central Library, Baroda Acc. No. 4110, is dated 1534 Saṁ = 1478 CE, and although credited to Gorakṣanātha appears to be earlier than any extant MS of *Gorakṣa-śataka*.

founder of the school. The most important of these are the *Yoga-bīja*, which is fully included in the *Yoga-śikhopaniṣad*, and the *Siddha-siddhānta-paddhati*, a somewhat later and quite different work.[1] *Yoga-bīja* appears to be from a parallel early school of *haṭha-yoga*, differing in various ways from our GŚ while showing a closer relation to the GŚo. It would appear that the later, more encyclopedic works on *haṭha*, in particular *Haṭha-yoga-pradīpikā* [HYP] of Svātmārāma, were composed in an attempt to harmonize these schools, along with others that existed during his time.

The popularity and influence of our GŚ or VM can be seen in the number of verses drawn from it that found their way into the Yoga Upanisads, particularly the *Yoga-bindu* and *Yoga-cuḍāmaṇi*, as well as in the *Haṭha-yoga-pradīpikā* in both its four-chapter and expanded ten-chapter versions (published simply as *Haṭha-pradīpikā* [HP]). We have attempted to give a concordance of the verses from these various sources in an appendix at the end of this book. Later *haṭha-yoga* compendia such as *Haṭha-tattva-kaumudī* and *Haṭha-ratnāvalī* have also referred to this work (GŚ) and borrowed from it extensively.

As is to be expected, variant readings in these different versions are extensive, but since our primary objective here in this edition has been to establish the correct reading of the *Yoga-taraṅgiṇī* and to translate it along with the original verses, we have restricted ourselves to commenting on the reading of the original text only where it was felt that to do so was necessary to explain a confused interpretation.

Yoga-taraṅgiṇī

When I first began teaching Sanskrit at Swami Rama Sadhaka Grama in 2007, I learned from Swami Veda Bharati of his attempts to collect a commentary on the *Gorakṣa-śataka* called *Yoga-*

[1] The latter is available in translation.

taraṅgiṇī. His guru, Swami Rama, had praised this commentary and instructed him that if he ever could manage to publish it, he would be most appreciative. Swami Veda had been working on this *guru-sevā* project for some time and had finally managed to gather four manuscripts from various libraries around the subcontinent—Benares, Nepal, Mysore and Bengal.[1]

Of these four, the first (our "A" manuscript) was from Benares. In actual fact this was a fairly recent (1930) Devanagari copy of a Telugu script held in the Adyar library in Chennai. It was the only one of our four MSS that was complete, covering the full 202 verses.

I typed out this Benares manuscript when it first was received in the ashram, but found it full of obvious mistakes, many of which were difficult to decipher or correct on a quick reading. Through the work in particular of Dr. Bibekanand Banerjee of the Asiatic Society of Bengal, this manuscript was collated with the B and C MSS and variant readings noted. These three manuscripts only covered the first *śataka*.

The fourth MS (D), which was obtained from the Nepali government collection through the efforts of Swami Rishikumar Panchsheel of Hansada Ashram (Benapa, Nepal), despite missing several pages and being riddled with errors, happily provided alternate readings for the second *śataka*, without which it would have been extremely difficult to establish a correct text for that part of the book.

The C and D manuscripts were both a terrible mess and on their own would have been almost completely useless, but were often correct in exactly those places where our primary MS text was confusing. Even where not correct, they were mistaken in ways that complemented A and made it possible to extract a decent reading.

One of the first things I noticed on examining these MSS was that additions and emendations had clearly been made by later

[1] For a full description of the manuscripts used, see the bibliography.

scribes. In most cases, the additions are minor and supplementary in nature, but in some cases show disagreement. One such example comes at verse 1.96, which is introduced as a description of *prāṇāyāma* in 22 verses in the A and C MSS. But this does not concur with the summary of contents found in the *Yoga-taraṅgiṇī*'s colophon. As observed in the notes there, this seems to be a case of the interpolator's not properly understanding the distinction being made between *prāṇāyāma* proper and *nāḍi-śodhana*.

It quickly became apparent that any hope of uncovering an Ur-text for the YT would not be tenable with the limited materials at hand. Because of the small number of manuscript resources, little could be done in the way of a *stemma codicum*. If any conclusion at all can be drawn, for what it is worth, it is that of those MSS we have in our possession, the "C" MS is likely the closest to the earliest version of the commentary.

After abandoning efforts at finding an Ur-text, I chose to include most of the later interpolations in our text in the interest of producing the most comprehensive commentary without too much care for establishing the intent of the original author. I determined that the best way forward was to simply come up with a text that scanned, i.e., yielded syntactically comprehensible language, and added the most insight into the original GŚ. Thus each individual variant reading has been adjudged for that which best fits this description.

The Mumbai *Gorakṣa-paddhati* [GP] mentioned above, which the Lonavla editors call the "Vulgate" edition, made use of the *Yoga-taraṅginī* along with another commentary, *Bāla-prabodhinī*, in producing its Hindi translation. The Lonavla GŚ [L] editors also refer to both these commentaries. Unfortunately, we did not have access to *Bāla-prabodhinī*, but the information available in the abovementioned sources leads us to suspect that it has considerable common ground with YT. No doubt the addition of *Bāla-prabodhinī* would have enriched this work further and made it more useful for our readers, but that work will unfortunately have to await another day.

As already intimated above, another major problem in editing and translating the text and commentary comes from clear inadequacies in the GŚ text that the YT commentator was using. It is apparent from the numerous other works that have made use of GŚ through quoting from it that a kaleidoscope of variant readings can be collected, not simply from the VM or GŚ, but also from those that directly quote or copy these sources, such as *Dhyāna-bindu Upaniṣad* [DBU], *Yoga-cūḍāmaṇi Upaniṣad* [YCU], *Haṭha-yoga-pradīpikā* [HYP] and its expanded, ten-chapter version, *Haṭha-pradīpikā* [HP]. I have refrained from giving all these alternative readings as our primary consideration was the provision of a clear text for the *Yoga-taraṅgiṇī* rather than *Gorakṣa-śataka*. Nevertheless, in the translation I have occasionally referred to the commentaries of these other works where they add contradictory or complementary information that was deemed useful.

Source texts referenced in the commentary

We know absolutely nothing about our commentator, nor can we make anything more that the most general conclusions about his time or place. The only indicators that we can use to localize him are the texts he quotes here and there in *Yoga-taraṅgiṇī*. Here is a list of the works to which he has referred:

Works on yoga

- *Yoga-sūtra* of Patañjali. Quoted directly or paraphrased at 1.7 and 1.82, 1.89, in all cases for definitions of the *yogāṅgas* and not for any philosophical propositions. This will be discussed below in the discussion of the contents of *Gorakṣa-śataka*.
- *Nitya-nātha-paddhati* [NNP]: Quoted once at 1.13. This text is not available to our knowledge. It clearly covers the same

territory as texts like *Siddha-siddhānta-paddhati* [SSP] and *Siddha-siddhānta-saṅgraha* [SSS]. The YT seems to assume that this work, also being ascribed to the Nātha tradition (SSP is usually attributed to Gorakhnath himself) is in agreement with GŚ, which is not the case. The fragments that our author cites from NNP also reveal some minor differences between these three *paddhati* texts.

- In the same part of YT (1.15-16), there is also an extended description of the *cakras*, the source of which cannot be established. To a great extent, it conforms with that of *Ṣaṭ-cakra-nirūpaṇa* [ṢCN], probably the most authoritative Tāntrika text on the subject, but since there are some minor differences we cannot state with certainty that this text was the one he used.

- *Yoga-cintāmaṇi:* Quoted three times, at 1.42 for a definition of *haṭha-yoga*, at 1.54 for a definition of celibacy, and at 1.57 for symptoms of the awakened *kuṇḍalinī*. We were unable to obtain copies of this or the following (*Yoga-sāra*).

- *Yoga-sāra* is the most cited book in YT, with nine quotes, mostly clarifying technical details.

- *Yogi-yājñavalkya* is only cited for the ten *yamas* and ten *niyamas* at 1.7, making up for their absence from the GŚ itself.

- *Mānasollāsa*: The work of this name is a commentary on the *Dakśiṇā-mūrti-stotra* attributed to Śaṅkarācārya, written by Sureśvarācārya, one of the four direct disciples of the founder of the Advaita school. It is quoted at 1.11, 1.20, and 1.30, primarily for clarification of anatomical details. Interestingly, I have found no reference to *Mānasollāsa* in other commentaries to yoga texts, such as Brahmānanda's *Jyotsnā* to *Haṭha-yoga-pradīpikā*.

Epics and Purāṇas

- GŚ 2.91 is a direct quote of Gītā 6.17, and another verse (2.24) paraphrases Gītā 2.58, but our commentator does not draw attention to the Gītā at all.
- *Nāradīya-purāṇa,* at 1.96. This single quote, which we could not find in our edition of the *purāṇa*, is on a relatively minor point describing the seat on which a yogi should engage in *prāṇāyāma* practice.
- *Bhāgavata-purāṇa* 3.25.15 (at 1.14). This quote from the teachings of Kapila is quoted to show the centrality of the mind to liberation and bondage. But our author is not interested in the broader purpose or theology of the *Bhāgavata.*

Other

- *Gobhila-gṛhya-sūtra* and *Nirṇayāmṛta.* In probably the only digression from the subject of yoga, at verse 1.100 the commentator goes into a discussion of the compound word *sūryācandramasau*, refering to Pāṇini and these two works on *karma-kāṇḍa* to make a somewhat arcane point. Elsewhere, in discussing mantras, he makes it clear that he does not approve of non-Brāhmaṇas chanting the Sāvitrī-mantra, recommending that they chant the mantras of their own sect, but other than this there is no particular bias to Brāhmaṇism (Cf. 2.2), though it seems clear that he was himself a Brāhmaṇa. Nātha-yoga itself seems to have been non-Vedic and non-Brāhmaṇical in its origins, though its practices were adapted and assimilated by Hindu sectarians. The *Yoga-yājñavalkya*, for instance, has a Vaishnava orientation. *Gorakṣa-śataka* shows little devotion to Hindu deities other than as titularies present in various locations in the body. Besides a single verse that is deemed an interpolation by the commentator himself (2.77), none of these are described in any great detail in elaborate meditations (*dhyānas*) such as those found in the Tantras.

- There are two references to an "Ācārya-caraṇa" (at 1.37) and one to Śaṅkarācārya (2.25), as well as a verse introduced as Krishna speaking to his father Nanda (at 2.25), none of which we have been able to locate or identify. These verses all describe an *advaita* philosophical vision. Kuvalayananda and Shukla observe in their comments that "according to the philosophy of Gorakṣa as it is to be found in this *śataka*... Śiva, Sadāśiva or Ādya Sadāśiva is broadly speaking the same as Brahman of the Vedantins." They refer to verses 2.58, 2.73, and 2.93 to establish this parallel.[1] YT appears to be more directly in the Advaitin school, but without making any reference to the principal Upaniṣads or any other essential Vedāntic text.
- *Tattva-saṅgraha*: In his remarks to the very last verse of the book, YT recommends getting further information about the true form of the Self (*ātma-svarūpa-nirṇaya*) from this book. There are at least two works of this name. One is that of the Bauddha Śāntirakṣita (8 CE), described in the following way: "Speaking in this work from the philosophical viewpoint of the Yogācāra-Mādhyamika-Svātantrika, Śāntirakṣita sought to refute all the rival philosophies of his time, both Buddhist and non-Buddhist."[2] The other *Tattva-saṅgraha* is by Sadyojyoti (9 CE) of the Śaiva-siddhānta school. This work seems to be primarily concerned with an analysis of the categories of elements, expanding from Sāṅkhya philosophy to 36. Of the two, this seems a likelier candidate for our YT author's *Tattva-saṅgraha*, but at this point nothing certain can be stated. The name itself could easily have been used by almost any author of any school to discuss any philosophical matter. *Alam.*

Other than one unascribed verse fragment (see GŚ 1.82), nothing from later texts like the *Haṭha-yoga-pradīpikā* is to be found here. The particular verse in question, which states the principle of

---

[1]Lonavla edition, page 52.

[2]Janice D. Willis, *Encyclopedia of Religions*, Vol. 13, p. 69. NY: Simon and Schuster Macmillan, 1995.

keeping one's spiritual practice and progress secret, is itself likely not original to HYP, which is a compendium drawn from numerous extant sources including GŚ itself. Our YT author was not interested in presenting an exhaustive treatise on *haṭha-yoga*, but only in understanding and explaining the verses he had before him. Nevertheless, the absence of such references could either mean he had no access to them or that he predates them. There are some signs, e.g., the introduction and comment to 2.16 (see below), where a particular posture is not described by the name known to the later tradition, which also could indicate its early date.

This scant information can only tell us that our author was an Advaitin scholar and yogi, most probably from south India. His dates are also impossible to determine, but I suspect that the absence of references to any of the later *haṭha-yoga* texts while drawing on ones lesser known indicate a fairly early origin for this commentary, pre-1350, the date given for HYP.

This Translation

Generally speaking, Sanskrit commentaries are already a translation of sorts; their primary purpose is to provide a gloss of the difficult words and clarify syntax, which in the verses might differ considerably from the normal prose word order. The *Gorakṣa-śataka* is a short work and its brief explanations and use of code words such as *candra* (moon), *sūrya* (sun), *agni* (fire), *ākāsa* (sky), etc., each of which may have more than one meaning, often require elucidation.

Since text and commentary are both given here, I have translated the verses as I saw them in as literal a manner as possible, and then allowed the commentator to offer his explanation. An exception is made in cases where the text is so obscure that I had to depend on the commentary to understand its meaning.

The yoga science, its anatomy and various practices, are all subjective in character, and thus the systems that developed over the years show idiosyncrasies and differences, even in direct contradiction to one another. Modern yoga researchers are doing their best to discover which practices can be harmonized with modern medical science, with many positive results and findings. But often understanding exactly what the original yogis were aiming for or what they actually experienced through their practices is not so easy.

This book, which is an early text describing such practices, also shows differences from other early *haṭha-yoga* texts like the "original" *Gorakṣa-śataka* and *Yoga-bīja*. Here and there we may comment on such differences, but in-depth research into these differences has and will be done by others. Here, our main task is simply to understand as clearly as possible what the *haṭha-yoga* system described in this *Gorakṣa-śataka* consists of.

In particular, the task of the textual historian consists of being vigilant not to attribute later understandings to either the *Gorakṣa-śataka* or the *Yoga-taraṅgiṇī*. Although in some cases, concepts in GŚ may have been clarified by later texts, we must be careful to separate later elucidations from the text before us.

The Contents of *Gorakṣa-śataka* Summarized

The *Gorakṣa-śataka* is a *paddhati-grantha,* i.e., a practitioner's manual or handbook, summarizing the fundamental practices of the Nātha-yoga sect. The word *paddhati* emphasizes this step-by-step character. As such, the text should be seen as sequential and cumulative. Like all *paddhati-granthas*, it is sequential, earlier practices being preconditions for the later; having been mastered, their benefits and gains assimilated. In other words, the practices, etc., described here are to be mastered in sequence and then integrated with the later ones, and not looked at in isolation.

After expanding on the *maṅgalācaraṇa,* the commentary accepts the authorship of Gorakṣa himself, even though verses 1.3-4 and 2.98 speak of him in the third person. Although it seems unlikely that Gorakṣa himself is the original author, he is acclaimed as the originator of the system that is being described. For simplicity's sake and to make the text readable, we have accepted him as the author and used his name to that end.

The Six Limbs of Yoga (1.7)

The author of GŚ begins his work proper by summarizing his system as having six parts or limbs (*aṅga*), which are exactly the same as the last six of Patañjali's classical *aṣṭāṅga* formulation. These six practices constitute the subject matter of the book and will be explained according to the tenets of the *haṭha-yoga* school.

Verse 1.7 excepts the *yamas* and *niyamas*, i.e., the first two of Patañjali's eight *aṅgas*, because, according to YT, they are irrelevant to the *Gorakṣa-śataka*, which is only concerned with the practices of *haṭha-yoga.* He allows that some of the activities contained within the scope of *yama* and *niyama* may also be integral to and supportive of other practices named in the book if so ordained by one's preceptor. Thus, for example, two of the *yamas*, *brahmacarya* and *mitāhāra* (chastity and controlled diet) are singled out for special attention in 1.54, and of the *niyamas*, the *japa* of Om, is covered in 1.83ff.

YT explains these six *aṅgas* in pretty much the same terms found in the second and third *pādas* of *Yoga-sūtra* (YS), with some additional specific details related to the *haṭha-yoga* practices that will be prescribed herein. These differences should be considered significant.

Pratyāhāra is explained in YT to 1.7 in accordance with the *Yoga-sūtra* definition, but YT adds the special definition given in GŚ 2.30ff (see below). YT also defines *dhāraṇā* somewhat differently from both GŚ and YS, emphasizing the single-pointed meditation on the navel center, etc., rather than the elements as given in 2.53-60. He also defines it as the *abhyāsa* of *samprajñāta-samādhi*, which seems somewhat out of sequence, unless one understands this to include all three of the *saṁyamas* as named in YS 3.4.

Dhyāna, however, is specifically described in YT here as concentration on the nine cakras just as it is later in this work (2.61-75). *Samādhi* is similarly described in a way that accommodates both the YS and later portions of the GŚ.

In 2.11-12, the principal attainments for each of these steps is noted: through *āsana* one destroys diseases, *prāṇāyāma* brings one freedom from past sins; *pratyāhāra* from the modifications (*vikāra*) of the mind; *dhāraṇā* gives steadiness of mind; *dhyāna*, a "supernatural consciousness" and *samādhi* liberation, the casting off of all auspicious and inauspicious karmas.

In the second century, *Gorakṣa-śataka* also gives a rough estimate of how much work is to be done at each level before proceeding: "*Dhāraṇā* [is reached] by two hours of control over the breath; *dhyāna* by twenty-four hours; *samādhi* by twelve days" (Cf. 2.13-14, 2.84).

Āsanas (1.8-12)

The *āsanas* are summarized in five verses and in fact only *siddhāsana* and *padmāsana* are explicitly mentioned as being the most important. *Siddhāsana* and *padmāsana* will be mentioned several times in relation to other activities like *śakti-cālana*, to be discussed below.

In communication with Prof. James Mallinson, I have heard that Nātha panthīs generally do not practice the *haṭha-yoga āsanas* assiduously, which would be borne out by the treatment given the subject here. YT's stated purpose of *āsana* is to remove illness, to achieve stillness and steadiness in the body, and to become free from disturbances (*sthiraṁ sukham anudvejakam*).[1] Since it is said that *āsanas* destroy the ills of the body (*āsanena rujo hanti* 2.11), it seems likely that a wider range of *āsanas* was in fact practiced.

In my personal experience, the continued maintenance of a sitting position for long sessions of meditation requires increasing the strength, balance, and flexibility of especially the back muscles, as well as a general reduction of fat, particularly in the belly and thighs. For most people who have been brought up in the West, the back muscles are weakened by the habit of lying in soft beds and sitting in comfortable chairs and sofas, and similarly the flexibility of the limbs is low. To make the body fit for sitting requires considerable training, a purpose that is served by the other *āsanas*. But like the *yamas* and *niyamas*, these are considered preparatory or peripheral to the principal practices of *haṭha-yoga* and are thus not mentioned in this abbreviated work.

Siddhāsana emphasizes placing pressure on the perineum with the heel, while the other foot places pressure on the genital from above, which implies the *mūla-bandha,* and the obvious reference to the *śakti-cālana* (*mokṣa-kavāṭa-bheda-janakaṁ*) is echoed later in 1.51. In the further text, *siddhāsana* is only mentioned once in association with what is introduced by YT as *samādhi-prakriyā*, in fact a version of what in the later tradition is known as *yoni-mudrā*, when the seven apertures on the head are closed off with the fingers (2.16).

---

[1]Lonavla (p. 50-51) elaborates on *āsana* as having two main divisions, cultural postures and meditative postures. GŚ is only interested in the latter, even where the *mudrās* and so on are added. "By prolonged practice, the meditative poses can be maintained for hours, without much discomfort. They offer a comfortable posture to the student of yoga for *prāṇāyāma, dhāraṇā, dhyāna* and *samādhi*, and in coordination with other yogic exercises, they help him in the awakening of the *kuṇḍalinī*. The traditional view is that a long and continued practice of the meditative poses is itself competent to rouse *kuṇḍalinī*." L. continues by listing three physiological benefits from such postures: (1) the erect spine eliminates compression of the abdominal viscera and frees the mind from "the burden of the body"; (2) richer blood supply for the pelvic region, toning up the coccygeal and sacral nerves, which helps awaken the *kuṇḍalinī* along with other practices, and (3) decreases carbon dioxide production due to the slowing of metabolism."

The *padmāsana* (1.12) described here is usually known as *baddha-padmāsana,* since along with crossing the legs and placing the feet on the opposite thighs, one also crosses the arms behind the back in order to grab the toes. The chin is pressed into the chest in *jālandhara-bandha.* This posture is particularly associated with *śakti-cālana* (1.52), the chanting of *oṁkāra* (1.83), *nāḍi-śodhana* (1.96), and *prāṇāyāma* (2.6-7 YT).

Other positions, like *mahā-mudrā* (1.77-78) and *viparīta-karaṇī* (2.32-34), which has a wide enough definition to include all the topsy-turvy postures like the headstand, shoulder stand and so on, are not spoken of as *āsanas*, but as *mudrās* (q.v.). I would hold that the *mudrās* are still being discussed within the general section concerned with *āsanas*. In fact the entire first century of this work could be said to deal with *āsana* (including *mudrās*) and preliminary breathing exercises, namely *haṁsa-mantra* and *nāḍi-śodhana.*

The Yoga Anatomy

Verses 1.13 to 46 give an introduction to the grossest portion of the process, i.e., the body itself. Although the ubiquitous yoga dictum that whatever exists in the macrocosm is found in the microcosm (*yad asti piṇḍe tad asti brahmāṇḍe*) is not stated overtly, the foundational sentiment itself is found here. The basic inspiration of the *haṭha* system is the human body, which is the abode of the conscious entity, the first basis for all spiritual practice.

This section describes the three principal categories of yoga anatomy, i.e., the *cakras* or psychic centers in the body (1.13-24), the *nāḍīs* or conduits of the *prāṇa* or energizing power through the body (1.25-32), and the ten airs (*vāyu*), through which the body's muscular operations or movements are conducted (1.33-46). The latter discussion will lead to the elaboration of various aspects of breath control (*prāṇāyāma, prāṇa-saṁrodha* or *kumbhaka*).

This process of visualizing the inner workings of the body and the inner movements of energy as perceived subjectively through meditation is the necessary basis for all subsequent practices. As verse 1.14 makes clear, this is the basic knowledge framework on which the *haṭha-yoga* system is founded.

> How can those yogis who do not know the home, which has a single pillar, nine doors and five divinities (*adhidaivata*), and is present in their own body, ever attain success?[1]

Later on, the *cakras* are given as the objects of *dhāraṇā* (2.54-59) and meditation (2.64-76) in a related but not exact same fashion. These descriptions are supplementary and expand the associations of the *cakras* to the great elements, tutelary deities, and so on.

Along with the *cakras*, special emphasis is given to the *yoni-sthāna* (also known as *kāma-rūpa* and *kāmākhya-pīṭha*, 1.17-18), the important center lying in the perineum between the genital and the anus, and to the *kanda* ("bulb") in the *maṇipūra* (i.e., navel center, 1.23), the nexus from which the vital airs are distributed through the body. Since it is presumed that one breathes abdominally, proper breathing brings mental focus into the navel area with the inhaled breath and one then feels this distribution of the vital energy emanating from that center. Both of these centers are connected to the *kuṇḍalinī*. It may be noted that the *siddhāsana* puts pressure on the *yoni*, the *baddha-padmāsana* on the *kanda*. It is likely for this reason that GŚ recommends the latter position for awakening the energies in *śakti-cālana*.

GŚ 1.47 says that the *kuṇḍalinī* remains above the *kanda*, coiled in eight rings and blocking the opening to the *suṣumṇā*. In the commentaries to 1.15ff, YT follows the more customary Tantric description that places the *kuṇḍalinī* in the *mūlādhāra* or *yoni*, in

---

[1] *eka-stambhaṁ nava-dvāraṁ gṛhaṁ pañcādhidaivatam |*
sva-dehe ye na jānanti kathaṁ siddhyanti yoginaḥ ||

particular quoting *Yoga-sāra*. But like many of the references taken from other sources in this early commentary, they do not appear to be in complete harmony with our text, which in 1.20 only emphasizes that this *yoni* or *kāmākhyā-pīṭha* is the locus of the "fire of Time" (*kālāgni*) and does not mention the *kuṇḍalinī*. In 2.64, however, one is advised to meditate on the *kuṇḍalinī* in the *mūlādhāra*.

Though these statements appear to be contradictory, they can be reconciled by understanding that the wakening of the *kuṇḍalinī* energy takes place in steps, something like a multistage rocket. But since the process of *śakti-cālana* is primarily connected to the tightening of the anal sphincter and the muscles at the root of the genital organ, the primary locus of the *kuṇḍalinī* must be recognized as the *mūlādhāra* itself. But the effect of the *kuṇḍalinī*'s awakening is principally felt in the snapping of the back to a more tightly erect position, which takes place from the *kanda*.

Nāḍis. The life airs contract and operate the muscular systems, reaching their destinations through the passageways known as *nāḍis*. This is why the contraction of the *mūlādhāra*, etc., is regulated according to the movements of the *prāṇa* and *apāna*. The number of *nāḍis* is given as 72,000, of which first 72, then 10, and finally three – the *piṅgalā, iḍā* and *suṣumṇā* – are said to be the most important.

Finally, the ten vital airs (*prāṇa-vāyu*) are discussed in several verses. Five are primary (from *prāṇa* to *vyāna*), five secondary. *Prāṇa* is the term that includes all the others, though *prāṇa* as a separate *vāyu* has its principal location in the heart. The names, principal functions and localizations of the ten life airs are given in Table 1.

Table 1

Name of air	Function	Location
prāṇa	inhaling and exhaling, coughing, etc., and including the digestion of food	heart; between the mouth and the nose, in the heart, in the navel area, around the *kuṇḍalinī*, and in the big toes
apāna	excretion of stool and urine	anus; genital, thighs, knees, belly, eyes, waist and navel
udāna	bodily growth	throat; all the joints, as well as in the hands and feet
samāna	nourishing the body	navel; combines with a portion of the fire of digestion and pervades the entire body. It creates a relationship with dualities such as one's happiness and distress and gives them form
vyāna	picking up and releasing	pervades whole body; ears, eyes, waist, ankles, sense of smell and throat
nāga	belching	
kūrma	opening of eyes	
kṛkara	sneezing	
devadatta	yawning	
dhanañjaya		pervades the body and does not leave the body even at death

The Individual Consciousness

The commentaries in relation to the individual soul (i.e., section 1.37-41) are among the most extensive in YT. In his explanation of the *jīva*, YT makes his greatest foray into philosophical territory.

We have translated the word *jīva* ("living being") as "fragmented consciousness" in keeping with the YT explanation. The GŚ is, philosophically, a Brahma-vādī text, which envisions perfection expressed in terms of merging the personal identity with Brahman rather than the *kaivalya-siddhi* of the *Yoga-sūtra*.

Verse 1.24 places the individual consciousness in the *anāhata-cakra*, i.e., the heart, where it "errs" (*bhramati*) or wanders in error for as long as it does not know the Truth. Then verse 1.37, GŚ uses the adjective *jīva-rūpiṇaḥ,* "in the form of the fragmented consciousness," to describe the ten airs themselves. YT clarifies that this should be understood as "giving form to the fragmented consciousness," i.e., the *prāṇas* are a constituent element of the subtle body as a part of the complex arrangement whereby the consciousness comes to identify with the body and is bound by this identification. They thus belong to the category of *upādhi*.

It is unlikely that the author of the *Gorakṣa-śataka* was himself here intending to present a comprehensive philosophy of the *jīva*. The commentary is probably correct in ascertaining his underlying assumptions, but the GŚ is here only seeking to clarify that the breath is the actual nexus of the living being's bondage, and causes it to remain in constant movement, never achieving stasis. The *jīva* consciousness bounces around within the body, finding a limited freedom with the exhalation when it goes out of the body, but then, bound by the *guṇas*, is returned, just like a falcon attached to its trainer by a string.

These verses are in fact intended as an introduction to the *haṁsa* mantra and *prāṇāyāma* more generally, which are the subjects covered in the next several verses, explaining the necessity for these practices. The idea, as expressed in 1.41, is that the unevenness of the breath, both in inhalation and exhalation as well as in the balancing of the *nāḍis*, is the main source of mental unsteadiness and thus establishes the relation of breath control to the conquest of the mind.

Haṁsa-mantra

The subsection of four verses describing the identity of the individual consciousness with the incoming and outgoing breaths then turns into a brief description of the *haṁsa* breath (1.41-46). This is the mantra *so'ham* ("That is I," or "The Truth that enters me in the form of the life air is the same as the 'I' or self that expresses itself outwardly," i.e., that which is without is also within), which is associated with respiration in its natural state, at about fifteen breaths per minute. The *so'ham* mantra is not elaborated on nor explained in any great detail, either as a practice or philosophically. As a practice it is apparently not meant to be primarily a mantra that is contemplated for its meaning. Its real function is to help achieve a constant awareness of the breath, one that becomes smooth, slow and drawn out, steady and even, without jerks or pauses, i.e., the merging of the inhaled and exhaled breaths.

YT refers to the *haṁsa-gāyatrī* as the *jīva-mantra*, since it is associated with the *jīva* as identified with the breath (See YT to 1.42). The *haṁsa mantra* is said to arise from the *kuṇḍalinī* (1.46), by which it would appear to mean that the ingoing and outgoing breath need to be connected to the *kuṇḍalinī* in order to awaken this energy and raise it upward.

The *haṁsa-mantra* is called a *gāyatrī mantra* in the sense that the singing (*gāya*) of it delivers one from material bondage (*trī*); it is the *prāṇa-vidyā* and *mahā-vidyā*, where *vidyā* means "spell" rather than just knowledge. It is also known as the *prāṇa-mantra.*

Saḥ is said to be the *prāṇa-bīja* or seed syllable of the incoming breath, *haṁ* the *apāna-bīja*; in other words the syllable *saḥ* is associated with the inward breath and *haṁ* with the outgoing.

The question arises: If the *haṁsa-mantra* is automatically associated with the natural breath, what is the purpose of this practice? The answer is that the inner and outer breath should be equalized (*ūrdhvādhaḥ saṁsthitāv etau saṁyojayati yogavit... saṁyojanam ekīkaraṇam*, 1.41). Indeed, our commentator quotes

Yoga-cintāmaṇi saying that the breathing exercise whereby the inward and outward breaths become one is the very definition of yoga (*candra-sūryākhyayoḥ prāṇāpānayor aikya-lakṣaṇaḥ prāṇāyāmo'yaṁ yoga ity ucyate*).

Though neither text nor commentary anywhere mention *kevala-kumbhaka*, which is what *ekīkaraṇaṁ* here seems to indicate, the *haṁsa-mantra* appears to primarily be an exercise in observing the breath, which is a usual preparatory for meditation.

This mantra is also called *ajapā* ("the non-uttered") because of its automatic nature, but nevertheless should be chanted by associating the respective sounds and their meaning with the ingoing and outgoing breaths. This mantra is thus meant to be the constant mental culture of the yogi.[1] Other than *praṇava*, it is the only mantra in GŚ, indicating once again that *haṭha* is meant to be a simplification of Tāntrika practices, in which multiple and complex mantras often play a central role, more important even than focusing on the breath. In *haṭha* the *mantra* serves the breath rather than vice versa.

Arousal of the Kuṇḍalinī Śakti (1.47-56)

The next section describes the process of arousing the *kuṇḍalinī śakti*, which is a simple yogic practice, perhaps its most famous, but one that has become clouded in mystification. The main statements covering the process itself are contained in 1.47-52; GŚ 1.53-55 are

[1]It may be observed that GŚo does not mention the *haṁsa-mantra. Yoga-bīja* (146-147) briefly notices it in connection with the four yoga systems, seen as a progression, and summarized as *mahā-yoga.* These are *mantra-yoga, haṭha-yoga, laya-yoga* and *rāja-yoga,* of which concentration on the breath in conjunction with the *haṁsa-mantra* is called *mantra-yoga*, the first of the four. There it is clearly said that the mantra's purpose is to balance the breath in the *suṣumṇā* whereby the sound *haṁsa* is reversed as *so'ham*. Each of the four yogas represents the unification of one set of opposites: the inward and outward breaths (*mantra-yoga*), the moon and sun, i.e., the left and right nostrils (*haṭha-yoga*), the individual and supreme consciousness (*laya-yoga*), and the male and female *bindus*, i.e., *śukra* and *rajas* in the body (*rāja-yoga*).

descriptive of some external regulations necessary for the activation of the *kuṇḍalinī*, in particular related to sexual activity and food, both of which should be controlled. This confirms the YT's earlier statement that of the rules and regulations (*yama-niyama*), only some are directly relevant to *haṭha-yoga's* principal exercises.

The *kuṇḍalinī* is sometimes described as being in the *yoni* (perineum) with 3½ coils (see YT 1.15), but in this section it is said to be within the *kanda* at the *maṇipūra*, with eight coils (1.47, 1.56). In either case, it is said to be sleeping and covering the doorway to the *suṣumṇā* with its mouth.

The process of this arousal (*śakti-prabodha*) is described in the main verses of this section (1.49, 1.52). The *kuṇḍalinī* is awakened by contact with fire. YT 1.49 says that the fire's flame is "sent forth by the *prāṇa*" (*prāṇa-preritānala-śikhā*). In 1.52, a rough description of the *bandha-traya*[1] is given and here again the emphasis is on raising the *apāna* air. *Apāna* here refers to the muscular functions used in ejaculation and excretion. This is combined with either the fire of Time in the *yoni* or that in the *maṇipūraka*, i.e., the *kanda*, (or both), awakening the *kuṇḍalinī*, which then removes its mouth from the entrance to the *suṣumṇā* channel.

Although the breathing exercises known as *kapāla-bhāti* (technically a purificatory *kriyā* in later works) and *bhastrikā* are not mentioned as they are in this context in some later works, they are clearly implied by the words *vāraṁ vāraṁ muñcan pūritam prāṇam* in the verse ("repeatedly lifts the *apāna* while releasing the

[1]The *bandha-traya,* i.e., *mūla-bandha, uḍḍīyāna-bandha* and *jālandhara-bandha.* Although all three of these are described in *Gorakṣa-śataka*, they are not combined as *bandha-traya* here as it is in GŚo (50-64) and *Yoga-bīja* (113-124). In the latter work, *bhastrikā* in combination with *bandha-traya* is given as the process for awakening the *kuṇḍalinī*. *Mūla-bandha* is the element most directly connected to the process, but in YB, only the pulling of the *apāna* air (i.e., the muscular functions connected to excretion and ejaculation) in the reverse direction is sufficient to awaken the *śakti*. The description given here with the addition of mind and fire are exclusive to our GŚ.

aïr that has been inhaled"). This would also be descriptive of *aśvinī-mudrā* as it appears in later yoga texts, which is a form of *mūla-bandha* that is held for a shorter period of time and repeated along with more rapid breathing such as in the bellows (*bhastrikā*). YT appears to favor a slower approach whereby the tightening of the sphincter is held for as long as possible before being released. Experimentation with both methods leads me to feel that each is useful, one preceding the other, the latter being the extended holding position that has the most direct effect on raising the *kuṇḍalinī*.

Once awakened, the *kuṇḍalinī* shoots up in a zigzag motion, and like a needle drawing thread, it goes through each *cakra*, and (according to YT) gathers up the presiding deities and all the elements in each of them until it reaches the *brahma-randhra* or crown of the head. One might also think of a vacuum tube pulling up whatever is placed before it.

The pressure of the *kuṇḍalinī śakti* remains constant and the sleeping *kuṇḍalinī*'s breath makes the body's breathing possible. But by simply removing it from the pipe that leads to the *brahma-randhra*, i.e., the *suṣumṇā* channel, it straightens out like a snake that has been struck by a stick.[1]

The awakening of this energy, which GŚ also names "the Supreme Goddess" (*parameśvarī*), is compared to the forceful (*haṭha*) opening of a door with a key (1.51). In India when this text was written, a key would have been a fairly gross affair requiring considerable physical strength to force a lock open. This is one of only two uses of the word *haṭha* in GŚ, but perhaps is the most realistic indicator of the central concept of *haṭha-yoga*, whereby physical mechanisms accompanied by mental concentration have an effect that is deemed spiritual.

A person devoted to the practice of yoga, i.e, someone constantly taking refuge in the practices of yoga alone and nothing

[1]This example is taken from GŚo 51: *tena kuṇḍalinī suptā saṁtaptā saṁprabudhyate | daṇḍāhata-bhujaṅgīva niḥśvasya ṛjutāṁ vrajet* ||

else, will attain success after one year, meaning that he will be able to raise the *kuṇḍalinī* energy at will (YT).[1] YT (1.57) also cites a passage from *Yoga-cintāmaṇi* giving one symptom of the awakened *śakti* as an itching or tingling sensation in the *suṣumṇā*.[2] Perhaps a more readily accessible sign of the awakened *kuṇḍalinī* is that the spine and all the attendant musculature suddenly stretches without any conscious effort, making sitting pleasant, natural and effortless; this is accompanied by a spurt of energy into the skull that stimulates meditation.

A minor point that is made in verse 1.53, which recurs in other *haṭha-yoga* literature in different contexts, is that one should massage into the skin the perspiration that results from the effort of the *śakti-cālana* exercises. Most other sources link this practice to *prāṇāyāma*.[3] The drinking of milk and eating bland foods are also said to be especially beneficial for this program.

Mudrās (1.57-82)

In all there are 26 verses describing the five *mudrās*. Although some of the five practices are named *bandhas*, usually translated as "locks," and others *mudrās* or "seals," GŚ gathers them all under

---

[1] Success in a practice is properly identified here. Swami Veda Bharati has given seven stages of mastery as follows: (1) One has internalized the technique. (2) The *kriyā* gets done in a shorter and shorter time and at an ever more subtle level. (3) During the *kriyā* the mind does not wander. (4) One can achieve the state of consciousness the *kriyā* imparts without actually doing the *kriyā*. (5) That state of consciousness then becomes the yogi's basic state at all times. (6) One is competent to guide others to reach the same depth and state of consciousness, even without words. (7) One who has reached the highest level of mastery can invoke that state of consciousness in another person simply by their presence.

[2] *pipīlikāyāṁ lagnāyām aṅge kaṇḍūr yathā bhavet*
suṣumṇāyāṁ tathābhyāsāt satataṁ vāyunā bhavet

[3] See, for instance, HYP 2.13, which places it after the equivalent context of our verse 2.6, where it is said that the middle-tiered practitioner of *prāṇāyāma* produces profuse perspiration. See also *Dhyāna-bindu Upaniṣad* 71, *Śāṇḍilyopaniṣad* 7.4, etc.

the rubric of *mudrā*. The term *bandha-traya*, i.e., the specific combining of the first three of these, does not appear. Though there may be specific characteristics by which these two categories (*mudrās* and *bandhas*) of yogic posture are distinguished from one another, I have yet to come across such a clear definition; nevertheless they are certainly separable from most *āsanas* in that they are not intended specifically for either physical culture or meditation.[1] Both *bandhas* and *mudrās* focus on internal muscular contractions, etc., that block or redirect the flow of life airs or body fluids; they may or may not be combined with the other postures.

The main points are as follows:

1. *Mūla-bandha* or *ādhāra-bandha* (1.58-59). This is the contracting of the anal sphincter to pull the *apāna* air upward (*apānam ūrdhvam ākṛṣya*). Thus wherever there is talk of lifting the *apāna* (as in 1.50 or 2.9, etc.), the *mūla-bandha* practice should be adduced. The central importance of *ādhāra-bandha* to the entire system of *haṭha-yoga* is made clear in 1.2, where it is singled out as the process whereby Mīnanātha attained perfection in yoga. The listed benefits are improved digestion and renewed youthfulness, and the union of inward and outward breath. This is the most basic and important of the *mudrās*, and therefore it is said (YT) that when one combines the different locks, one should start with the *mūla-bandha* and afterwards add the others, and release it only after the other locks have been released.
2. *Uḍḍīyāṇa-bandha* (1.60-61), "the flying lock." This *bandha* is well-known, but the information given here is somewhat sketchy, perhaps resulting from the confusion apparent in the textual tradition. The clearest explanation of the verses should probably be taken from the *Yoga-bīja* which indicates that the meaning of "flying up" is that this practice results in

[1] *Śiva-saṁhitā* (4.15), for instance, lists ten *mudrās* (*mudrā-daśakam*), but like our *Gorakṣa-śataka* contains both *mudrās* and *bandhas* in its list.

the *prāṇa* air "flying up the *suṣumṇā nāḍī*."[1] The actual *bandha* requires that one press the abdominal viscera against the spine while exhaling, then hold the position for as long as possible. The prior and following *bandhas* naturally accompany the forceful pressure exerted by the abdominal muscles.

3. *Jālandhara-bandha* (1.62-63). This is the chin lock, or constriction of the throat. The main feature of this *mudrā* is said to be that it prevents "the nectar of the moon" from falling downward "into the fire," which according to YT means that it remains in the *kapāla-kuhara,* the cavity in the skull. The intention appears to be that one prevents the saliva from being swallowed but holds and absorbs it in the mouth. This practice of preventing the nectar from falling into the fire comes up again in different forms, such as in the *khecarī-mudrā* immediately following, but in all cases some form of *jālandhara* is involved. YT here mentions that the constriction of the throat also entails obstructing the movement of the air. Certainly *kumbhaka* or holding of the breath, is generally accompanied by *jālandhara*, but of course nasal breathing is not prevented by constructing the throat.

4. *Khecarī-mudrā* (1.64-76). "The sky-going seal." Also called *nabho-mudrā*, or "sky seal." This *mudrā* requires the tongue be turned up and back within the mouth while one gazes at the point between the eyebrows. This is the longest subsection in the discussion on *mudrās* since it includes a discussion on the *bindu*, about which more below. Notable for its absence is any discussion of the *sarasvatī-cālana* or any other system of cutting the lingual frenum or pulling and lengthening the tongue so that it can reach the described destination, namely the recess above the uvula, i.e., the soft palate or cavity at the back of (and above) the palatal bone that forms the roof of the mouth. According to

---

[1] *kumbhakādau recakānte kartavyas tūḍḍīyānakaḥ |*
baddho yena suṣumṇāyāṁ prāṇas tūḍḍīyate tataḥ ||
tasmād uḍḍīyāṇākhyo'yaṁ yogibhiḥ samudāhṛtaḥ |
uḍḍīyānaṁ tu sahajaṁ guruṇā kathitaṁ sadā || (*Yoga-bīja*, 118-119)

the *haṭha-yogīs*, this spot is called the *kapāla-kuhara* or "the hollow of the skull." For one who masters this technique, the semen (*bindu*) is not spilled, even if engaged directly in sexual activity. YT (1.57) quotes *Yoga-sāra* saying that the benefit of the *khecarī* is to send the *kuṇḍalinī* to its natural resting place in the *brahma-randhra*, where the word *kha* or sky is identified with the *brahma-randhra*, the topmost point in the *cakra* system.[1]

5. *Mahā-mudrā* (1.77-81, with main verse 1.78). In this seated posture, one alternates stretching the legs and taking hold of the large toe with both hands. Though this appears like an *āsana*, it is a *mudrā* because it incorporates or should incorporate the other *bandhas* for awakening the *kuṇḍalinī*, in particular the placing of the heel in the *yoni*. It should also be pointed out that this position facilitates *nāḍi-śodhana*.

With the exception of the *mahā-mudrā*, it should probably be taken as given that all these practices accompany *āsanas* in general and meditational postures in particular. *Khecarī* is to be kept at all times.

[1]The *khecarī mudrā* has an interesting and complex history, for which James Mallinson's scholarship on *The Khecarīvidyā of Ādinātha* (Delhi: Indica Books, 2010) is an excellent resource that should be consulted. The *Gorakṣa-śataka* predates the *Khecarī-vidyā* and its presentation of the subject is considerably less elaborate. Mallinson concludes from his ethnographic research that the practice of cutting the frenum is not widespread, but some yogis still do it. Theos Bernard (1950: 68-69) describes his own experiments with *khecarī*. My own experience, without engaging in the cutting, is that one naturally curls the tongue inward and enjoys the sensation that is produced by its contact with the receding portions of the palate. Indeed, even though the tongue cannot curl all the way into the upper chamber of the nasal sinuses, the pressure exerted on the palate seems to create an energetic sensation that penetrates into the skull. Like Bernard, I find that I became habituated to curling the tongue upward, which makes talking a disagreeable disturbance and helps control one's physical hunger.

The Bindu

Now we come to the difficult subject of the *bindu* ("the drop, point"), which is usually translated as semen; indeed, verse 1.69 does not allow for any other interpretation. This *bindu* is to be differentiated from the orthographic *bindu* associated with the *nāda* vibration in the *omkāra*, the point towards which the nasal hum of the *om* sound leads and into which it merges. The *bindu* is the root cause of the body itself, not simply because it impregnates the woman, but because (according to YT) it is the ongoing source of the vital energy the nerves (*śirāḥ*) carry to every part of the body (1.68). The primary effect of the *khecarī-mudrā* is that it blocks the outward flow of the semen even if one is engaged in sexual activity.

Verse 1.70 further states that as long as the *bindu* is held within, the body remains alive, and death is induced by the loss of the *bindu*. Further on, a similar verse (1.91) conflates the *bindu* with the *prāṇa*: for as long as the vital force (*prāṇa*) is in the body, it stays alive; when the *prāṇa* moves, the *bindu* moves, when the former is still, so too the latter. In other words, mastery of the breath leads to control over the semen and irregular breathing leads to its being spilt. If the *bindu* is set into motion and falls into "the fire," it can be stopped by the *yoni-mudrā*, which here means a variant of the root lock or *mūla-bandha*.

YT (at 1.15) quotes the *Yoga-sāra* saying that the *bindu* has its origin in the *yoni* between the *mūlādhāra* and *svādhiṣṭhāna*. And again at 1.19, he quotes the same work which says the *kuṇḍalinī* has "the form of the *bindu*" (*kuṇḍalī bindu-rūpiṇī*). That same verse also indicates that this *bindu* is the reflection of a jewel-like point in the brain.

Further verses in this sequence next make it clear that the *bindu* is something more than simply the gross male ejaculate. The *khecarī-mudrā* or tongue lock is meant to block a stream of "nectar" that drips constantly from "the moon," which according to YT is equivalent to the *viśuddha-cakra* or otherwise the *kapāla-kuhara*.

The female *bindu*, which is given the same name as the menstrual fluid in a woman (*rajas*), is said to be present in the male body also, but in the region of the navel. GŚ says that "their union is most rarely achieved." The means for achieving this union is not different from the *śakti-cālanam* already described above (1.75).

"The *bindu* is Śiva, *rajas* Śakti. The *bindu* is the moon, *rajas* the sun. Only through the union of both [*bindu* and *rajas*] is the supreme state attained."[1] YT (1.74) elaborates by saying that "in the basic definition of *haṭha-yoga*... as the union of sun and moon, of the *prāṇa* and *apāna*, or of the individual soul and the Supreme Soul (*jīvātma-paramātmanoḥ*), it should be taken that these are all intended as synonyms for one another." YT then repeats this (1.76) by saying that the union of *bindu* and *rajas* is the very definition of yoga (*tayor yogasyaiva yoga-pada-vācyatvāt*).[2]

I understand this to mean that the *haṭha-yogīs* conceived of the external control of the ejaculate to be dependent on the internal control of another, subtler fluid that flows from the brain itself, the former being the gross form of the latter. The *bandha-traya* combined with *khecarī* is the process by which the grosser energies are turned inwards and the inner *bindu* is assimilated and spread throughout the body, producing many beneficial effects.

Sun and Moon

For the ordinary reader, there appears to be a bit of confusion here about the terms "sun" and "moon." These are most commonly identified with the *piṅgalā* and *iḍā*, respectively, but here (1.74, 1.76) we see the terms standing in for the respective characteristics of their site of provenance, i.e., the cooling and nectar-dripping moon in the *viśuddha-cakra* and the fiery and all-consuming

---

[1] *binduḥ śivo rajaḥ śaktir bindur indū rajo raviḥ |*
ubhayoḥ saṅgamād eva prāpyate paramaṁ padam ||

[2] One of the Bhagavad-Gītā's (2.48) definitions of yoga is "equilibrium" (*samatvam*).

digestive fire in the *maṇipūra*. The idea presented here is that the yogi is to bring the sun/fire of the *rajas* up to the *śukra/amṛta* that drips from the moon, and prevent its normal downward flow, which would be the destruction of the *bindu*. The same subject of drinking the *soma-kalāmṛta* arises further on in the context of the *viparīta-karaṇī mudrā* (Cf. 2.42).

There are also references to the moon in connection with *nāḍi-śodhana* exercises, where the yogi is again advised to meditate on the sun and moon in the *maṇipūra* and *viśuddha-cakras* respectively. In all these cases, the object of meditation is a center of either heating or cooling energy. In 1.32, the *suṣumṇā* is also identified with fire, which can be seen as a helpful hint for further understanding.

A table for the different meanings of sun and moon (See YT 1.74).

Table 2a

1. Moon (*candra*)	2. Sun (*sūrya*)
Iḍā (left)	Piṅgalā (right)
Śakti	Śiva

Table 2b

2. Moon (*candra*)	2. Sun (*sūrya*)
bindu (*śukra*)	*bindu* (*rajas*)
viśuddha and upward	*maṇipūra* and downward
Śiva	Śakti

Statements about *yoga* that emphasize terms like *aikyaṁ, samatvaṁ, ekatvaṁ, samarasatvam*, etc., all synonyms for the unification of the above-listed—and other—dualities or pairs of opposites, are oft repeated in the *haṭha-yoga* literature. One of the *Bhagavad-gītā*'s (2.48) basic definitions of yoga is "equilibrium" (*samatvam*). Here it is said that the union of the two *bindus*, *śukra* and *rajas* is the purpose of yoga. The symbol of fertile sexual union is perhaps most direct here, as the verse itself makes clear by likening the two to Śiva and Śakti, but in fact the union of opposites in various psycho-physical spheres is frequently given as the object of this yoga.

yo'pāna-prāṇayor aikyaṁ sva-rajo-retasos tathā
sūryācandramasor yogo jīvātma-paramātmanoḥ
evaṁ tu dvandva-jālasya saṁyogo yoga ucyate

> The union of the *prāṇa* and *apāna*, one's own *rajas* and *retas*, the sun and the moon [i.e., *iḍā* and *piṅgalā*] as well as the individual and Supreme Self (*jīvātmā* and *paramātmā*), and in this way the combination of the entire network of dualities, is called *yoga*. (*Yoga-śikhopaniṣad*, 68)

ha-kāraḥ kīrtitaḥ sūryaṣ ṭha-kāraś candra ucyate
sūrya-candramasor yogād haṭha-yogo nigadyate

> *Ha* refers to the sun and *ṭha* to the moon. Because [this process] results in the union of the sun and the moon, it is called *haṭha-yoga*. (*Siddha-siddhānta-paddhati* 1.69)[1]

YT to 1.75: "By that wind (*vāyu*) that activates the *śakti*, the *rajas* is impelled or raised upward, where it enters into permanent union with the *bindu*. In other words, the two achieve a state of equilibrium." Such equilibrium is later given as one of the characteristics of *samādhi*.[2] Interestingly, YT's use of the expression

---

[1] See *Philosophy of Hatha Yoga*, page 2. union of *ha* and *ṭha*.
[2] Cf. 2.86 = HYP 4.6.
yadā saṁkṣīyate prāṇo mānasaṁ ca pralīyate |
tadā samarasatvaṁ ca samādhir abhidhīyate ||

haṭha-yoga-prakaraṇe in this context also implicitly identifies *haṭha-yoga* with *samādhi*, rather than as a means to *rāja-yoga* as is often found in the later literature.[1]

Again, in 1.97 and 1.99 meditations on *candra* and *sūrya* are given to accompany *kumbhaka* during the *nāḍi-śodhana* breathing exercise. The first follows the inhalation through *iḍā*, the latter though *piṅgalā*. The first of these does not give a place for this *candra* to be meditated on, the latter places the *sūrya* at the navel center (*nābhi*). The natural conclusion would be that the *candra* spoken of here is to be meditated on in the *viśuddha-cakra* or *sahasrāra*, but YT (1.97) says that this too is to be localized in the navel area.[2]

Verse 1.99 appears in *Yoga-cūḍāmaṇi Upaniṣad* (97) with the word *hṛdi* ("in the heart") in the place of *nābhi*. But YCU 98 (= GŚ 1.100) refers to "the two *bindus*" (*bindu-dvayam*) whereas our text has *bimba-dvayam* ("the two disks"). If one looks for consistency, it would be necessary to read *bindu-dvayaṁ* and to place the moon in the *viśuddha* and sun in *maṇipūraka*; it seems unnecessarily confusing to add a meditation that does not correspond to previously given information. To add to this general confusion, YT 2.7 writes,

> In this position he should salute his guru and Lord Śiva, fixing his gaze at the tip of the nose, which according to the statement "the orb of the moon is between the brows" (*bhrū-madhye śaśabhṛd-bimbam*) means one should gaze at this point where the orb of the moon is dripping nectar.

---

[1] HYP 1.1-2, 1.67, 2.76, 4.79, etc. See also infra 2.85-86, HYP 4.7.

[2] These meditations are not duplicated in the later works, perhaps due to this confusion. *Haṭha-yoga-pradīpikā* seems to have deliberately removed them from its contextual discussion.

Starting in verse 2.31 the section on *viparīta-karaṇī* speaks of "a woman come from the moon" which is glossed by YT as the flow of nectar from the *viśuddha cakra*. Then 2.32-33:

> One, the sun, dwells in the navel region, made of the power to burn. And the moon, made of nectar, is always situated at the base of the palate. The moon, with its face downward, showers [the nectar]; the sun, facing upward, swallows it. This being the case, one should know the means [or posture] by which this ambrosia can be intercepted.

The practice of praṇava (1.83-89).

This short section contains instructions on chanting japa of *om*, the glories of this *bīja mantra* in five verses, and a final verse giving the principal benefit of the practice, which is to be freed from past sins. The only stipulation is that one should sit in the *padmāsana*. *Japa* of the *praṇava* is one of the practices that is included in the *Yoga-sūtra* (*taj-japas tad-artha-bhāvanam*, 1.28), but the GŚ treatment of the subject differs from the one given there and appears to follow other sources; the glorification of *praṇava* consists in breaking its three syllables into various other triads, such as the three Vedas, or the *trimūrti* of gods and their energies.

The *Gorakṣa-śataka* is not particularly interested in the theological concept of *īśvara*, so the *Yoga-sūtra*'s statement that *praṇava* is the *vācaka* or indicator of God or *īśvara* (YS 1.27), i.e., a devotional act, is not mirrored in any way. Rather, though YT accepts the next *sūtra* of YS, "[*Praṇava*] should be recited and its meaning contemplated" (YS 1.28), he summarizes,

> With the mind, one should always remember that very light in the form of the Supreme Brahman, that self-effulgent consciousness that is the resting place (*adhiṣṭhāna*) of the three worlds, the three times, the

> moon, sun and fire deities, the three Vedas, the three gods Brahmā, Viṣṇu and Rudra, and the three energies of action, will and wisdom, and not to allow any other desires to enter the mind, but whenever encountering any object from the phenomenal universe, whether gross or subtle, should remember the self-revealed and all-pervading consciousness that is indicated by the *praṇava* syllable. This is the purport of this entire section. (YT 1.88)

As in the *Yoga-sūtra*, this practice of *japa* is considered separate from meditation proper, as is the remembering of the *haṁsa* mantra. Indeed, the chanting of *praṇava* is to be done not only with the voice, but with body and mind also. YT explains,

> One should practice the *praṇava* with one's body: One should think of the *praṇava* as Brahman with attributes and endowed with the power of action (*kriyā*). Then in a way that is conducive to this understanding of the mantra, one should remain with the body positioned in the *siddhāsana* or some other *āsana*. Action, will and wisdom were mentioned in the previous verse, so *kriyā* or action has been accepted as a component of the *praṇava*. Thus it is clear that any actions or practices that are favorable to the chanting of Om are also considered a part of the practice of Om.

It should be noted that since the repetition of *praṇava* appears to function as integral to the system of counting used in the descriptions of *nāḍi-śodhana* and *prāṇāyāma,* it is not to be chanted in the drawn out manner that one tends to hear frequently in yoga circles, but merely as an utterance taking not more than a second or the time of a heartbeat to complete. GŚ says the benefit of chanting is to be released from sin rather than, as in YS, a privileged way of attaining *samādhi*.

Introduction to Prāṇāyāma; Nāḍi-śodhanam (1.90-101)

The next four verses talk about mastering the breath and the eight that follow of purifying the *nāḍis*. Those that glorify *prāṇa-saṁrodha* have the refrain, "Therefore one should restrain the wind" (*tato vāyuṁ nirodhayet*). The ruling idea is that since the presence of the *prāṇa* in the body is the sign of life, one should keep it within the body by controlling the breath. This indicates that *kumbhaka* is the main element in the practice.

This then leads to a cursory discussion of *nāḍi-śodhanam*. There is some confusion in the commentary about this section probably due to later emendations. At 1.96, one version of YT claims that "after glorifying *prāṇāyāma*, the author now describes its method over the next 22 verses." But verse 1.96 clearly states that the purification of the *nāḍis* is a necessary prerequisite to *prāṇāyāma* proper and the last two verses of the *śataka* confirm that *nāḍi-śodhanam* was indeed the subject by first telling us that by the previously described practice the *nāḍis* will be purified in at least three months, and then telling us of its benefits, namely improved digestion, the manifestation of the *nāda* sound, and freedom from disease.

For *nāḍi-śodhanam* it is also necessary to sit in *padmāsana*. One inhales through one nostril and exhales through the other after holding to capacity. The nostrils are identified with the moon (left, *īḍā*) and the sun (right, *piṅgalā*). This instruction is accompanied by two meditations, on the shining white orb of the moon [which is in the *viśuddha-cakra*] and on the blazing sun in the navel, respectively. In the YT to 1.99, our commentator places both these meditations in the navel, which is somewhat unusual.

YT also states that the same counts that are prescribed for *prāṇāyāma* in 2.4ff also apply here, i.e., twelve repetitions of *praṇava* for the inhalation (*pūraka*), sixteen for the holding of breath (*kumbhaka*), and ten for exhalation (*recaka*). It would seem, however, that if *nāḍi-śodhanam* is to be differentiated from *prāṇāyāma* (which is also, in the first instance, described as alternate nostril breathing), that difference would lie in that no counting is specifically advised here and that one should hold the breath for as long as one can rather than according to a specific count. On the other hand, verse 1.100 does use the word *parimitaṁ*, indicating some measure is to be made. In neither context do *Gorakṣa-śataka* or *Yoga-taraṅgiṇī* advise using the fingers to block off the nostrils, even for beginners.

The word *sthāṇutvam* ("pillar-like motionlessness") in verse 1.90 should be noted as one of the principal benefits of *prāṇāyāma* (just as earlier in 1.11, it is given as a characteristic of the *siddhāsana*). YT says that this means that the yogi "is able to tolerate opposites like heat and cold and sustain his yoga practice over a long period of time."

The commentator adds that there is no need for any of the six purificatory tasks (*ṣaṭ karma*) if one's channels are clear (*nāḍi-śodhana*), and no necessity for even *nāḍi-śodhana* exercises if the three humors are in balance.

Prāṇāyāma (2.1-21)

The second *śataka* begins with 21 verses describing *prāṇāyāma*. The centrality of *prāṇāyāma* to the entire *haṭha-yoga* system will be confirmed in 2.84, where further progress is expressed in multiples of one's *prāṇāyāma* practice. It would seem from this statement that *prāṇāyāma* itself is the essential practice that leads eventually to *samādhi*. Indeed, as was already made clear,

Verse 2.3 speaks of the balance of the two nostrils (sun and moon), i.e., the results of *nāḍi-śodhana*, as the necessary prerequisite to *prāṇāyāma*. Then 2.4 goes on to makes the distinction between *prāṇāyāma* proper and *nāḍi-śodhana*, by specifying that when there is a specific count for the inhalation, holding of the breath and the exhalation, it is the former. The word usually used in this context is *mātrā*, which simply means a measure and is calculated differently in different traditions. Here the unit of time used is how long it takes to say Om.

One is supposed to inhale twelve measures, hold for sixteen and then exhale ten *mātrās*. One cycle including both sides, left and right, is a single *prāṇāyāma*. A beginner maintains this measure, a more advanced practitioner doubles it, and the superior *sādhaka* triples it. The beginner is said to experience profuse sweating, in the middle stage there is trembling and the most advanced is said to "rise up," which our commentator says means simply "he rises from his seated position." This seems a somewhat anodyne attainment for someone capable of following this difficult practice; similar verses in other books goes as far as to say that this means levitation. (See notes to verse 2.6.)

The gaze is to be fixed on the tip of nose between the eyes (2.7), which means (YT) "the orb of the moon is between the brows" (*bhrū-madhye śaśabhṛd-bimbam*), i.e., one should gaze at this point where the orb of the moon is dripping nectar.

Verse 2.8 returns us to one of the recurring themes of the entire *haṭha* practice as it tells us to draw up the *apāna* air, place it in the *prāṇa*, then lead it upward by the *kuṇḍalinī* power. This clearly shows how the author conceives the development of the practice. One starts with the gross physical aspects of the *bandhas* and *śakti-cālana*. Then, as one masters the breath, one becomes capable of effecting the same *kriyās* on subtler and subtler levels. The mind is captured stage by stage through these meditations on progressively subtler manifestations of the gross and subtle body until one is catapulted into *samādhi*. This is further supported by the contents of verses 2.13-14, which have already been discussed.

The descriptions of *prāṇāyāma* contain two further instructions or practices, 2.9 and 2.16, the principal verses of the section, both of which are in the privileged long meter of *śārdūla-vikrīḍita*. The first of these verses is introduced by YT as instruction in the practice of *kumbhaka*, i.e., what is to be done while the breath is being held during the retention phase of the *prāṇāyāma*. Here again, there is the by-now familiar exhortation to retain the inhaled air firmly, then to activate it with the *kuṇḍalinī* power, lift it together with the *apāna* air and the fire (*vahni*) up to the sky (*ākāśa*), and then place the *prāṇa* firmly in the *brahma-randhra.*

A bit further on in 2.17, also for the first time, the *nāda* is spoken of. Verse 2.73 clarifies that the *nāda* is connected to "space" (*ākāśa*), since the *tanmātra* of the *mahābhūta ākāśa* is *śabda*, and then identifies its place as the *ājñā-cakra.*

Here again the problem of the meaning of *ākāśa* can best be resolved by understanding it to include both the *ājñā* and the *sahasrāra.* This makes sense if we accept Kuvalayananda and Shukla's argument that the *suṣumṇā* "passes through the *meru-daṇḍa* until it emerges from it when it bifurcates, one branch going directly to *brahma-randhra* and the other to *brahma-randhra* via the *ājñā-cakra.*"[1]

The above verse furthermore brings in, for the first time, "meditating on the Self" as a part of the process. When the *prāṇa*, etc., are in the *brahma-randhra*, one "should focus his attention on his own true spiritual identity" there.

Both of these verses (2.9 and 2.16) include the concept, though unnamed in either *mūla* or commentary, of the *yoni-mudrā* or *ṣaṇmukhī-karaṇa*, which entails using the fingers of both hands to cover the ears, eyes, and nostrils in order to promote internalization and concentration on the breath. The latter verse specifies furthermore the *śītalī* breath, also unnamed, whereby one creates a funnel with the tongue and breathes in slowly through the mouth before exhaling through the nostrils. This is further differentiated by the sitting posture and the holding of the *prāṇa* in the chest or heart *cakra* along with the *apāna* and the fire, before lifting it to the head as before.

Verses 2.10 and 2.11 emphasize the principal result of breath control as the burning of sin. [Therefore] the yogis always call it

---

[1] L. p. 88.

"the great bridge over the ocean of existence." The purificatory nature of *prāṇāyāma* is said by YT to come from the purification of the basis or substratum (*adhiṣṭhāna*) of the *prāṇa*.

The section concludes with warnings to take care in doing *prāṇāyāma*, for just as a wild animal can only be tamed by an expert exercising great prudence, without which it may cause the death of its putative trainer, so it is with one seeking mastery over the *prāṇa*.

Pratyāhāra (2.22-51)

The *pratyāhāra* section is the longest of all, containing thirty verses. This length is principally due to a long subsection discussing the *viparīta-karaṇī-mudrā*, which we will deal with separately.

The GŚ gives two separate definitions of *pratyāhāra* or withdrawal,[1] the third of Gorakṣa's six *aṅgas*: one that follows the general concept as given by Patañjali in YS 2.54-55, as the act of separating mental processes from sense percepts, without which complete control of the senses cannot be accomplished.

GŚ gives the analogy of the sun withdrawing rays in the late afternoon, and also gives another, like Gita 2.58, comparing the process to a tortoise withdrawing its limbs into the shell (2.24).

The procedure for *pratyāhāra* is repeated in five verses, one for each of the knowledge-acquiring senses. The formula, perhaps the most psychological of all in the book, is the same in each case: "Whatever one hears [sees, touches, tastes, or smells], whether good or bad, is to be recognized as a product of the self, and therefore one should withdraw it within the self."

The technique is akin to a process of *jñāna-yoga*, whereby one identifies the sense perceptions as the products of one's own consciousness. Once they are identified as the self, they are no longer separate from one's self and so withdrawn into oneself (2.25-29). YT appropriately takes the opportunity here to give a

---

[1]Swami Veda Bharati gives an extensive analysis of different understandings of *pratyāhāra* in Appendix V of his *Yoga-sūtras*, Vol. II, 742.

brief explanation of *vivarta-vāda*, the Advaita theory that sees the creation as an illusory construct existing within the Self.

> One should recognize that [the sense objects] are part of oneself, the substratum of consciousness onto which the illusion of non-self (*vivarta*) is superimposed... When one is established in recognition of the truth, one withdraws [from the illusory reality].

The second, specialized definition of *pratyāhāra* involves reversing the flow of the lunar nectar, already mentioned above in relation to the *khecarī-mudrā*. As in verse 1.71, the problem is expressed as avoiding the consumption of this lunar *amṛta* by the fire in the navel. This *amṛta* is there identified with the semen or *bindu*. GŚ 2.30 tells us that the original enjoyer of this *amṛta* is the moon, the next is the sun, but the yogi should be the third to do so, whereby he attains freedom from old age and death.

Viparīta-karaṇī mudrā (2.30-51)

GŚ here introduces a second meaning to *pratyāhāra*, more relevant to the concerns of *haṭha-yoga* than the simple act of withdrawing the senses from their objects. "The sun consumes the stream of lunar ambrosia (*amṛta*). The withdrawal of this torrent is called *pratyāhāra*." (2.30).

From verse 2.33 onward, the process of this *pratyāhāra* is identified with the *viparīta-karaṇī mudrā*, whereby one raises the legs above the body so that the head is lying with the chin against the chest in *jālandhara-bandha*, the stomach above the throat. In this position, one is to apply the *khecarī-mudrā*, placing the tongue in the cavity in the *brahma-randhra*, i.e., the *brahma-dvāra*, and there moving the tongue within it, taking the nectar that falls directly on it. Verse 2.37 gives the most complete description:

> The yogi who while meditating on the Supreme Śakti according to the prescribed method turns his face upward and places his tongue [in the cavity[1]] and drinks the drops from the exceedingly clear stream of moon liquor as it trickles down from the head to the sixteen-petaled lotus, and which has then been acquired forcefully (*haṭhāt*) from the *prāṇa* and taken on the tongue after being stirred by it, develops a body that is as soft as the stem of a lotus and lives a very long time.

Here again, one drinks in the air through the mouth, as in verses 2.9 and 16. The *kāka-cañcū mudrā* is introduced in 2.38, appearing to be here a practice intended to complement this kind of breathing through the mouth. This appears to include a variation of the *ujjāyī* breath, which is not so named herein.[2]

Since the purpose of the exercise can be seen as a further elaboration or extension of the *khecarī*, which is included within it, nothing much further need to be said here. Various names have been given for the destination of the tongue in these practices, and indeed these destinations are different. The *Khecarī-vidyā* places the *gagana-dvāra* in the nasal cavity above the palate, which is the actual destination of the tongue's activity here, but I cannot say with complete conviction that the *Gorakṣa-śataka* goes beyond the

---

[1]Here the verse is ambiguous. The word *vidhivat*, here translated "according to the prescribed method," and read with "meditating," etc., is replaced by *vivare*, "in the cavity," read with "places his tongue" in many versions of the verse (e.g., VM 118, HYP 3.51, HP 5.74). Our commentator's gloss *nāsikordhva-vivare*, "the cavity above the nostrils," is a reference to the fully extended *khecarī mudrā*, whereby the tongue has been stretched and turns upward at the throat. This then feels to the meditator as though the tongue is touching and connected to the root of the nose, not from below but from behind, i.e., it has entered the sinus cavities. Something analogous can be experienced through mental concentration on the relevant areas of the gross and subtle bodies, though the actual physical touch is no doubt a stronger stimulus for triggering the intended psychosomatic response. Brahmānanda in *Jyotsnā* (HYP 3.51) gives the synonym *kapāla-kuhare*. *Nāsānta-suṣira* is mentioned in 2.42-43 below.

[2]See footnote to 2.39.

viśuddha-cakra or throat and the complex of centers found there. Nevertheless, it is most likely that the terms and descriptions here should be understood in the light of *Khecarī-vidyā.*[1]

Dhāraṇā. (2.52-60)

The process of *dhāraṇā* also takes on a specific meaning in the *Gorakṣa-śataka* that is somewhat distinct from the *Yoga-sūtra*'s description, which is "Fixing the mind on a particular locus is called *dhāraṇā* or holding a focus" (*deśa-bandhaś ca dhāraṇā*, YS 3.1). True to the insight of the *haṭha-yoga* school, these loci are all in the body. These are given in sequence from gross to subtle, in the method of *pratisañcara*, or reversed devolution.

The YS offers a number of objects for concentration in its first chapter, but GŚ is specific about concentrating for two hours (five *ghaṭikās*) on each of the five great elements, which are each described with their accompanying symbols: the *devatā*, seed mantra (*bīja*), geometrical figure and color, etc. Most of these are the same as given in other source materials and also here by YT in the early portion of the book. The principal difference here is that these elements are associated with different places in the body from their usual *cakra* locations as given elsewhere. This is how Gorakṣa describes them:

Table 3

Element	Location	Color	*Bīja*	Shape	Deity
Earth	Heart	yellow	*la*	square	Brahmā
Water	Throat	white	*va*	half-moon	Viṣṇu
Fire	Palate	red	*ra*	triangle	Rudra
Air	Ajñā-cakra	black	*ya*	circle	Īśvara
Ether	Brahmarandhra	clear	*ha*	---	Sadā-śiva

[1]See Mallinson's historical overview of *khecarī-mudrā*, *Khecarīvidyā of Ādinātha*, pp. 16-33.

Dhyāna (2.61-84)

Dhyāna is defined by *Yoga-sūtra* as an enhanced version of *dhāraṇā*, principally characterized by continuity:

tatra pratyayaika-tānatā dhyānam

> In that concentration on its locus, a single unbroken continuous flow is called meditation. (YS 3.2)

GŚ first instructs the proper posture for meditation, the *dhyāna-mudrā*.

> Keeping the lower [part of the body] firmly established in a comfortable posture (*sukhāsana*), the mind fixed inward and the gaze outward, and the [upper] body straight—this is called the meditative position (*dhyāna-mudrā*). (2.63)

GŚ 2.62 makes a distinction between formless meditation, i.e., on light, and meditation on gods and the such. The author then proceeds to what YT calls a description of the loci of meditation in eleven verses, 2.64-74. Verse 2.76 says that each of these meditations contain both an *upādhi* (limiting adjunct or attribute) and the *tattva* (essential truth), which according to YT refers respectively to the descriptors given in these verses.

At the end of these meditations, there is a recapitulation of the nine loci of meditation in one verse (2.75). This list corresponds for the most part to the first nine verses of the eleven; the tenth being a further explanation of the ninth and the eleventh being the non-localized formless and all-pervading Self. The recapitulation helps clarify the original intention, while at the same time leaving a few questions. I present a summary chart here without any further comment.

TABLE 4

Vs.	Place	Description of place	Object of meditation	Describers of object of meditation	Further info.	Benefit	2.75-76
2.64	*mūlādhāra*	with Kundalini, like gold, four petals	The *ādhāra* itself.	as given		released from all stains	anus
2.65	*svādhiṣṭhāna*	6 petals, red ruby	The Self			becomes happy	genital organ
2.66	*maṇipūra*	moon that shines like sun.	The Self			sets world trembling	navel
2.67	*hṛd-ākāśa*		Śambhu	Lustrous like the fierce sun.		one with Brahman	heart lotus
2.68	*hṛt-padma*	Like lightning.	The Self		*prāṇāyāma-vibhedataḥ*	one with Brahman	above that (?)
2.69	*viśuddha*	Shining like a lamp in uvula.	The Self			free from death	the uvula
2.70	*bhrū-madhya*		The Self, Deva	Like a ruby		filled with bliss	the palate (?)
2.71	*bhrū-madhya*		The Self, Parameśvara	Like a sapphire.	*vijita-prāṇo*	attains yoga	Between eyebrows.
2.72	*gagane*		Śiva	without qualities, peaceful, all-pervading.	*ekākī*	one with Brahman	*brahma-randhra*)
2.73	*ākāśe ājñā-cakre*		The Self /Śiva			attains yoga	
2.74	Everywhere		The Self	spotless, all-pervading like sky		attains liberation	

YT concludes his comment to 2.76 by saying, "There [in the *brahma-randhra*] alone does [the yogi] enter into the emptiness of the sky of consciousness (*cid-ākāśa*) and dissolve."

Verses 2.77 and 2.78 are lengthier verses that appear to be interpolated, since verse 2.79 begins with the word *eṣu*, which refers back to the nine loci of meditation listed in 2.76. 2.79 is once again a *nirguṇa* meditation where one concentrates on the divine light of Śiva, which is non-different from Brahman. The verse and commentary make clear that one is meant to meditate on both *saguṇa* and *nirguṇa* forms in each of the loci. The words *upādhi-tattva-yuktāni* ("associated with [both] adjuncts and substance") here are further indicative of these two kinds of meditation.

YT agrees that these verses are interpolated, but adds that he has retained them for the "excellence of their meaning." The first of the two cannot truly be spoken of as a meditation, as it recapitulates the entire procedure as it has been given for rising through the *cakra* system to enter the "sky," which here must mean the *brahma-randhra*. The sky is where the Supreme Truth is present as Maheśa or Sadāśiva. This conforms with other descriptions, and simply places the emphasis on the *brahma-randhra* and the attainment of Sadāśiva as the ultimate goal. "There alone does [the yogi] enter into the emptiness of the sky of consciousness (*cid-ākāśa*) and dissolve."

The next verse is a meditation on the goddess Chinnamastā, who is said to reside above the lotus navel in the "pure region of the fierce-rayed sun." Being primarily a glorification of this particular deity, it is quite out of character for the *Gorakṣa-śataka*. Chinnamastā Devī is otherwise unmentioned in this book and, as far as I have been able to see, any other literature connected to the *haṭha-yoga* tradition. However, since the first of these two verses shows more of the stylistic characteristics of the rest of the composition, it is quite possibly original to the work.

YT points out in the commentary to 2.79 that "the light of Śiva is the light (*jyotiḥ*) that has the nature of Śiva, identified [particularly] with the heart lotus and *ājñā-cakras.*" This is perhaps an indicator that the name of Śambhu and Śiva are specifically given in relation to the meditations on those locations.

GŚ concludes by emphasizing the highest object of meditation as the "unequalled light of Śiva, the luster that is identical with Brahman" and then glorifying *dhyāna* as having more than 16 times the value of an *aśvamedha* sacrifice (2.80).

Some readings of verse 1.13, which in our version mentions six *cakras*, have the word nine in the place of six. Nine *cakras* are named in the *Siddha-siddhānta-paddhati*, which is probably the original source of the verse.[1] The nine *cakras* given in that work (see 2.1-9) are (1) the *brahma-cakra* in the *mūlādhāra*, (2) *svādhiṣṭhāna*, (3) *maṇipūra,* (4) *anāhata,* (5) *kaṇṭha-cakra*, i.e., the *viśuddha,* (6) *tālu-cakra*, i.e., the palate, (7) between the eyebrows, (8) *nirvāṇa-cakra* in the *brahma-randhra*,[2] and (9) *ākāśa-cakra*, which seems to be visualized outside the body. Here again the correspondence does not appear to be exact, but nevertheless useful for comparison.

Samādhi. (2.81-97)

GŚ begins its discussion of *samādhi* (according to YT) by explaining the *vastu-sthiti*, differentiating the *upādhis* from the *tattva.* In other words, one may meditate on the *upādhis*, primarily the *mahā-bhūtas,* for the *upādhi* is the locus within which the Self, the *tattva* or Reality, is revealed – as was said in 2.76 in relation to *dhyāna.* Here, however (2.81-82), the distinction between *dhyāna* and *samādhi* is made: the *upādhis* need to be destroyed. Thus,

> As long as the sense objects [*tanmātras* or subtle elements] such as sound are present to the ears and other

---

[1]See the footnote to this verse.

[2]Though it is sometimes described as being within the subtle complex of either the *ājñā* or the *sahasrāra*. See Goswami, *Laya Yoga,* p. 244, 253, 282.

senses, that is called meditation. *Samādhi* is beyond that. (2.82)

Tattva is further described in 2.92. "The knowers of Reality know It to be without beginning or end, without any support, undevolved, without any substratum, without any ills, and formless." YT: "The Reality (*tattva*) means the unity of the separated consciousness (the *jīva*) and the Self (*ātmā*), i.e., the essential being of the Self, which is the meaning intended by the word *yoga*."

The YT here includes a reference to the YS definition: "When the senses have been submerged in the Self and one is in the state where there is only the flash of meaning,[1] then the word *samādhi* can [appropriately] be employed." This means, in YS language, that the *vṛttis* have been stopped: "When in meditation the true nature of the object shines forth, not distorted by the mind of the perceiver, that is absorption (*samādhi*)" (*tad evārtha-mātra-nirbhāsaṁ svarūpa-śūnyaṁ iva samādhiḥ*, YS 3.3).

Samādhi is further defined (2.85) as the state wherein there is complete unification of all dualities [and] of the individual self with the Supreme Self, and all desire-ideation (*saṅkalpa*) has been completely banished. Through turning inward (*antar-mukhatayā*) [i.e., yoga], the functions of the mind take the shape of the Self, and thus oneness or union of the mind and the Self is achieved. This state is called *samādhi*. When the *prāṇa* is dissolved and the mind merges, then the complete equilibrium (*samarasatva*) [that results] is called *samādhi*.

The yogi stops the activities of mind and breath together and contemplates the Self. "When his breath is dissolved," i.e., even

---

[1]*Artha-mātrāvabhāsa*. This is taken from Patañjali's *Yoga-sūtra* 1.43, which defines the *nirvitarkā samāpatti*: *smṛti-pariśuddhau svarūpa-śūnyevārtha-mātra-nirbhāsā nirvitarkā*. "When there has occurred complete and all-round purification of memory and the mind-field is, as it were, devoid of its own form and illuminative of only the object signified, it is called *samādhi* without gross thought." Translation by Swami Veda Bharati, *The Yoga-sūtras of Patañjali*, Vol. I, p. 387.

without applying the *jālandhara-bandha* and other techniques, he is unable to observe any movement of exhalation, in other words the breath becomes merged into the Self. Furthermore, when the mind or inner instrument merges or attains a formless state, there is no fluctuation (*vṛtti*) at all.

The person in *samādhi* is not aware of the sense percepts, nor of himself as a distinct entity, or anyone else. He is unaffected by any external problems, whether physical, mental or magical. Time and past deeds do not influence him, nor can he be controlled by any other person.

Verse 2.91 interestingly cites the Gītā 6.17: "Yoga ends the suffering of one who is balanced in eating and leisure activity, who is balanced in his efforts in karmas, and balanced in sleeping and waking." YT contextualizes the verse by asking how *samādhi* can be achieved and this is the answer. After the elaborate techniques that have formed the subject of the GŚ, this verse seems a little out of place here, perhaps simply a reminder to practice diligently, but with patience as in 2.20-21, which advised the yogī to not rush his *prāṇāyāma* practices.

The teaching on *samādhi* comes to its conclusion in 2.92-95, where the *tattva* is described in completely impersonal terms, a point that is further emphasized in 2.96-97, where (according to YT) the author combats the argument that the individual soul maintains any separate identity after liberation. Oneness with Brahman means literally merging.

Final Conclusion (2.98-101)

And finally the benefit of studying the *Gorakṣa-śataka* is spoken of in four verses. Though 2.98 once again mentions Gorakṣa as the author, 2.100 submits that Ādinātha is the actual author.

Verse 2.101 gives a final glorification of yoga, which stands above all other ritual processes or practices. This was already stated in Verse 2.80:

A thousand horse sacrifices or a hundred *vājapeya* sacrifices are not worth even one-sixteenth part of a single yogic meditation.

snātaṁ tena samasta-tīrtha-salile dattā dvijebhyo dharā
yajñānāṁ ca hutaṁ sahasram ayutaṁ devāś ca saṁpūjitāḥ
satyaṁ tena sutarpitāś ca pitaro svargaṁ ca nītāḥ punar
yasya brahma-vicāraṇe kṣaṇam api prāpnoti dhairyaṁ manaḥ

2.101. One whose mind has attained even a moment's stillness while deliberating on Brahman has bathed in the water of all the places of pilgrimage, has given the [entire] earth in charity to the Brāhmaṇas, has performed thousands of millions of sacrifices and worshiped all the gods. Truly, he has properly pleased the forefathers and led them to heaven.

The important verse (verses in longer meters):

One way of assessing points of importance is through the metrical language. Ordinary information is conveyed by means of *anuṣṭubh* verses (eight syllables to a line); longer verses immediately attract the attention by a change in rhythm and the weightiness of their diction. Of the 202 verses in *Gorakṣa-śataka*, all but 19 are in *anuṣṭubh*; the "weightier" verses are all in the *śārdūla-vikrīḍitā* meter. These verses, extracted from the text, would in themselves form a fairly strong summary of the entire *Gorakṣa-śataka*, with all the more important practices such as *mūla-bandha, khecarī,* etc., being emphasized repeatedly even within this selection.

- 1.2 The *maṅgalācaraṇa* to Ādinātha.
- 1.11 *Padmāsana.*
- 1.12 *Siddhāsana.*
- 1.52. *Śakti-cālana.*
- 1.78 *Mahāmudrā.*

- 1.100 *Nāḍi-śodhanam.*
- 2.9 *Kumbhaka.*
- 2.16 *Yoni-mudrā.*
- 2.37 *Khecarī, soma-pānam.*
- 2.43 *Khecarī, viparīta-karaṇī.*
- 2.48 *Khecarī, viparīta-karaṇī.*
- 2.54-58 Five kinds of *dhāraṇā.*
- 2.77 Obeisances to Śiva in the *brahma-randhra.*
- 2.78 Obeisances to Chinnamastā Devī.
- 2.101 Glorification of yoga in the final verse.

The Phala-śrutis.

There are traditionally six characteristics by which one is advised to determine the purpose of a particular text,

upakramopasaṁhārāv abhyāso'pūrvatā phalam
artha-vādopapattī ca liṅgaṁ tātparya-nirṇaye

> The six-fold criteria by which one can establish the meaning [of a text] are 1) opening and concluding statements; 2) frequently repeated statements; 3) original statements; 4) the benefits it proclaims; 5) those things that are particularly singled out for praise; and 6) conclusions made by argumentation.

As already mentioned above, verses 2.10-11 give the specific goals of each of the six aṅgas of the yoga system outlined here.

āsanena rujo hanti prāṇāyāmena pātakam |
vikāraṁ mānasaṁ yogī pratyāhāreṇa muñcati ||11||
dhāraṇābhir mano-dhairyaṁ dhyānāc caitanyam adbhutam |
samādhau mokṣam āpnoti tyaktvā karma śubhāśubham ||12||

> The yogī destroys diseases through *āsana*, sin through *prāṇāyāma*, and becomes free from the modifications (*vikāra*) of the mind through *pratyāhāra*. Through *dhāraṇā* [the yogi] attains steadiness of mind, from *dhyāna* a supernatural consciousness, and in *samādhi* he attains liberation, having cast off all auspicious and inauspicious karmas. (2.11-12)

No less than 72 verses in the *Gorakṣa-śataka* state the benefits of one practice or another. For the sake of this analysis, we have divided these benefits into five categories: Liberation or bliss, physical health, mystic powers, some intermediate benefit, and "other."

Liberation by far dominates with 33 promises that a certain practice will lead to liberation, which is expressed as freedom from grief, freedom from suffering and death, the taint of *karmas* or the touch of sin or stains; the conquest of time, attaining yoga or success in yoga (*yoga-siddhi*), attaining a state beyond decay and death where there are no more comings and goings, attainment of the highest state (*paramaṁ padam*), and becoming the same or one with Brahman. Three of these verses express this state as one of supreme bliss (*paramānanda*).

The benefits of reading GŚ itself are given as the attainment of the highest state (*paramaṁ padam*) in 1.4, liberation from all sins and success in yoga (*yoga-siddhi*) in 2.99, i.e., the introductory and concluding portions of the book. Yoga in general brings supreme joy (1.3), pacifies worldly sufferings (1.6) and eliminates misery (2.91).

Table 5

1.12	*padmāsana*	the destroyer of disease and disturbances
1.59	*mūla-bandha*	One's bodily excretions are diminished. Even an old man becomes young.
1.62	*Jālandhara*	removes diseases of the throat
1.65	*khecarī*	One does not experience disease, death, sleep, hunger, thirst, or fainting.
1.78	*mahā-mudrā*	destroys diseases
1.80	*mahā-mudrā*	One has the ability to digest even poison.
1.81	*mahā-mudrā*	One gets rid of tuberculosis, leprosy, constipation, enlargement of the spleen and improper digestion.
1.101	*nāḍi-śodhanam*	the ability to hold the breath, kindling the fire of digestion, the manifestation of the subtle inner vibration (*nāda*), and freedom from disease
2.3	*prāṇāyāma*	removes defects (*doṣa*)
2.11	*āsana*	destroys diseases
2.18	*prāṇāyāma*	freedom from disease
2.37	*viparīta-karaṇī*	One develops a body that is as soft as the stem of a lotus and lives a very long time, devoid of defects of body and mind.
2.38	*Kākacañcū*	does not age
2.39	*viparīta-karaṇī*	All illnesses are destroyed.
2.43	*viparīta-karaṇī*	One will never know decay or diminution.

Of the practices that are particularly singled out for *phala-śrutis* related to attaining liberation are *siddhāsana, uḍḍīyāna, khecarī, viparīta-karaṇī,* chanting of the *ajapā mantra, praṇava japa, prāṇāyāma, dhāraṇā, dhyāna,* and *samādhi*. Of these, all the nine kinds of *dhyāna* are said to lead to some kind of *mukti*: attaining yoga, freedom from suffering and oneness with Brahman. *Viparīta-karaṇī* (in the *pratyāhāra* section), which is said to bring freedom from old age and death, *prāṇāyāma*, the removal of sin, and *samādhi*, the end of repeated birth and death and liberation, are each glorified as the cause of liberation in at least three different verses each.

Table 6

1.5	reading GŚ	The mind turns away from sense pleasure and becomes attached to Paramātmā, deceives time.
1.52	*śakti-cālana*	attains unequalled understanding
1.57	*Bandhas*	becomes eligible for liberation
1.69	*khecarī*	the *bindu* does not flow out
1.75	union of *bindu* with *rajas*	the body becomes divine
1.77	*Mahā-mudrā*	purification of the net of channels, the arousing of the sun and moon, as well as the drying up of the juices,
1.90	*prāṇāyāma*	*sthāṇutvam*
1.92	*prāṇāyāma*	purity of mind (*citta-nirmalatvam*), freedom from fear of death
1.95	*nāḍi-śodhanam*	capable of controlling or stilling the breath (*prāṇa-saṅgrahaṇe kṣamaḥ*)
2.11	*dhāraṇā*	steadiness of mind
2.11	*pratyāhāra*	overcoming mental modifications
2.12	*dhyāna*	an amazing state of consciousness
2.46	*danta-bila*	become poet-philosopher
2.58	*dhāraṇā (ākāśa)*	opens the door to liberation
2.89	*samādhi*	cannot be pierced by any weapon, killed by any embodied being, nor be controlled by any spell (*mantra*) or occult diagram (*tantra*).
2.90	*samāḍhi*	not bound by time, tainted by action, nor can he be influenced by anyone or anything

The second major category of *phala-śruti* promises the removal of various diseases. As indicated in 2.11, *āsana* is the main practice that removes physical obstacles presented by the mind, and *prāṇāyāma* that of the body. If we include the *bandhas* and *mudrās* in the category of *āsana*, then the correspondence is clear. In particular, *mahā-mudrā* appears to be singled out as effective in ridding one of negative effects and *viparīta-karaṇī* in giving one a body that is healthy and long-lived. There is some overlap here, as freedom from the fear of death or death itself can be viewed as a benefit related to the body itself (*cidānandāyate tanuḥ*).

Six verses speak of mystic powers. These are all in connection with *dhyāna* and *dhāraṇā*, and all are found in verses 2.54-66. Only verse 2.76 speaks directly of the eight *siddhis* and the other verses speak of mastery of the elements. These are manifest in the higher strata of the six practices.[1]

Other benefits are usually expressed in other terms.

---

[1]The last three of the eight *aṅgas* of yoga (*dhyāna*, *dhāraṇā* and *samādhi*) are the *antaraṅga* or its most intimate practices. See *Yoga-sūtra* 3.7.

Acknowledgements

First I should acknowledge the debt that I have personally to Swami Veda Bharati, who not only brought me to Rishikesh but gave me an education in yoga and meditation in the guise of employing me as a Sanskrit teacher in the Gurukula for three years (2007-2010). Having the opportunity to live closely to him and observe his self-discipline, commitment to his guru, to his practice, to his mission, to his disciples and seekers who come to him, and most of all to his scholarship, all convinced me of his true character as a *siddha-yogi*. It was his grace on me that I had the opportunity to not only do this work, but surely whatever understanding or *yoga-sādhanā* I have gained are directly attributable to his blessings.

Thanks are due to Swami Rishi Kumar Panschsheel of Hansada Ashram, Nepal, who obtained a *Yoga-taraṅgiṇī* manuscript from the National Library of Kathmandu, to Dr. Bibekananda Banerjee of the Asiatic Society of Bengal, whose expertise in manuscript work led to the first draft of the critical edition. Pandit Chandramani and Pandit Sanjay Shastri both contributed in many ways, especially by helping sort out difficult passages. Suresh Shetty has been invaluable in doing various research tasks, formatting and generally mediating between myself and Swami Veda. Mamta Nakoti of the AHYMSIN Library at Swami Rama Sadhaka Grama deserves special thanks for tolerating me during the times I worked there and for her helpful attitude in finding books, etc. And of course I must mention Mei Wan Soh (Medha), Swamiji's personal secretary, for her helpful attitude in all matters practical.

I would like to repeat my gratitude to the help that came through the good graces of professors Mark Singleton and James Mallinson, whose insights were greatly helpful in clarifying many matters in this book.

yogena yogo jñātavyo yogo yogāt pravartate
yo'pramattas tu yogena sa yoge ramate ciram

Yoga is to be understood through yoga practice. Yoga manifests from yoga itself. One who has become vigilant through the practice of yoga delights in yoga for a long time.

Jagadananda Das
Vrindavan, India
3/26/2014

॥ श्रीगणेशाय नमः ॥

॥ गोरक्षशतकम् ॥

॥ प्रथमं शतकम् ॥

अथ ग्रन्थारम्भः

[1]श्रीशंभुं श्रीगुरुं[2] सूर्यं हेरम्बं जगदीश्वरीम्।
प्रणम्य शतकव्याख्यां कुर्मो योगतरङ्गिणीम्॥

तत्र[3] योगस्य प्रकरणमारभमाणो[4] भगवान् गोरक्षः श्रीगुरुपादाभिवन्दनात्मकं मङ्गलं ग्रन्थनिर्विघ्नतासिद्धये[5] शिष्यशिक्षायै निबध्नाति, अर्थाद्विषयप्रयोजने च सूचयति—

श्रीगुरुं परमानन्दं वन्दे स्वानन्दविग्रहम्।
यस्य सान्निध्यमात्रेण चिदानन्दायते तनुः ॥ १ ॥

---

[1] B. commentary begins: ओं श्रीगणेशाय नमः। ओं नमः शिवाय। अथ गोरक्षशतकं लिख्यते।

[2] श्रीहरिं (B,C)

[3] पूर्वश्लोकमत्रास्थातव्यम्। श्रीशम्भुं। तरङ्गिणीं। व्याख्यामङ्गलश्लोकोऽयम् (C)

[4] प्रकरणारम्भं (B)

[5] ग्रन्थ... सिद्धये (B only)

अहं गोरक्षः तं श्रीगुरुं श्रीमांश्चासौ, श्रीः परम आनन्दो यस्मादिति विग्रहे तु परमानन्दस्य जन्यतापत्तिरिति,[1] गुरुश्च श्रीगुरुः परिपृच्छमानानामात्मतत्त्वावबोधनशक्तियुक्तः, तं वन्दे अभिवादये।[2]

ननु कोऽसौ गुरुः यस्याभिवादनं मङ्गलप्रदम् ? इत्याकाङ्क्षायामाह—कथंभूतं श्रीगुरुं ? परमानन्दं परमश्चासावानन्दश्च परमानन्दः, निरतिशयानन्दरूपः परमात्मा, तम्। अनेन श्रीगुरोः ब्रह्मरूपत्वं दर्शितम्।

ननु ब्रह्मणि शरीरेन्द्रियसम्बन्धायोग्यतया, गुरौ च तत्सम्बन्धयोग्यतया, तयोर्भेदोपलब्धेः स्फुरत्वात्[3] कथमभेदः[4] प्रतिपाद्यते ? तत्राह—पुनः कथंभूतं श्रीगुरुं ? स्वानन्दविग्रहं स्वेषामात्मीयानामानन्दः स्वानन्दः स्वानन्दाय विग्रहो देहो यस्य स स्वानन्दविग्रहः प्रत्यगात्मा, तम्। अनेन भक्तानुकम्पया स्वीकृतशरीरस्य श्रीगुरोः ब्रह्मत्वं[5] निर्विवादमित्यभिहितं[6] भेदस्य काल्पनिकतया प्रत्यगात्मताया आपेक्षिकत्वं[7] चाभिहितम्।[8]

तदभिवादनस्य फलं उत्तरार्धेन दर्शयति—यस्येति। यस्य श्रीगुरोः सान्निध्यमात्रेण शिष्यः, तनुः कर्मभूतं जडमपीति भावः। चिदानन्दायते चिदानन्दमिव करोति। किमुत चिरमुपासनेनात्मानं चिदानन्दं न कुर्यात् ? अपि तु कुर्यादेवेत्यर्थः, तम्। अत्र स्वानन्दविग्रहं परमानन्दमिति[9] पदद्वये सामानाधिकरण्येन जीवब्रह्मणोरेकत्वलक्षणे विषयः चिदानन्दायते तनुरिति निरतिशयानन्दप्राप्तिरूपं प्रयोजनं च सूचितम्॥ १॥

---

[1] श्रीः... इति (C only). C follows with ऋजोक्तिः श्री पौसा (?)

[2] B. inserts इत्यन्वयः क्रियया कर्तुः परस्य लाभात्

[3] स्फुरत्वात् not in B,C.

[4] न भेदः (B)

[5] ब्रह्माभिन्नत्वं (B)

[6] निर्विवादमिति (A)

[7] प्रत्यगात्मतायापेक्षिकत्वं (ed.)

[8] भेदस्य...चाभिहितम् not in B,C.

[9] चिरमुपा... परमानन्दं not in B,C. C has चिरमुपासनेनात्मानं कुर्यादित्यर्थः, तम्.

संप्रति पूर्वसूचितविषयप्रयोजनप्रेक्षावत्प्रत्ययाय[1] योगाङ्गैः संपादितप्रयोजनं[2] मीननाथं नमस्कुर्वन्[3] प्रयोजनस्य सुलभतां दर्शयति[4]—

अन्तर्निश्चलितात्मदीपकलिकास्वाधारबन्धादिभिः
यो योगी युगकल्पकालकलनातत्त्वं च जेगीयते।
ज्ञानामोदमहोदधिः समभवद्यत्रादिनाथः स्वयं
व्यक्ताव्यक्तगुणाधिकं तमनिशं श्रीमीननाथं भजे॥ २॥

तं प्रसिद्धं श्रीमीननाथं अनिशं निरन्तरं अहं भजे कायमनोवचोभिः समाश्रये। तं कं ? यो योगी आधारबन्धादिभिः आधारोड्डीयाणजालन्धरबन्धैर्वक्ष्यमाणलक्षणैः कृत्वा, अन्तः हृत्कमलादिषु निश्चलितात्मदीपकलिकासु निश्चलं यथा भवति तथा स्थापिता या आत्मदीपकलिका[5], आत्मा एव दीपः[6] प्रकाशकत्वात्, तस्य कलिका इव, कलिकाः कलिकाकाराणि, ज्योतींषि, तास्तथोक्ताः, तासु सतीषु युगकल्पकालकलनातत्त्वं[7], युगश्च कल्पश्च युगकल्पौ, तावेव कालः, तस्य युगरूपस्य कल्परूपस्य कालस्याकलनात्मकं कालात्मतत्त्वं जेगीयते अतिशयेन गायति, निःशेषं जानातीत्यर्थः[8]।

तं च पुनः यो योगी यत्र यासु निश्चलितात्मदीपकलिकासु सतीषु ज्ञानामोदमहोदधिः ज्ञानानन्दसागरः विदिताखिलात्मतत्त्व[9] इति यावत्, अत एव आदिनाथः[10], स्वयमभवत्।

तं पुनः कथंभूतं ? तमत एव च व्यक्ताव्यक्तगुणाधिकं, व्यक्तानि पृथिव्यादीनि स्थूलभूतानि, अव्यक्तानि बुद्ध्यहंकारादीनि च तथोक्तानि। यद्वा, व्यक्तं पञ्चीकृत[11]भूतोत्थं स्थूलशरीरं,

---

[1] सम्प्रति पूर्वसूचितविषयनिरतिशयानन्दप्रयोजनप्रेक्षावत् प्रवृत्तये (C), ... प्रयोजने प्रेक्षवत् प्रेवृत्तये (B)

[2] सम्पादितविषयं (B)

[3] नमस्करोति (B,C)

[4] प्रयोजनस्य सुलभतां दर्शयति not in B,C.

[5] निश्चलं...आत्मदीपकलिका not in C.

[6] देवः (C)

[7] -तत्त्वे (C)

[8] निरन्तरमभ्यस्यतीत्यर्थः (C)

[9] विदिताखिलतत्त्व (C)

[10] अनादिनाथः (C)

[11] -पञ्चीभूत- (A)

अव्यक्तमपञ्चीकृतभूतोत्थं सूक्ष्मशरीरं[1], गुणाः नश्वरत्वपरिणामित्वादयः स्वभावाः[2]तेभ्योऽधिकः, तैरनभिभूतः[3], तथोक्तः तमित्यर्थः[4]॥२॥

विषयप्रयोजनेऽभिधाय स्वनामाधिकारिसम्बन्धानाह[5]—

नमस्कृत्य गुरुं भक्त्या गोरक्षो ज्ञानमुत्तमम्।
अभीष्टं योगिनां ब्रूते परमानन्दकारकम्॥३॥

स एव गोरक्षः पूर्वोक्तलक्षणं श्रीगुरुं भक्त्या पुनः पुनः नमस्कृत्य योगिनां पूर्वजन्मानुवृत्तयोगवासनावतां अभीष्टं संमतं यतः परमानन्दकारकं अद्वैतबोधजनकं, अत एव उत्तमं सर्वोत्कृष्टं ज्ञानं, ज्ञानसाधनप्रकरणं[6] ब्रूते कथयति। ज्ञानस्यात्युपकारकत्वात् ज्ञानसाधनमपि ज्ञानत्वोपचार[7] इत्यर्थः। अत्र परमानन्दकारकं ज्ञानमित्युक्त्या कर्मोपासनाभ्यां सम्पादितान्तःकरणशुद्धिकः[8] पुरुषोऽधिकारीति। ब्रूते इत्युक्त्या वाच्यवाचकभावलक्षणः सम्बन्ध इति सूचितम्। गोरक्ष इति स्वनामाभिहितम्[9]॥३॥

योगिनामभीष्टं ज्ञानं[10] ब्रूते इत्युक्तं, तत् किम् ? इत्याकाङ्क्षायां[11] प्रारीप्सितस्य प्रकरणस्य नाम लिखति—

गोरक्षशतकं वक्ति योगिनां हितकाम्यया ।
ध्रुवं यस्यावबोधेन जायते परमं पदम्॥४॥

---

[1] यद्वा... सूक्ष्मशरीरं not in C.

[2] तेषामेव स्वभावाश्च (B), तेषां गुणा नश्वरत्वपरिणामित्वादिभिः (C)

[3] तैरभिभूतः (C)

[4] C. here has the following after तयोक्तानि (as given): तेषां गुणाः नश्वरत्वपरिणमित्वादिभिः तेभ्यो अधिकः तैरभिभूतः तयोक्तस्तमित्यर्थः।

[5] -सम्बन्धमाह (C)

[6] ज्ञानसाधकप्रकरणं (C)

[7] C. drops ज्ञानसाधनमपि and reads ज्ञानसाधकत्वोपचार for ज्ञानत्वोपचारः।

[8] शुद्धितः (C)

[9] A,C here read ...सम्बन्ध इति । गोरक्ष इति स्वनाम इति सूचितम्।

[10] ज्ञानं in B only.

[11] योगि... इत्याकाङ्क्षायां not in C.

स एव गोरक्षः योगिनां पूर्वोक्तलक्षणानां हितकाम्यया हितं कामयते हितकाम्या अनुकम्पा तया गोरक्षशतकनामप्रकरणं वक्ति कथयति। कथंभूतं शतकं यस्य शतकस्य अवबोधेन गुरूपदेशतो यथार्थज्ञानेन, ध्रुवं निश्चयेन, यद्वा ध्रुवं पुनरावृत्तिरहितं, परमं पदं शाश्वतं स्थानं जीवन्मुक्तत्वादिकमित्यर्थः। "मुक्त एव हि मुच्यत" इति श्रुतेः।[1] जायते प्रादुर्भवति तदित्यर्थः॥४॥

एतच्छतकोक्तार्थानुष्ठानात् परमानन्दप्राप्तिरित्यभिधाय संप्रत्यवश्यसेव्यत्वमभिधत्ते[2]—

एतद्विमुक्तिसोपानमेतत् कालस्य वञ्चनम्।
यद्व्यावृत्तं मनो भोगादासक्तं परमात्मनि॥५॥

एतच्छतकं स्वोक्तकर्मानुष्ठानद्वारा कालस्य प्राणोत्क्रमणव्यापाराश्रयत्वेन संभावितस्य वञ्चनं, तत्सम्बन्धनिवर्तकं सत्, चिरकालयोगाभ्याससाधनद्वारा विमुक्तिसोपानं विशिष्टायां कैवल्यरूपायां मुक्तौ सोपानमिव सुमेधा[3]विचारणादिभूमिकाक्रमेण शीघ्रप्रापकं, यथा प्रासादादिषु सोपानमनायासेन प्रापकं तद्वदित्यवश्यसेव्यमित्यर्थः[4]।

तर्हि सर्वैरप्येतदेव कुतो न सेव्यते ? तत्राह—यदिति। यत्[5] यदि मनः भोगात् विषयास्वादाद्व्यावृत्तमन्तर्मुखतयोपरतं सत् परमात्मनि आसक्तं भवेत्, तस्यैव नान्यथेति। अनेन शमदमादिसिद्धभक्तिवैराग्याद्यैस्तत् फलं प्राप्यं[6], न तु विषयासक्तैरिति अधिकारिस्वरूपमिति[7] दर्शितम्॥५॥

ननु मोक्षसाधने वेदबोधितदानव्रतयागादिबहुतरयत्नेषु सत्स्वपि योगमेव किमस्तौषीत्[8] ? इत्याकाङ्क्षायां, नैतद्दानादिवत् साधारणं कारणं, किन्तु विशिष्टं दुर्लभं चेत्याह —

---

[1] This quote not in B,C.

[2] अभिधीयते (B)

[3] शुभे (C)

[4] तद्वदित्यवश्यमभ्यसेदित्यर्थः (B)

[5] यत् not in B,C.

[6] प्राप्यते (B)

[7] अधिकारिस्वरूपमिति B. only.

[8] Corrected from अस्तौतीति (B) and किमिति स्तौषीत् (A,C)

द्विजसेवितशाखस्य श्रुतिकल्पतरोः फलम्।
शमनं भवतापस्य योगं भजत सत्तमाः ॥ ६ ॥

हे सत्तमाः ! भवतापस्य संसारचक्रपरिवर्तनश्रमस्य[1] शमनं नाशनं योगं भजत॥[2] ननु श्रौतस्मार्तविधिनैवं कृतार्था अनवकाशाश्च वयं कथं योगं भजामः ? तत्राह—द्विजेति। कथंभूतं योगं ? द्विजसेवितशाखस्य द्विजैः ब्राह्मणैः सेविता उपासिता शाखा अवयवा यस्य सः। तथा तस्य श्रुतिकल्पतरोः, श्रुतिः वेदः, स एव कल्पतरुः कल्पवृक्षो विचित्रफलप्रदत्वात्, तस्य श्रुतिकल्पतरोः समग्रस्येत्यर्थः, फलमतश्चैकैकशाखामात्रावलम्बिनामतिदुर्लभमिति भावः ॥ ६ ॥

प्रकृतशास्त्रस्य[3] स्वरूपकथनाय अङ्गानि दर्शयति—

आसनं प्राणसंरोधः प्रत्याहारश्च धारणा।
ध्यानं समाधिरेतानि योगाङ्गानि वदन्ति षट् ॥ ७ ॥

- आसनमिति। आस्यते अनेनेत्यासनं पद्मादि। तच्च यथा स्थिरं सुखमनुद्वेजकं च भवति तदा योगाङ्गतां भजते। तस्य भेदं लक्षणं चाग्रे वक्ष्यते।
- प्राणसंरोध इति। प्राणस्य औदर्यप्रभञ्जनस्य संरोधः श्वासप्रश्वासगतिभङ्गः प्राणसंरोधः[4], प्राणायाम इत्यर्थः।
- प्रत्याहार इति। विषयं विषयं प्रति गच्छतामिन्द्रियाणां, बहिर्मुखानामित्यर्थः, आ समन्तात्, हरणमन्तर्मुखतया स्वस्वरूपेऽवस्थापनं प्रत्याहारः। तथा सति चित्[5]स्वरूपानुकारीणि सर्वेन्द्रियाणि भवन्ति।
- धारणेति। नाभिचक्रादौ वृत्त्यन्तरपरिहारेण चित्तस्यैकाग्रतया धारणं धारणा। तया च संप्रज्ञातसमाधेरभ्यासो भवति।

---

[1] -श्रमज्वरस्य (C)

[2] ...योगं भजनां अतिदुर्लभमिति भावः (C)

[3] शास्त्रप्रतिपाद्य- (A)

[4] प्राणसंरोधः not in B.

[5] चित्त- (A,C)

- ध्यानमिति। मूलाधारादिवक्ष्यमाणनवचक्रादौ विजातीयप्रत्ययपरिहारेण सजातीयप्रत्ययप्रवाहकरणं ध्यानम्।

- समाधिरिति। सम्यग् आधीयते, एकाग्रीक्रियते विक्षेपान्परिहृत्य यत्र मनः, स समाधिः। अयमर्थः—तदेव ध्यानं [1]यथार्थमात्रस्यावभासमानं तिरोहितज्ञानाद्यखिलेन्द्रिय-वृत्तिस्वरूपतया बहिःशून्यतामिव[2] सम्पद्यते, स समाधिरिति।

एतानि षट् योगाङ्गानि वदन्ति॥

न च "यमनियमासनप्राणायामप्रत्याहारधारणाध्यानसमाधयोऽष्टावङ्गानि" [यो.सू. २.२९] इति पातञ्जलसूत्रादावष्टाङ्गता-श्रवणात् कथं षडङ्गत्वकथनमिति वाच्यम्। अत्र हठाभ्यासावसरे प्रातःस्नानोपवासादिकायक्लेशानां निषेधस्य सर्वसम्मततया अहिंसा सत्यमस्तेयमित्यादियमानां, तपः सन्तोष आस्तिक्यमित्यादिनियमानां च निवृत्तिनिरतस्य पूर्वकाण्डतोऽनुस्मृततया[3]न्येषां यस्य यस्य यदा यदा अनुष्ठेयत्वं, तस्य तस्य तदा तदा गुरुमुखावगम्यत्वस्य चावश्यकतयाङ्ग्योरपि यमनियमयोरिह ग्रन्थे अनभिधानं बोध्यम्॥ तयोः स्वरूपं च—

अहिंसा सत्यमस्तेयं ब्रह्मचर्यं दयार्जवम्।
क्षमा धृतिर्मिताहारः शौचं चेति यमा दश॥ [यो.या. १.४९]
तपः सन्तोष आस्तिक्यं दानमीश्वरपूजनम्।
सिद्धान्तश्रवणं चैव ह्रीर्मतिश्च जपो व्रतम्॥
दशैते नियमाः प्रोक्ताः। [यो.या. २.१-२]

एतेषामङ्गानां भेदानाह याज्ञवल्क्यः—

यमश्च नियमश्चैव दशधा संप्रकीर्तितः। आसनान्युत्तमान्यष्टौ त्रीणि तेषूत्तमानि तु॥
प्राणायामस्त्रिधा प्रोक्तः प्रत्याहारश्च पञ्चधा॥ धारणा पञ्चधा प्रोक्ता ध्यानं षोढा प्रकीर्तितम्।[4]
त्रीणि तेषूत्तमान्याहुः समाधिस्त्वेकरूपतः॥ [यो.या. १.४६-४८] इति॥७॥

---

[1] Should probably be यदा...

[2] A. तिरोहितज्ञानाद्यखिलेन्द्रियस्वरूपतया शून्यतामिव

[3] B. अनुस्यूततया

[4]This is the B. reading, which matches our YY. Others have षोडश कीर्तितम्.

अथ आसनम्

तत्रासनानां भेदान् दर्शयति त्रिभिः[1]—

आसनानि च तावन्ति यावन्तो जीवजन्तवः ।
एतेषामखिलान् भेदान् विजानाति महेश्वरः ॥ ८ ॥

यावन्तो जीवजन्तवो जीवस्योपाधिभेदास्तावन्त्येव आसनानि च सन्तीति शेषः। तत्तदुपवेशनप्रकाराणां पार्थक्यस्यौचित्यात्[2]। एतेषामासनानामखिलान्भेदान्महेश्वर एव जानाति,[3] नान्यः। जन्तुशब्दोऽत्र जीवपदसमभिव्याहारे उपाधिमात्रपरः ॥ ८ ॥

तर्हि[4] महेश्वरज्ञानमात्रविषयाणामासनानां कथं योगाङ्गत्वं, योगस्येतरजनसाधारणत्वात् ? इत्याशङ्क्य साधारणासनानि[5] सङ्क्षिप्य दर्शयति द्वाभ्यां—

चतुरशीतिलक्षाणामेकैकं समुदाहृतम्।
ततः शिवेन पीठानां षोडशोनं शतं कृतम् ॥ ९ ॥

चतुरशीतिलक्षाणां जीवोपाधीनामेकैकं प्रत्युपाधि भिन्नं भिन्नमासनमुदाहृतं कथितम्। ततस्तेभ्यः पीठानां षोडशोनं शतं चतुरशीतिसङ्ख्याकं प्रति लक्षमेकैकं सर्वसारभूतं शिवेन सर्वसाधारणतया कृतमभिहितम्। एतेनेतरजनानुष्ठितानामप्यासनानामङ्गत्वमित्युक्तम्[6] ॥ ९ ॥

ततोऽपि सारभूतमासनद्वयमाह—

आसनेभ्यः समस्तेभ्यो द्वयमेतदुदाहृतम्।
एकं सिद्धासनं प्रोक्तं द्वितीयं कमलासनम् ॥ १० ॥

---

[1] त्रिभिः Not in A.

[2] पार्थक्यात् (C)

[3] B inserts सर्वान्तर्यामितया. C. reads विरचितानिति.

[4] Not in C.

[5] इत्याशङ्क्यासाधारणासनानि (?A), इत्याशङ्क्यासनानि (B), इत्यासनानि (C)

[6] एते ... मित्युक्तम् not in B,C.

समस्तेभ्यः आसनेभ्य एतदासनद्वयमुत्तममुदाहृतं मुख्यं कथितम्[1]। तस्मिन्नासनद्वये एकं सिद्धासनं, द्वितीयं कमलासनं पद्मासनम्[2] इत्यर्थः ॥ १० ॥

तत्र सिद्धासनस्य लक्षणमाह—

योनिस्थानकमङ्घ्रिमूलघटितं कृत्वा दृढं विन्यसेन्
मेढ्रे पादमथैकमेव नियतं कृत्वा समं विग्रहम्।
स्थाणुः संयमितेन्द्रियोऽचलदृशा पश्यन्भ्रुवोरन्तरं
चैतन्मोक्षकवाटभेदजनकं सिद्धासनं प्रोच्यते ॥ ११ ॥

योनिस्थानकं गुदमेढ्रान्तरालस्थानं। तदुक्तं मानसोल्लासे (४.१०)—

गुदाच्च द्व्यङ्गुलादूर्ध्वं मेढ्राच्च द्व्यङ्गुलादधः। योनिस्थानमिति ख्यातम् ॥ इति।

दृढं यथा स्यात् तथा अङ्घ्रिमूलेन पादपार्ष्णिना घटितं पीडितं कृत्वा, एकं पादं विन्यसेत् स्थापयेत् ॥ अथ[3] अपरं पादं मेढ्रे लिङ्गमूले नियतं स्थिरं कृत्वा विन्यसेत् स्थापयेत्। विग्रहं शरीरं ऋजु कृत्वा स्थाणुः कायचाञ्चल्यशून्यः संयमितेन्द्रियः चित्तचाञ्चल्यशून्यः सन्, अचलदृशा बद्धैकतानाभ्यां दृग्भ्यां भ्रुवोरन्तरं पश्यन्नासीत। एतत् मोक्षकपाटस्य कुण्डलिनीनिरुद्धसुषुम्णामुखस्य उद्घाटकं जीवब्रह्मणोरेकत्वाधायीत्यर्थः[4]। सिद्धासनं प्रोच्यते कथ्यते[5] ॥ ११ ॥

अथ पद्मासनस्य लक्षणम्—

वामोरूपरि दक्षिणं च चरणं संस्थाप्य वामं तथा
दक्षोरूपरि पश्चिमेन विधिना धृत्वा कराभ्यां दृढम्।
अङ्गुष्ठौ हृदये निधाय चिबुकं नासाग्रमालोकयेद्
एतद्व्याधिविकारनाशनकरं पद्मासनं प्रोच्यते ॥ १२ ॥

---

[1] मुख्यं कथितम् not in C.

[2] पद्मासनम् not in B,C., इत्यर्थः only in C.

[3] अथ not in B.

[4] जीवब्रह्मणोरेकत्वाधायीत्यर्थः not in C.

[5] C. has शिवेनोच्यते in the place of कथ्यते

वामोरूपरि[1] वामपादोरुमूलप्रदेशे दक्षिणं चरणं उत्तानपादतलं यथा भवति तथा संस्थाप्य, तथा वामचरणं दक्षोरुमूले संस्थाप्य पश्चिमेन विधिना पृष्ठभागावलम्बिताभ्यां कराभ्यां पादयोरङ्गुष्ठौ दृढं यथा स्यात् तथा गृहीत्वा, अयमर्थः[2]—वामोरुगतं दक्षिणपादाङ्गुष्ठं पृष्ठभागवेष्टितेन दक्षकरेण एवं दक्षोरुगतं वामपादाङ्गुष्ठं पृष्ठभागवेष्टितेन वामकरेणेत्येवं गृहीत्वेति, चिबुकं हृदये निधाय स्थितः सन् पूर्ववदचलदृशा नासाग्रमालोकयेत्, एतत् पद्मासनं यमिनां व्याधिविकारनाशनकरं, व्याधयः धातुवैषम्यनिमित्ता ज्वरादयो, विकाराः कामक्रोधादिजनिता मानसिका विक्षेपाः, तेषां नाशकरं भवति। अत एव "आसनेन रुजो हन्ति" (2.11) इति वक्ष्यते॥ १२॥

अथ षट्चक्रम्

इदानीं विषयवासनाकलितस्य[3] मनसो निरोधमन्तरेण स्वस्वरूपानुपलब्धेः[4] तन्निरोधस्य च विनावलम्बनेनाशक्यतया[5] तदवलम्बनभूतमान्तरीयं षट्चक्रादिकं दर्शयति—

षट्चक्रं षोडशाधारं द्विलक्ष्यं[6] व्योमपञ्चकम्।
स्वदेहे ये न जानन्ति कथं सिध्यन्ति योगिनः॥ १३॥

षट्चक्रमग्रे वक्ष्यते। षोडशाधारमिति। तदुक्तं नित्यनाथपद्धतौ—

१- तत्र प्रथमं पादाङ्गुष्ठाधारं,[7] तत्र तेजो ध्यायेत्। दृष्टिः स्थिरा भवति।

२- द्वितीयं मूलाधारं, पादपार्ष्णिना तदापीड्य तिष्ठेदग्निदीपनं भवति।

३- तृतीयं गुदाधारं, तस्य संकोचविकासमभ्यसेत्। अपानवायुः स्थिरो भवति।

४- चतुर्थं मेढ्राधारं, तस्य सङ्कोच मभ्यसेत्। पश्चिममार्गेण वज्रगर्भाख्यनाड्यां प्रविष्टः पवनो ब्रह्मग्रन्थित्रयं भित्त्वा भ्रमरगुहायां विश्रान्त ऊर्ध्वतः शङ्खबिन्दुं[8] स्तंभयति।

---

[1] वामोरूपरि not in B,C.

[2] अयमर्थः not in C.

[3] व्याकुलितस्य (B,C)

[4] स्वरूपलब्धेः (C)

[5] For तन्निरोधस्य...शक्यतया, C. has तन्निरोधमन्तरेणावलम्बनेनाशक्यतया.

[6] त्रिलक्ष्यं (B)

[7] B. here inserts तन्मूये पादान्तरेण क्रम स्थित्वा (Sic)

[8] विश्रान्तस्तदभिमुखमायन्तं ते मूर्द्धतः (B)

५- पञ्चममुड्डीयमाणाधारं, तस्यासनादिषु बन्धनेन मलमूत्रकृमीणां नाशनं भवति।

६- षष्ठं नाभिमण्डलाधारं, तत्र चिद्रूपं ध्यात्वा प्रणवं जपेन्नादोदयो भवति।

७- सप्तमं हृदयाधारं, तत्र प्राणनिरोधनेन हृत्पद्मविकाशो भवति।

८- अष्टमं कण्ठाधारं, तत्र चिबुकं गाढं नियोजयेदिडापिङ्गलयोर्वायुप्रवाहः स्थिरो भवति।

९- नवमे घण्टिकाधारे जिह्वाग्रं प्रवेशयेच्चन्द्रगलितामृतकलालाभो भवति।

१०- दशमे ताल्वाधारे छेदनदोहनाभ्यां दीर्घीकृतां जिह्वां प्रवेशयेत् काष्ठा भवति।

११- एकादशं जिह्वाधोभागं जिह्वाग्रेण मन्थयेदमृतं प्रादुर्भवति दिव्यकविता भवति।

१२- द्वादशे ऊर्ध्वदन्तमूलाधारे जिह्वाग्रं धारयतोऽखिलरोगशान्तिर्भवति।

१३- त्रयोदशं नासाग्राधारं लक्षयेत् मनः स्थिरं भवति।

१४- चतुर्दशे नासिकामूलाधारे दृष्टिं धारयेत्। षण्मासाज्ज्योतिः प्रत्यक्षं भवति।

१५- पञ्चदशं भ्रूमध्याधारमवलोकयेत्। किरणाकारं ज्योतिः प्रत्यक्षं भवति। एतस्य दृढाभ्यासे सूर्याकाशे मनो लीयते।

१६- षोडशं नेत्राधारं तन्मूलेङ्गुल्या चालनेनापाङ्गप्रदेशे[1] ज्योतिः दृश्यते। सदा तदवलोकने ज्योतिः साक्षाद्भवति इति षोडशाधाराः॥

अथ द्विलक्ष्यम्। लक्ष्यं द्विविधम्। बाह्यमाभ्यन्तरं च। तत्र बाह्यं नासाग्रभ्रूमध्यादि। आभ्यन्तरं मूलाधारहृत्पद्मादि।

अथ व्योमपञ्चकं। तदुक्तं नित्यनाथपद्धतौ—

आकाशं च पराकाशं महाकाशं तृतीयकम्।
तत्त्वाकाशं चतुर्थं स्यात् सूर्याकाशं च पञ्चमम्॥
श्वेतं रक्तं तथा धूम्रं नीलं विद्युन्निभं पुनः।
एकैकं ज्योतीरूपं तु स बाह्याभ्यन्तरं स्मरेत्॥ इति॥ १३॥

---

[1] चालनेनायामप्रवेशे (A,C)

किं च —

एकस्तम्भं नवद्वारं गृहं पञ्चाधिदैवतम्।
स्वदेहे ये न जानन्ति कथं सिध्यन्ति योगिनः॥ १४॥

स्तंभो हि गृहं निवासयोग्यं करोति। तत्सदृशं चात्र देहे[1] सकलवासनाधिकरणत्वान्मन एव। तदुक्तं श्रीभागवते—

चेतः खल्वस्य बन्धाय मुक्तये चात्मनो मतम्।
गुणेषु सक्तं बन्धाय रतं वा पुंसि मुक्तये॥ [भा.पु. ३.२५.१६] इति।

नवद्वारमिति। मुखमेकं चक्षुर्नासिकाश्रोत्राणां द्वयं द्वयमिति ऊर्ध्वद्वाराणि सप्त। गुदं मेढ्रमित्यधोद्वारे द्वे इति नवद्वाराणि।

गृहमिति पञ्चाधिदैवतं पञ्च अधिदेवता यस्मिन् तद्गृहं शरीरम्। अधिदेवताश्च ब्रह्मा विष्णू रुद्र ईश्वरः सदाशिवः इति पञ्च। तदुक्तं योगसारे—

चतुरस्रधरण्यादौ ब्रह्मा तत्राधिदेवता[2]। अर्धचन्द्राकृतिर्जलं विष्णुस्तत्राधिदेवता[3] ॥
त्रिकोणमण्डलं वह्नौ रुद्रस्तत्राधिदेवता। वायोर्बीजं तु षट्कोणमीशस्तत्राधिदेवता॥
आकाशमण्डलं वृत्तं देवतास्य सदाशिवः॥ इति पञ्चाधिदैवतमिति।

एतानि वस्तूनि स्वशरीरे ये योगिनो न जानन्ति[4] न पश्यन्ति, ते कथं केन प्रकारेण सिध्यन्ति ? अपि न सिध्यन्तीत्यर्थः॥ १४॥

षट्चक्रमाह—

चतुर्दलं स्यादाधारं स्वाधिष्ठानं च षट्दलम्।
नाभौ दशदलं पद्मं सूर्यसङ्ख्यादलं हृदि॥ १५॥

---

[1] देहे Not in A.

[2] B. throughout prefers -दैवतं

[3] C. adds स्मृता (not metrical).

[4] न जानन्ति not in C.

आधारचक्रं पीतवर्णमधोमुखं चतुर्दलं पङ्कजम् । दलानि च पीतवर्णैर्वशषसैरुपशोभितानि। तत्कर्णिकायां शूलाष्टकवेष्टितायां पीतवर्णायां[1] चतुःकोणभूमण्डलान्तर्गतेन गजेन्द्राधिरूढेन चतुर्बाहुना धराबीजाङ्कगतेन चतुर्वक्त्रेण ब्रह्मणा[2] तच्छक्त्या च डाकिन्याख्यया कोटिसूर्यप्रकाशया समलङ्कृतायां देदीप्यमानं त्रिकोणमण्डलं कामाख्यानाम पीठं[3] समुल्लसति। यस्य मध्ये पश्चिमाभिमुखं स्वयंभूर्नाम महालिङ्गं विलसति। यस्मिन् लिङ्गे विद्युत्प्रभोज्ज्वला कुण्डलीशक्तिः सार्धत्रिवलयाकारतया वेष्टितं स्वमुखेन[4] सुषुम्णामुखमाच्छाद्य स्वपिति। तस्या एव श्वासोच्छ्वासात् प्राणापानादिसंभवः। तदुक्तं योगसारे—

यस्मादुत्पद्यते वायुः यस्मादुत्पद्यते मनः। यस्मादुत्पद्यते हंसो यस्माद्वह्निः प्रजायते॥

यस्मादुत्पद्यते बिन्दुः यस्मान्नादः प्रवर्तते। तदेव कामरूपाख्यं पीठं कामफलप्रदम्॥ इति ॥

॥ इति मूलाधारचक्रम्॥

अथ स्वाधिष्ठानं। लिङ्गमूले रक्तवर्णं षड्दलमूर्ध्वमुखं पङ्कजं बादिलान्तैर्वर्णैरुपशोभितं, तत्कर्णिका च शुक्लवर्णार्धचन्द्राकारा वंबीजाधिष्ठितजलमण्डलालङ्कृता। तस्यां च वंबीजाङ्कदेशे श्रीवत्सकौस्तुभ-पीताम्बरालङ्कृतश्चतुर्भुजो विष्णुर्निजशक्त्या राकिनीसंज्ञया सहितस्तिष्ठति॥

॥ इति स्वाधिष्ठानम्॥

नाभिमूले नीलवर्णं दशदलमूर्ध्वमुखं मणिपूरकं नाम चक्रं। नीलैः डादिफान्तैरुपशोभितं। तत्कर्णिकायामरुणवर्णं तेजोमण्डलं यद्वह्निः स्वस्तिकाकारे[5]मेषारूढं सूर्यसंकाशं चतुर्भुजं वह्निबीजमस्ति। तस्य चाङ्कदेशे रक्तवर्णो भस्मालिप्ताङ्गो महारुद्रो नीलवर्णया चतुर्भुजया लाकिनीनामशक्त्या सहितस्तिष्ठति॥

॥ इति मणिपूरकचक्रम्॥

---

[1] पीतवर्णायां B. only.

[2] ब्रह्मणा B. only.

[3] -पीठे (A)

[4] चतुर्मुखेन

[5] स्वस्तिकाकारे (A)

तदूर्ध्वंहृत्प्रदेशे रक्तवर्णं कादिठान्तद्वादशवर्णघटितद्वादशदलैरलङ्कृतमूर्ध्वमुखमनाहतं नाम द्वादशदलपद्मं। तत्कर्णिकायां धूम्रवर्णषट्कोणं वायुमण्डलं तस्य मध्ये धूम्रवर्णं चतुर्बाहुकं वायुबीजं कृष्णमृगारूढं[1] काकिनीशक्तिसहितमस्ति तस्याङ्कदेशे वराभयकर ईश्वरोऽस्ति, तत्कर्णिकागतत्रिकोणमण्डले कनकवर्णं बाणलिङ्गमस्ति। इदमेव पूर्णगिरिपीठम्।

॥ इति अनाहतचक्रम्॥ १५॥

कण्ठे स्यात् षोडशदलं भ्रूमध्ये द्विदलं तथा।
सहस्रदलमाख्यातं ब्रह्मरन्ध्रे महापथे॥ १६ ॥

तदूर्ध्वं कण्ठमूले रक्तवर्णैः षोडशस्वरैरलङ्कृतं षोडशदलमूर्ध्वमुखं स्फटिकाभं विशुद्धाख्यं चक्रं। तत्कर्णिकायां पूर्णचन्द्राकारं वृत्तं नभोमण्डलम् । तत्रैव निष्कलङ्कं[2] पूर्णचन्द्रमण्डलम् । तस्य मध्ये शुक्लगजारूढं शुक्लं पाशाङ्कुशवराभयकरमाकाशबीजं साकिन्याख्यया[3] शक्त्या सह तिष्ठति। इदं जलन्धरं नाम पीठम् ।

॥ इति विशुद्धचक्रम्॥

तदूर्ध्वं भ्रूमध्ये देशे द्विदलं श्वेतवर्णं हक्षाभ्यां समलङ्कृतमाज्ञानामचक्रमूर्ध्वमुखं तिष्ठति। तत्कर्णिकायां हाकिनीशक्त्यलङ्कृतायां[4] योनिमण्डलं विलसति। यस्यां योनौ इतराख्यं शिवलिङ्गं तिष्ठति। एतच्चक्रं मनसः स्थानं इदमेवोड्डीयाणनामकं पीठं भवति॥

॥ इति आज्ञाचक्रम्॥ इति षट्चक्रम्॥

क्रमप्राप्तं सहस्रदलमाह—सहस्रदलमिति। महापथे ब्रह्मरन्ध्रे सहस्रदलं शुभ्रं पूर्णचन्द्रसन्निभमधोवक्त्रं परमानन्दरूपं कमलमस्ति। तत्कर्णिकायां च अकारादिवर्णविन्यासने हलक्षाङ्कितकोणत्रयात्मकेनोपलक्षिता अधोऽग्रकोणा[5] योनिरस्ति। तस्यां योनौ स्फुरज्ज्योत्स्नाजालालङ्कृतं पूर्णेन्दुमण्डलमुल्लसति। तन्मध्ये विद्युदाकारमतिशयानन्दराशीभूतं स्फुरज्ज्योति-

---

[1] कृष्णमृगीरूढं (B)

[2] निष्कलं (B)

[3] शकिन्याख्यया (A,B) शक्तिन्याख्यया (C)

[4] हाकिनीशक्तिसमलङ्कृतायां (B)

[5] This word only appears in the B manuscript.

रुल्लसति। तत्र चिदानन्दरूपी सकलवेदान्तैकवेद्यः परमशिवो विजयते। तस्याङ्कदेशे सहस्त्रसूर्यप्रकाशसूक्ष्मानि स[1]प्रबोधरूपार्धचन्द्रभङ्गुरतनुर्निर्वाणकला[2] विलसति। यस्या अन्तः कोटिसूर्यप्रकाशकेशाग्रस्य कोटिभागैकरूपा यस्या उन्मीलननिमीलनाभ्यां जगदुत्पत्तिप्रलयौ जायेते। सेयं पूर्णनिर्वाणशक्तिः परिलसति। अस्या एवान्तरे योगमात्रैकगम्यमवाङ्मनस-गोचरमतिशयानन्दरूपं परात्परतरं[3] परमशिवपदं यस्यैवानन्दलेशेन ब्रह्मादयोऽप्यानन्दवन्तो भवन्ति॥

॥ इति सहस्त्रदलचक्रम्॥ १६॥

कामरूपपीठं तदधिष्ठितौ शक्तिशिवौ च दर्शयति त्रिभिः —

आधारं प्रथमं चक्रं स्वाधिष्ठानं द्वितीयकम्।
योनिस्थानं द्वयोर्मध्ये कामरूपं निगद्यते॥ १७॥

मूलाधारं स्वाधिष्ठानं चेति चक्रद्वयमपि प्रागुक्तम्। तयोर्द्वयोः स्वाधिष्ठानमूलाधारयोर्मध्ये[4] कामरूपं नाम पीठं निगद्यते कथ्यते॥ १७॥

किं तयोर्मध्ये तृतीयं स्थानं ? नेत्याह—

आधाराख्यं गुदस्थानं पङ्कजं च चतुर्दलम्।
तन्मध्ये प्रोच्यते योनिः कामाख्या सिद्धवन्दिता॥ १८॥

गुदस्थानं यत् आधाराख्यं चतुर्दलं पङ्कजं, तन्मध्ये तत्कर्णिकायां कामाख्या नाम योनिर्मातृकाक्षरमयी सुषुम्णान्तर्गताऽधोगतेन तृतीयकोणाग्रसंस्पृष्टमूलाधारकर्णिकामध्य-भागेत्यर्थः। अत उक्तं द्वयोर्मध्य इति।[5] सर्वसिद्धैरपि वन्दिता नमस्कृता प्रोच्यते कथ्यते॥ १८॥

---

[1] The best sense I can make here would be -सूक्ष्मानिश-

[2]–कलं (A).

[3] परतरं महानिर्वाणसंज्ञं (B)

[4] तयोर्द्वयोर्मध्ये (A)

[5] From योनि... A,C have only योनिर्मातृकाक्षरमित्यर्थः

योनिमध्ये महालिङ्गं पश्चिमाभिमुखं स्थितम्।
मस्तके मणिवद्बिम्बं यो जानाति स योगवित्॥ १९॥

तस्या योनेर्मध्ये पश्चिमाभिमुखं सुषुम्णावदनाभिमुखं यथा स्यात् तथा स्थितं स्वयंभूर्नामकं महालिङ्गमस्तीति शेषः। मस्तके तस्य लिङ्गस्य शिरःप्रदेशे मणिवद्देदीप्यमानं बिम्बम्। तदुक्तं योगसारे—

या मूलाधारगा शक्तिः कुण्डली बिन्दुरूपिणी।
मस्तके मणिवद्बिम्बं यो जानाति स योगवित्॥ इति।[1]

एतद्द्वयं यो जानाति स योगवित् योगज्ञो भवति। योगानभिज्ञैरनभिज्ञेयमेतद्द्वयमिति[2] भावः॥ १९॥

तत्रैव कालाग्नेः स्थानं दर्शयति —

तप्तचामीकराभासं तडिल्लेखेव विस्फुरत्।
त्रिकोणं तत्पुरं वह्नेरधोमेढ्रात् प्रतिष्ठितम्॥ २०॥

मेढ्रात् लिङ्गमूलादधोभागे आधारकर्णिकायां लिङ्गं प्रतिष्ठितं[3] तप्तचामीकराभासं तप्तकनकसन्निभं तडिल्लेखेव विद्युल्लतेव विस्फुरद्देदीप्यमानं, तत्पूर्वोक्तं[4] वह्नेः कालाग्नेः पुरं स्थानं भवति। तदुक्तं सुरेश्वराचार्येण — "मूले तिष्ठति कालाग्निः" [मानसोल्लास ९.१०] इति। योगसारे च —

पातालानामधोभागे कालाग्निर्यः प्रतिष्ठितः।
स मूलाग्निः शरीरेऽस्मिन् यस्मान्नादः प्रवर्तते॥ इति॥ २०॥

कालाग्निमेव समाधिपूर्वक्षणे चराचरप्रपञ्चात्मकं विश्वं प्रणवद्वारा चिदात्मनि योजनाय व्यापकत्वेन ध्यानविषयीकृतं विशेषरूपं कालाग्निमेव दर्शयति[1]—

---

[1] अत्राप्यस्तीति योज्यं (B). It would appear that the second line of this verse is being seen by B. as the insertion of the second line of the GŚ verse.
[2] B. drops एतद्द्वयम्.
[3] लिङ्गं निप्रतिष्ठितं (A); लिङ्गत्रिकोणयोर्मध्ये इत्यर्थः (B); आधारकर्णिकायां इत्यर्थः। प्रतिष्ठितं... (C)
[4] प्रोक्तं (A)

यत् समाधौ परं ज्योतिरनन्तं विश्वतोमुखम्।
तस्मिन् दृष्टे महायोगे यातायातं न विद्यते॥ २१॥

यत् योगिनः समाधौ अनन्तं[2] निरवच्छिन्नं विश्वतोमुखं विश्वव्यापकं सत् परं[3] ज्योतिरुत्तमं तेजः प्रादुर्भवति। तदेव कालाग्निरूपमिति शेषः। महायोगे धारणाद्यङ्गत्रये[4] शक्तिचालनद्वारा साधने वा, तस्मिन् ज्योतिषि दृष्टे सति यातायातं जननमरणं[5] संसारचक्रपरिवर्तनमिति यावत् न विद्यते॥ २१॥

स्वाधिष्ठानं विवृणोति—

स्वशब्देन भवेत् प्राणः स्वाधिष्ठानं तदाश्रयः।
स्वाधिष्ठानाश्रयादस्मात् मेढ्रमेवाभिधीयते॥ २२॥

स्वशब्देन वाच्यः प्राणः हंसरूपी भवेत्। तस्याधिष्ठानमाश्रयः[6], अस्मात् पदात् मेढ्रमेवाभिधीयते प्रमीयते। तदेव द्वितीयं चक्रमित्यर्थः॥ २२॥

मणिपूरकमाह—

तन्तुना मणिवत् प्रोतो यत्र कन्दः सुषुम्णया।
तन्नाभिमण्डलं चक्रं प्रोच्यते मणिपूरकम्॥ २३॥

तन्तुना सूत्रेण[7] प्रोतः मणिरिव यत्र यस्मिन्सुषुम्णया गुम्फितः कन्दोऽस्ति, तन्नाभिमण्डलं मणिपूरकं नाम चक्रं प्रोच्यते॥ २३॥

---

[1] कालाग्निमेव दर्शयति (C); कालाग्निमेव समाधिपूर्वक्षणे चराचरप्रपञ्चात्मकप्रणवद्वारा चिदात्मनि योजनाय व्यापकत्वेन ध्यानविषयीकृतं विशेषरूपं दर्शयति (A).

[2] यद् यस्मिन् त्रिकोणे समाधा अनन्तरं निरन्तरं (C)

[3] तत्परं (B)

[4] B, C here insert महायोगस्य.

[5] जन्ममरणं (B)

[6] स्वाधिष्ठानमाश्रयः (C)

[7] तंत्रेण (C)

अनाहतचक्रमाह—

द्वादशारे महाचक्रे पुण्यपापविवर्जिते।
तावज्जीवो भ्रमत्येव यावत् तत्त्वं न विन्दति॥ २४॥

द्वादशारे द्वादशदले पुण्यपापरहिते अनाहताख्ये महाचक्रे बुद्धिकर्मेन्द्रियप्राणानां पञ्चकैर्मनोबुद्धिभ्यां चोपलक्षितो जीवस्तावदेव भ्रमति यावत्पर्यन्तं तत्त्वमात्मतत्त्वं[1] न विन्दति न प्राप्नोति॥ २४॥

अथ दश नाड्यः

पुर्वोक्तं कन्दमाह—

ऊर्ध्वं मेढ्रादधो नाभेः कन्दयोनिः खगाण्डवत्।
तत्र नाड्यः समुत्पन्नाः सहस्राणां द्विसप्ततिः॥ २५॥

मेढ्राल्लिङ्गदेशादूर्ध्वं नाभेरधः कन्दो योनिरिव योनिः सकलनाड्युत्पत्तिस्थानं खगाण्डवत् पतङ्गानामण्डाकारमस्तीत्यर्थः। तत्र सहस्राणां द्विसप्ततिः नाड्यः समुत्पन्ना इतस्ततः प्रसृताः सन्तीत्यर्थः[2]॥ २५॥

तेषु नाडीसहस्रेषु द्विसप्ततिरुदाहृताः।
प्रधानाः प्राणवाहिन्यो भूयस्तासु दश स्मृताः॥ २६॥

तेषु द्विसप्ततिसहस्रेषु द्विसप्ततिनाड्यः प्राणवाहिन्यः सन्ततं प्राणव्यापाराविशिष्टाः, अत एव प्रधानाः। भूयः पुनरपि तासु द्विसप्ततिनाडीषु दशनाड्यः प्रधानतराः स्मृताः॥ २६॥

पूर्वोक्तानां दशनाडीनां नामानि स्थानानि च दर्शयति पञ्चभिः—

इडा च पिङ्गला चैव सुषुम्णा च तृतीयका।
गान्धारी हस्तिजिह्वा च पूषा चैव यशस्विनी॥ २७॥

---

[1] आत्मतत्त्वं (C)

[2] संवृत्ता इत्यर्थः (C)

अलम्बुषा कुहूश्चैव शङ्खिनी दशमी स्मृता।
एतन्नाडीमयं चक्रं ज्ञातव्यं योगिभिः सदा॥ २८॥

इडा पिङ्गला सुषुम्णा गान्धारी हस्तिजिह्वा पूषा यशस्विनी अलम्बुषा कुहूः शङ्खिनी। एतन्नाडीमयं नाडीजालवितानभूतं नाडीचक्रं योगिभिः सदा ज्ञातव्यम्। एतत्सञ्चारी वायुश्च ज्ञातव्यः। तयोरविरोधेन पवनादियोगमभ्यसेदित्युभयोरर्थः॥ २७-२८॥

स्थानान्याह—

इडा वामे स्थिता भागे पिङ्गला दक्षिणे स्थिता।
सुषुम्णा मध्यदेशे तु गान्धारी वामचक्षुषि॥ २९॥

इडा वामे भागे स्थिता, पिङ्गला दक्षिणे भागे स्थिता, सुषुम्णा तयोर्मध्ये मेरुदण्डमाश्रित्य स्थितेत्यर्थः। एतन्नाडीत्रयं मूलाधारगतयोन्याः कोणत्रयात् समुद्भूतम्। तत्र वामकोणादिडा[1], दक्षिणकोणात् पिङ्गला, पश्चिमकोणात् सुषुम्णा समुद्भूता। तत्रेडापिङ्गले सुषुम्णायां समालिङ्गिते स्वस्वभागगतनासिकाबिलाभ्यां विनिःसृते। सुषुम्णा तु मूलाधारात् ब्रह्मरन्ध्रपर्यन्तमागतेत्यर्थः। तदुक्तं सुरेश्वराचार्यैः—

> मूलाधाराग्रकोणोत्था सुषुम्णा ब्रह्मरन्ध्रगा। तत्पार्श्वकोणयोर्जाते द्वे इडापिङ्गले स्थिते॥
>
> नाडीचक्रेण संस्फूर्ते नासिकान्तमुभे गते॥ इति।

अग्रकोणोत्था पश्चिमकोणोद्भूताः, अन्यास्तु नाभिचक्रकन्दादुद्भूताः। ततो वामचक्षुःपर्यन्तं गान्धारी॥ २९॥

दक्षिणे हस्तिजिह्वा च पूषा कर्णे च दक्षिणे।
यशस्विनी वामकर्णे ह्यानने चाप्यलम्बुषा॥ ३०॥

दक्षचक्षुःपर्यन्तं हस्तिजिह्वा। तथा दक्षिणकर्णपर्यन्तं पूषा, वामकर्णपर्यन्तं यशस्विनी। आनने मुखे अलम्बुषा॥ ३०॥

---

[1] वाम भागगतकोणादिडा (B,C)

कुहूश्च लिङ्गदेशे तु मूलस्थाने तु शङ्खिनी।
एवं द्वारं समाश्रित्य तिष्ठन्ति दश नाडयः[1] ॥ ३१ ॥

लिङ्गदेशे च कुहूः। मूलस्थाने च शङ्खिनी। इमे द्वे नाड्यौ नाभिचक्रीयकन्दादधोमुखतया गतेत्यर्थः। एवममुना प्रकारेण भिन्नं भिन्नमेकैकं द्वारं प्राणवायोर्मार्गभूतं समाश्रित्य दश नाड्यस्तिष्ठन्तीत्यर्थः ॥ ३१ ॥

निरन्तरं प्राणवाहितया एताभ्योऽपि प्रधानभूतं नाडीत्रयमाह—

इडापिङ्गलासुषुम्नाः प्राणमार्गसमाश्रिताः।
सन्ततं प्राणवाहिन्यः सोमसूर्याग्निदेवताः ॥ ३२ ॥

इडापिङ्गलासुषुम्णा एता नाड्यः प्राणस्य श्वासोच्छ्वासरूपतया प्रवेशनिर्गमरूपव्यापाराश्च यस्य मार्गे समाश्रिता मार्गत्वेन स्थिता इत्यर्थः। कथंभूतास्ताः ? सोमसूर्याग्नयो देवता यासां तास्तथोक्ताः। इडायाश्चन्द्रो देवता, पिङ्गलायाः सूर्यः, सुषुम्णाया अग्निर्देवतेत्यर्थः ॥ ३२ ॥

अथ सव्यापाराश्च वायवः

दशवायूनाह चतुर्दशभिः[2] —

[3]प्राणोऽपानः समानश्चोदानव्यानौ वायवः।
नागः कूर्मोऽथ कृकरो देवदत्तो धनञ्जयः ॥ ३३ ॥

प्राणः, अपानः, उदानः, समानः, व्यानः, नागः, कूर्मः, कृकरः, देवदत्तः, धनञ्जय इति दश। तत्र प्राणाद्याः पञ्च वायवः प्रधानाः। तत्र कर्माणि तु श्वासोच्छ्वासकाशादि, अन्नादिपाचनपर्यन्तानि[4]

---

[1] नाडिकाः (L, Briggs)

[2] चतुर्दशभिः only in B.

[3] Verses 33-49 are missing in C.

[4] पाचतर्पयन्तानि (all)

प्राणस्य, विण्मूत्रादिविसर्जनमपानस्य, हानोपादानादिचेष्टा व्यानस्य, शरीरवृद्ध्यादिकमुदानस्य, पोषणादि[1] समानस्य। अन्येषां मूले वक्ष्यते॥ ३३॥

पूर्वोक्तदशवायूनां मध्ये पञ्चानां स्थानानि दर्शयति—

हृदि प्राणो वसेन्नित्यमपानो गुदमण्डले।
समानो नाभिदेशे तु उदानः कण्ठमध्यतः॥ ३४॥
व्यानो व्यापी शरीरे तु प्रधानाः पञ्चवायवः।
प्राणाद्याः पञ्च विख्याता नागाद्याः पञ्चवायवः॥ ३५॥

प्राणो नाम वायुः नित्यं हृदि वसेत् वसति। अपानो नित्यं गुदमण्डले आधारचक्रे वसति[2]। समानो नित्यं नाभिमण्डले वसति । उदानः कण्ठमध्ये वसतीति सङ्क्षेपेणोक्तम्। वस्तुतस्तु मुखनासिकयोर्मध्ये हृन्मध्ये नाभिमध्यमे कुण्डल्याः परितः पादाङ्गुष्ठे प्राणः सदा वसेदिति प्राणवायोः स्थानानि। एवं गुदमेढ्रोरु[3]जानूदरेक्षणकटिनाभिषु अपानः। श्रोत्राक्षिकटिगुल्फघ्राणगले व्यानः। सर्वसन्धिस्थाने हस्तयोः पादयोरप्युदानः। समानवायुश्च जाठराग्निकलासम्मिलितः सर्वाङ्गं व्याप्य तिष्ठति, [स्वगतसुखदुःखादिद्वन्द्वं सम्बन्धं विधाय रूपवन्तं कुर्वन्][4]। अत एवैते पञ्चवायवः प्रधानाः कथिताः। नागाद्यास्तु[5] पञ्चवायवः त्वगस्थ्यादिषु तिष्ठन्ति॥ ३४-३५॥

नागादीनां कर्माण्याह—

उद्गारे नाग आख्यातः कूर्म उन्मीलने स्मृतः।
कृकरं क्षुतकृत् ज्ञेयो देवदत्तो विजृंभणे॥ ३६॥

उद्गारो नागस्य कर्म। उन्मीलनं नेत्रपक्ष्मव्यापारः, तच्च कूर्मस्य। क्षुतं कृकस्य, विजृंभणं देवदत्तस्य॥ ३६॥

---

[1] शोषणादि (all?) See YY 4.68.

[2] वसति here and after नाभिमण्डले (B. only)

[3] गुदमेढ्र ऊरु- (all)

[4] The portion between brackets not found in B,C.

[5] नागाद्याः (A)

न जहाति मृतं चापि सर्वव्यापी धनंजयः।
एते सर्वासु नाडीषु भ्रमन्ते जीवरूपिणः॥ ३७॥

सर्वशरीरव्यापी धनञ्जयो धनञ्जयो नाम वायुः मृतं शवभूतमपि शरीरं न जहाति न विमुञ्चति। एते दशवायवो जीवमवच्छिन्नं चैतन्यं[1] रूपयन्ति, स्वस्मिन् ताद्रूप्याध्यासेन स्वमतसुखदुःखादिद्वन्द्वं सम्बन्धं विधाय रूपवन्तं कुर्वन्ति[2]। ते जीवरूपिणो अहं सुखी अहं दुःखीति च यः सूक्ष्मशरीरगतजीवव्यवहारस्तस्य साधनीभूताः सन्तः सर्वासु नाडीषु भ्रमन्ते, एकत्रावस्थानं नालभन्त इत्यर्थः[3]।

[4]अत्र यद्यपि अविद्यावच्छिन्नं चैतन्यं जीवो न च तत्र भ्रमणादिकं संभवति, तथाप्युपाधिभूत एवोदकगतं[5] चाञ्चल्यादिकं तत्प्रतिफलितं चन्द्रादाविव[6] जीवोपाधिभूतहंसाकारबुद्धिवृत्ति-सञ्चलितप्राणादिगतं चलनादिकं तदुपहितजीव-चैतन्येऽध्यारोप्यते[7]। जीवोपाधिश्च मनोबुद्धिज्ञानकर्मेन्द्रियप्राणपञ्चकरूपे लिङ्गदेहः। अत एवायमपि चिदाभासरूपो जीव इति व्यपदिश्यते। तथा च लिङ्गदेहावयवीभूतप्राणनिष्ठव्यापारस्य तत्तादात्म्यापन्न[8]जीवचैतन्येऽभ्युपगमो न विरुद्धः।

अत्र जीवस्य त्रैविध्यं प्रसिद्धम्। तदुक्तमाचार्यस्वामिचरणैः[9]—

अवच्छिन्नश्चिदाभासस्तृतीयः स्वप्नकल्पितः। विज्ञेयस्त्रिविधो जीवस्तत्राद्यः पारमार्थिकः॥ इति॥

अवच्छिन्नो घटाकाशादिवत् प्राणादिसङ्घातावच्छिन्नश्चिदात्मेत्येकविधो जीवः। चिदाभास उदक इव सूर्यादेरुपाधौ चित्प्रतिबिम्ब उपाधिधर्मास्कन्दितो जीवो द्वितीयविधः[10]। अयमेव जीवोऽत्र

---

[1] अवच्छिन्नं चैतन्यं only in B.

[2] The portion स्वमतसुखदुःखादिद्वन्द्वं सम्बन्धं विधाय रूपवन्तं कुर्वन्ति only in B.

[3] After नाडीषु B reads only भ्रमन्त इत्यर्थः.

[4] C commentary to this verse stops here.

[5] A has incorrect तथाप्युपाधिभूतशसर्वाङ्गगतं

[6] चन्द्रादावपि (A)

[7] ऽप्यारोप्यते (A)

[8] A has only तादात्म्यापन्न-

[9] The manuscripts appear to have gotten their pages mixed up at this point. This has, I think, been now restored to the proper order here.

[10] -विधः not in B.

विवक्षितः। तृतीयस्तु स्वप्नप्रकल्पितो देवोऽहं मनुष्योऽहमित्येवं स्वप्न इव स्थूलसंघाताभेदेन[1] कल्पित इति त्रिविधो जीवः। तत्राद्यः पारमार्थिको जीव इति तदर्थः। तथा च सिद्ध एव लिङ्गदेहे जीवव्यवहारः। तत्राद्यस्य पारमार्थिकत्वमपि[2] तैरेवोक्तम्—

> अवच्छेदः कल्पितः स्यादविच्छिद्यं तु वास्तवम्।
>
> तस्मिन् जीवत्वमारोपात् ब्रह्मत्वं तु स्वभावतः॥ इति॥३७॥

उक्तप्रकारेण प्राणादिरूपतापन्नस्य जीवस्यानेकविधमस्वस्थत्वं सदृष्टान्तं दर्शयति—आक्षिप्त इति चतुर्भिः।

आक्षिप्तो भुज[3]दण्डेन यथोच्चलति कन्दुकः।
प्राणापानसमाक्षिप्तस्तथा जीवो न तिष्ठति॥३८॥

यथा वारविलासिनीभिः भुजदण्डेन करतलेनाक्षिप्तस्ताडितस्तासां लीलोपकरणरूपः कन्दुक उच्चलति, भूतलप्रतिघातेन ऊर्ध्वमुत्तिष्ठति, एवं मुहुस्ताडितः करभूतलयोराघात-प्रतिघातैरेकत्रावस्थानमलभमान एव विलासिनीमनो विलासयन्विलसति। तथा प्राणप्रदेश-गतोऽपानेनापानप्रदेशगतश्च प्राणेनेत्येवं प्राणापानाभ्यां स्वस्वप्रदेशमाकृष्टो जीवोऽप्येकत्र न तिष्ठति। स्वस्वाकारमात्र-प्रतिफलिततया प्राणापानाभ्यां स्वस्वप्रदेशमाकृष्ट एकत्रावस्थानमलभमान एवाभिमानिनामनुकूलरूपं विलसतीत्यर्थः। एवं चात्र यथा कन्दुकस्य वारविलासिनीकरपरतन्त्रता, तथा जीवस्याप्यविद्याकार्यप्राणादिपराधीनत्वमिति भावः॥३८॥

अत एवाह—

प्राणापानवशो जीवो ह्यधश्चोर्ध्वं च धावति।
वामदक्षिणमार्गेण चञ्चलत्वान्न दृश्यते॥३९॥

---

[1] स्थूलसंपाताभेदे (A)

[2] पारमार्थिकमपि (A)

[3] Lonavla here reads भुवि, which does seem to make better sense, though not our commentator's reading. All others have the same as our text.

जीवो हि यतः प्राणापानयोर्वश अधीनः अतः कारणात् वामदक्षिणमार्गेण इडापिङ्गलाद्वारेण कृत्वा अधो मूलाधारपर्यन्तं, ऊर्ध्वं मुखनासिकाविवरपर्यन्तं च धावति। अतश्चञ्चलत्वात् प्राणापानवशतया अस्थिरत्वात् न दृश्यते। असंयतप्राणस्य हृत्पङ्कजादिषु ध्यानविषयो न भवति। दृशिरत्र ज्ञानार्थः[1] ॥ ३९ ॥

इदानीं सुषुप्तौ जीवोपाधिभूताविद्याकार्यलये जीवभावविनिर्मुक्तस्य ब्रह्मणः पुनर्जीवभावं सदृष्टान्तं दर्शयति—

रज्जुबद्धो यथा श्येनो गतोऽप्याकृष्यते पुनः।
गुणबद्धस्तथा जीवः प्राणापानेन कृष्यते ॥ ४० ॥

यथा रज्ज्वा चरणादौ बद्धः श्येनः पक्षिविशेषो यो गतोऽपि[2] बन्धनस्थानात् प्रचलितोऽपि तया रज्ज्वा पुनराकृष्यते तत्रैव स्थाप्यते, तथा गुणैर्मायांशैरवशिष्टारब्ध[3]कर्मफलभोगवासनारूपैर्बद्धो रूढसम्बन्धो जीवश्चिदाभासात्मा गतोऽपि लीनायां बुद्धिवृत्तौ पूर्वोक्तोपाधिविनिर्मुक्तोऽपि प्राणापानेनोक्तभोगार्थमवशिष्टेन कृष्यते[4], जाग्रतस्तद्बुद्धायां[5] बुद्धिवृत्तौ पुनर्जीवभावमानीयत इत्यर्थः। यद्वा, प्राणप्रदेशगतस्यापानप्रदेशप्राप्तौ, अपानप्रदेशगतस्य जीवस्य प्राणप्रदेशप्राप्तौ जाग्रत्येव[6]। दृष्टान्तः श्येनः ॥ ४० ॥

अपानः कर्षति प्राणं प्राणोऽपानं च कर्षति।
ऊर्ध्वाधः संस्थितावेतौ संयोजयति योगवित् ॥ ४१ ॥

अपानो मूलाधारगतवायुः प्राणमाज्ञागतवायुं[7] कर्षति। स्वप्रदेशमानयति तथा प्राणश्च अपानं मूलाधारगतवायुं कर्षति स्वप्रदेशमानयतीत्यर्थः। एवमसंयतप्राणस्यावस्थामभिधाय संयतप्राणस्तु

---

[1] दर्शनार्थः (C)

[2] पक्षिविशेषो यो गतोऽपि not in C.

[3] गुणैरवशिष्टप्रारब्ध- (C)

[4] गुणैरवशिष्टप्रारब्धकमफलभोगवासनारूपैर्जावोऽपि प्राणापानैराकृष्यत इत्यथः (C) C ends here.

[5] Conjecturally: जाग्रत्यामुद्बुद्धायां

[6] यद्वा, प्राणप्रदेशगतस्य जीवस्य प्राणप्रदेशप्राप्तौ जाग्रत्येव। (A,C)

[7] प्राणमागतं (B)

नैवंविध[1]दुःखैरभिभूयत इति सूचयन्नुपसंहरति—ऊर्ध्वेति। योगवित् पुरुषस्तूर्ध्वाधः आज्ञामूलाधारयोः[2] संस्थितौ एतौ प्राणापानौ वक्ष्यमाणप्रकारेण संयोजयति एकीकरोति। अयमेव हठयोगः। तदुक्तं योगचिन्तामणौ—"चन्द्रसूर्याख्ययोः प्राणापानयोरैक्यलक्षणः प्राणायामो हठयोग"[3] इत्युच्यत इति॥४१॥

तर्हि किं तत् ? इत्याकाङ्क्षायां[4] प्राणापानयोर्निर्गमप्रवेशप्रतिफलितं हंसमन्त्रमाह—

हकारेण बहिर्याति सकारेण विशेत् पुनः।
हंसहंसेत्यमुं मन्त्रं जीवो जपति सर्वदा॥४२॥

स एव प्राणवायुसारूप्यमापन्नो जीवश्चिदाभासरूपः[5] हकारेण प्राणबीजेन बहिर्याति स्वाधिष्ठानतो निःसरति। पुनः सकारेण बीजेन अन्तर्विशति मूलाधारादिप्रदेशं गच्छति। [6]अमुना प्रकारेण सर्वदा हंसः हंस अमुं मन्त्रं जपति। अतोऽयं जीवमन्त्र इति विश्रुतः। अत्र विसर्गान्तत्वस्यावश्यकत्वादिति शब्दिनः सन्धिरार्षः ॥४२॥

तस्य मन्त्रस्याहोरात्रसञ्जातजपसङ्ख्यामाह[7]—

षट् शतानि त्वहोरात्रे सहस्राण्येकविंशतिः।
एतत् संख्यान्वितं मन्त्रं जीवो जपति सर्वदा॥४३॥

जीवः प्राग् उक्तः। सर्वदा अहोरात्रे अहोरात्रमध्ये एकविंशति सहस्राणि, पुनः षट् शतानि षट्शताधिकैकविंशतिसहस्राणीत्यर्थः। एतत्सङ्ख्यान्वितं मन्त्रं जपति मन्त्रजपं करोतीत्यर्थः।[8]॥४३॥

---

[1] नैवं विविध- (B)

[2] आज्ञाधिष्ठानयोः (A,C)

[3] लक्षणं प्राणायामोऽहंयोग (A)

[4] First portion not found in A.

[5] चिदाभासरूपः (not in C)

[6] From here to end C has एवंप्रकारेण हंस इति मन्त्रं सर्वदा जपतीत्यर्थः.

[7] मन्त्रस्य सङ्ख्यामाह (C)

[8] Last sentence not in C.

एतन्मन्त्रस्य माहात्म्यं[1] दर्शयति त्रिभिः।

अजपा नाम गायत्री योगिनां मोक्षदायिनी।
अस्याः सङ्कल्पमात्रेण सर्वपापैः प्रमुच्यते॥ ४४॥

इयं अजपा नाम गायत्री। अस्या अजपागायत्र्याः सङ्कल्पमात्रेण, जपं विनापीत्यर्थः, सर्वपापैः, अकृत्यकरणादिजनितैरित्यर्थः[2], प्रमुच्यते। अत एव इयमजपा गायत्री योगिनां मोक्षदा भवतीत्यर्थः॥ ४४॥

अनया सदृशी विद्या अनया सदृशो जपः।
अनया सदृशं ज्ञानं न भूतं न भविष्यति॥ ४५॥

अनया अजपागायत्र्या सदृशी तुल्या जीवब्रह्मणोरभेदप्रतिपादिका। अन्या विद्या तथा एतज्जपसदृशोऽन्येनायासेन बहुफलप्रदो जपः तथा अनया सदृशं स्वरूपेणैवाद्वैतानुभवजनकं ज्ञानं ज्ञानसाधकमन्यत् किमपि न भूतं न भविष्यति॥ ४५॥[3]

कुण्डलिन्याः समुद्भूता गायत्री प्राणधारिणी।
प्राणविद्या महाविद्या यस्तान्वेत्ति स योगवित्॥ ४६॥

इयं यतः प्राणधारिणी कुण्डलिन्याः सकाशात् समुद्भूता गायत्री, अतः प्राणविद्या, अत एव महाविद्या। तामिमां यो वेत्ति स एव योगवित् योगार्थतात्पर्यवेत्ता भवतीत्यर्थः[4]॥ इत्यजपाप्रकरणम्॥ ४६॥

---

[1] एतज्जीवमाहात्म्यं (C)

[2] इत्यर्थः is not found in B.

[3] अजपागायत्रीसदृशी विद्या नास्तीत्यर्थः (C, entire commentary)

[4] C. only has इत्यर्थः for योगार्थतात्पर्यवेत्ता भवतीत्यर्थः

अथ शक्तिचालनम्

दशभिः[1] श्लोकैः शक्तिचालनप्रकरणस्योद्धाटनाय[2] अपरं कुण्डलिनीस्थानमाह—

कन्दोर्ध्वे कुण्डली शक्तिरष्टधा कुण्डलाकृतिः।
ब्रह्मद्वारमुखं नित्यं मुखेनाच्छाद्य तिष्ठति॥ ४७॥

कन्दस्य सकलनाडीनां योनिभूतस्य ऊर्ध्वदेशे मणिपूरककर्णिकायामित्यर्थः॥ अष्टधा कुण्डलाकृतिः कुण्डली शक्तिः ब्रह्मद्वारमुखं स्वमुखेनाच्छाद्य पिधाय नित्यं तिष्ठति॥ ४७॥

किं च,

येन द्वारेण गन्तव्यं ब्रह्मस्थानमनामयम्।
मुखेनाच्छाद्य तद्द्वारं प्रसुप्ता परमेश्वरी॥ ४८॥
प्रबुद्धा वह्नियोगेन मनसा मरुता सह।
सूचीवद्गुणमादाय व्रजत्यूर्ध्वं सुषुम्णया॥ ४९॥

येन द्वारेण येन मार्गेण कृत्वा अनामयं जननमरणादिदुःखचिन्तारहितं ब्रह्मस्थानमखण्डानन्दपदं गन्तव्यं, तद्द्वारं मुखेनाच्छाद्य प्रसुप्ता परमेश्वरी कुण्डली शक्तिः वह्नियोगेन प्राणप्रेरितानल-शिखासम्बन्धेन कृत्वा प्रबुद्धा त्यक्तनिद्रा सती मनसा मरुता प्राणेन च सह युक्ता सुषुम्णया मध्यमनाड्या कृत्वा ऊर्ध्वं सहस्रदलाभिमुखं व्रजति। दृष्टान्तमाह—सूचीवदिति यथा सूची स्वसंयुक्तं[3] गुणमादाय ऊर्ध्वं पटस्य प्रतितन्त्वन्तरालं व्रजति, तद्वदियमपि स्वकल्पितषट्चक्रं तदधितिष्ठति, तत्तद्देवतादिसकलप्रपञ्चं संहृत्य व्रजति॥ ४८-४९॥

तस्याः स्वरूपं गतिं चाह—

प्रस्फुरद्भुजगाकारा पद्मतन्तुनिभा शुभा।
प्रबुद्धा वह्नियोगेन व्रजत्यूर्ध्वं सुषुम्णया॥ ५०॥

---

[1] षड्भिः (B)

[2] -प्रकरणस्योपपादनाय (B), -प्रकरणस्योद्धाटनापनयनमाह C)

[3] स्वसंसक्तं (A)

सा च वह्नियोगेन अपानप्रेरिताया मूलाधारगतकालाग्निशिखाया योगेन प्रबुद्धा, अत एव प्रस्फुरद्भुजगाकारा प्रस्फुरन् यो भुजगः, तदाकारा रभसयुक्तसर्प इव वक्रगत्या व्रजन्तीत्यर्थः। पद्मतन्तुनिभा पद्मतन्तुसदृशी सूक्ष्मा ज्योतिर्मयी चेत्यर्थः। शुभा शुभस्वरूपा सती सुषुम्णया सुषुम्णामार्गेण ऊर्ध्वं व्रजतीत्यर्थः॥५०॥

तथा चानया कुण्डलिन्या सुषुम्णामुखं भेदयेदिति सदृष्टान्तमाह—

उद्घाटयेत् कवाटं तु यथा कुञ्चिकया हठात्।
कुण्डलिन्या तथा योगी मोक्षद्वारं प्रभेदयेत्॥५१॥

यथा गृही जनः कवाटं गृहद्वारं मुद्राङ्कितमिति शेषः कुञ्चिकया कृत्वा हठादेवोद्घाटयेत्, कुञ्चिकां विना तु न कथंचिदपीति तुशब्दार्थः, तथा योगी कुण्डलिन्या कृत्वा मोक्षद्वारं सुषुम्णामुखं प्रभेदयेत् कुण्डलिनीं विना तु न कथंचिदपीति दृष्टान्तप्रतिफलितोऽर्थः॥५१॥

अथ पूर्वश्लोके कुण्डलिन्या मोक्षद्वारं प्रभेदयेदित्युक्तम्। तच्च कुण्डलिन्यां प्रबुद्धायां संभवेत्। अतस्तत्प्रबोधनोपायभूतं पद्मासनं विशेषमाह—

कृत्वा संपुटितौ करौ दृढतरं बद्ध्वा तु पद्मासनं
गाढं वक्षसि सन्निधाय चिबुकं ध्यात्वा च तच्चेप्सितम्।
वारं वारमपानमूर्ध्वमनिलं प्रोच्चारयेत् पूरितं
मुञ्चन्प्राणमुपैति बोधमतुलं शक्तिप्रबोधान्नरः॥५२॥

करौ संपुटितौ कृत्वा तयोर्मूलप्रदेशाभ्यां वक्षसि संयोजितं पद्मासनं दृढतरं यथा स्यात् तथा बद्ध्वा तु, पुनश्चिबुकं वक्षस्येव गाढं यथा स्यात् तथा निधाय, यदीप्सितं तच्च ध्यात्वा, अपानमनिलं अपानवायुं वारं वारं ऊर्ध्वमुच्चारयेत् पुनः पुनः ऊर्ध्वमुत्थापयेत्। पूरितमपानेन सहैकीकृत्य यथाशक्ति धारितं प्राणवायुं मुञ्चन् त्यजन् सन् अनन्तरमेवेत्यर्थः। नरः अतुलमपरिमितं बोधमुपैति ज्ञानं प्राप्नोति। कस्मात्? शक्तिप्रबोधात् अर्थादेतदभ्यासाच्छक्तिप्रबोधो भवति तस्मादित्यर्थः॥५२॥

तस्मिन् कर्मणि नियमानाह द्वाभ्यां—

अङ्गानां मर्दनं कुर्याच्छ्रमजातेन वारिणा।
कट्वम्ललवणत्यागी क्षीरभोजनमाचरेत्॥ ५३॥

श्रमजातेन परिश्रमोत्पन्नेन वारिणा घर्मोदकेनाङ्गानां मर्दनं कुर्यात्। कट्वम्लवणादिनिषिद्धद्रव्यत्यागी सन् क्षीरमात्रं तत्प्रचुरं[1] भोजनमाचरेत्॥ ५३॥

किं च,

ब्रह्मचारी मिताहारी त्यागी योगपरायणः।
अब्दादूर्ध्वं भवेत्सिद्धो नात्र कार्या विचारणा॥ ५४॥

अत्र ब्रह्मचर्यं मैथुनत्यागः, स च स्वाश्रमानुसारेणानुष्ठेयः। तदुक्तं योगचिन्तामणौ—

सर्वत्र मैथुनत्यागो ब्रह्मचर्यं प्रचक्षते। ब्रह्मचर्याश्रमस्थानां यतीनां नैष्ठिकस्य च॥

ऋतावृतौ स्वदारेषु सङ्गतिर्या विधानतः। ब्रह्मचर्या तु सैवोक्ता गृहस्थाश्रमवासिनाम्॥ इति।

मिताहारलक्षणमनुपदं वक्ष्यते।[2] त्यागी विषयानुरागरहितः फलानुसन्धानशून्य इति यावत्। योग एव परमतिशयितं अयनं स्थानं आश्रयो यस्य सन्ततं योगमात्राश्रित इत्यर्थः॥ एतादृशो योगी अब्दात् वत्सरादूर्ध्वं सिद्ध इच्छामात्रोत्थितशक्तिको[3] भवेदित्यत्र विचारणा भविष्यति वा न वेति चिन्ता न कार्या[4] इत्यर्थः॥ ५४॥

मिताहारलक्षणमाह—

सुस्निग्धं मधुराहारं चतुर्थांशविवर्जितम्।
भुञ्जते सुरसंप्रीत्यै मिताहारः स उच्यते॥ ५५॥

स्नेहप्रचुरं मधुरं अम्ललवणवर्जितं यदाहारं चतुर्थांशविवर्जितम्। तदुक्तम्—

---

[1] B,C क्षीरप्रचुरं

[2] This sentence not in C.

[3] -शक्तिदो (A); इच्छामात्रोत्थितशक्तिको not in C.

[4] अत्र संशयो न वक्तव्यः (C)

द्वौ भागौ पूरयेदन्नैस्तोयेनैकं प्रपूरयेत्। प्राणवायोः प्रचारार्थं चतुर्थमवशेषयेत्॥ इति

सुराणां संप्रीत्यै तेभ्यो निवेदितमित्यर्थः। [1]"अनिवेद्य न भुञ्जीत मत्स्यमांसादिकं त्यजेत्" इत्यादिवाक्यात्। एवंविधं यमाहारं योगिनो भुञ्जते स मिताहार उच्यते॥ ५५॥

सैव पूर्वोक्ता कुण्डली उक्तप्रकारेण बोधिता सती मोक्षदा भवतीत्याह—

कन्दोर्ध्वे कुण्डली शक्तिरष्टधा कुण्डलाकृतिः।
बन्धनाय च मूढानां योगिनां मोक्षदा सदा॥ ५६॥

पूर्वार्धं पूर्वं व्याख्यातम् (४७)। सा च ब्रह्मद्वाराच्छादनेन मूढानां योगकर्मानभिज्ञानां सदा सर्वदा, सत्यपि तपोयोगादिकर्मान्तरे इति भावः,[2] बन्धनाय भवति। शक्तिचालनाद्युपायमभिजानतां योगिनां तु ब्रह्मप्रापकतया सदा मोक्षदा जननमरणादिजीवभावनिवर्तयित्री भवतीत्यर्थः॥ ५६॥

अथ महामुद्रादिपञ्चकम्

महामुद्रादिपञ्चकं शक्तिचालनेऽवश्यमपेक्षितमित्याह—

महामुद्रां नभोमुद्रामुड्डियानं जलंधरम्।
मूलबन्धं च यो वेत्ति स योगी मुक्तिभाजनम्॥ ५७॥

महामुद्रां नभोमुद्रा खेचरीमुद्रा तां उड्डीयाणं बन्धनं जलंधरं बन्धं मूलबन्धमेतन्मुद्रापञ्चकं यो वेत्ति स योगी मुक्तिभाजनं मुक्तिपात्रमिति। एतन्मुद्रापञ्चकं ज्ञात्वैव शक्तिं चालयेत्तेनैव मुक्तिभाजनो भवति, नान्यथेत्यर्थः। एतदभ्यासे शक्तिः प्रचलिता न वेति जिज्ञासायामुक्तं योगचिन्तामणौ—

पिपीलिकायां लग्नायामङ्गे कण्डूर्यथा भवेत्। सुषुम्णायां तथाभ्यासात् सततं वायुना भवेत्॥ इति।

एवमहरहो यथाशक्ति समभ्यस्याभ्यासावसाने महामुद्राखेचर्यादिकं शनैः शनैरुत्सृज्य मूलबन्धमुत्सृजेत्, न तु प्रागेव। तथा च योगसारे ईश्वरवचनम्—

यदा विघटयेन्मुद्रां खेचरीं योगवित् ततः। शक्तिः स्वस्थानमभ्येति पूर्वोद्दिष्टेन कर्मणा॥ इति॥ ५७॥

---

[1] From here to end not in C.

[2] For तपोयोगादिकर्मान्तरे इति भावः, C has योगादिषु.

इदानीं मूलबन्धानि मुद्रापञ्चकानां लक्षणानि क्रमेणाह--

पार्ष्णिभागेन संपीड्य योनिमाकुञ्चयेद्गुदम्।
अपानमूर्ध्वमाकृष्य मूलबन्धो विधीयते॥ ५८॥

अपानं वायुमूर्ध्वमाकृष्य पादस्य पार्ष्णिभागेन योनिं गुदमेढ्रान्तरालस्थानं संपीड्य गुदं मूलद्वारमाकुञ्चयेत् सङ्कोचयेत्। पुनरपानमधोदेशे यथा न गच्छेत् तथा कुर्यादित्यर्थः। एवं मूलबन्धो विधीयते॥ ५८॥

प्रसङ्गात् मूलबन्धमात्र[1]स्याभ्यासे यत् फलं तदाह—

अपानप्राणयोरैक्यात् क्षयान्मूत्रपुरीषयोः।
युवा भवति वृद्धोऽपि सततं मूलबन्धनात्॥ ५९॥

सततं मूलबन्धनात् मूलबन्धस्य निरन्तराभ्यासात् वृद्धोऽपि वलीपलितादिग्रस्तोऽपि युवा षोडशवार्षिको[2] भवति। तत् कस्मात्? मूलबन्धाभ्यासात् यदपानप्राणयोरैक्यमेकव्यापारः, तस्माच्च यः मूत्रपुरीषयोः क्षयो नाशः, तस्मात्॥ ५९॥

उड्डीयाणबन्धमाह—

उड्डीनं कुरुते यस्मादविश्रान्तं महाखगः।
उड्डीयाणं तदेव स्यान्मृत्युमातङ्गकेसरी॥ ६०॥

यस्मादुड्डीयाणबन्धात् तेन बन्धेन रुद्धो महाखगः प्राणः अविश्रान्तं यथा भवति तथा सुषुम्णायामुड्डीनं उड्डीय गमनं कुरुते। तत् तस्मात् मृत्युरेव मातङ्गः तस्मिन्केसरी सिंह इव मृत्युनिवर्तकोऽयं उड्डीयाणं नाम बन्धो भवतीत्यर्थः॥ ६०॥

---

[1] -मात्र- not in C.

[2] For वलीपलितादिग्रस्तोऽपि युवा षोडशवार्षिको C has only युवा.

अयं बन्धः कुत्र विधीयते ? इत्याकाङ्क्षायामाह—

उदरात् पश्चिमभागे त्वधोनाभेर्निगद्यते।
उड्डीयाणस्य बन्धोऽयं तत्र बन्धो विधीयते॥ ६१॥

उदरात् पश्चिमे भागे नाभेरधःप्रदेशे अयं उड्डीयाणः, तस्य बन्धो निगद्यते, सिद्धैरिति शेषः। तस्मादयं बन्धस्तत्रैव विधीयते नान्यत्र॥ ६१॥

जालन्धरबन्धस्य फलमाह—

बध्नाति हि शिराजालं नाधो याति[1] नभोजलम्।
ततो जालन्धरो बन्धः कण्ठदुःखौघनाशनः॥ ६२॥

जालन्धरबन्धः कण्ठे यानि दुःखानि तेषामोघस्य समूहस्य नाशनो नाशकर्ता सन् शरीरे शिराणां नाडीनां जालं बध्नाति स्तंभयति नभोजलं चन्द्रकलामृतं अधो न याति, कपालकुहरान्न[2] पतति॥ ६२॥

जालन्धरस्य लक्षणमाह—

जालन्धरे कृते बन्धे कण्ठसंकोचलक्षणे।
पीयूषं न पतत्यग्नौ न च वायुः प्रकुप्यति॥ ६३॥

कण्ठस्य सङ्कोचः प्राणगतिनिरोधनं लक्षणं यस्य तस्मिन्जालंधरे बन्धे कृते सति पीयूषं चन्द्र-कलामृतं अग्नौ, सूर्यरूपे इत्यर्थः, न पतति। वायुश्च न प्रकुप्यति, विरुद्धो न भवतीत्यर्थः॥ ६३॥

---

[1] -मधोगामि is the reading found in our text, but the commentary follows this variant given above, found in the V edition of GP, *Viveka-mārtaṇḍa, Haṭha-yoga-pradīpikā.*

[2] MSS have incorrect गुहरान्.

अथ खेचरीमुद्रायाः फलं लक्षणं चाह कपालेति त्रयोदशभिः[1]—

कपालकुहरे जिह्वा प्रविष्टा विपरीतगा।
भ्रुवोरन्तर्गता दृष्टिः मुद्रा भवति खेचरी॥ ६४॥

विपरीतगा सती कपालकुहरे लम्बिकोर्ध्वविवरे प्रविष्टा जिह्वा, भ्रुवोरन्तः भ्रूमध्ये गता दृष्टिर्निश्चलमवस्थिता दृष्टिरियं खेचरी मुद्रा भवति॥ ६४॥

खेचरीफलमाह षड्भिः—

न रोगो मरणं तस्य न निद्रा न क्षुधा तृषा।
न च मूर्च्छा भवेत् तस्य यो मुद्रां वेत्ति खेचरीम्॥ ६५॥

यो योगी उक्तलक्षणां खेचरीमुद्रां वेत्ति, चिरमभ्यस्यतीत्यर्थः, तस्य योगिनः रोगः कफवातादिप्रकोप[2]जन्यज्वरादि[3], मरणं प्राणोत्क्रमणावस्थाविशेषः, निद्रा मूर्च्छावस्थाविशेष एव, क्षुधा तृषा एतानि किमपि न संभवतीत्यर्थः॥ ६५॥

पीड्यते न स शोकेन लिप्यते न स कर्मणा।
बाध्यते न स कालेन[4] यो मुद्रां वेत्ति खेचरीम्॥ ६६॥

यो योगी उक्तलक्षणां खेचरीमुद्रां वेत्ति गुरूक्तमार्गेणानुतिष्ठति, स योगी शोकेन न पीड्यते। मायाप्रपञ्चातीतत्वात् स कर्मणा कर्मफलेन सुखदुःखेन न लिप्यते न स्पृश्यते।[5] कालेनापि जगदन्तकारेणापि न बाध्यते॥ ६६॥

---

[1] This reading only in B. A, C have खेचरीलक्षणमाह.

[2] -प्रयोग- (A)

[3] ज्वरादि not in A or C.

[4] केनापि in GP.

[5] कर्मफलेन न लिप्यते सुखदुःखादिभिर्न स्पृश्यते (C)

खेचरीति नाम विगृह्णाति[1]—

चित्तं चरति खे यस्मात् जिह्वा चरति खे गता।
तेनैव खेचरीमुद्रा सर्वसिद्धैर्नमस्कृता॥ ६७॥

यस्मात् कारणात् चित्तं ब्रह्मैकतानात्मकमन्तःकरणं[2] खे शून्ये चरति[3]। जिह्वा च रसना खे आकाशे चरति, चन्द्रामृतं पिबति गच्छति वा। तेनैव कारणेनान्तःकरणस्य विषयसम्बन्ध-निवारकत्वेनेत्यर्थः। खेचरीमुद्रा सर्वसिद्धैरपि नमस्कृता पूजिता॥ ६७॥

बिन्दुमूलं शरीरं तु शिरास्तत्र प्रतिष्ठिताः।
भावयन्ति शरीरं या ह्यापादतलमस्तकम्॥ ६८॥

शरीरे बिन्दुर्मूलं कारणं यस्य, तत् बिन्दुमूलं, बिन्दुनैव संरक्षितमित्यर्थः। तत् कथं भवेत्? तत्राह[4]—हि यस्मात् कारणात् याः शिरा आपादतलमस्तकं शरीरं भावयन्ति, बिन्दुना सिञ्चनेन कृत्वा जीवयन्तीत्यर्थः। ताः शिरास्तत्र प्रतिष्ठितास्तद्धेतौ[5] अतः शरीरं बिन्दुमूलमित्यर्थः॥ ६८॥

खेचर्या मुद्रितं येन विवरं लंबिकोर्ध्वतः।
न तस्य क्षरते बिन्दुः कामिन्यालिङ्गितस्य च॥ ६९॥

तथा च येन योगिना कण्ठनालस्य विवरं छिद्रं लम्बिकोर्ध्वतः लम्बिकाया उर्ध्वभागे खेचर्या मुद्रिकया कृत्वा मुद्रितं रुद्धं, तस्य योगिनः कामिन्यालिङ्गितस्यापि बिन्दुर्न क्षरते, न स्रवतीत्यर्थः॥ ६९॥

---

[1] निरुक्तिमाह (C)

[2] ब्रह्मैकतदात्मकमन्तःकरणं (B)

[3] यस्मात् चित्तं ब्रह्मैकतानं सत् शून्ये चरति। (C)

[4] तत् कथं भवेत्? तत्राह not in C.

[5] स्तद्धेतौ not in C.

बिन्दुर्न क्षरते इत्युक्तं, किं तेन ? इत्याकाङ्क्षायामाह—[1]

यावद्बिन्दुः स्थितो देहे तावन्मृत्युभयं कुतः।
यावद्बद्धा नभोमुद्रा तावद्बिन्दुर्न गच्छति॥ ७०॥

यावत्पर्यन्तं देहे बिन्दुः स्थितोऽस्ति, तावत्पर्यन्तं देहे[2] मृत्युभयं कुतो भवेत् ? न कुतोऽपीत्यर्थः।[3] व्योमचक्रोपरि[4] बिन्दुस्थानं। तत्र कालस्य[5] प्राप्तेरभावादिति भावः। बिन्दुश्च कियत्कालं स्थिरो भवेत् ? तत्राह—यावदिति। यावत्कालपर्यन्तं नभोमुद्रा खेचरीमुद्रा बद्धा भवति, तावत्पर्यन्तं बिन्दुर्न गच्छति, न स्रवति[6]॥ ७०॥

चलितोऽपि यदा बिन्दुः संप्राप्तश्च हुताशनम्।
व्रजत्यूर्ध्वं हतः शक्त्या निरुद्धो योनिमुद्रया॥ ७१॥

यदा कदाचित् चलितोऽपि बिन्दुः हुताशने सूर्यमण्डले प्राप्तोऽपि तत्क्षणे एव स्वस्थानादुत्थापितया शक्त्या हतः सन् ऊर्ध्वं व्रजति। ततश्च योनिमुद्रया निरुद्धः सुस्थितो भवतीत्यर्थः॥ ७१॥

तस्य भेदमाह—

स पुनर्द्विविधो बिन्दुः पाण्डुरो लोहितस्तथा।
पाण्डुरं शुक्रमित्याहुः लोहिताख्यं महारजः॥ ७२॥

स बिन्दुः पाण्डुरलोहित इति भेदेन द्विविधः। तत्र पाण्डुरः बिन्दुः[7] शुक्रमित्याहुः, लोहिता आख्या यस्य तत् महारजः रजोरूपं भवतीत्यर्थः॥ ७२॥

---

[1] Not in C.

[2] देहे C only.

[3] न कुतोऽपीत्यर्थः। not in C.

[4] व्योमचक्रपरितो (B)

[5] कामस्य (B)

[6] न स्रवति not in C.

[7] पाण्डुरं बिन्दुं (C)

तयोः स्थानभेदं दर्शयति—

सिन्दूरद्रवसंकाशं रविस्थाने स्थितं रजः।
शशिस्थाने स्थितो बिन्दुः तयोरैक्यं सुदुर्लभम्॥ ७३॥

सिन्दूरस्य यो द्रवः तैलादिमिश्रणे[1] संभूतः तत्संकाशं तत्समानवर्णं रजोरूपं बिन्दू रविस्थाने नाभिप्रदेशे स्थितं भवति। बिन्दुः शुक्रं शशिस्थाने षोडशारचक्रे[2] स्थितः। तयोरैक्यं वक्ष्यमाणोपायसाध्यं च सुष्ठु दुर्लभं भवति। तस्य फलमग्रे वक्ष्यते॥ ७३॥

जगतः शिवशक्त्यात्मकत्वादिश्रुतं प्रमाणयति—

बिन्दुः शिवो रजः शक्तिर्बिन्दुरिन्दू रजो रविः।
उभयोः सङ्गमादेव प्राप्यते परमं पदम्॥ ७४॥

बिन्दुः पाण्डुरः प्रागुक्तः शिवो भवति। रजो लोहितं शक्त्यंशः। पुनः स बिन्दुश्चन्द्रो भवति। रजो लोहितं रविः सूर्यो भवति। तथा च चन्द्रसूर्ययोरपि शिवशक्त्यात्मकत्वमुक्तम्। अत एव हठयोगनिरूपणप्रकरणे[3] चन्द्रसूर्ययोः प्राणापानयोर्वा जीवात्मपरमात्मनोर्वा एकत्वं योग इति[4] पर्यायेणोक्तिरुपपद्यते,[5] उभयोस्तयोः सङ्गमादेकत्वादेव[6] परमं पदं प्राप्यते॥ ७४॥

तयोर्बिन्दुरजसोरेकत्वे उपप्रापकं[7] फलमाह—

वायुना शक्तिचारेण प्रेरितं तु यदा रजः।
याति बिन्दोः सहैकत्वं भवेद्दिव्यं वपुस्तदा॥ ७५॥

[1] Corrected from -मिश्रेण

[2] षोडशदलचक्रे (C)

[3] - कारेण (A,C)

[4] एकत्वेति (A) एकत्वं योगमिति (C)

[5] पर्यायतोक्तिरुपपद्यते (B) पर्यायोक्तिरुपपद्यते (C)

[6] उभयोः संगादेकत्वादेव (B) तयोः संगमादेहात्वादेव (C)

[7] उपायं (B,C)

शक्तिं चारयतीति शक्तिचारः, तेन शक्तिं चालयता वायुना प्रेरितमूर्ध्वमुत्थापितं रजः स्त्रीधर्मिण्या रक्तं यदा बिन्दोः सह, बिन्दुनेति पाठस्तु नित्यमेकत्वं याति,[1] समरसत्त्वं प्राप्नोति। तदा दिव्यं दाहच्छेदादिरहितं वलिपलितादिरहितं च वपुः शरीरं[2] भवेत्॥ ७५॥

किं च,

शुक्रं चन्द्रेण संयुक्तं रजः सूर्येण संयुतम्।
तयोः समरसैकत्वं यो जानाति स योगवित्॥ ७६ ॥

शुक्रं बिन्दुरूपं चन्द्रेण संयुक्तं सममवस्थितं रजश्च सूर्येण संयुतं समं स्थितं, तयोः चन्द्रसूर्यरूपतयावस्थितयोः बिन्दुरजसोः समरसतया एकत्वं यो जानाति स योगविदिति, तयोः योगस्यैव योगपदवाच्यत्वात्[3]॥ ७६॥

॥ इति खेचरीमुद्राप्रकरणम्॥[4]

अथ महामुद्राप्रकरणम्। तत्रादौ फलं[5]—

शोधनं नाडिजालस्य चालनं चन्द्रसूर्ययोः।
रसानां शोषणं चैव महामुद्राभिधीयते॥ ७७॥

नाडीजालस्य नाडीनां विस्तारस्य शोधनं तदाश्रितवातपित्तादिदोषस्य निःसारणं शशिसूर्ययोश्चन्द्रादित्ययोश्चालनं एकत्र करणं च पुनः रसानां भुक्तपीतान्नपानादिपाकजातानां शोषणं नाशनं च[6] यया मुद्रया भवति सेयं महामुद्रा अभिधीयते कथ्यते॥ ७७॥

---

[1] After बिंदोः, बिंदुना शुक्रेण सह एकत्वमेति (B), बिन्दुरिति पाठस्तु स्फुटितः। एकत्वं याति (C)

[2] शरीरं not in C.

[3] तयोः योगस्यैव योगपदवाच्यत्वात् not in C.

[4] इति खेचरीमुद्रा (C)

[5] तत्रादौ नाडिशोधनं (C)

[6] दृढीकरणं (B) for नाशनं च.

संप्रति महामुद्राया लक्षणमाह—

वक्षोन्यस्तहनुः प्रपीड्य सुचिरं योनिं च वामाङ्घ्रिणा
हस्ताभ्यामनुधारयन्प्रसरितं पादं तथा दक्षिणम्।
आपूर्य श्वसनेन कुक्षियुगलं बद्ध्वा शनै रेचयेद्
एषा व्याधिविनाशिनी सुमहती मुद्रा नृणां कथ्यते॥ ७८॥

वक्षोन्यस्तहनुः वक्षसि स्थापितचिबुकः योगी वामाङ्घ्रिणा वामपादपार्ष्णिना योनिं पूर्वोक्तां सुचिरं नितरां प्रपीड्य प्रसरितं दक्षिणं पादं हस्ताभ्यामनुधारयन् गृह्णन् सन् कुक्षियुगलं श्वसनेन प्राणेन आपूर्य पूरयित्वा बद्ध्वा यथोक्तकालं कुंभयित्वा, अनन्तरं शनैःशनै रेचयेत्। एषा नृणां योगिनां व्याधिविनाशिनी सकलरोगक्षयकारिणी सुमहती मुद्रा महामुद्रा इति कथ्यते अभिधीयते॥ ७८॥

तस्या अभ्यासक्रममाह—

चन्द्रांशेन समभ्यस्य सूर्यांशेनाभ्यसेत् पुनः।
यावत् तुल्या भवेत् सङ्ख्या ततो मुद्रां विसर्जयेत्॥ ७९॥

इमां महामुद्रां पूर्वं चन्द्रांशेन समभ्यस्य अभ्यासं कृत्वा[1], पुनः सूर्यांशे अभ्यसेत्। चन्द्रांशेन वामाङ्गेन सूर्यांशेन दक्षिणाङ्गेनेत्यर्थः। यावत्पर्यन्तं सङ्ख्यामात्रा तुल्या भवेत्, वामदक्षिणयोरङ्गयोः समा भवेत्, तावत्पर्यन्तमभ्यसेदित्यर्थः[2]। ततस्तदनन्तरं[3] मुद्रां विसर्जयेत् दैनन्दिनिकमभ्यासं त्यजेदित्यर्थः॥ ७९॥

तस्या एव फलमाह पुनस्त्रिभिः—

न हि पथ्यमपथ्यं वा रसाः सर्वेऽपि नीरसाः।
अपि भुक्तं विषं घोरं पीयूषमिव जीर्यति॥ ८०॥

---

[1] अभ्यासं कृत्वा not in C.

[2] इति तात्पर्यम् (C)

[3] तदनन्तरं not in C.

अस्यां महामुद्रायामभ्यस्तायां पथ्यमपथ्यं वा न विचारणीयम्। सर्वे रसाश्च कट्वम्ललवणादयः नीरसाः स्वं स्वगुणदोषजनने असमर्था भवन्तीत्यर्थः। हि यतो[1] घोरमपि विषादिकं भुक्तं चेत्[2] स्वदोषमुन्मादादिकमनुत्पाद्य पीयूषमिव शरीरानुकूल्येनैव जीर्यति, किं पुनरन्ये रसाः करिष्यन्तीति भावः॥८०॥

अत एव रसानामनुकूलत्वात्[3] क्षयकुष्ठादयोऽपि सुस्था भवन्तीत्याह—

क्षयकुष्ठगुदावर्तगुल्माजीर्णपुरोगमाः।
रोगास्तस्य क्षयं यान्ति महामुद्रां च योऽभ्यसेत्॥८१॥

यो योगी महामुद्रामभ्यसेत्, तस्य योगिनः क्षयकुष्ठगुदावर्तगुल्माजीर्णपुरोगमाः सर्वे रोगाः क्षयं यान्ति विनश्यन्ति॥८१॥

उपसंहरति—

कथितेयं महामुद्रा महासिद्धिकरी नृणाम्।
गोपनीया प्रयत्नेन न देया यस्य कस्यचित्॥८२॥

नृणामुपासकानां महासिद्धिकरी इयं महामुद्रा मया कथिता। प्रयत्नेन गोपनीया रक्षणीया॥ "गुप्ता वीर्यवती ज्ञेया निर्वीर्या स्यात् प्रकाशिता" (ह.यो.प्र. १.११) इति सर्वसम्मतत्वात्। [4]अतो यस्य कस्यचिन्न देया साधकाय इयं[5] देया इत्यर्थः॥८२॥

॥ इति महामुद्राप्रकरणम्॥[6]

---

[1] जीर्यते (A); ह्रियते (B)

[2] तत् (C)

[3] अननुकूलत्वात् (A,C)

[4] Here to end of comment not in C.

[5] एव (B)

[6] इति महामुद्रा (B)

अथ प्रणवाभ्यासः

मनोवासनाविनाशार्थं प्रणवाभ्यासं सप्तभिः श्लोकैराह—

पद्मासनं समारुह्य समकायशिरोधरः।
नासाग्रदृष्टिरेकान्ते जपेदोंकारमव्ययम्॥ ८३॥

कान्ते निर्जनप्रदेशे पूर्वोक्तलक्षणं पद्मासनं सम्यग् आरुह्य समकायशिरोधरः ऋजुशरीरग्रीवो नासाग्रदृष्टिः नासाग्रमवलोकयन् सन् अव्ययं ओंकारं प्रणवं जपेत्॥ ८३॥

कथंभूतमोंकारं जपेत्? इत्यत आह—

भूर्भुवःस्वरिमे लोकाः सोमसूर्याग्निदेवताः।
यस्य मात्रासु तिष्ठन्ति तत्परं ज्योतिरोमिति॥ ८४॥

अस्य ओंकारस्य मात्रासु अकार-उकार-मकारेषु भूर्लोकभुवर्लोकस्वर्लोका इति लोकाः, सोमः सूर्योऽग्निरिति देवताश्च क्रमेण तिष्ठन्ति। तत्परं कारणरूपं ज्योतिर्ज्योतिर्मयं[1] चैतन्यं[2] ओमिति साकारं बीजं भवतीत्यर्थः॥ ८४॥

त्रयः कालास्त्रयो वेदाः त्रयो लोकास्त्रयः स्वराः।
त्रयो देवाः स्थिता यत्र तत्परं ज्योतिरोमिति॥ ८५॥

पुनः कथंभूतं ओं? त्रयः कालाः भूतवर्तमानभविष्यद्रूपाः। त्रयो वेदाः ऋग्यजुःसामरूपाः। त्रयो लोका त्रिविधा लोका इत्यर्थः। ते च स्वेदजाण्डजजरायुजाः, लतागुल्मादीनां जरायुजेष्वन्तर्भाव इत्यर्थः, स्वर्गमृत्युपातालं वा।[3] त्रयः स्वराः उदात्तानुदात्तस्वरिताः। त्रयो देवा ब्रह्मविष्णुरुद्राश्च। यत्र यस्मिन् [4]प्रणवे अकारादिमात्रासु क्रमेण[1] स्थिता भवन्ति तद्ब्रह्मरूपं परं ज्योतिःस्वरूपं ओमिति बीजं जपेदित्यर्थः॥ ८५॥

---

[1] ज्योतिर्ज्योतिर्मयं (C only)

[2] चैतन्यं not in C.

[3] From त्रिविधा लोका to वा not in C.

[4] From here to end C reads प्रतितिष्ठन्ति तद् ब्रह्मरूपं प्रणवं जपेदित्यर्थः

क्रिया इच्छा तथा ज्ञानं ब्राह्मी रौद्री च वैष्णवी।
त्रिधा शक्तिः स्थिता यत्र तत्परं ज्योतिरोमिति॥ ८६॥

पुनः कथंभूतमोम् ? इति क्रिया इच्छा ज्ञानमिति भेदेन त्रिविधा, ब्राह्मी रौद्री वैष्णवीति भेदवती शक्तिर्यत्र प्रणवे [2]अकारादिमात्रासु क्रमेण स्थिता तत् परं ज्योतिरोमिति॥ ८६॥

अकारश्च उकारश्च मकारो बिन्दुसंज्ञकः।
त्रिधा मात्रा स्थिता यत्र तत्परं ज्योतिरोमिति॥ ८७॥

पुनः कथंभूतमोम् ? इति अकार उकार बिन्दुसंज्ञको मकारश्च इति त्रिविधा मात्रा यत्र यस्मिन् ज्योतिषि स्थिता भवन्ति, तत् परं ज्योतीरूपम [3]ओमिति बीजं भवतीत्यर्थः॥ ८७॥

किं च,

वचसा तज्जपेद्बीजं वपुषा तत् समभ्यसेत्।
मनसा तत् स्मरेन्नित्यं तत्परं ज्योतिरोमिति॥ ८८॥

वचसा तदेव प्रणवं बीजं निखिलप्रपञ्चस्य कारणं भावयन् जपेत्। कारणत्वं च प्रणवात् सप्त[4]व्याहृतयो भवन्ति। व्याहृतिभ्यो गायत्री भवति, गायत्र्याः सावित्री भवति। सावित्र्याः सरस्वती भवति। सरस्वत्या वेदा भवन्ति। वेदेभ्यो ब्रह्मा भवति। ब्रह्मणो लोका भवन्ति। "ततो लोकाः प्रवर्तन्त" इति श्रुतेः। वपुषा शरीरेण च तदेव प्रणवं समभ्यसेत्। क्रियाशक्तिविशिष्टं सगुणब्रह्मरूपं प्रणवं संभावयन् तदर्थानुचिन्तनानुकूलेन[5] सिद्धाद्यासनारूढेन[6] वपुषा तिष्ठेदित्यर्थः। क्रिया इच्छा तथा ज्ञानमिति च पूर्वश्लोकेन क्रियाया प्रणवाङ्गकत्वकथनात् तदनुकूलक्रियाभ्यासस्य प्रणवाभ्यासत्वं स्पष्टमिति भावः।

---

[1] अकारादिमात्रासु क्रमेण not found in B or C.

[2] From here to end C reads only तादृशेत्यर्थः.

[3] From here to end not in C.

[4] सम- (A)

[5] From प्रणवं C reads प्रणवार्थं चिन्तयन् आनुकूल्येन

[6] -अनुरुद्धेन (B), -अनुरूढेन (A)

मनसा तदेव परब्रह्मरूपं[1] ज्योतिः स्वप्रकाशचैतन्यं भूरादि[2]लोकानां वर्तमानादिकालानां[3] सोमसूर्याग्निरूपदेवानां[4] ऋगादिवेदत्रयस्य[5] ब्रह्मादिदेवत्रयस्य क्रियेच्छादिशक्तित्रयस्य अकारादिमात्रात्रयस्य सकलप्रपञ्चस्य अधिष्ठानतया व्यापकरूपं नित्यं संस्मरेत्। इतरविषयिणीं वासनां मनसि[6] नारोहयेत्, किंतु चराचरस्य[7] स्थूलसूक्ष्मरूपस्य कस्यापि वस्तुनः साक्षात्कारे प्रणवप्रतिपादितं व्यापकरूपं स्वप्रकाशं चैतन्यमेवानुसन्दध्यादिति प्रकरणार्थः ॥ ८८ ॥

प्रणवजपस्य फलं[8] दर्शयति—

शुचिर्वाप्यशुचिर्वापि यो ज़पेत् प्रणवं सदा।
न स लिप्यते[9] पापेन पद्मपत्रमिवांभसा ॥ ८९ ॥

शुचिः बाह्याभ्यन्तरशौचयुक्तः, अशुचिः तद्रहितो वापि यः पुरुषः सदा प्रणवं पूर्वोक्तलक्षणं बीजं जपेत्, तदर्थं भावयेत् पुनः पुनश्चेतसि विनिवेशयेदित्यर्थः, तदुक्तं पतञ्जलिना— "तज्जपस्तदर्थभावनम्" [यो.सू. १.२८] इति, [10]स योगी पापेन निषिद्धानिषिद्धकर्मजनितादृष्टेन न लिप्यते न सम्बध्यते। केन किमिव ? अंभसा पद्मपत्रमिव, यथा अम्भसि जले वर्तमानमपि पद्मपत्रं अंभसा जलेन न लिप्यते न स्पृश्यते तद्वदित्यर्थः। अत्र पापेनेत्युपलक्षणं पुण्यस्यापि[11] यथा पापस्याविद्यामूलत्वात् सद्यः प्रतिफलिततेजोरूपस्य प्रणवस्याभ्यासेन नाशः, तथा विद्यामूलत्वाविशेषात् पुण्यस्यापि[12] नाशः समुचित इत्यर्थः ॥ ८९ ॥

---

[1] तत्परं ब्रह्मरूपं (A)

[2] गुणादि- (A)

[3] -कालत्रयस्य (B)

[4] देवत्रयस्य (B) सोमादिदेवत्रयस्य (C)

[5] Not in C.

[6] मनसा (A)

[7] Not in C.

[8] फलबाहुल्यं (B)

[9] Corrected everywhere from लिप्यति.

[10] From here to end C. has स योगी पापेन निषिद्धकर्मजनितादृष्टेन अम्भसा पद्मपत्रमिव न लिप्यत इत्यर्थः। इदं पुण्यस्याप्युपलक्षणम्।

[11] प्रणवस्यापि (A,C)

[12] प्रणवस्यापि (A,C)

अथ प्राणायामप्रशंसनम्

अथ वायुनिरोधं चतुर्भिः श्लोकैः प्रस्तौति—

चले वाते चलो[1] बिन्दुर्निश्चले निश्चलो भवेत्।
योगी स्थाणुत्वमाप्नोति ततो वायुं निरुद्धयेत्[2]॥ ९०॥

वाते प्राणवायौ चले श्वासोच्छ्वासरूपव्यापारविशिष्टे[3] सति बिन्दुः पूर्वोक्तलक्षणं "शुक्रं बिन्दुरुच्यते" सोऽपि चलो भवति। प्राणवायौ निश्चले व्यापाररहिते सति बिन्दुरपि निश्चलः स्थिरो भवति। तथा सति निरोद्धा स्थाणुत्वं स्थाणुवत् शीतोष्णादिसहिष्णुत्वं, चिरकालयोगाभ्यासक्षमत्वमित्यर्थः। आप्नोति प्राप्नोतीत्यर्थः। ततस्तस्मात् कारणात् योगी वायुं प्राणवायुं निरुद्धयेत्॥ ९०॥

किं च,

यावद्वायुः स्थितो[4] देहे तावज्जीवनमुच्यते।
मरणं तस्य निष्क्रान्तिस्ततो वायुं निरुन्धयेत्॥ ९१॥

यावत्कालपर्यन्तं वायुः प्राणः देहे शरीरे श्वासोच्छ्वासरूपव्यापारासक्ततया कुंभितत्वेन वा[5] स्थितो भवति, तावत्पर्यन्तं जीवनमित्युच्यते। तस्य वायोर्निष्क्रान्तिः [6]शरीरान्निर्गमनमेव मरणमित्युच्यते। ततस्तस्माज्जीवनमरणयोः प्राणवाय्वधीनत्वात् तं प्राणवायुमवश्यं निरुन्धयेत्॥ ९१॥

किं च,

यावद्बद्धो मरुद्देहे यावच्चित्तं निरामयम्।
यावद्दृष्टिर्भ्रुवोर्मध्ये तावत् कालाद्भयं कुतः॥ ९२॥

---

[1] चलेद् in the text. चलो is the reading preferred by the commentary.

[2] This and the next verse have the incorrect forms निरुन्धयेत् and निरुद्धयेत्. Other readings, which are more correct, are नियन्त्रयेत्, निबन्धयेत् or निरोधयेत्.

[3] विश्लेषे (A)

[4] स्थिरो (A). The commentary follows the given reading.

[5] कुंभितत्वेन वा not in B.

[6] शरीरान् Not in A.

यावत्पर्यन्तं मरुत्[1] प्राणवायुः देहे बद्धः पूर्वोक्तव्यापारासक्तः पूर्वोक्तप्राणायामेन[2] कुंभितो वा भवति, यावत्पर्यन्तं च[3] चित्तं निरामयं स्वसमीहितार्थाकारवृत्त्यपेक्षया[4] विषयान्तराकारवृत्त्यन्तरापत्तिरामयस्तादृशवृत्त्यन्तररहितं भवति[5], यावत्पर्यन्तं च भ्रुवोर्मध्ये दृष्टिर्निश्चला भवति, तावत्पर्यन्तं कालात् मृत्युरूपात् भयं कुतः ? अपि तु न कुतश्चिदपीत्यर्थः।

अत्र यद्यपि यः प्राणपवनस्पन्दश्चित्तस्यान्तःसराबहीति [?] चित्तप्राणयोरेक-व्यापाराश्रयणात् [6]यावच्चित्तमिति द्वितीयः पादोऽधिक इवाभाति, तथापि चित्तस्य विषयान्तरानुसन्धानराहित्ये तथा[7] ज्ञेयम्। विषयान्तरानुसन्धाने तु सत्यपि, कुंभके चित्तस्य व्यापारान्तराश्रयणे [8]बाधकाभावात् एकीक्रियते। [एवं कृते][9] योगी कालेन न बाध्यते इत्यर्थः॥९२॥

एवं कृते योगी कालेन न बाध्यते इत्यर्थं प्रमाणयति[10]—

अतः कालभयाद्ब्रह्मा प्राणायामपरायणः।
योगिनो मुनयश्चैव ततो वायुं निरुद्धयेत्॥९३॥

अतः कारणात् जीवनमरणौ प्राणाधीनौ। अतः कारणात् कालभयात् ब्रह्मा, योगिनः सनकादयः, मुनयः कश्यपादयः, अन्ये च कालभयभीताः सर्वेऽपि प्राणायामपरायणाः प्राणायामरता भवन्ति। ततस्तस्मात् कारणात् अन्योऽपि जनः कालभयभीतश्चेत् वायुं निरुद्धयेत् प्राणायामं कुर्यात् येन जरामरणवर्जितो भवतीत्यर्थः॥९३॥

---

[1] मरुत् not in A,C.

[2] पूर्वोक्तप्राणायामेन only in B.

[3] च not in B.

[4] -प्रत्यपेक्षया (A,C)

[5] After निरामयं C has दशभिर्वृतिभी रहितो भवति.

[6] यावद्बद्धो मरुदित्युक्तौ चित्तस्य निरामयतासिद्धेः (B)

[7] राहित्यतया (B)

[8] From here to the end of this commentary, B reads तथा च चित्तस्य विषयान्तरावलम्बन-निषेधफलको द्वितीयपादः।

[9] Added from the next line of B. See next footnote.

[10] Only प्रमाणयति— (A). C. stops here. Its next verse is our 2.96.

इदानीं प्राणवायोः हंसस्य समानरूपत्वं दर्शयति—[1]

षड्विंशदङ्गुलो हंसः प्रयाणं कुरुते बहिः।
वामदक्षिणमार्गेण ततः प्राणोऽभिधीयते॥ ९४॥

षड्विंशदङ्गुलः षड्विंशदङ्गुलपरिमाणः[2] प्राणापानभेदविशिष्टः हंसः वामदक्षिणमार्गेण इडापिङ्गलाभ्यां बहिः प्रयाणं कुरुते निःसरतीत्यर्थः। ततस्तस्मात् प्रयाणरूपव्यापाराश्रयणात् प्राण इत्यभिधीयते कथ्यते। तथा च प्राणापानयोरेव[3] हंसरूपत्वं, न तु हंसः कश्चिदन्य इति भ्रमितव्यमिति भावः॥ ९४॥

शुद्धिमेति यदा सर्वं नाडीचक्रं मलाकुलम्।
तदैव जायते योगी प्राणसङ्ग्रहणे क्षमः॥ ९५॥

यदा मलाकुलं मलेन व्याप्तं सर्वमपि नाडीचक्रं पूर्वोक्तनाडीशोधनप्रकारेण शोधितं सत् शुद्धिमेति मलजालं विमुञ्चति,[4] तदा एव योगी प्राणसङ्ग्रहणे प्राणवायोः स्तंभने क्षमः समर्थो भवेत्। अन्यथा प्राणरक्षणक्षमो न भवतीत्यर्थः॥ ९५॥

एवं प्राणायामं प्रस्तुत्य संप्रति प्राणायामप्रकारं दर्शयति[5]—

बद्धपद्मासनो योगी प्राणं चन्द्रेण पूरयेत्।
धारयित्वा यथाशक्तिर्भूयः सूर्येण रेचयेत्॥ ९६॥

अत्र आवश्यकमपि कुशाद्यास्तरणं ग्रन्थगौरवभिया नोपदर्शितम्। तदुक्तं नारदीयपुराणे—

> कुशैश्च सुमृदुभिश्छिन्नैः पवित्रेणाथ चर्मणा। तत्रोपविष्टः सततं योगाङ्गानि समभ्यसेत्॥ इति।

---

1 इदानीं प्राणायामस्य प्रकारं दर्शयति— (B)

2 -परिणामः (A)

3 प्राणापानयोः (A)

4 विमुक्तमलजालं भवति (B,D)

5 द्वाविंशतिभिः श्लोकैः (A)

योगसारे च—"कुशचैलाजिनास्तीर्ण" इति। एवं कुशाजिनचैलक्रमेणास्तीर्णे आसने उक्तप्रकारेण बद्धपद्मासनो योगी चन्द्रेण इडामार्गेण प्राणवायुं पूरयेत्। शनैः शनैरवेगेनेव तं[1] वायुं प्रवेशयेत्, यथाशक्ति धारयित्वा कुंभयित्वा[2], भूयः पुनः सूर्येण पिङ्गलामार्गेण रेचयेत् त्यजेत्[3] ॥ ९६ ॥

अथ चन्द्रमार्गाभ्यस्त[4]प्राणायामे ध्यानमाह—

अमृतं दधिसंकाशं[5] गोक्षीरधवलोपमम्[6]।
ध्यात्वा चन्द्रमसो बिम्बं प्राणायामी सुखी भवेत् ॥ ९७ ॥

प्राणायामी पुरुषः दधिसंकाशं दधिवदाभासमानं[7] गोक्षीरवद्धवलं अमृतरूपं चन्द्रमसो बिम्बं ध्यात्वा सुखी भवेत्। सुखाकारान्तःकरणवृत्तिपरिणामात् सन्ततं सुखानुभवो भवतीत्यर्थः ॥ ९७ ॥

चन्द्राङ्गाभ्यासमभिधाय सूर्याङ्गाभ्यासमभिधत्ते—

दक्षिणे श्वासमाकृष्य पूरयेदुदरं शनैः।
कुंभयित्वा विधानेन पुनश्चन्द्रेण रेचयेत् ॥ ९८ ॥

दक्षिणे दक्षिणेनेत्यर्थः। चन्द्रेणेत्यनुरोधात् तथा च पिङ्गलाख्यया दक्षिणनाड्या श्वासं बाह्यवायुं शनैरनतिवेगेन आकृष्य उदरं पूरयेत्। विधानेन विध्युक्तकुंभकमात्रासङ्ख्याया कुंभयित्वा पुनश्चन्द्रेण इडाख्यवामनाड्या रेचयेत् पूरितं प्राणं त्यजेत् ॥ ९८ ॥

अथ सूर्याङ्गाभ्यस्तप्राणायामे ध्यानमाह—

प्रज्वलज्ज्वलनज्वालापुञ्जमादित्यमण्डलम्।
ध्यात्वा नाभिस्थितं योगी प्राणायामी सुखी भवेत् ॥ ९९ ॥

---

[1] बाह्यं (D)

[2] कुंभयित्वा not in D.

[3] त्यजेत् not in B.

[4] चन्द्राङ्गाभ्यस्त- (B,D)

[5] अमृतोदधिमध्यस्थं (VM)

[6] - रजतोपमम् (GP)

[7] -भासं (A,C)

प्राणायामी योगी प्रज्वलन् यो ज्वलनो वह्निः, तस्य ज्वालानां पुञ्जं समूहमिव नाभिपद्मे स्थितमादित्यस्य मण्डलं, वह्निप्रचुरमित्यर्थः, ध्यात्वा सुखी भवेत्।

श्लोकद्वयेनैतदुक्तं भवति—पूर्वं इडया अधममध्यमोत्तमेषु अन्यतममात्रया द्वादशप्रणवैर्बाह्यवायुमापूर्य षोडशप्रणवैः कुंभयित्वा दश प्रणवैः शनैर्निःशेषं रेचयेत्। अत्र कुंभके पूर्वोक्तं चन्द्रमण्डलं नाभौ ध्यायेत्। एवं पिङ्गलया द्वादशप्रणवैः पूरयित्वा षोडशप्रणवैः कुंभयित्वा दशप्रणवै रेचयेत्। अत्रापि उक्तविधं सूर्यमण्डलं कुंभकसमये नाभौ ध्यायेदिति॥९९॥

श्लोकचतुष्टयोक्तमर्थं सङ्क्षिप्यैकेन दर्शयति—

प्राणं चेदिडया पिबेत् परिमितं भूयोऽन्यया रेचयेत्
पीत्वा पिङ्गलया समीरणमथो बद्धा त्यजेद्वामया।
सूर्याचन्द्रमसोरनेन विधिना बिम्बद्वयं ध्यायतां
शुद्धा नाडिगणा भवन्ति यमिनां मासत्रयादूर्ध्वतः॥ १००॥

चेद्यदि प्राणं समीरणं पूर्वोक्तमात्राकालपरिमितं इडया वामनाड्या पिबेत्। तर्हि परिमितकालं बद्धा कुम्भयित्वा अन्यया पिङ्गलया परिमितकालेन शनै रेचयेत्। न तु इडयैवेत्यर्थः। भूयः पुनः पिङ्गलया परिमितं प्राणं पीत्वा कुंभयित्वा पूर्ववत् वामया रेचयेत्। अथो अनेन विधिना प्राणायामं कुर्वन् वामनाड्या पूरितस्य कुंभके चन्द्रबिम्बं, दक्षिणनाड्या पूरितस्य कुंभके सूर्यबिम्बम्, एवं सूर्याचन्द्रमसोः बिम्बद्वयं[1] ध्यायतां यमिनां मासत्रयादूर्ध्वतः मासत्रयानन्तरं नाडीगणाः शुद्धा भवन्ति। तथा च नाडीशुद्ध्यर्थं षट् कर्मपरिश्रमो नादर्तव्यः। कफादिदोषसाम्ये तु एवं तस्यापि नावश्यकत्वमिति भावः।

अत्र "देवताद्वन्द्वे च" [६.३.२६] इति सूत्रे "आनङृतौ द्वन्द्वः" [६.३.२५] इति सूत्रात् द्वन्द्वपदानुवृत्तौ पुनर्द्वन्द्वपदं प्रसिद्धसाहचर्यस्य परिग्रहार्थं तेनैकहविर्भागित्वासाहचर्यस्य प्रसिद्धत्वान्मित्रावरुणावित्यत्रानङ् भवतीति स्थिते सूर्याचन्द्रमसोस्तु तादृशसाहचर्यस्याप्रसिद्धतयानङः प्राप्तौ छान्दसं रूपमिति केचिदाहुः, तन्न, तयोरपि सन्निकर्षविप्रकर्षाभ्यां दर्शपौर्णमासीनिरूपकत्वसाहचर्यस्य लोकत्रयप्रसिद्धस्योपलभ्यमानतया

[1] B, D here insert प्रानापानस्वरूपं "असौ वा आदित्यः प्राणः" इति श्रुतेः। ["असौ वा आदित्यो बहिरात्मान्तरात्मा प्राणः" इत्यादि मैत्रायणी उपनिषद् (६.१) द्रष्टव्यम् । यद्वा, "आदित्यो ह वै प्राणः" इत्यादि प्रश्नोपनिषद् (१.५)]

आनङ्गवृत्तौ बाधकाभावात्। तथा च गोभिलः-"यः परो विप्रकर्षः सूर्याचन्द्रमसोः सा पौर्णमासी, यः परः सन्निकर्षः साऽमावास्या" इति। विस्तरश्चायमर्थो निर्णयामृते "न चादित्यचन्द्रौ" इत्यादावपि तच्छङ्ख्यमदित्यपत्यत्वापरपर्यायस्यादित्यत्वस्य इन्द्रोपेन्द्रादिसाधारणतया तत्रातिथिनिरूपकतावच्छेदकत्वव्यभिचाराद् इत्यलमतिबाललीलाविलासनेति॥ १००॥

नाडीशुद्धेः फलं दर्शयति—

यथेष्टं धारणं वायोरनलस्य प्रदीपनम्।
नादाभिव्यक्तिरारोग्यं जायते नाडिशोधनम्॥ १०१॥

नाडीशोधनानन्तरं यथेष्टं स्वाभीष्टमात्रापरिमितकालपर्यन्तं वायोः प्राणस्य धारणं अन्तर्नाड्यां शोभनमित्यर्थः। तथा अनलस्य जठराग्नेः प्रदीपनमुद्बोधनं तथा नादस्य अभिव्यक्तिः स्पष्टतया श्रवणं तथा आरोग्यं कफवातादिजनितबाधाशून्यत्वं एतत् सर्वं जायते तेनोत्तराङ्गाभ्यासाधिकारसंपन्नो भवतीत्यर्थः॥ १०१॥

॥ इति गोरक्षशतकव्याख्यायां योगतरङ्गिण्यां प्रथमशतकं समाप्तम्॥ [1]

[1] इति जोर्षशतक पूर्वशतकटीका सम्पूर्णम्। संवत् १९३० भादौमासे कृष्ण पक्षे ४ सोमवासरे काश्यायां धर्मेश्वर निकटे शुभम्। श्री ६५०. (B)

॥ श्रीः ॥

गोरक्षशतके

॥ द्वितीयशतकम् ॥

अथ प्राणायामः

श्रीगणेशाय नमः।

महेशं रमेशं दिनेशं गणेशं परेशीं गिरीशां गुरुज्ञानमूर्तिम्।
झषेन्द्रादिसिद्धान्मुनीन्काश्यपादीन् पुरीः सत्यगङ्गादितीर्थानि नौमि॥

इत्थं शुद्धनाडीगणः साधितयमनियमासनाङ्गत्रितयो ज्ञातषट्चक्रषोडशाधारादिपरिचितनाडीजाल-तत्सञ्चारिवायुगणो योगी चन्द्रताराद्यनुकूले सुमुहूर्ते गुरुगणेशादिपूजनपूर्वकमङ्गलपाठ-स्वस्तिवाचनादिकं कारयित्वा श्रीगुरुमाराध्य तदनुज्ञया प्राणायामं कुर्यादिति प्राणायाममेकविंशति-श्लोकैः प्रपञ्चयति[1]—

प्राणो देहे स्थितो वायुरपानस्य निरोधनात्॥
एकश्वसनमात्रेणोद्घाटयेद्गगने गतिम्॥ १॥

प्राणो नाम देहे स्थितः शरीरान्तर्वर्ती वायुः अपानस्य मूलाधारवर्तिनो अपान-वायोर्निरोधनादूर्ध्वमुत्थापनात् एकश्वासमात्रेण एकेन श्वासोच्छ्वासरूपव्यापारेण[2] गगने

---

[1] प्रपञ्चन्नादौ तस्य मात्रादिभेदं चिह्नफलं च दर्शयति (D)

[2] निरुद्धेनेति शेषः (D)

सुषुम्णान्तर्गतचिदाकाशे गतिमुद्घाटयेत्। कुण्डलिनीरुद्धसुषुम्णामुखमुद्घाट्य गगने गतिं प्रापयेदित्यर्थः। एतच्च सति प्राणायामाभ्यासे कुंभकावस्थायां संभवति॥ १॥

इदानीं पूर्वसूचितप्राणायामस्य भेदानादौ दर्शयति—

रेचकः पूरकश्चैव कुंभकः प्रणवात्मकः।
प्राणायामो भवेत् त्रेधा मात्राद्वादशसंयुतः ॥ २॥

रेचक इति। स च प्राणायामस्त्रेधा त्रिविधो भवति। रेचकपूरककुंभकभेदात्। तत्र पूरको बाह्यवायोरन्तः प्रवेशेन रूपः। कुंभकः पूरितस्यान्तर्निरोधनरूपः। रेचको निरुद्धस्य तस्यैव बहिर्गमनरूपः। किंभूतः प्राणायामः ? मात्राद्वादशसंयुतः सकृत् प्रणवजपकालो मात्रेत्युच्यते। तथा च द्वादशप्रणवजपकालेन पूरित इत्यर्थः। जपो मनसा प्रसङ्ख्यानम्। जप्यस्वरूपं च ब्राह्मणानां सप्रणवसप्तव्याहृतिपूर्विकाशिरोऽन्तिमा गायत्री प्रणव एव वा अन्येषां च शैववैष्णवादिमन्त्राः। तत्र प्रणवजपेऽपि पूरके अकारं कुंभके उकारं रेचके मकारं स्मरन्प्रणवं जपेत्। तदेवाह—कथंभूतः प्राणायामः ? प्रणवात्मकः प्रणवरूपः॥ २॥

इदानीं प्राणायामाभ्यासयुक्तस्य नाडीषु मलोदये येन केनापि हेतुना संभवे पुनः पुनर्नाडीशुद्धि-प्रकारेणोक्तं प्राणायामं कुर्यादिति तदेव स्मारयति—

मात्राद्वादशसंयुक्तौ निशाकरदिवाकरौ।
दोषजालमपघ्नन्तौ ज्ञातव्यौ योगिभिः सदा॥ ३॥

मात्राणां द्वादश मात्राद्वादश, तैर्मात्राद्वादशभिः संयुक्तौ द्वादशसङ्ख्याकप्रणवजपरूपमात्राभिः वाम-दक्षिणनाडीक्रमेण पूरितप्राणायामेन संयुक्तौ स्वस्वाङ्गाभ्याससमये ध्यानयोगेन योजितौ निशाकर-दिवाकरौ चन्द्रसूर्यौ दोषाणां नाडीमलानां जालमपघ्नन्तौ नाशयन्तौ योगिभिः सदा ज्ञेयौ॥ ३॥

त्रिविधं प्राणायामं विवृणोति—

पूरके द्वादशीं कुर्यात् कुंभके षोडशी भवेत्।
रेचके दश ओंकारान्प्राणायामः स उच्यते॥ ४॥

अस्य प्राणायामस्य पूरके द्वादशीं द्वादशोंकारवतीं मात्रां कुर्यात्। कुंभके षोडशोंकारवती मात्रा भवेत्। रेचके दश ओंकारान् जपेदिति शेषः। स एष प्रत्येकं त्रिविधोऽपि एकः प्राणायाम उच्यते॥४॥

अयं प्राणायामोऽभ्यासतारतम्येन पुनस्त्रिविधः अधममध्यमोत्तमभेदादित्यभिप्रेत्यैतद्भेदघटकं मात्राभेदं दर्शयति—

अधमे द्वादशी मात्रा मध्यमे द्विगुणा मता।
उत्तमे त्रिगुणा प्रोक्ता प्राणायामस्य निर्णयः॥५॥

इयं पूर्वोक्तद्वादशी मात्रा अधमे प्राणायामे मता मध्ये प्राणायामे तद् द्विगुणमता एवमुत्तमे प्राणायामे त्रिगुणा मात्रा ज्ञेयेत्यर्थः। एवं च अधममध्यमोत्तमेषु क्रमेण द्वादश १२। चतुर्विंशति २४। षट्त्रिंशदिति ३६। पूरके, षोडश १६। द्वात्रिंशत् ३२। अष्टाचत्वारिंशत् ४८। कुंभके, दश १०। विंशति २०। त्रिंशत् ३०। इति ओंकारः रेचके प्रोक्ता इति प्राणायामस्य त्रिविधस्य मात्रायाश्च निर्णय इत्यर्थः॥५॥

अथ त्रिविधप्राणायामस्य चिह्नानि दर्शयति—

अधमे प्रचुरो घर्मः कम्पो भवति मध्यमे।
उत्तिष्ठत्युत्तमे योगी ततो वायुं निरुन्धयेत्॥६॥

अधमे सद्यः समारब्धोभ्यासके प्राणायामेन तु द्वादशमात्राके तत्रापि चराभ्यासे आसनोत्थानासंभवात्[1] प्रचुरो घर्मः प्रस्वेदो भवति, मध्यमे प्राणायामे प्राणायामाभ्यासे कंपो गात्राणां विशिष्टस्य शरीरस्य वा प्रचलनं भवति। उत्तमे प्राणायामे बद्धपद्मासनो योगी उत्तिष्ठति, आसनादुत्थानं लभते। ततस्तस्मात् कारणात् प्राणवायुं निरुद्धयेत्, प्राणायाममभ्यसेत्॥६॥

[1] Both our manuscripts (A, D) have आसनोत्थानसंभवात्, which we have emended.

इदानीं योगाङ्गं प्राणायामं दर्शयति—

बद्धपद्मासनो योगी नमस्कृत्य गुरुं शिवम्।
नासाग्र[1]दृष्टिरेकाकी प्राणायामं समभ्यसेत्॥ ७॥

बद्धं पद्मासनं येन स योगी एकाकी निर्जने मठादौ पूर्वोक्तकुशाजिनचैलसंपाते सुसमे भूतले पद्मासनेनोपविश्य आसने स्थित्वा, गुरुं शिवं च नमस्कृत्य, नासाग्रे भ्रूमध्ये दृष्टिः सन् भ्रूमध्ये शशभृद्बिम्बमित्युक्तेः स्रवत्पीयूषं चन्द्रबिम्बं भ्रूमध्ये चक्षुर्भ्यामवलोकयन्नित्यर्थः। द्विजश्चेत् पूर्वोक्तं प्रणवं गायत्रीं वा अन्यश्चेत् शैववैष्णवादिमन्त्रं जपेत्। पूर्वोक्तमात्रानुसारेण प्राणायामं समभ्यसेत्। अनवच्छेदेनाभासं कुर्यादित्यर्थः॥ ७॥

ऊर्ध्वमाकृष्य चापानवायुं प्राणे नियोजयेत्।
ऊर्ध्वमानीयते शक्त्या सर्वपापैः प्रमुच्यते॥ ८॥

किं अपानवायुं आधारसङ्कोचनादिना ऊर्ध्वमाकृष्य प्राणे नियोजयेत्, प्राणेनैकीकुर्यात्। अपानेन मिलितः प्राणः शक्त्या कुण्डलिन्या ऊर्ध्वमानीयते चेत् सर्वपापैः प्रमुच्यते॥ ८॥

तस्यैव कुंभकप्रकारं प्रपञ्चयति—

द्वाराणां नवकं निरुध्य मरुतं पीत्वा दृढं धारितं
नीत्वाकाशमपानवह्निसहितं शक्त्या समुच्चालितं।
आत्मध्यानयुतस्त्वनेन विधिना विन्यस्य मूर्ध्नि ध्रुवं
यावत् तिष्ठति तावदेव महतां सङ्घेन संस्तूयते॥ ९॥

द्वाराणां नवकं नवद्वाराणि पूर्वोक्तानीत्यर्थः। निरुध्य वक्ष्यमाणप्रकारेण निरुध्य मरुतं पीत्वा, वायुनोदरं पूरयित्वेत्यर्थः। मूलाधारगतेन वह्निना अपानवायुना च सहितं यथा स्यात् तथा मूलाधारचक्रे दृढं धारितं तत्र स्थिरतामापादितं, ततः शक्त्या कुण्डलिन्या समुच्चालितं ऊर्ध्वमुत्थापितं प्राणं आकाशमाज्ञाचक्रोर्ध्वप्रदेशं नीत्वा, ध्रुवं स्थिरं यथा स्यात् तथा मूर्ध्नि सहस्रदले विन्यस्य स्थापयित्वा, आत्मध्यानयुतस्तत्रैव लक्ष्यीकृतात्मस्वरूपो योगी अनेन विधिना

[1] भ्रूमध्ये (GP)

एतत्प्रकारेण यावत् तिष्ठति यावत्कालपर्यन्तं निश्चलः सन्नात्मानं ध्यायति, तावदेव महतामात्मध्याननिरतानां सङ्घेन संस्तूयते सम्यक् स्तूयते,[1] एवंविधस्य स्तुत्यत्वादिति भावः॥९॥

प्राणायामो भवत्येवं पातकेन्धनपावकः।
भवोदधिमहासेतुः प्रोच्यते योगिभिः सदा॥१०॥

एवममुना प्रकारेण सदा अनुष्ठीयमानः प्राणायामः पातकानि ब्रह्महत्याप्रमुखानि इन्धनानि तूलतृणादीनीव सद्य एव भस्मसात्कर्तुमुचितानि यस्य, एवंविधः पावकोऽग्निर्भवति। अयं प्राणायामः योगिभिः भवः संसार एवोदधिः समुद्रः, तस्मिन्महासेतुः सेतुरिव सद्य उत्तारकः प्रोच्यते॥१०॥

पातकापहारित्वं द्रढयति —

आसनेन रुजो हन्ति प्राणायामेन पातकम्।
विकारं मानसं योगी प्रत्याहारेण मुञ्चति॥११॥

योगी आसनेन मयूरमत्स्येन्द्रादिना दोषशमनद्वारा रुजो दैहिकबाधा हन्ति नाशयति। प्राणायामेन उक्तप्रकारेण पातकं हन्ति, अधिष्ठानशुद्धिद्वारा[2] नाशयति। प्रत्याहारेण मानसं विकारं विषयसम्बन्धनिवर्तनद्वारा मुञ्चति त्यजति॥११॥

धारणाभिर्मनोधैर्यं ध्यानाच्चैतन्यमद्भुतम्।
समाधौ मोक्षमाप्नोति त्यक्त्वा कर्म शुभाशुभम्॥१२॥

धारणाभिः वक्ष्यमाणाभिः मनसो धैर्यं वर्धयति इति शेषः। ध्यानादद्भुतं चैतन्यमुत्तमं ज्ञानं प्राप्नोति समाधौ शुभाशुभं कर्म तत्फलं च अभिमानत्यागद्वारा त्यक्त्वा मोक्षं कैवल्यरूपमाप्नोति॥१२॥

इदानीं प्राणायामेनैव प्रत्याहाराभ्यासफलं दर्शयति[3]—

प्राणायामद्विषट्केन प्रत्याहारः प्रकीर्तितः।
प्रत्याहारद्विषट्केन जायते धारणा शुभा॥१३॥

---

[1] सम्यक् स्तूयते Not in A.

[2] अधिष्ठानानि शुद्धद्वारा (A) अधिष्ठानबुद्धिद्वारा (D)

[3] प्रत्याहारादीनां कालमुपलक्षयति (D)

प्राणायामानां द्विषङ्केन द्वादशप्राणायामेनाभ्यस्तेन[1] प्रत्याहारः प्रकीर्तितः, प्रत्याहारफलोदयः कथित इत्यर्थः। तथा प्रत्याहाराणां द्वादशप्राणायामरूपानां द्विषङ्केन द्वादशगुणितेन चतुश्चत्वारिंशदधिक-शतसङ्ख्याकप्राणायामरूपा[2] धारणा जायते, धारणाजनितफलोदयो भवतीत्यर्थः[3]॥ १३॥

यावत्कालावस्थित्या धारणादित्रयं भवति—[4]

धारणा द्वादश प्रोक्तं ध्यानं ध्यानविशारदैः।[5]
ध्यानद्वादशकेनैव समाधिरभिधीयते॥ १४॥

ध्यानविशारदैः षड्विधध्याननिपुणैः द्वादशधारणाः द्वादशप्रत्याहाररूपाया पूर्वोक्तधारणा सैव द्वादशभिर्गुणिता सती अष्टाविंशत्यधिकसप्तदशशतसङ्ख्याकप्राणायामरूपं ध्यानं प्रोक्तं कथितं। तदेवं ध्यानं द्वादश गुणितं सत् षड्त्रिंशदधिकसप्तशतोत्तरविंशतिसहस्रप्राणायामरूपं संपद्यते। स एव द्वादशाहोरात्रसाध्यसमाधिरित्यभिधीयते कथ्यते सामान्यम्[6]॥ १४॥

समाधिस्वरूपं दर्शयति—

यत् समाधौ परं ज्योतिरनन्तं विश्वतोमुखम्।
तस्मिन्दृष्टे क्रियाकर्म यातायातं न विद्यते॥ १५॥

पूर्वं व्याख्यातम्[१.२१ संख्यकश्लोको द्रष्टव्यः]॥ १५॥

समाधिप्रक्रियां दर्शयति—

सम्बद्धासनमेढ्रमङ्घ्रियुगलं कर्णाक्षिनासापुट-
द्वाराण्यङ्गुलिभिर्नियम्य पवनं वक्त्रेण संपूरितम्।

---

[1] D. here inserts ...यावान् कालो भवति तावता कालेन...

[2] D. reads यावान् कालो भवति तावता कालेन in place of चतुश्चत्वारिंशद्...रूपा.

[3] धारणा... भवतीत्यर्थः not in D.

[4] A. ध्यानमाह—

[5] D. reads the verse as follows: धारणा द्वादशायामा ध्यानं द्वादशधारणा। ध्यानद्वादशकर्मा च समाधिरभिधीयते॥ १४॥

[6] D. इत्यर्थः for सामान्यम्.

धृत्वा वक्षसि वह्न्यपानसहितं मूर्ध्नि स्थितं धारयेद्
एवं याति विशेषतत्त्वसमतां योगीश्वरस्तन्मयः॥ १६॥

सम्बद्धे आसनमेढ्रे यथा स्यात् तथा अङ्घ्रियुगलं पादद्वयं संस्थाप्य सिद्धासनमारुह्येत्यर्थः। अत्रासनं योनिस्थानं तल्लक्षणे योनिस्थानकमङ्घ्रिमूलघटितं कृत्वेत्युक्तत्वात् कर्णाक्षिनासापुटद्वाराणि अङ्गुलिभिः नियम्य संरुध्य तदित्थं कर्णविवरे करद्वयगताङ्गुष्ठाभ्यामक्षिद्वयं तर्जनीभ्यां नासिकाद्वयं मध्यमाभ्यामपराभ्यां मुखं निरुध्येत्यर्थः पूर्वं वक्त्रेण मुखेन संपूरितं पूर्वोक्तरीत्या मूलाधारस्थितवह्न्यपानाभ्यां सहितं ताभ्यां संमीलितं पवनं प्राणवायुं वक्षसि हृत्सरोजे धृत्वा ततोऽप्यूर्ध्वं नीतं मूर्ध्नि स्थितं सहस्त्रदलादौ स्थापितं धारयेत्। एवमभ्यसन्योगीश्वरस्तन्मयो वह्न्यपानसंमीलितप्राणमयो भूत्वा विशेषतत्त्वेन समतां तुल्यतां याति सर्वदृगान्तरात्मना साक्षीभूतेन तदविशेषो भवतीत्यर्थः॥ १६॥

गगनं पवने प्राप्ते ध्वनिरुत्पद्यते महान्।
घण्टादीनां प्रवाद्यानां तदा सिद्धिरदूरतः॥ १७॥

एवंरीत्या पवने प्राणे गगनमाकाशं प्राप्ते सति महान् ध्वनिः घण्टाभेरीमद्दलप्रमुखानां प्रवाद्यानां शब्द उत्पद्यते। तदा तादृशचिह्ने उपलब्धे सति सिद्धिः अदूरतः सन्निधावेवोपस्थिता भवतीत्यर्थः॥ १७॥

एवं प्राणायामं निरवच्छेदमभ्यसेदित्याह—

प्राणायामेन युक्तेन सर्वरोगक्षयो भवेत्।
अयुक्ताभ्यासयोगेन सर्वरोगस्य संभवः॥ १८॥

युक्तेन यथायोग्यं अभ्यस्तेन प्राणायामेन सर्वेषां पूर्वानुवृत्तानां सद्य उत्पन्नानां च रोगानां क्षयो भवेत्। अयुक्ताभ्यासेन अनियताभ्यासेन तु सर्वरोगस्य संभवो भवेत्॥ १८॥

के रोगास्ते ये अयुक्ताभ्यासे संभवन्ति ? इत्यत्राह—

हिक्का कासस्तथा श्वासः शिरःकर्णाक्षिवेदनाः।
भवन्ति विविधा रोगाः पवनस्य व्यतिक्रमात्॥ १९॥

पवनस्य व्यतिक्रमात् अयुक्ताभ्यासेन विरोधात् हिक्का कासः श्वासः शिरःकर्णयोर्नेत्रयोश्च वेदनास्तत्र तत्र शूलविशेषाः तथान्येऽपि विविधा मूकत्वाङ्गस्फुटनत्वादयो रोगा भवन्ति॥ १९॥

शनैरभ्यसेदिति सदृष्टान्तमुपदिशति—

यथा सिंहो गजो व्याघ्रो भवेद्वश्यः शनैः शनैः।
अन्यथा हन्ति योक्तारं तथा वायुरसेवितः॥ २०॥

व्याघ्रः सिंहः गज इत्यादिर्विरुद्धोऽपि जन्तुः यथा शनैः अनुकूललालनया योजितश्चेद्वश्यः स्वेच्छानियोगयोग्यो भवति, अननुकूलनियोजने तु योक्तारं हन्ति, तथा वायुरपि विधिवत् सेवितश्चेद्वश्यो भवति, अन्यथा यथोक्तनियमपरित्यागेनाभ्यस्तश्चेद्योक्तारं योगाभ्यासनिरतं जनमुक्तरोगादिना निहन्ति॥ २०॥

पूर्वं लघुमात्रादिनाभ्यसेदित्याह—

युक्तं युक्तं त्यजेद्वायुं युक्तं युक्तं च पूरयेत्।
युक्तं युक्तं च बध्नीयादेवं सिद्धिमवाप्नुयात्॥ २१॥

वायुं प्राणं युक्तं युक्तमतिवेगरहितं नासिकाग्रस्थितकरे स्थापितसक्तुकणप्रकंपमात्रं योग्यं रेचयेत् त्यजेत्। एवं कुंभकपूरकयोरपि बोध्यम्। अत्र युक्तं युक्तमिति वीप्सा मध्यमप्राणायामसमर्थोऽपि योगी कतिचित्कालं अधमप्राणायाममेवाभ्यसेत्। एवमुत्तमप्राणायामसमर्थोऽपि मध्यमेनैव प्राणायामेनाभ्यसेदित्यर्थः सूचितः॥ २१॥

अथ प्रत्याहारः

अथ प्रत्याहारमाह त्रिंशद्भिः श्लोकैः—

चरतां चक्षुरादीनां विषयेषु यथाक्रमम्।
यत् प्रत्याहरणं तेषां प्रत्याहारः स उच्यते॥ २२॥

विषयेषु स्वस्वविषयेषु रूपरसगन्धस्पर्शशब्देषु चरतां तदेकाग्रतया प्रवृत्तानां चक्षुरादीनामिन्द्रियाणां यथाक्रमं[1] क्रममनतिक्रम्य यथाक्रम[2]मासनप्राणायामाङ्गद्वयसाधनानन्तरम्। यद्वा, दूरे स्थितेभ्यः स्वल्पतरेभ्यश्च[3] विषयेभ्यो यत् प्रत्याहरणं तेभ्यो विषयेभ्यो[4] निवर्तनमनभिमुखीकरणं स प्रत्याहार उच्यते॥ २२॥

एतदेव सदृष्टान्तं दर्शयति—

यथा तृतीयकालस्थो रविः प्रत्याहरेत् प्रभाम्।
तृतीयाङ्गस्थितो योगी विकारं मानसं तथा॥ २३॥

यथा तृतीयकालस्थो दिवसावसानस्थो रविः सूर्यः, पूर्वपर्वताभिमुखं प्रसृतमित्यर्थः,[5] प्रभां दीप्तिं प्रत्याहरेत् तथा तृतीयाङ्गस्थितः प्रत्याहाराभ्यासयुक्तो योगी मानसं विकारं विषयवासनारूपं[6] प्रत्याहरेत्, विषयसम्बन्धाद्विघटयेत्॥ २३॥

दृष्टान्तान्तरेणाह—

अङ्गमध्ये यथाङ्गानि कूर्मः संकोचयेद्ध्रुवम्।
योगी प्रत्याहरत्येवमिन्द्रियाणि तथात्मनि॥ २४॥

कूर्मोऽङ्गानि चरणशिरांसि यथा यद्वत् अङ्गमध्ये सङ्कोचयेत्, एवं तद्वत् योगीन्द्रियाणि चक्षूरसनादीनि आत्मनि ध्रुवं स्थिरं अनुद्विग्नं यथा स्यात् तथा प्रत्याहरति विनिवर्तयति[7]॥ २४॥

यं यं शृणोति कर्णाभ्यामप्रियं प्रियमेव वा।
तं तमात्मेति विज्ञाय प्रत्याहरति योगवित्॥ २५॥

---

[1] यथाक्रमं not in D.

[2] यथाक्रमं not in D.

[3] Not in D.

[4] Not in D.

[5] D only.

[6] विषयेषु मनोऽभिनिवेशरूपम् (D)

[7] प्रत्याहरेत् विनिवर्तयेत् (D)

कर्णाभ्यां यं यं शब्दजातं प्रियं स्वानुकूलार्थप्रतिपादकमप्रियं प्रतिकूलार्थाभिधायकं शृणोति श्रवणेन्द्रियद्वारा साक्षात्करोति तं तमात्मेति विज्ञायात्मत्वेन विनिश्चित्य। तथा हि विवर्ताधिष्ठान-चैतन्यमात्मा। विवर्तश्चाधिष्ठानसमसत्ताकोऽन्यथाभावः, यथा रज्ज्वां सर्पबुद्धिः स्थाणौ पुरुषबुद्धिः, तथा पूर्णानन्दरूपे आत्मचैतन्ये जगद्देहादिबुद्धिरिति नात्मनोऽतिरिक्तं किञ्चिदिति सिद्धम्। प्रत्याहरति विषयत्वेऽङ्गीकुर्वन्तीं धीवृत्तिं भ्रान्तित्वेन परित्यज्य, तदनुप्रवृत्तां श्रोत्रवृत्तिं निवर्तयतीत्यर्थः। एवं च विवर्तस्याधिष्ठानाभिन्नतया प्रपञ्चस्यात्मरूपत्वात् शब्दादीन् आत्मत्वेन विनिश्चित्येत्यर्थः स्पष्टः। तथा च नन्दं प्रति श्रीकृष्णवाक्यं—

विवर्तो ब्रह्मणः प्रोक्तो देहादी रज्जुसर्पवत्। न भिन्नो रज्जुतः सर्पो ब्रह्मणो न जगत्तथा॥ इति।

शङ्कराचार्यश्चाह—

सृष्टिर्नाम ब्रह्मरूपे सच्चिदानन्दवस्तुनि। अम्बुफेनादिवत् सर्वं नामरूपप्रसारणम्॥ इति॥ २५॥

अगन्धमथवा गन्धं यं यं जिघ्रति नासिका।
तं तमात्मेति विज्ञाय प्रत्याहरति योगवित्॥ २६॥
अमेध्यमथवा मेध्यं यं यं पश्यति चक्षुषा।
तं तमात्मेति विज्ञाय प्रत्याहरति योगवित्॥ २७॥
अस्पृश्यमथवा स्पृश्यं यं यं स्पृशति चर्मणा।
तं तमात्मेति विज्ञाय प्रत्याहरति योगवित्॥ २८॥
लवण्यमलवण्यं वा यं यं रसति जिह्वया।
तं तमात्मेति विज्ञाय प्रत्याहरति योगवित्॥ २९॥

एवं च अगन्धं अननुकूलं गन्धं अनुकूलं गन्धं वा नासिकया जिघ्रति, एवममेध्यमपवित्रं मेध्यं पवित्रं वा यं यं श्वानशैलेत्यादिरूपवत् पिण्डं चक्षुषा पश्यति, एवमस्पृश्यं शवदेहादिकं स्पृश्यं गोविप्रादिकं वा यं यं चर्मणा त्वगिन्द्रियेण स्पृशति, एवं लवण्यं लवणादिसंपन्नतया स्वादिष्टं अलवण्यं तद्रहितं जिह्वया स्पृशति आस्वाद्यति, तं तं सर्वमपीन्द्रियवृत्तिविषयं उक्तरीत्या आत्माभिन्नत्वेन विनिश्चित्य योगवित् योगतात्पर्यः पुरुषः प्रत्याहरति, स्वस्वविषयव्यावृत्ता इन्द्रियवृत्तिः प्रतीपमात्मसन्निधिमाहरति विषयेभ्यो विनिवर्तयतीत्यर्थः॥ २६॥

योगमात्र[1]साधारणं प्रत्याहारमभिधाय चन्द्रमण्डलगलितामृतधाराहरणादिरूपं हठयोगसाध्य-प्रत्याहारं नानाप्रकारैर्दर्शयति—

चन्द्रामृतमयीं धारां प्रत्याहरति भास्करः।
यत् प्रत्याहरणं तस्याः प्रत्याहारः स उच्यते॥ ३०॥

चन्द्रामृतमयीं कण्ठस्थितचन्द्रगलितामृतस्य धारां नाभिस्थितः भास्करः प्रत्याहरति—तस्या धाराया वक्ष्यमाणप्रकारेण यत् प्रत्याहरणं स्वस्य जिह्वायां समानयनं स एव प्रत्याहार उच्यते॥ ३०॥

एका स्त्री भुज्यते द्वाभ्यामागता चन्द्रमण्डलात्।
तृतीयो यः पुनस्ताभ्यां स भवेदजरामरः॥ ३१॥

एका स्त्री चन्द्रमण्डलात् षोडशदलमध्यस्थादागता स्रवपीयूषधारारूपेत्यर्थः। द्वाभ्यां चन्द्रसूर्याभ्यां भुज्यते। ताभ्यां तृतीयो यः तस्या भोक्ता भवेत्। स जरामरणवर्जितो भवेत्। अयमर्थः—कण्ठस्थितचन्द्रबिम्बादमृतं स्रवति। तच्च नाभिस्थितसूर्यबिम्बे पतति। तच्च वक्ष्यमाणया विपरीतकरण्या स्वमुखे यः समानयेत्, स जरामरणवर्जितो भवेदिति ॥ ३१॥

याभ्यां सा स्त्री भुज्यते, तौ द्वौ कथयन् विपरीतकरणीं सूचयति त्रिभिः—

नाभिदेशे वसत्येको भास्करो दहनात्मकः।
अमृतात्मा स्थितो नित्यं तालुमूले च चन्द्रमाः॥ ३२॥

एको दहनात्मको वह्निप्रचुरो भास्करो नाभिदेशे वसति। अन्यो अमृतात्मा अमृतरूपश्चन्द्रो नित्यं तालुमूले विशुद्धचक्रे स्थितो भवति॥ ३२॥

वर्षत्यधोमुखश्चन्द्रो ग्रसत्यूर्ध्वमुखो रविः।
ज्ञातव्या करणी तत्र यया पीयूषमाप्यते॥ ३३॥

---

[1] मात्र- Not in A. D. reads मात्रा-.

सोऽधोमुखश्चन्द्रो वर्षति अमृतधारां स्रवति। स रविरूर्ध्वमुखः सन् ग्रसति चन्द्रगलितामृतधारां पिबति। तत्र यया पीयूषमाप्यते प्राप्यते, सा करणी विपरीतकरणी ज्ञातव्या गुरुमुखादवगन्तव्या इत्यर्थः॥ ३३॥

कीदृशी सा करणी ? इत्यत्राह—

ऊर्ध्वं नाभिरधस्तालुरूर्ध्वं भानुरधः शशी।
करणी विपरीताख्या गुरुवाक्येन लभ्यते॥ ३४॥

नाभिः ऊर्ध्वं ऊर्ध्वप्रदेशे तालुस्तालुमूलं विशुद्धचक्रमधोऽधःप्रदेशे। एवं भानुः नाभिदेशस्थः सूर्य ऊर्ध्वमुपरिभागे, शशी तालुमूलस्थश्चन्द्रोऽधोऽधःप्रदेशे। एवं विपरीतं यथा स्यात् तथा[1] विपरीताख्या विपरीत इति नामधेया करणी भवतीत्यर्थः। अस्याः संकेतस्तु गुरुवाक्येनैव लभ्यते इत्यर्थः॥ ३४॥

खेचरीप्रदर्शनाय अनाहतं चक्रमाह—

त्रिधा बद्धो वृषो यत्र रोरवीति महास्वनः।
अनाहतं च तच्चक्रं हृदये योगिनो विदुः॥ ३५॥

यत्र यस्मिंश्चक्रे त्रिधा त्रिःप्रकारेण बद्धो वृष इवानभिज्ञत्वाद्वृषो[2] गुणत्रयात्मिकायां प्रकृतौ[3] प्रतिबिम्बितो जीवो महास्वनो मध्यमशक्तिकनादविशिष्टः सन् रोरवीति अतिशयेन रौति, निरन्तरं शब्दं करोतीत्यर्थः। तदुक्तं योगसारे—

हृदये वाद्यते घोषो गर्जत्पर्जन्यसन्निभः। तत्र स्थिता महादेवी मध्यमेत्यभिधीयते॥ इति।

हृदये अनाहतं नामकं तच्चक्रं योगिनोऽन्तर्ध्याननिरता विदुर्जानन्ति॥ ३५॥

---

[1] ह्रियमाणं (D)

[2] वृष इव परतन्त्रत्वाद्विषयानभिज्ञत्वाद् (D)

[3] मायायां (D)

खेचरीमुद्रायाममृतपानमुपदिशति द्वाभ्याम्—

अनाहतमतिक्रम्य चाक्रम्य मणिपूरकम्।
प्राप्ते प्राणे महापद्मं योगित्वममृतायते॥ ३६॥

उक्तरीत्यापानमुत्थाप्य, तेनैकीकृते प्राणे मणिपूरकमाक्रम्यारुह्य, अनन्तरमनाहतमतिक्रम्योल्लङ्घ्य, चकारोऽनुक्तयोर्विशुद्धाज्ञयोः समुच्चयार्थः, विशुद्धामाज्ञां चातिक्रम्येत्यर्थः। महापद्मं सहस्रदलाख्यं ब्रह्मस्थानं प्राप्ते सति, योगित्वमत्र त्व-प्रत्ययार्थौ न विवक्षितः। योगीत्यर्थः। अमृतायते जननमरणवर्जितो भवतीत्यर्थः॥ ३६॥

मूर्ध्नः षोडशपत्रपद्मगलितं प्राणादवाप्तं हठाद्
ऊर्ध्वास्यो रसनां निधाय विधिवत्[1] शक्तिं परां चिन्तयन्।
उत्कल्लोलकलाजलं सुविमलं जिह्वाकुलं यः पिबेन्
निर्दोषः स मृणालकोमलतनुर्योगी चिरं जीवति॥ ३७॥

एवं महापद्मं संप्राप्तप्राणो यो योगी मूर्ध्नः शिरसः सहस्रदलात् षोडशपत्रं यत् पद्मं, तस्मिन्विशुद्धचक्रे इत्यर्थः, गलितं पतितं हठात् ऊर्ध्वमुत्थापितात् प्राणात् अवाप्तं नासिकोर्ध्वविवरे[2] नीतं। तत्र रसनां जिह्वां निधाय ऊर्ध्वविवरे प्रवेश्य ऊर्ध्वास्यः ऊर्ध्वमुखः सन् विधिवत् परां शक्तिं सहस्रदले प्राणेन सह प्राप्तां कुण्डलीशक्तिं चिन्तयन् ध्यायन् सन्, तस्यां प्रविष्टायां ये कल्लोला अमृताम्बुनो बृहदूर्मयः, तेषां कलाजलं लेशाम्बु सुविमलमतिनिर्मलं जिह्वाकुलं जिह्वाया निर्मथनेनाकुलं अमृतजलं पिबेत्। स योगी मृणालकोमलशरीरो निर्दोषः कायिकमानसिकदोषैर्दद्रुकुष्ठरागद्वेषादिभी रहितः सन् चिरं चिरकालपर्यन्तं जीवति॥ ३७॥

अथ जरामररोगादिशान्तये शीतलीप्रमुखाः क्रिया दर्शयति—

काकचञ्चूवदास्येन शीतलं सलिलं पिबेत्।
प्राणापानविधानेन योगी भवति निर्जरः॥ ३८॥

---

[1] विवरे (HYP)

[2] - खेचरे (A)

काकचञ्चूसमानाकारेण मुखेन कृत्वा प्राणापानयोर्विधानेन पूर्वोक्तरीत्या एकीकरणप्रकारेण शीतलं शीतलं सलिलं बाह्यवायुं यः पिबेत् पूरयेत् स योगी निर्जरो, जरा वृद्धत्वं, तद्रहितो भवतीत्यर्थः॥ ३८॥

रसनातालुमूलेन यः प्राणमनिलं पिबेत्।
अब्दार्धेन भवेत् तस्य सर्वरोगस्य संक्षयः॥ ३९॥

एवं रसनातालुमूलेन रसना जिह्वा, तत्सहायभूतेन[1] तालुमूलेन कृतं यद्विवरं, तेन कृत्वा यः योगी प्राणमनिलं प्राणवायुं पिबेत् पूरयेत्, तस्य योगिनोऽब्दार्धेन षण्मासेन सर्वरोगाणां नाशः क्षयो[2] भवेत्॥ ३९॥

रविमुखं वञ्चयित्वामृतकलापानप्रकारमाह—

विशुद्धे पञ्चमे चक्रे ध्यात्वा सोमकलामृतम्।
उन्मार्गेणाहृतं याति वञ्चयित्वा मुखं रवेः॥ ४०॥

विशुद्धे कण्ठदेशवर्तिनि पञ्चमे चक्रे सोमकलामृतं मनसा ध्यात्वा उन्मार्गेण ऊर्ध्वमार्गेणाहृतं सत्[3] रवेर्मुखं वञ्चयित्वा स्वस्योदरप्रदेशं याति, तत्र जीर्णम्। तदपि जरारोगादिकं नाशयतीत्यर्थः॥ ४०॥

विशुद्धपदं विवृणोति—

वि-शब्देन स्मृतो हंसो नैर्मल्यं शुद्धिरुच्यते।
अतः कण्ठे विशुद्धाख्यं चक्रं चक्रविदो विदुः॥ ४१॥

वि-शब्दः पक्षिवाचकः, तेन वाच्यो हंसः स्मृतः। नैर्मल्यं निर्मलत्वं शुद्धिशब्देनोच्यते। अतः कारणात् कण्ठदेशे विः पक्षी शुद्धो निर्मलो यस्मिन्, तद्[4] विशुद्धं नाम चक्रं चक्रविदश्चक्रतात्पर्यज्ञा योगिनो विदुर्जानन्ति॥ ४१॥

---

[1] तत्सहायभूत- (A)

[2] सर्वरोगसंक्षयो (D)

[3] ऊर्ध्वमाकृष्य क्रमेणाहृतं (D)

[4] विपक्षि शुद्धे निर्मले यस्मिन् तद् is the A reading, not found in D. We have emended the text here.

अमृतं कन्दरे कृत्वा नासान्तसुषिरे क्रमात्।
स्वयमुच्चालितं याति वर्जयित्वा मुखं रवेः॥ ४२॥

विशुद्धचक्रस्थितममृतं पूर्ववदुत्थापितप्राणेनोच्चालितं कन्दरे लम्बिकोर्ध्वविवरे कृत्वा, ततोऽपि क्रमेण नासान्तसुषिरे नीतं सत् रवेर्नाभिमण्डलस्थस्य सूर्यस्य मुखं वर्जयित्वा, स्वयमेव भुक्तान्नपानादिवज्जाठराग्निप्रदेशं याति॥ ४२॥

किं च—

बद्धं सोमकलाजलं सुविमलं कण्ठस्थलादूर्ध्वतो
नासान्ते सुषिरे नयेच्च गगनद्वारं ततः सर्वतः।
ऊर्ध्वास्यो भुवि सन्निपत्य नितरामुत्तानपादः पिबेद्
एवं यः कुरुते जितेन्द्रियगणो नैवास्ति तस्य क्षयः॥ ४३॥

कण्ठस्थलादूर्ध्वदेशे बद्धं संरुद्धं सुविमलं सोमकलाजलं चन्द्रामृतं नासान्ते सुषिरे नयेत् प्रापयेत्। च पुनः। सर्वत उपरि गगनद्वारं आज्ञाप्रदेशं नयेत्, तत ऊर्ध्वास्य ऊर्ध्वमुखः भुवि भूमौ सन्निपत्य उत्तानपादः सन् पिबेत्। जितेन्द्रियगणो यो योगी नितरां निरन्तरमेवं कुरुते, तस्य योगिनः क्षयो मरणं नैवास्ति कदाचिदपि, न म्रियत इत्यर्थः॥ ४३॥

किं च—

ऊर्ध्वजिह्वां स्थिरां कृत्वा सोमपानं करोति यः।
मासार्धेन न सन्देहो मृत्युं जयति योगवित्॥ ४४॥

जिह्वामूर्ध्वलम्बिकोपरि विवरे स्थिरं कृत्वा यः योगी सोमपानममृतपानं करोति, स योगवित् योगक्रियाकुशलः पुरुषः मासार्धेन पक्षमात्राभ्यासेन मृत्युं जयति, संप्राप्तोऽपि मृत्युस्तस्मिन्नसमर्थो भवति। अत्र सन्देहो न कर्तव्य इत्यर्थः॥ ४४॥

बद्धं मूलबिलं येन तेन विघ्नो विदारितः।
अजरामरमाप्नोति यथा पञ्चमुखो हरः॥ ४५॥

येन योगिना मूलबिलं मूलद्वारं सुषुम्णारूपं[1] बद्धं संरुद्धं, तेन विघ्नो जरामरणादिरूपो विदारितः विशेषेण नाशितः, तेन जरामरणादिसहितं देहात्मभावं विहाय अजरामरं जरामरणरहितं शुद्धात्मभावं प्राप्नोति यथा पञ्चमुखो हरो देहाहंभावजरामरणादिरहितः तद्वदित्यर्थः ॥ ४५ ॥

किं च—

संपीड्य रसनाग्रेण राजदन्तबिलं महत्।
ध्यात्वामृतमयीं देवीं षण्मासेन कविर्भवेत् ॥ ४६ ॥

रसनाग्रेण जिह्वाग्रेण राजदन्तबिलं महत् संपीड्य अमृतमयीं देवीं वागीश्वरीं[2] ध्यात्वा षण्मासेन षण्मासाभ्यासेन[3] कविर्विचित्रकविताविलासी भवेत् ॥ ४६ ॥

वक्ष्यमाणाः पञ्चधारणा अभ्यसतोऽपि योगिनोऽयमेव प्रकार इति दर्शयति—

सर्वद्वाराणि बध्नाति तदूर्ध्वं धारितं महत्।
न मुञ्चत्यमृतं क्वापि स पन्थाः पञ्चधारणाः ॥ ४७ ॥

योगी तत् महत् रसनाग्रेन संपीडितं राजदन्तबिलं रुन्धन् सन् सर्वद्वाराणि नाडीमुखानि बध्नाति रुणद्धि। तदूर्ध्वं धारितं धाराकारममृतं[4] क्वापि न मुञ्चति। वक्ष्यमाणधारणमभ्यसतोऽपि योगिनः सोऽयमेव पन्था[5] मार्गो भवतीत्यर्थः। यथा चन्द्रगलितामृतस्याहरणं प्रत्याहार उच्यते, तथा तस्यामृतस्य लम्बिकोर्ध्वविवरे धारणं धारणेत्युच्यत इति भावः ॥ ४७ ॥

किं च—

चुम्बन्ती यदि लम्बिकाग्रमनिशं जिह्वा रसस्यन्दिनी
सक्षारं कटुकाम्लदुग्धसदृशं मध्वाज्यतुल्यं तथा।

---

[1] सुषुम्णारूपं Not in A.

[2] कुण्डलिनीं (D)

[3] षण्मासाभ्यन्तर एव (D)

[4] धाराद्वारममृतं (D)

[5] पुण्यो (D)

व्याधीनां हरणं जरान्तकरणं शास्त्रागमोद्दीरणं[1]
तस्य स्यादमरत्वमष्टगुणितं सिद्धाङ्गनाकर्षणम् ॥ ४८ ॥

यस्य जिह्वा सक्षारं[2] कदाचित् क्षाररसयुक्तं कटुकाम्लदुग्धसदृशं कटुकरसयुक्तं कदाचित् आम्लरसयुक्तं कदाचित् दुग्धसदृशं कदाचित् मधुसदृशं कदाचित् घृततुल्यमिति नानारसयुक्तं लम्बिकाग्रं यदि अनिशं निरन्तरं चुम्बन्ती सती रसस्यन्दिनी तत्तद्रसयुक्ता भवेत्, तर्हि तस्य पुरुषस्य[3] व्याधीनां पूर्वोक्तानां हरणं नाशनं जरायाः वृद्धावस्थायाः अन्तःकरणं व्ययसामर्थ्यं शास्त्राणामागमानां चोद्दीरणं तत्र तत्रस्थितसिद्धान्तानां यन्त्रमन्त्राणां चाश्रुतपूर्वाणां व्याख्यानं तथा अष्टगुणा अणिमाद्यष्टसिद्धयः सञ्जाता अस्मिन्नित्यगुणितमष्टगुणोदयः, विशिष्टममरत्वं देवत्वमित्यर्थः[4]। तथा सिद्धाङ्गनानां ध्यानमात्रेण कर्षणं च स्यादित्यर्थः ॥ ४८ ॥

प्रकरणम्[5] उपसंहरन् प्रत्याहारस्य फलं दर्शयति श्लोकत्रयेण—

अमृतापूर्णदेहस्य योगिनो द्वित्रिवत्सरात्।
ऊर्ध्वं प्रवर्तते रेतोऽप्यणिमादिगुणोदयः ॥ ४९ ॥

एवमुक्तरीत्या अमृतेन आ समन्तात् पूर्णदेहस्य योगिनो द्वित्रिवत्सराभ्यासादेव रेतो वीर्यमूर्ध्वं प्रवर्तते, ऊर्ध्वं गच्छति। अणिमादिगुणानामुदयोऽपि जायत इत्यर्थः ॥ ४९ ॥

इन्धनानि यथा वह्निस्तैलवर्तीं च दीपकः।
तथा सोमकलापूर्णं देहं देही न मुञ्चति ॥ ५० ॥

वह्निरिन्धनानि शुष्ककाष्ठानि तथा दीपस्तैलोपसिक्तां वर्तीं यथा न मुञ्चति, तथा देही जीवात्मा पूर्वोक्तरीत्या सोमकलाभिः पूर्णं देहं शरीरं न मुञ्चति न त्यजति ॥ ५० ॥

नित्यं सोमकलापूर्णं शरीरं यस्य योगिनः।

---

[1] शास्त्रागमोद्धारणं (A)

[2] साक्षात्कारं (A)

[3] रसस्य (D)

[4] विशिष्टममरत्वं देवत्वमित्यर्थः not in D.

[5] धारणम् (A)

तक्षकेनापि दष्टस्य विषं तस्य न सर्पति॥ ५१॥

यस्य योगिनः शरीरं नित्यं सोमकलापूर्णं भवति, तस्य योगिनः तक्षकेन दष्टस्यापि शरीरे विषं तदुद्गीर्णं न सर्पति, सर्वाङ्गं न व्याप्नोतीत्यर्थः॥ ५१॥

अथ धारणा

एवमभ्यस्ताङ्गत्रितयो योगी धारणां समभ्यसेदिति नवभिः श्लोकैर्दर्शयति—

आसनेन समायुक्तः प्राणायामेन संयुतः।
प्रत्याहारेण सम्पन्नो धारणां च समभ्यसेत्॥ ५२॥

आसनेन समायुक्तः अनुद्वेजकतयाभ्यस्तपूर्वोक्तान्यतमासनः, एवं प्राणायामेनापि संयुतस्योत्तममध्यमाधमान्यतमलक्षणलक्षितः, तथा प्रत्याहारेण संपन्नो विधिवत् प्रत्याहृतेन्द्रियवृत्तिर्योगी धारणां सम्यग् अभ्यसेत्॥ ५२॥

हृदये पञ्चभूतानां धारणं च पृथक् पृथक्।
मनसो निश्चलत्वेन धारणा साभिधीयते॥ ५३॥

हृदये हृत्प्रदेशे मनसः, चकारः प्राणस्य समुच्चयार्थः, तथा च प्राणमनसोर्निश्चलत्वेन[1] पञ्चभूतानां पृथक् पृथक् संधारणं[2], सैव धारणेत्यभिधीयते॥ ५३॥

तत्रादौ पृथिवीधारणामाह—

या पृथ्वी हरितालहेमरुचिरा पीता लकारान्विता
संयुक्ता कमलासनेन हि चतुष्कोणा हृदि स्थायिनी।
प्राणं तत्र विलीय पञ्चघटिकं चित्तान्वितं धारये-
देषा स्तंभकरी सदा क्षितिजयं कुर्याद्भुवो धारणा॥ ५४॥

---

[1] प्राणस्य च निश्चलत्वेन प्राणस्य (A)

[2] D inserts here क्रियते.

या पृथ्वी हरितालहेमवत् रुचिरा रमणीया, अतः पीता लकारबीजेनान्विता, कमलासनेन ब्रह्मणा संयुक्ता समधिष्ठिता, चतुष्कोणाकारा हृदि स्थायिनी, तत्र ध्यानविषयीकृतेत्यर्थः, तत्र तस्मिन्भूमण्डले स्वयमपि विलीय लीनो भूत्वा, तत्तत्त्वमयो भूत्वेत्यर्थः, चित्तान्वितं चित्तेन संमिलितं प्राणं पञ्चघटिकाकालं यावत् धारयेत्। एषा भुवो धारणा स्तंभकरी गुरुहेतुकपतनस्तंभिका[1] सदानुष्ठिता सती क्षितिजयं कुर्यात्। स्तंभनप्रकारस्तु गुरुमुखात् ज्ञेयः॥५४॥

वारुणीं धारणामाह—

अर्धेन्दुप्रतिमं च कुन्दधवलं कण्ठेऽम्बुतत्त्वं स्थितं
यत् पीयूषवकारबीजसहितं युक्तं सदा विष्णुना।
प्राणं तत्र विलीय पञ्चघटिकं चित्तान्वितं धारये-
देषा दुःसहकालकूटदहनी स्याद्वारुणी धारणा॥५५॥

अर्धेन्दोः प्रतिमेव प्रतिमा यस्य तद्[2] अर्धेन्दुप्रतिमं अर्धचन्द्रभङ्गुराकारमित्यर्थः। कुन्दवत् धवलवर्णं पीयूषरूपी यद्वकारबीजं, तेन सहितं विष्णुना स्वतत्त्वाभिमानि नायुक्तं कण्ठे विशुद्धचक्रे स्थितं यत् अम्बुतत्त्वं, तत्र स्वयं प्रविलीय[3] चित्तान्वितं प्राणं विलीय प्रविलाप्य पञ्चघटिकावधि धारयेत्। एषा दुःसहस्य कालकूटस्य दहनी भस्मकारिणी, तस्य उद्वेजकत्वशक्तिनाशिनीति यावत् वारुणी धारणा स्यात्॥५५॥

तैजसीं धारणामाह—

यत् तालुस्थितमिन्द्रगोपसदृशं तत्त्वं त्रिकोणानलं
तेजो रेफयुतं प्रवालरुचिरं रुद्रेण यत् सङ्गतम्।
प्राणं तत्र विलीय पञ्चघटिकं चित्तान्वितं धारये-
देषा वह्निजयं सदा वितनुते वैश्वानरी धारणा॥५६॥

---

[1] Not in D.

[2] अर्धेन्दोः ... तद् Not in D.

[3] स्वयं विलीय (No तत्र) (D)

त्रिकोणाकारं इन्द्रगोपसदृशं प्रवालवत् रुचिरं रक्तं[1] तेजोरूपं यत् रेफबीजं तेन युतं रुद्रेण तत्तत्त्वाभिमानिना सङ्गतं तालुस्थितं यदनलमाग्नेयं तत्त्वं, तत्र स्वयं विलीय चित्तान्वितं प्राणं पञ्चघटिकं यावत् धारयेत्। एषा वैश्वानरी धारणा सदाभ्यस्ता वह्निजयं वह्निजनितदाहादिराहित्यं वितनुते विस्तारयतीत्यर्थः॥५६॥

वायवीं धारणामाह—

यद्भिन्नाञ्जनपुञ्जसन्निभमिदं वृत्तं भ्रुवोरन्तरे
तत्त्वं वायुमयं यकारसहितं तत्रेश्वरो देवता।
प्राणं तत्र विलीय पञ्चघटिकं चित्तान्वितं धारये-
देषा खे गमनं करोति यमिनां स्याद्वायवी धारणा॥५७॥

वृत्तं वर्तुलाकारं भिन्नं विदीर्णमञ्जनस्य पुञ्जं तद्वदिति नीलवर्णं यकारबीजेन सहितं ईश्वरेण तत्तत्त्वाभिमानिना सहितं भ्रुवोरन्तरे स्थितं यदिदं वायुमयं तत्त्वं तत्र स्वयं विलीय चित्तान्वितं प्राणं पञ्चघटिकं पूर्ववद्धारयेत्। एषा वायवी धारणा यमिनां खे गमनमाकाशगतिं करोति जनयति॥५७॥

आकाशधारणामाह—

आकाशं सुविशुद्धवारिसदृशं यद् ब्रह्मरन्ध्रे स्थितं
तन्नादेन सदाशिवेन सहितं तत्त्वं हकारान्वितम्।
प्राणं तत्र विलीय पञ्चघटिकं चित्तान्वितं धारयेद्
एषा मोक्षकपाटपाटनपटुः प्रोक्ता नभोधारणा॥५८॥

सुविशुद्धमकलुषम् । यद्वारि तत्सदृशं स्वच्छं नादेन तत्र व्यक्तिमागतेन सदाशिवेन तत्तत्त्वाभिमानिना सहितं हकारबीजेन अन्वितं मिलितं ब्रह्मरन्ध्रे स्थितं यत् आकाशतत्त्वं, तत्र पूर्ववत् स्वयं विलीय चित्तान्वितं प्राणं पञ्चघटिकं धारयेत्। एषा मोक्षकपाटस्य पाटनमुत्पाटनं, तत्र पटुः कुशला नभोधारणा प्रोक्ता। यत् तद्धारयतो मोक्षरूपं फलं भवतीत्यर्थः॥५८॥

---

[1] Not in A.

पञ्चभूतधारणायाः प्रत्येकं फलं दर्शयति—

स्तम्भिनी द्राविणी चैव दहनी भ्रामिणी तथा।
शोषिणी च भवन्त्येता भूतानां पञ्च धारणाः॥५९॥

स्तंभनादिकं पृथिवीधारणादीनां फलं क्रमेण बोध्यम्॥५९॥

कर्मणा मनसा वाचा धारणाः पञ्च दुर्लभाः।
विज्ञाय सततं योगी सर्वदुःखैः प्रमुच्यते॥६०॥

कर्मणा अनुष्ठानरूपेण, मनसा चिन्तनरूपेण, वाचा इत्थमिति निदर्शनात्मकवचनरूपेण, प्राप्तुं दुर्लभाः पञ्चधारणाः विज्ञाय योगी सर्वदुःखैः प्रमुच्यते॥६०॥

अथ ध्यानम्

अथ चतुर्विंशतिभिः श्लोकैः ध्यानस्य प्रकरणमुत्थापयन्[1] प्रथमं चिन्तार्थकधातुं दर्शयति—

स्म्रित्येव सर्वचिन्तायां धातुरेकः प्रपद्यते।
यच्चित्ते निर्मला चिन्ता तद्धि ध्यानं प्रचक्षते॥६१॥

स्मृ इति धातुरेव सर्वचिन्तायां प्रपद्यते, चिन्तासामान्यवाचकतया कथ्यते इत्यर्थः। व्याकरणे इति शेषः। तथा च चित्ते निर्मला अनाच्छन्नविषया चिन्ता शास्त्रोक्तप्रकारेण स्मरणमिति यावत्। हि निश्चये। तदेव ध्यानमिति प्रचक्षते उच्यते॥६१॥

तदेव ध्यानं सगुणनिर्गुणभेदेन द्विविधं भवतीत्याह—

द्विविधं भवति ध्यानं सकलं निष्कलं तथा।
सकलं वर्णभेदेन निष्कलं निर्गुणं भवेत्॥६२॥

द्विविधमिति तद्ध्यानं द्विविधं भवति। एकं सकलया सत्त्वादिगुणरूपवर्णमुद्राकारादिरूपया सहितं सकलं सगुणं चतुर्बाहुपञ्चवक्त्रादिरूपं तद्रहितं निष्कलं निर्गुणं ज्योतीरूपं भवेदित्यर्थः॥६२॥

---

[1] From श्लोकैः only in D.

ध्यानसमयेऽवस्थानप्रकारमाह—

अन्तश्चेतो बहिश्चक्षुरधः स्थाप्य सुखासनम् ।
समत्वं च शरीरस्य ध्यानमुद्रेति कथ्यते॥ ६३॥

अन्तर्वक्ष्यमाणाधारचक्रादिषु चेतोऽन्तःकरणं बहिर्नासाग्रादिषु चक्षुर्नेत्रम् अधस्तु समे भूतले सुखदमासनं पूर्वोक्तप्रकारेण संस्थाप्य शरीरस्य समत्वं विधाय समकायशिरोधरः सन् ध्यायेत्। इयं ध्यानमुद्रा इति कथ्यते इत्यर्थः॥ ६३॥

अथाधारादिध्यानस्थानभेदं दर्शयति आधारमित्यादिभिः—

आधारं प्रथमं चक्रं स्वर्णाभं च चतुर्दलम्।
कुण्डलिन्या समायुक्तं ध्यात्वा मुच्येत किल्बिषैः॥ ६४॥

आधारं मूलाधाराख्यां प्रथमं स्वर्णवर्णं चतुर्दलं यच्चक्रं कुण्डलिन्या समायुक्तं, तद् ध्यात्वा योगी किल्बिषैः पातकैर्मुच्यते, निष्कल्मषो भवतीत्यर्थः। अत्राधारशब्देन तत्रत्यस्वयंभूलिङ्गविशिष्टस्य ग्रहणम्॥ ६४॥

स्वाधिष्ठाने च षड्दले सन्माणिक्यसमप्रभे।
नासाग्रदृष्टिरात्मानं ध्यात्वा योगी सुखी भवेत्॥ ६५॥

स्वाधिष्ठाने इति। षड्दले सन्माणिक्यप्रभया तुल्यप्रभे सुष्ठुरक्तवर्णे इत्यर्थः। स्वाधिष्ठाने नासाग्रदृष्टिः सन् आत्मानं सगुणमिष्टरूपं निर्गुणं वा ज्योतिःस्वरूपं ध्यात्वा योगी सुखी भवेत्॥ ६५॥

किं च,

तरुणादित्यसङ्काशे चक्रे च मणिपूरके।
नासाग्रदृष्टिरात्मानं ध्यात्वा सङ्क्षोभयेज्जगत्॥ ६६॥

पुनस्तरुणः सद्यःसमुदितो य आदित्य आरक्तमण्डलो रविः, तद्वत् सङ्काशते दीप्यते इति तरुणादित्यसङ्काशः, तस्मिन्मणिपूरके चक्रे नासाग्रदृष्टिः सन् आत्मानं[1] ध्यात्वा योगी निखिलं जगत् सङ्क्षोभयेत्॥ ६६॥

हृदाकाशे स्थितं शंभुं प्रचण्डरवितेजसम्।
नासाग्रे दृष्टिमाधाय ध्यात्वा ब्रह्ममयो भवेत्॥ ६७॥

हृदाकाशे हृत्सरोजविवरे अनाहताख्यचक्र इत्यर्थः। स्थितं प्रचण्ड उत्कटकिरणो यो रविः सूर्यः तद्वत् तेजो यस्य तं शम्भुं बाणलिङ्गरूपमित्यर्थः। नासाग्रदृष्टिमाधाय स्थापयित्वा ध्यात्वा ब्रह्ममयो निरस्तसमस्तोपाधिगुणो भवेदित्यर्थः॥ ६७॥

विद्युत्प्रभे च हृत्पद्मे प्राणायामविभेदतः।
नासाग्रदृष्टिरात्मानं ध्यात्वा ब्रह्ममयो भवेत्॥ ६८॥

पुनः विद्युत्प्रभे तं तडिल्लतेवाभासमाने पूर्वोक्ते हृत्पद्मे प्राणायामविभेदतः प्राणायामोक्तप्रकारेण नासाग्रदृष्टिः सन्नात्मानं पूर्वोक्तरीत्या ध्यात्वा योगी ब्रह्ममयो भवेत्॥ ६८॥

सततं घण्टिकामध्ये विशुद्धे दीपकप्रभे।
नासाग्रदृष्टिरात्मानं ध्यात्वा मृत्युं प्रमुञ्चति॥ ६९॥

घण्टिकामध्ये कण्ठमूलप्रदेशे विशुद्धे चक्रे दीपकसमानप्रभे नासाग्रदृष्टिः सन्नात्मानं सततं निरन्तरं ध्यात्वा योगी मृत्युं मरणं प्रमुञ्चति, अमरो भवतीत्यर्थः॥ ६९॥

किं च,

भ्रुवोरन्तर्गतं देवं सन्माणिक्यशिखोपमम्।
नासाग्रदृष्टिरात्मानं ध्यात्वानन्दमयो भवेत्॥ ७०॥

भ्रुवोरन्तर्गतमाज्ञाचक्रे स्थितं सन्माणिक्यस्य शिखावदारक्तवर्णमात्मानं नासाग्रदृष्टिः सन् ध्यात्वा आनन्दमयो विगलितद्वन्द्ववेदनो भवेत्॥ ७०॥

---

[1] आसने (!D)

ध्यायेन्नीलनिभं नित्यं भ्रूमध्ये परमेश्वरम्।
आत्मानं विजितप्राणो योगी योगमवाप्नुयात्॥ ७१॥

भ्रूमध्ये आज्ञाचक्रे नीलनिभं नीलवर्णं परमेश्वरं शिवमात्मानं परमात्मानं विजितप्राणः सन् नित्यं ध्यात्वा योगी योगं जीवात्मपरमात्मनोरैक्यमावाप्नुयात् प्राप्नुयात्॥ ७१॥

निर्गुणं च शिवं शान्तं गगने विश्वतो मुखम्।
नासाग्रदृष्टिरेकाकी ध्यात्वा ब्रह्मसमो भवेत्॥ ७२॥

गगने आज्ञाचक्रस्थाने निर्गुणं कर्तृत्वभोक्तृत्वाद्यभिमानकलारहितम्, अतएव शान्तं, विश्वतोमुखं विश्वव्यापकं, शिवं नासाग्रदृष्टिः सन् एकाकी जनसंपर्कशून्यस्थो योगी ध्यात्वा ब्रह्मसमो जीवभावप्रदगुणधर्मरहितो भवेत्। व्यवहारदशायामपीति भावः॥ ७२॥

आकाशे यत्र शब्दं स्यात् तदाज्ञाचक्रमुच्यते।
तत्रात्मानं शिवं ध्यात्वा योगी मुक्तिमवाप्नुयात्॥ ७३॥

आकाशे आकाशतत्त्वनिलये यत्र यस्मिन् स्थाने शब्दः नादरूपो व्यक्तः स्यात्, तदेव भ्रूमध्ये गतमाज्ञाचक्रमुच्यते। तत्र तस्मिन् चक्रे स्थितं शिवं शिवरूपिणमात्मानं पूर्वोक्तरीत्या ध्यात्वा योगी मुक्तिं कैवल्यरूपामवाप्नुयात्। एतदाकाशमण्डलम्। अतो नादं चात्रैव व्यक्तो भवति। शब्दस्याकाशगुणत्वात् तदुक्तं योगसारे—

आकाशमण्डलं वृत्तं देवतास्य सदाशिवः। नादरूपं भ्रुवोर्मध्ये मनसो मण्डलं विदुः॥ इति॥ ७३॥

आज्ञाचक्रोपरिगतशून्यस्थाने सकलचक्रवत् साधारणं ध्यानमाह—

निर्मलं गगनाकारं मरीचिजलसन्निभम्।
आत्मानं सर्वगं ध्यात्वा योगी मुक्तिमवाप्नुयात्॥ ७४॥

निर्मलं स्वरूपतिरोधायकमलसम्बन्धरहितं, अत एव गगनाकारं निरभ्रगगनसदृशं मध्येऽवच्छेदकाभावात् सर्वत्रैकाकारतया व्यापकमित्यर्थः, अत एव सर्वगम्। ननु किं स्वरूपशून्यता ? इत्याह—मरीचिजलसन्निभं मृगतृष्णिकोदकवत् स्फुरत्तेजोरूपमित्यर्थः। एतादृशमात्मानं ध्यात्वा योगी मुक्तिं प्राप्नुयात्॥ ७४॥

उक्तध्यानस्य स्थानमाह द्वाभ्यां—

गुदं मेढ्रश्च नाभिश्च हृत्पद्मं च तदूर्ध्वतः।
घण्टिका लम्बिकास्थानं भ्रूमध्यं च नभोबिलम्॥ ७५॥

गुदं मूलाधारं, मेढ्रः स्वाधिष्ठानं, नाभिः मणिपूरकं हृत्पद्ममनाहतं तदूर्ध्वतः विशुद्धं घण्टिकामूलं लम्बिकास्थानं भ्रूमध्ये आज्ञाचक्रं नभोबिलं तदुपरि शून्यस्थानमिति॥ ७५॥

कथितानि नवैतानि ध्यानस्थानानि योगिभिः।
उपाधितत्त्वयुक्तानि कुर्वन्त्यष्टगुणोदयम्॥ ७६॥

उपाधिना पृथिव्यादिमण्डलेन तत्त्वेन आत्मना च, आभ्यां युक्तानि एतानि नवध्यानस्थानानि योगिभिः कथितानि ध्यानयोगेन सेवितानि अष्टगुणानां[1] अणिमादीनामुदयं कुर्वन्ति॥ ७६॥

नाभौ संयम्य चित्तं पवनगतिमधो रोधयेत्[2] संप्रयत्ना-
दाकुञ्च्यापानमूलं हुतवहसदृशं तन्तुवत् सूक्ष्मरूपम्।
तद्भित्त्वा हृत्सरोजे तदनु चरणके[3] तालुके ब्रह्मरन्ध्रे
भित्त्वान्ते याति शून्यं प्रविशति गगने यत्र देवो महेशः॥ ७७॥

चित्तमन्तःकरणं नाभौ मणिपूरके चक्रे संयम्य स्थिरीकृत्य, अपानमूलं मूलविवरं संप्रयत्नादुत्तमप्रयत्नेन सङ्कोचयित्वा, अधो मूलविवरे पवनगतिमपानसञ्चारं रोधयेत् वारयेत्,[4] ऊर्ध्वमेवानीय मनःप्राणाभ्यामेकीकुर्यादित्यर्थः। हुतवहो वह्निः, तत्सदृशं स्फुरत्तेजोरूपमित्यर्थः। तन्तुवत् सूक्ष्मरूपं सूक्ष्मतन्तुसमानाकारं तत्र चिन्तयेदित्यर्थः। तदनु तदनन्तरं तत् नाभिचक्रं भित्त्वा भेदयित्वा हृत्सरोजे याति पुनश्चरणके विशुद्धचक्रे एवं तालु ब्रह्मरन्ध्रे क्रमेण यातीत्यर्थः। अन्ते शरीरत्यागसमये च भित्त्वा ब्रह्मरन्ध्रे भेदयित्वा यत्र महेशो देवः परमशिवस्तिष्ठति। तत्रैव शून्यं चिदाकाशं विशति तत्र लीयत इत्यर्थः॥ ७७॥

---

[1] अष्टगुणेन (A) गुणानां (D)

[2] धारयेत्

[3] दलनके (GP)

[4] धारयेत् ?

नाभौ शुभ्रारविन्दं तदुपरि विमलं मण्डलं चण्डरश्मेः
संसारस्यैकरूपां त्रिभुवनजननीं धर्मदात्रीं नराणाम्।
तस्मिन्मध्ये त्रिमार्गे त्रितयतनुधरां छिन्नमस्तां प्रशस्तां
तां वन्दे ज्ञानरूपां मरणभयहरां योगिनीं ज्ञानमुद्राम्॥ ७८॥

नाभौ मणिपूरके चक्रे शुभ्रारविन्दे श्वेतं कमलं विचिन्त्येत्यर्थः। तदुपरि तस्मिन् कमले चण्डरश्मेः सूर्यस्य विमलं मण्डलं सञ्चिन्त्य तस्मिन् मध्ये तस्मिन् मण्डलमध्ये त्रिमार्गे गुणत्रयोपाधिभेदेन त्रैविध्यापन्ने सुषुम्णाविवरे इत्यर्थः। त्रितयतनुधरां यतः ज्ञानरूपः, अतः प्रशस्तां योगिनीं योगमात्रगम्यां ज्ञानमुद्रां ज्ञानमात्रोपध्यवच्छिन्नां, अत एव मरणभयहरां तां छिन्नमस्तां वन्दे, अभिवादये इत्यर्थः। प्रक्षिप्तमपि पद्यद्वयमर्थप्राशस्त्याद्व्याख्यातम् ॥ ७८॥

एषु ब्रह्मात्मकं तेजः शिवज्योतिरनुत्तमम्।
ध्यात्वा ज्ञात्वा विमुक्तः स्यादिति गोरक्षभाषितम्॥ ७९॥

एषु नवस्थानेषु अनुत्तमं न उत्तमं यस्मात् तदनुत्तमं सर्वोत्कृष्टमित्यर्थः। शिवज्योतिः शिवात्मकं ज्योतिर्हृत्कमलाज्ञाचक्रयोरभिहितं[1] साकारमित्यर्थः तथा ब्रह्मात्मकं तेजो निराकारं निर्गुणं ब्रह्मेत्यर्थः। उक्तरीत्या ध्यात्वा तत्तद्विधस्य तत्तत्स्थानेषु स्थितं ज्ञात्वा च विमुक्तः संसारानुवृत्तिरहितं स्यादिति गोरक्षेण भाषितं प्रतिज्ञातमतो नात्र सन्देहः कार्य इति भावः॥ ७९॥

उपसंहरति—

अश्वमेधसहस्राणि वाजपेयशतानि च।
एकस्य ध्यानयोगस्य कलां नार्हन्ति षोडशीम्॥ ८०॥

अश्वमेधानां सहस्राणि तथा वाजपेयानां शतानि च, हिंसाप्रचुराणीत्यार्थः, एकस्य ध्यानयोगस्य षोडशीं कलां नार्हन्ति। एतत् षोडशांशतुल्यफलप्रदानसमर्थानि न भवन्तीत्यर्थः॥ ८०॥

[1] अधिष्ठितं?

अथ समाधिः

पञ्चदशभिः श्लोकैः समाधिं दर्शयन् चतुर्भिर्वस्तुस्थितिमभिधत्ते—

उपाधिश्च तथा तत्त्वं द्वयमेतदुदाहृतम्।
उपाधिः प्रोच्यते वर्णस्तत्त्वमात्माभिधीयते॥ ८१॥

उपाधिः उप समीपे आधीयते सर्वावयवेन धार्यते आत्मा अस्मिन्नित्युपाधिरात्म[1]प्रकाशस्थानं, तथा तत्त्वमात्मचैतन्यमेतद्द्वयमुदाहृतं कथितम्। तत्र उपाधिरकारादिरूपः प्रणवरूपो वा वर्णं प्रोच्यते, तत्त्वमात्माभिधीयते कथ्यते॥ ८१॥

तदेव स्पष्टयति—

उपाधेरन्यथा ज्ञानं तत्त्वसंस्थितिरन्यथा।
समस्तोपाधिविध्वंसी सदाभ्यासेन जायते॥ ८२॥

उपाधेर्हेतुभूतात् ज्ञानं यथार्थविषयकमपि अन्यथा वैपरीत्यबोधकं भवति यथा जपाकुसुमसन्निधाने रक्तस्फटिक इति। यथा वा चिदाभासात्माभ्युपगमे अहं सुखी अहं दुःखीति। तत्त्वसंस्थितिस्तत्त्वस्य संस्थानं अन्यथेव भवति। यथा रक्ततयाभासमानस्फटिकोऽपि तत्त्वतः शुक्ल एव, न रक्त इति। यथा वा सुखदुःखादीन्द्रियधर्मास्कन्दितोऽपि जीवो वस्तुतो ज्ञानानन्दरूपो न सुखदुःखसम्बन्धवानिति। एवमुक्तयोगानां सदाभ्यासेन कृत्वा योगी समस्तोपाधिविध्वंसी जायते॥ ८२॥

समाधिं लक्षयति—

शब्दादीनां च तन्मात्रं यावत् कर्णादिषु स्थितम्।
तावदेव स्मृतं ध्यानं समाधिः स्यादतः परम्॥ ८३॥

ध्यानस्थस्य योगिनः कर्णादीन्द्रियेषु शब्दादीनां विषयानां तन्मात्रं यावत्स्थितं उपलब्धं तावदेव ध्यानं स्मृतं,[1] लीनेन्द्रियस्यात्मनि अर्थमात्रावभासदशायां तु समाधिपदेन व्यवहारः स्यादित्यर्थः॥ ८३॥

---

[1] अस्मिन्निरुपाधिस्वात्म (A)

प्रसङ्गतो धारणादिप्रमाणं दर्शयति—

धारणा पञ्चनाडीभिः ध्यानं च षष्टिनाडिभिः।
दिनद्वादशकेन स्यात् समाधिः प्राणसंयमात्॥ ८४॥

निरुद्धप्राणव्यापारादिभिः पञ्चनाडीभिः धारणा भवति। एवंविधाभिः एव षष्टिनाडीभिः ध्यानं भवति। दिनद्वादशकेन अहोरात्रद्वादशकेन कालेन प्राणसंयमात् समाधिः स्यात्॥ ८४॥

समाधिस्वरूपमाह—

यत् सर्वद्वन्द्वयोरैक्यं जीवात्मपरमात्मनोः।
समस्तनष्टसङ्कल्पः समाधिः सोऽभिधीयते॥ ८५॥

यत् सर्वद्वन्द्वयोः सुखदुःखशीतोष्णादिरूपयोरैक्यं, तदुत्थजगतः[2] शून्यतया कारणमात्ररूपत्वं, तद्वदेव जीवात्मपरमात्मनोः यदैक्यं, स एव समस्तसङ्कल्परहितः समाधिरित्यभिधीयते॥ ८५॥

जीवात्मपरमात्मनोरैक्यं सदृष्टान्तं दर्शयति—

अम्बुसैन्धवयोरैक्यं यथा भवति योगतः।
तथात्ममनसोरैक्यं समाधिरभिधीयते॥ ८६॥

अम्बूनि जले सैन्धवस्य प्रक्षेपे कृते सति योगात् तत्संयोगतः अम्बुसैन्धवयोः यथा येन प्रकारेणैक्यं भवति, अभेदः संपद्यते, तथा तेन प्रकारेण अन्तर्मुखतयात्माकारवृत्तिके मनसि सति आत्ममनसोरैक्यं संपद्यते, स एव समाधिरित्यभिधीयते॥ ८६॥

निर्विकल्पसमाधिमाह—

यदा सङ्क्षीयते प्राणो मानसं च प्रलीयते।
यदा समरसत्वं च समाधिः सोऽभिधीयते॥ ८७॥

---

[1] शिव- (A)

[2] तदुत्पे जगता (A; D folio missing here.)

मनःप्राणावेकत्र सन्निरुध्यात्मानं भावयतो योगिनो यदा तु प्राणो वायुः सङ्क्षीयते विनापि जालन्धरादिना रेचकास्पन्दराहित्यमनुसन्धत्ते आत्मन्येवलीयत इत्यर्थः। च पुनः यदा मानसमन्तःकरणं प्रलीयते यत्किञ्चिद्वृत्तिं विना निराकारतामापद्यते। एतावत्सविकल्पेऽपि भवति। निर्विकल्पकसाधारणं विशेषमाह[1]—यदा च समरसत्वं जलसैन्धवयोरिव जीवात्मपरमात्मनोरभिन्नस्वरूपत्वं सम्पद्यते[2], स एव समाधिरित्यभिधीयते॥ ८७॥

तदानीन्तनां योगिनोऽवस्थां दर्शयति—

न गन्धं न रसं रूपं न च स्पर्शं न निःस्वनम्।
नात्मानं न परं वेत्ति योगी युक्तः समाधिना॥ ८८॥

समाधिना युक्त एकत्वापन्नो योगी सर्वेन्द्रियाणां मनसा सहैव लीनतया तत्तद्विषयगन्धरसादीन्न वेत्ति, तद्वदात्मानं ध्यातृत्वेन, परं परमात्मानं ध्येयत्वेन, चकारेण ध्यानमपि, न वेत्ति न जानाति विषयज्ञानस्येन्द्रियजन्यत्वादात्मनश्चाविषयत्वादिति भावः॥ ८८॥

अभेद्यः सर्वशस्त्राणामवध्यः सर्वदेहिनाम्।
अग्राह्यो मन्त्रतन्त्राणां योगी युक्तः समाधिना॥ ८९॥

युक्तसमाधिर्योगी सर्वशस्त्राणां अभेद्यो भेदनायाशक्यो भवति। तथा सर्वदेहिनां सिंहगजादीनामवध्यो वधायायोग्यो भवति। मन्त्रतन्त्राणामाभिचारविधिना प्रयुक्तानामग्राह्यो मरणमोहनरूपव्यापारसम्बन्धरहितो भवतीत्यर्थः॥ ८९॥

बाध्यते न स कालेन लिप्यते न स कर्मणा।
साध्यते न च केनापि योगी युक्तः समाधिना॥ ९०॥

स समाधिना युक्तो योगी कालेन जरामरणादिरूपावस्थाजनकेन न बाध्यते। तथा कर्मणा सदसत्फलहेतुना न लिप्यते। जरामरणयोः सदसत्कर्मफलयोश्चाश्रयो न भवतीत्यर्थः। अत एव च केनापि ब्रह्मणापि न साध्यते। विषयवासनासंसिद्धो न क्रियत इत्यर्थः॥ ९०॥

---

[1] एतावत् ... आह not in D.

[2] Not in A.

एवंविधो योगः कथं प्राप्यते ? तत्राह—[1]

युक्ताहारविहारस्य युक्तचेष्टस्य कर्मसु।
युक्तस्वप्नावबोधस्य योगो भवति दुःखहा॥ ९१॥

युक्ताहारेति युक्तौ आहारविहारौ यस्य सः। तथा तत्र युक्ताहारत्वं पूर्वोक्तमितभोजनादिकं, युक्तविहारत्वं लौकिकव्यापारमाद्यं (?), कर्मसु नित्यनैमित्तिकेषु युक्तचेष्टस्य अत्यासक्तिरहितस्य युक्तस्वप्नावबोधस्य परिमितं सुप्तस्य[2] परिमितमवबुद्धस्य योगिनः दुःखहा जननमरणादिश्रम[3]नाशको योगो भवति॥ ९१॥

कोऽसौ योगः ? तत्राह द्वाभ्यां—[4]

निराद्यन्तं निरालम्बं निष्प्रपञ्चं निराश्रयम्।
निरामयं निराकारं तत्त्वं तत्त्वविदो विदुः॥ ९२॥

निराद्यन्तमाद्यन्तवर्जितं, निरालम्बमवलम्बनशून्यं, निराश्रयमाश्रयरहितं प्रपञ्चवन्मायानधिष्ठित-मित्यर्थः। निष्प्रपञ्चं द्वैतकल्पनादिप्रपञ्चशून्यम्। निरामयमामयः पतनमरणादिजन्यदुःखं तद्रहितं निराकारं आकारः करचरणादिपरिणामविशेषस्तद्रहितं तत्त्वमेव जीवात्मनोरेकतापन्नं योगपद-वाच्यमात्मस्वरूपं तत्त्वविदो[5] योगिनो विदुः जानन्ति॥ ९२॥

किं च—

निर्मलं निश्चलं नित्यं निष्क्रियं निर्गुणं महत्।
व्योमविज्ञानमानन्दं ब्रह्म ब्रह्मविदो विदुः॥ ९३॥

निर्मलं कर्मफलवासनारूपमलरहितं, निश्चलं संयोगवियोगानुकूलचेष्टारहितं, निष्क्रियं व्यापारसामान्यशून्यं, निर्गुणं सत्त्वरजस्तमोगुणसम्बन्धरहितं, महद्देशकालादिकृतपरिच्छेदशून्यं,

---

[1] एवंविधो योगः कथञ्चित् प्राप्नोति आहारविहारसानुकूलश्चेत् फलतीत्याह (D)

[2] परिमितं सुप्तस्य Not in A.

[3] -भ्रम- (D)

[4] कोऽसौ योगीति दर्शयन्स्वरूपमाह (D)

[5] For आत्मस्वरूपं तत्त्वविदो, D. has आत्मतत्त्वविदो.

व्योम चिदाकाशरूपं विज्ञानं बोधः तत्स्वरूपमेतादृशमद्वैतानन्दरूपं ब्रह्म ब्रह्मविदो योगिनो विदुर्जानन्ति॥ ९३॥

केन किमिव वा ज्ञायते ? तत्राह—

निरातङ्के निरालम्बे निराधारे निरामये।
योगी योगविधानेन परे ब्रह्मणि लीयते॥ ९४॥

योगी षडङ्गयोगस्य विधानेन यथाविध्यभ्यासेन आतङ्कालम्बाधारामयै रहिते परे ब्रह्मणि लीयते ताद्रूप्यं प्राप्नोति॥ ९४॥

हेतुदृष्टान्तनिर्मुक्तमनोबुद्ध्योरगोचरम्।
व्योमविज्ञानमानन्दतत्त्वं तत्त्वविदो विदुः॥ ९५॥

साक्षात्कारहेतुना दृष्टान्तेन च निर्मुक्तं रहितं बुद्ध्योरगोचरं अविषयं व्योमविज्ञानमानन्दतत्त्वं तत्त्वविदो विदुः॥ ९५॥

लीयत इत्युक्तं। तत्र जले पाषाण इव विरूपस्तिरोहितो भवति किं ? नेत्याह—

यथा घृतं घृते क्षिप्तं घृतमेव हि जायते।
क्षीरे क्षीरं तथा योगी तत्त्वमेव हि जायते॥ ९६॥

यथा घृतं घृते क्षिप्तं घृतमेव नान्यथा,[1] एवं क्षीरे क्षिप्तं क्षीरं,[2] तथा तत्त्वरूपे ब्रह्मणि लीनो योगी तत्त्वमेव जायते, जीवब्रह्मणोरुभयोरपि उपाधिकृतभेदे सत्यपि उपाधिविलये[3] चिद्रूपत्वाविशेषात्॥ ९६॥

---

[1] जायते नान्यत् (C,D)

[2] क्षीरमेव (C); क्षीरमेव जायते (D)

[3] उपाधि... विलये not in A,C.

जीवब्रह्मणोर्नाममात्रकृतो भेद इति सूचयितुमेकस्यैव वस्तुनो नामभेदेन दृष्टान्तं दर्शयति—[1]

दुग्धे क्षीरं घृते सर्पिरग्नौ वह्निरिवार्पितः।
तन्मयत्वं व्रजत्येव योगी लीनः परे पदे॥९७॥

अग्नौ वह्नौ अर्पितो वह्निरिव यथा दीपद्वयसंयोगिज्योतिरेकाकारं संपद्यते तद्वदित्यर्थः। शेषं स्पष्टम्[2]॥९७॥

गोरक्षशतकाभ्यासफलम्

इदानीं श्रोतॄन् अभिमुखीकुर्वन् फलप्रदर्शनेन उपसंहरति—[3]

भवभयहरं नृणां मुक्तिसोपानसंज्ञकम्।
गुह्याद्गुह्यतरं गुह्यं गोरक्षेण प्रकाशितम्॥९८॥

नृणां जनानां भवभयहरं[4] भवो जननमरणादिरूपः संसारः, तज्जन्यभयहरं मुक्तिसोपानसंज्ञकम्, एतत्संज्ञार्हं तत्क्रियाकारितादित्यर्थः। अत एव गुह्याद्गुह्यतरं त्रिवर्गप्रदेभ्यः सर्वगुह्येभ्योऽपि गुह्यतरम्। गोरक्षेण गां वाणीं रक्षतीति गोरक्षो मितभाषीत्यर्थः। तेनापि गुह्यं यथा भवति तथा प्रकाशितं योगविद्भ्य एव कथितमित्युत्तरान्वयिपद्यम्[5]॥९८॥

इति गोरक्षशतकं योगशास्त्रं जनः पठेत्।
सर्वपापविनिर्मुक्तो योगसिद्धिं लभेद्ध्रुवम्॥९९॥

इति पूर्वोक्तप्रकारं[6] गोरक्षशतकं नाम योगशास्त्रं यो जनः पठेत्। सर्वपापैर्विनिर्मुक्तः सन् ध्रुवं निश्चयेन योगसिद्धिं लभेत्॥९९॥

---

[1] Not in A,C.

[2] D. only.

[3] This portion not in A,C.

[4] From here to कथितं, A,C read: संसारे जननमरणजन्यभीतिहरं मुक्तौ सोपानमिव शीघ्र-प्रापकमित्यर्थः। सकलगुह्येभ्योऽतिगुह्यमित्यर्थः गोरक्षेण योगिना प्रकाशितं...

[5] कथितमित्युत्तरात्॥ (D)

[6] पूर्वोक्तं (A)

अन्यशास्त्राणां स्वल्पफलप्रदत्वात् तानि विहायैतदेवाभ्यसेदित्याह—[1]

योगशास्त्रं पठेन्नित्यं किमन्यैः शास्त्रविस्तरैः।
यत् स्वयं चादिनाथस्य निर्गतं वदनाम्बुजात्॥ १००॥

योगी इदं[2] योगशास्त्रं नित्यं पठेत्। अन्यैः शास्त्रविस्तरैः किं फलं स्यात् ? [3]ननु अस्मिन्शास्त्रे यथोक्तं फलमस्तीत्यत्र किं प्रमाणम् तत्राह—यत आदिनाथस्य वदनाम्बुजान्निर्गतम्। अत्राम्बुज-पदेनानुभवः सूच्यते। हृदयाम्बुजेऽनुभूतं वदनाम्बुजान्निर्गतमिति प्रामाणिकमेवेत्यर्थः॥ १००॥

साक्षान्मोक्षप्रतिपादके अस्मिन् शतके सर्वमधिकृतं स्यादित्यत आह—[4]

स्नातं तेन समस्ततीर्थसलिले दत्ता द्विजेभ्यो धरा
यज्ञानां च हुतं सहस्रमयुतं देवाश्च संपूजिताः।
सत्यं तेन सुतर्पिताश्च पितरो स्वर्गं च नीताः पुन-
र्यस्य ब्रह्मविचारणे क्षणमपि प्राप्नोति धैर्यं मनः॥ १०१॥

तेन पुरुषेण गङ्गादीनां सलिले जले स्नातं च पुनः द्विजेभ्यो ब्राह्मणेभ्यो धरा पृथ्वी दत्ता यज्ञानां सहस्रमयुतं च हुतं देवाश्च ब्राह्मणादयः सर्वे पूजिताः। सर्वे पितरः तेन सन्तर्पिताः स्वर्गं च नीताः प्रापिताः सत्यमेतत् तेन। केन यस्य मनः ब्रह्मविचारणे स्वस्वरूपचिन्तने क्षणमपि धैर्यं अचाञ्चल्यं प्राप्नोति अवलम्बते तेनेति ॥[5]एतत् गङ्गादितीर्थस्नानादिकं यावत् फलं ददाति तावत् तावत् फलं क्षणमात्रेणापि आत्मचिन्तनरूपो योगो ददातीत्यर्थः। आत्मस्वरूपनिर्णयस्तु तत्त्वसङ्ग्रहेण यो निर्णीतस् तत एव ज्ञातव्यः॥ १०१॥

॥ अथानुक्रमणम्॥

श्लोकैः पञ्चभिराख्यातमनुबन्धचतुष्टयम्। योगस्यैकेन तु फलं षडङ्गान्यपरेण तु॥ १॥

[1] Not in A.

[2] योगी इदं Not in A.

[3] From here to end of comment, यस्मादिदं योगशास्त्रं आदिनाथस्य मुखाम्बुजात् विनिःसृतं निर्मितमित्यर्थः (A)

[4] साक्षान्मोक्षप्रतिपादकं योगशास्त्रमधीत्य सर्वं कृतमित्याह (D)

[5] From here to end only in D.

आसनं पञ्चभिः श्लोकैः षट्चक्रं सप्तपञ्चभिः। दश नाड्यस्तथा तासां स्थानान्यपि तथाष्टभिः॥२॥
चतुर्दशभिराख्याताः सव्यापाराश्च वायवः। आख्यातं दशभिः श्लोकैः शक्तिचालनमुत्तमम्॥३॥
षड्विंशतिभिराख्यातं महामुद्रादिपञ्चकम्। सप्तभिः प्रणवाभ्यासः प्राणायामप्रशंसनम्॥४॥
चतुर्भिः प्राणसंरोधो नाडीशुद्धौ तथाष्टभिः। एकविंशतिभिः श्लोकैः प्राणायामो निरूपितः॥५॥
प्रत्याहारश्च त्रिंशद्भिः धारणा नवभिस्तथा। चतुर्विंशतिभिर्ध्यानं समाधिश्चाष्टपञ्चभिः॥६॥
गोरक्षशतकाभ्यासफलं श्लोकचतुष्टये। एवं क्रमानुसारेण व्याख्यातं शतकं मया॥७॥
यदत्र चापलं मेऽस्ति क्षन्तव्यं तच्च साधुभिः। योगीश्वरमहावाक्ये कथं न क्षुभ्यतां मनः॥८॥
खलाय भक्तिशून्याय शिश्नोदरपराय च। इदं रहस्यं परमं न दातव्यमिति ध्रुवम्॥९॥

॥ इति गोरक्षशतकं॥

॥ समाप्तम्॥[1]

[1] Our B manuscript has the scribe's signature and date: नारायणस्वामिशास्त्री २४.१.१९३०.

Gorakṣa-śataka with Yoga-taraṅgiṇī commentary

Granthārambhaḥ

śrī-śambhuṁ śrī-guruṁ sūryaṁ herambaṁ jagad-īśvarīm |
praṇamya śataka-vyākhyāṁ kurmo yoga-taraṅgiṇīm ||

After bowing to Śambhu Śiva, to Śrī Guru, to the Sun god, to Gaṇeśa, and to the Mother Goddess, I commence this commentary on the Century of Gorakṣa named *Yoga-taraṅgiṇī*.

As he begins his discourse on yoga, the illustrious Gorakṣa first composes an auspicious invocatory verse in praise of his guru for the purpose of teaching his disciples [the proper etiquette]. [At the same time] through the meaning of the words, he indicates both the subject and purpose of his treatise.

śrī-guruṁ paramānandaṁ vande svānanda-vigraham |
yasya sānnidhya-mātreṇa cidānandāyate tanuḥ ||1||

1.1. I bow down to the splendorous Guru who is [both] the supreme bliss and the embodiment of his own bliss. Simply by proximity to him, one's body takes on the quality of such spiritual bliss.

I, namely Gorakṣa, bow down to the Guru, who is here named "Śrī" Guru. The implication of the word *śrī* ("splendorous") is that the guru possesses the ability to instill knowledge of the self in those who make inquiries from him. To him I offer my salutations.

Who then is this Guru to whom the offering of salutations bestows auspiciousness? In response to this expected question, Gorakṣa describes the Guru's nature. He is "supreme bliss" (*paramānandaṁ*), meaning that he is both the Supreme and blissful; he is the Supreme Soul himself, in the form of unexcelled joy. By this statement, the author shows that the Guru is the direct manifestation of Brahman.

Now since it is improper to speak of Brahman having any connection to either body or senses, whereas the Guru does indeed have such a relation, there is surely a distinct difference between the two. So how can one try to establish that they are the same?

In response, the author asks, "Again, what is the nature of the Guru?" And answers: "He is the embodiment of his own bliss" (*svānanda-vigrahaṁ*). Here *sva* ("his own") should be taken to mean those who are closely related to him [such as his disciples]. He is their bliss, and his [taking a] body or form is entirely for their bliss; this means he is the inward soul or *pratyag-ātmā*.

By this it is being shown that the Brahma-being of Śrī Guru is indisputable, as he has accepted a body out of kindness for the devotee. Thus since any difference [between him and Brahman] is only imagined, his appearance as an individual soul or *pratyag-ātmā* is secondary or dependent on it.

In the second half of the verse, [the author] reveals the benefits of such salutations to the guru, "Simply by proximity to him." The disciple [is here understood to be the subject], while body (*tanuḥ*), which is without consciousness (*jaḍa*), is the object. Simply by proximity to the guru, the disciple effectively makes his body take on the quality of spiritual bliss, making it become as though made of the bliss of pure consciousness. [Since mere proximity has this result] then would not [such a disciple] imbue his very self with spiritual bliss by worshiping the guru for an extended period of time? Of course he most certainly would.

Since here both the adjectives used to describe the guru, namely *svānanda-vigrahaṁ* (supreme bliss) and *paramānandam* (embodiment of his own bliss) are read together [in apposition], the indication is that the subject of this book is the oneness of the individual soul with Brahman, and by the words *cidānandāyate tanuḥ* ("one's body takes on the quality of spiritual bliss"), it is shown that its ultimate purpose is the attainment of unexcelled joy.[1]

Now, in order to make the above indicated subject and purpose of this work as clear as though directly perceived, [the author] bows down to Mīnanātha, who attained the ultimate goal through the exercise of the different limbs of yoga and thereby demonstrates the facility of attaining that goal:

antar-niścalitātma-dīpa-kalikāsv ādhāra-bandhādibhiḥ
yo yogī yuga-kalpa-kāla-kalanā-tattvaṁ ca jegīyate |
jñānāmoda-mahodadhiḥ samabhavad yatrādināthaḥ svayaṁ
vyaktāvyakta-guṇādhikaṁ tam aniśaṁ śrī-mīna-nāthaṁ bhaje ||

1.2. I constantly offer homage to Śrī Mīnanātha, who is greater than the attributes of manifest and unmanifest, the yogi who in the buds of the flame of the Self made still within through the practices [of *haṭha-yoga*] like *ādhāra-bandha*, heartily sings the truth that is the impeller of time in its various forms as *yuga* and *kalpa*, wherein the original master of yoga, Ādinātha,[2] the

---

[1]Normally a commentary will elucidate from the opening verses the *anubandha-catuṣṭaya*, the four "binding reasons" for a text. They are its *viṣaya* or subject matter, the *prayojana*, i.e., goal or purpose of the work, *adhikārī* (the qualified reader or intended audience of the work) and *sambandha*, the interconnections of the three.

[2]Ādinātha is almost universally identified with Lord Śiva in the Nāthayoga texts. But since the commentary has not specifically made that connection, we have refrained from making it directly in the translation.

great ocean of the pleasure of wisdom, is himself revealed.

I worship him, the celebrated Mīnanātha; I take shelter of him in body, mind and words. Who is he? He is the one who through the practices of the *ādhāra-bandha* (i.e. *mūla-bandha*) and other locks like the *uḍḍiyāna*-and *jālandhara-bandhas* that are to be described subsequently [here in this book],

- "within"(*antaḥ*), in the lotus of the heart and elsewhere;[1]
- "in the buds of the flame of the Self made still" (*niścalitātma-dīpa-kalikāsu*); the buds (*kalikā*) are the rays which are like flowerbuds, i.e., they are shaped like flowerbuds. Here the Self verily *is* the flame because it has the nature of illumination. "Made still" (*niścalita*) means established therein in such a way that [this flame] is motionless.
- "heartily sings" (*jegīyate*): [since this is the intensive form of the verb √*gai* meaning to sing[2]] he sings in abundance; in other words, he knows [this subject] to its very limit,
- "the truth that is the impeller of time in its various forms as *yuga* and *kalpa*" (*yuga-kalpa-kāla-kalanā-tattvaṁ*): *Yugas* and *kalpas* taken together are verily identified with time. The impeller of this time in the form of *yugas* and in the form of *kalpas*, is its essence; thus, [what he sings is] the truth that is the soul of time.

Again, [I offer homage to Mīnanātha], the yogī wherein (*yatra*), i.e., in the aforementioned buds of the flame of the Self made still, appeared none other than [Ādinātha, the person qualified as] "the

---

[1]A reference to the various centers or *cakras* that are focal points for meditation as will be described further on.

[2]Defined in *Sarva-darśana-saṅgraha* (3.224 etc.) as "asserted obstinately." See Monier Williams, *sui verbis*.

great ocean of the pleasure of wisdom" (*jñānāmoda-mahodadhiḥ*), the ocean of the bliss of knowledge, by which we can infer that he knows the full extent of essential knowledge related to the Self (*ātmā*) and for that reason is verily [worthy of the title] "the original master of yoga" (*ādi-nātha*).

What more can be said about Mīnanātha? Because of all the above, he is "more than the attributes of manifest and unmanifest" (*vyaktāvyakta-guṇādhikaṁ*): "manifest" here refers to the gross elements like earth, etc., and "unmanifest" to the subtle elements like intelligence and ego; or alternatively, the manifest can refer to the gross body produced from the creation of the five elements after their division and expansion, and the unmanifest to the subtle body produced when the same elements are undivided.[1] The attributes (*guṇa*) refered to here are their natural tendencies to destruction and transformation. [Mīnanātha] is more than them, i.e., he is not overcome by them. I bow down to one such as this.

Having stated the subject and purpose of the text, the author now reveals his own name as well as the qualified student (*adhikārī*) and the interrelations (*sambandha*) [of subject, purpose and student][2]—

[1]According to the Yoga-sāṅkhya philosophy, the phenomenal universe devolves from an unmanifest state of primordial nature, whereby the five primary elements—ether, air, fire, water and earth—are first manifested in an inchoate form. When these elements are mixed, they take the various individual and changing forms visible in the world. The terms *pañcī-bhūta* or *pañcīkṛta* refer to this mixing or combining of the elements, their manifest state, while the opposite, *apañcī-kṛta* or *apañcī-bhūta* refers to elements in their unmixed or simple state. The description of the subtle body as being *apañcībhūta* is found summarized in Śaṅkarācārya's *Ātma-bodha* (12): *pañca-prāṇa-mano-buddhi-daśendriya-samanvitam | apañcīkṛta-bhūtotthaṁ sūkṣmāṅgaṁ bhoga-sādhanam ||* "The subtle body, the instrument of the soul's experience, consists of the five *prāṇas*, the ten organs, *manas* and *buddhi*, all formed from the rudimentary elements before their subdivision and combination with one another." Trans. Swami Nikhilananda. Madras: Sri Ramakrishna Matha, 1947. p. 139.

[2]These are again the other two of the four *anubandha-catuṣṭaya* mentioned earlier.

namaskṛtya guruṁ bhaktyā gorakṣo jñānam uttamam |
abhīṣṭaṁ yogino brūte paramānanda-kārakam ||3||

1.3. After bowing to Śrī Guru with devotion, Gorakṣa speaks the most elevated wisdom sought after by the yogīs, that which produces the ultimate bliss.

The very same Gorakṣa[1], after having bowed with devotion, i.e., repeatedly, to the Śrī Guru possessing the characteristics described above, speaks or expounds the wisdom (*jñānam*), i.e., the teaching of the means to attaining such wisdom as is most elevated or superior to all others because it "produces the ultimate bliss" (*paramānanda-kārakaṁ*), namely awakens an awareness of the non-dual reality. For this reason, it is "sought after by the yogīs" (*abhīṣṭaṁ yogināṁ*) or approved by those whose instincts for yoga are carried over from previous lifetimes. The idea is that the practices leading to wisdom are extremely beneficial for their attainment, and that therefore the word "wisdom" (*jñāna*) can [legitimately] be used to refer to both the end and the means.

By refering to this wisdom as the producer of ultimate bliss, the author indicates that the person who has completed the purifications of the inner instrument (*antaḥ-karaṇa*, i.e., body, mind, intellect and *citta*) [as far as is] attainable through works (*karma*) and worship (*upāsanā*) is the proper candidate (*adhikārī*) for receiving it. He also implies the interrelation of these three, characterized as the signified, signifier and actual state of being (*bhāva*).[2] With the word *gorakṣa* [the author] states his own name.

[1]The commentator accepts uncritically that the author is using his own name in the third person. Modern scholars, of course, hold that the author was someone other than Gorakṣa and was collating the fundamental teachings attributed to Gorakṣa some time after his disappearance.

[2]*Vācya, vācaka, bhāva.* This is sometimes given as *sādhya-sādhana-bhāvaḥ*. One is the object (*prayojana*) which is to be obtained, the next is the means (*vācaka*) and the third the actual status, i.e., of the practitioner, *sādhaka* or *adhikārī*.

It was stated that this is "the wisdom desired by yogis." What is that [wisdom]? In order to further elaborate on this, [the author] writes the name of the treatise that he is about to commence —

gorakṣa-śatakaṁ[1] *vakti yogināṁ hita-kāmyayā |*
dhruvaṁ yasyāvabodhena jāyate paramaṁ padam ||4||

1.4. Out of a wish to benefit the yogis, [he] recites the *Gorakṣa-śataka*, from the clear understanding of which, [attainment of] the highest station surely comes about.

The selfsame Gorakṣa, "out of a wish to benefit" (*hita-kāmyayā*), that is, out of compassion, for "the yogis," the characteristics of whom have already been described, speaks or recites the treatise named *Gorakṣa-śataka.*

What is the nature of this century of verses? It is the one hundred verses[2] "by the clear understanding of which," that is, by the proper knowledge [of which] gained through the instruction of the spiritual master, "the highest attainment," the permanent state, i.e., the state of living liberation (*jīvan-mukti*), for the Śruti says, "Only one who is already liberated is set free,"[3] "surely" (*dhruvaṁ*), with certainty, "comes about" ["is born"] (*jāyate*) or becomes manifest.[4]

Alternatively, the word *dhruvam* [can here be taken as an adjective modifying "the highest attainment" instead of as an

---

[1]The Mumbai edition of *Gorakṣa-paddhati*, which is the published work (with Hindi translation) that most closely matches this one, here reads *saṁhitāṁ*.

[2]The commentator does not seem disturbed by the fact that there are more than 200 verses in the extant text for which he is writing a commentary.

[3]I have not found the source of this quotation, *mukta eva hi mucyate*. The meaning taken by the commentator here is that liberation after death does not take place without first achieving a state of living liberation. The alternative meaning is that the soul is never in truth bound, so his liberation is merely a question of recognizing what already is his true state.

[4]That is to say, it is not something that arises anew, but is the natural state that is being revealed.

adverb, in which case it] meansa state [of certainty] wherein being born again in this world does not occur.

Having stated that attainment of the supreme bliss comes about through following the discipline prescribed in this *Śataka*, he now states the necessity of attending to it.

[1]*etad vimukti-sopānam etat kālasya vañcanam |*
yad vyāvṛttaṁ mano bhogād[2] *āsaktaṁ paramātmani ||5||*

1.5. This is the stairway to liberation and to deceiving Time, the way by which the mind is turned away from sense pleasure (*bhoga*) and becomes attached to the Supreme Self (*paramātmā*).

This *Śataka*, i.e., by through executing the actions prescribed in it, is "the cheating" (*vañcanaṁ*)" of Time" (*kālasya*), i.e., it causes the cessation of any relationship to any possibility arising from matters related to the departure of the life airs [i.e., death][3]; and by means of the sustained and lengthy practice of yoga, it is the "stairway to liberation" (*vimukti-sopānaṁ*). Here the sense of the prefix *vi-* is that it is a special kind of liberation, namely *kaivalya*. This book is thus a staircase to such liberation, which means that by following the progressive sequence of various stages beginning with the intelligent examination [of the *Gorakṣa-śataka*'s contents], this liberation is quickly attained, in the same way that a staircase is the

[1]This is the first verse of *Viveka-mārtaṇḍa.*
[2] *mohāt* (B, L v.2)
[3]Lonavla (p.48): "The aim of the Yogi is to transcend Time. [citing Brahmānanda to HYP 4.17] *Prāṇa* moves through the *piṅgalā* for about an hour and then through the *iḍā* for an equal period. So these two hours form day and night from the *yaugika* point of view. Our ordinary day thus consists of twelve such days and nights. Now when *prāṇa* leaves *iḍā* and *piṅgalā* and remains only in *suṣumṇā*, then there is no Time. So *suṣumṇā* is said to swallow Time. The yogi, knowing beforehand the time of his death, takes his *prāṇa* to the *brahma-randhra* and defies Time, i.e., death."

easiest means to get to the roof of a house. As such, one should definitely undertake its study.

One may then ask, why does not everyone study it then? In answer, [Gorakṣa] says, "If," taking the indeclinable *yat* in that sense.[1] "If the mind is turned away from sense pleasure" (*yad vyāvṛttaṁ mano bhogāt*), i.e., if one's mind has ceased relishing the sense objects by becoming inward looking, and then becomes "attached to the Supreme Soul" (*āsaktaṁ paramātmani*), then only will a person study it, not otherwise.

By this it is shown that these benefits only accrue to those who have attained virtues such as devotion and dispassion through accomplishment in the culture of practices such as sense and mind control and not to those who are attached to sensuality.

The question then arises, "Why has [the author] praised yoga when there are so many performances that lead to liberation advised in the Vedas, such as charity, solemn vows such as fasting, performance of sacrifices and so on?" Expecting such a question, [Gorakṣa] answers by saying that this is not an ordinary cause or means like charity [i.e., such as those prescribed by common morality or religious injunction], etc., but is quite different and rare. To this end he recites the next verse:

dvija-sevita-śākhasya śruti-kalpa-taroḥ phalam |
śamanaṁ bhava-tāpasya yogaṁ bhajata sattamāḥ ||6||

1.6. O most honest of men! Resort to yoga, the fruit of the wish-fulfilling tree of the Śruti, whose branches are

[1]*Yat* has a multitude of possible meanings. This interpretation is somewhat unusual, as *yasmāt* ("because, since" is a more common adverbial meaning that would convey pretty much the same sense. It seems the commentator is limiting the effectiveness of the process to those who are free from desire, rather than crediting the process for freeing one from desire, which would seem to be the original intent of the author. The next sentence shows however, that he takes both meanings: "If through the process of *haṭha-yoga* taught in this book one becomes purified, then for such a person it is the stairway to liberation."

frequented by the twice-born, and the pacifier of worldy sufferings.

O most honest of men (*sattamāḥ*)! "Resort to yoga" (*yogaṁ bhajata*), which is "the pacifier" (*śamanaṁ*) or destroyer "of worldly sufferings" (*bhava-tāpasya*), the toil and travail that comes with the turning of the wheel of *saṁsāra*.

Should someone say, "But I am quite fulfilled in this way through following the rules of the Śrutis and Smṛtis, and this leaves me no further time, so how will I resort to yoga?" The first half of the verse is the answer to this: How can this yoga be described?

It is "the fruit of the wish-fulfilling tree of the Śruti" (*śruti-kalpa-taroḥ phalam*); Śruti means the Vedas, which are verily a wish-fulfilling tree because they bestow all manner of benefits, "whose branches are frequented by the twice-born" (*dvija-sevita-śākhasya*),[1] namely its different divisions are practiced or revered by the brāhmaṇas. The idea is that since this treatise on yoga is the fruit of the entire tree of the Veda, it is difficult [to follow] for those who only adhere to one or the other division of the Veda.

Now in order to enter into the actual substance of this topic for study, [Gorakṣa] lists the different limbs [of yoga that will be described therein]:

> *āsanaṁ prāṇa-saṁrodhaḥ pratyāhāraś ca dhāraṇā* |
> *dhyānaṁ samādhir etāni yogāṅgāni vadanti ṣaṭ* ||7||

1.7. They say there are six limbs of yoga: these are posture (*āsana*), breath restraint (*prāṇa-saṁrodha*),

[1]The commentator does not trouble himself to explain the rather common pun on the word *dvija* ("twice-born"), which can means either a Brāhmaṇa or a bird, along with a number of other meanings. A bird is twice born because it is born once with the laying of the egg, a second time when the egg hatches. Technically, a *dvija* refers to any of the three upper castes, but most commonly just for Brāhmaṇas.

withdrawal of the senses (*pratyāhāra*), concentration (*dhāraṇā*), meditation (*dhyāna*) and full absorption (*samādhi*).

Postures are those methods by which one sits, such as the *padmāsana*. When such postures are stable, comfortable and not a cause of agitation,[1] then they are qualified as a limb of yoga. Divisions and characteristics of sitting postures will be given further on.

Breath restraint (*prāṇa-saṁrodha*) is the control of the breath, the air that enters the abdomen, breaking the normal rhythms of inhalation and exhalation.[2] This is also known as *prāṇāyāma*.

Withdrawal of the senses (*pratyāhāra*). The prefix *prati*-refers to the externally facing senses that go out towards their different objects; the [next] prefix, *ā*-, means completely, and the verb root √*hṛ* means to gather. Taken together, the word *pratyāhāra* means to establish the senses in one's own essential being through the process of turning inward. When that is done, then all the senses follow or imitate the essential spiritual nature.[3]

Concentration (*dhāraṇā*) means to hold the attention on the psychic centers (*cakra*) such as the navel center through the process of giving up all other mental fluctuations and remaining single-pointed. By this one comes to the practice of "cognitive absorption" (*saṁprajñāta-samādhi*).[4]

Meditation (*dhyāna*) refers to the maintenance of a continuous flow of the same image focused in [any of] the nine centers, which are to be described further on, through giving up all dissimilar images or impressions.[5]

---

[1]Paraphrasing *Yoga-sūtra* 2.46.
[2]The commentator is here paraphrasing *Yoga-sūtra* 2.49.
[3]Cf. *Yoga-sūtra* 2.54.
[4]*Yoga-sūtra* 3.1. Here our commentary is much more specific than YS with the mention of the *cakras*. See infra 2.
[5]Here too, the commentary is more specific than YS 3.2, giving a distinctly *haṭha-yoga* tenor to the concept.

Full absorption (*samādhi*) is derived from *sam*, "completely, thoroughly" and the verb *ā√dhā*, to place or establish. When the mind is completely focused and all distractions are discarded, that is called *samādhi*.

The meaning is this: *Samādhi* is that very same meditation (*dhyāna*) when it illuminates the object alone and seems to attain a state of emptiness due to the disappearance of all one's knowledge and the natural essence of all the sense functions.[1]

These then are said to be the six limbs of yoga. One should not object that only six limbs are here listed, whereas Patañjali names eight such limbs in his *Yoga-sūtra* (2.29), namely the codes of regulation (*yamas*), restraints and disciplines (*niyamas*), sitting postures (*āsana*), breath control (*prāṇāyāma*), withdrawal of the senses (*pratyāhāra*), concentration (*dhāraṇā*), meditation (*dhyāna*) and full absorption (*samādhi*).

Only *haṭha-yoga* practices are under consideration in this book. It is agreed by all authorities that any practice that afflicts the body such as taking early morning bath and fasting,is prohibited, and that the *yamas* such as non-violence, truthfulness, non-theft, and the *niyamas* such as austerity, contentment and religious faith are [to have been] assimilated from previous [preparatory] practices by [the yogi] who is now turning away from worldly involvements. For such persons, whenever any other practice is to be undertaken, it should of necessity be comprehended through direct instruction from the spiritual master. Otherwise it should be understood that the *yamas* and *niyamas* are not of relevance to this treatise.

Those *yamas* and *niyamas* are given as follows:

ahiṁsā satyam asteyaṁ brahmacaryaṁ dayārjavam |
kṣamā dhṛtir mitāhāraḥ śaucaṁ ceti yamā daśa ||

---

[1]*Yoga-sūtra* 3.3: .*tad eva dhyānaṁ yathā artha-mātrasyāvabhāsamānaṁ tirohita-jñānādy-akhilendriya-vṛtti-svarūpatayā bahiḥ-śūnyatām iva sampadyate.*

The ten *yamas* are non-violence, truthfulness, non-acquisitiveness, celibacy, mercy, simplicity, forgiveness, patience, controlled eating, and cleanliness. (*Yogi-yājñavalkya*, 1.49)

tapaḥ santoṣa āstikyaṁ dānam īśvara-pūjanam |
siddhānta-śravaṇaṁ caiva hrīr matiś ca japo vratam |
daśaite niyamāḥ proktāḥ...

The ten *niyamas* are austerity, contentment, religious belief, charity, worship of God, hearing the philosophical conclusions, modesty, faith, chanting of mantras and following vows. (*Yogi-yājñavalkya*, 2.1-2)

Yājñavalkya further summarizes the subdivisions of the other six limbs of yoga as follows:

yamaś ca niyamaś caiva daśadhā saṁprakīrtitaḥ |
āsanāny uttamāny aṣṭau trīṇi teṣūttamāni tu ||
prāṇāyāmas tridhā proktaḥ pratyāhāraś ca pañcadhā ||
dhāraṇaṁ pañcadhā prokto dhyānaṁ ṣoḍaśa kīrtitam |
trīṇi teṣūttamāny āhuḥ samādhis tv eka-rūpataḥ ||

The *yamas* and *niyamas* are both said to be tenfold. The most important *āsanas* are eight in number and of those three are the best. *Prāṇāyāma* has three divisions, *pratyāhāra* has five. *Dhāraṇā* is also fivefold, while *dhyāna* has sixteen divisions. Of those, three are the best. *Samādhi* takes only one form. (YY 1.46-48)

Āsana

Next, Gorakṣa speaks of the divisions of *āsana*.

āsanāni ca tāvanti yāvanto jīva-jantavaḥ|
eteṣām akhilān bhedān vijānāti maheśvaraḥ ||8||

1.8 [There are] as many postures as [there are species of] living being. Maheśvara alone knows all their divisions.

"As many as there are living beings." "Living being" refers to the various bodily identifications (*upādhi*) possible for a living entity or *jīva* to acquire. That is how many sitting postures there are. The verb "to be" is understood. This is because each species appropriately has different ways of sitting. Only Maheśvara and no one else knows all these divisions of *āsana* completely. The word *jantu* ("creature"), joined in a compound with *jīva* ("living entity, the soul itself"),[1] must be taken to mean the *upādhi* of the jīva soul, i.e., the false identification of the soul with these different bodily forms.

Then the question arises, "If the *āsanas* are only known to Maheśvara, then how can they be considered limbs of yoga; since then they would then be exactly like the sitting postures of the non-yogis?"[2] In order to deal with this, he briefly mentions the common ways of sitting over the next two verses:

caturāśīti-lakṣāṇām ekaikaṁ samudāhṛtam |
tataḥ śivena pīṭhānāṁ ṣoḍaśonaṁ kṛtaṁ śatam ||9||

1.9. One sitting posture was designated for each of the 84 lakhs [species], and from them, 84 kinds of seats (*pīṭha*) were created by Śiva.

---

[1]Even though the two words are practically synonymous, they should not be seen as a mere repetition.

[2]Since each species has its own way of sitting, then the 400,000 kinds of human beings must also have their own. But these would simply be natural ways of sitting and have nothing to do with the purpose of yoga.

Of the 84 lakhs (8,400,000) of kinds of bodies (*upādhi*)[1] taken by the jīvas, for each body one of each (*ekaikam*), that is, a different one for each different body, was designated (*udāhṛtam*) or mentioned. Then from out of those, sixteen less that one hundred, in other word 84 in number, one seat for each lakh (100,000) was selected by Śiva as essential and applicable to everyone [and not just that species alone]. Since these seating postures are not practised by ordinary people or non-yogis, they are accepted as limbs of yoga.

And of all these postures, two again are again said to be the essence of them all,[2]

āsanebhyaḥ samastebhyo dvayam etad udāhṛtam |
ekaṁ siddhāsanaṁ proktaṁ dvitīyaṁ kamalāsanam ||10||

1.10. Of all the postures, the following two were [specially] designated [for yoga practice]. One is called *siddhāsana*,"the posture of the accomplished," and the second is *kamalāsana* or "the lotus posture."

These two *āsanas* are selected as being superior to all the others, that is they are said to be the chief postures [for the yogi]. Of the two, one is *siddhāsana*, the other *kamalāsana* or *padmāsana*.

The characteristics of the *siddhāsana* are given as follows:

---

[1]*Upādhi* means an "overlay" or false identification of pure consciousness with particular names and forms, which principally means the bodily designations, etc.

[2]Above, *Yoga-yājñavalkya* named three essential postures. YY is a later text. Other such discrepancies will be apparent later.

yoni-sthānakam aṅghri-mūla-ghaṭitaṁ kṛtvā dṛḍhaṁ vinyasen
meḍhraṁ pādam athaikam eva niyataṁ kṛtvā samaṁ vigraham[1] |
sthāṇuḥ saṁyamitendriyo'cala-dṛśā paśyan bhruvor antaraṁ
caitan mokṣa-kavāṭa-bheda-janakaṁ siddhāsanaṁ procyate ||11||

1.11. When one firmly places the base of the foot against the perineum (*yoni-sthāna*), while placing the other heel above the penis, making his body straight, keeping still, his senses restrained, and looking [at the spot] between the eyebrows with a steady gaze, then this is the *siddhāsana* or posture of the accomplished adept, by which the door to liberation [is made to] burst open.

The *yoni-sthāna* or perineum is the spot beween the genital and the anus. This is described in the *Mānasollāsa* (4.10)—

gudāc ca dvy-aṅgulād ūrdhvaṁ
meḍhrāc ca dvy-aṅgulād adhaḥ
yoni-sthānam iti khyātam

> The place that is two fingers above the anus and two fingers below the genital is called the *yoni-sthāna*, the "womb place."

The word *dṛḍhaṁ* "firmly" is an adverb describing the act of placing (*ghaṭitaṁ*) or pressing the base of the foot (*aṅghri-mūla*) or heel. One should so place one foot [there on the *yoni-sthāna*].

Now then one should fix the other foot at the genital, i.e., at the [upper] base of the penis. Then he should sit, making the body straight and remaining motionless (*sthāṇu*), without any restlessness in the body, the senses controlled (*saṁyamitendriyaḥ*), i.e.without any mental restlessness, "with a fixed gaze" (*acala-*

---

[1]Many editions of *Gorakṣa-śataka* here read *hṛdaye kṛtvā hanuṁ susthiram*, "placing the chin motionless over the heart," i.e., pressing the chin into the clavicle.

dṛśā), i.e., the eyes controlled and fixed continually on the point between the eyebrows.

This [posture], called *siddhāsana* or the posture of the accomplished adept, is that "by which the door to liberation [is made to] burst open," i.e., it uncovers the mouth of the *suṣumṇā nāḍī*, which is being blocked by the [slumbering] *kuṇḍalinī* and brings [the yogi] awareness of the oneness of the individual soul and Brahman.

Now Gorakṣa gives the characteristics of the *padmāsana*:

vāmorūpari dakṣiṇaṁ ca caraṇaṁ saṁsthāpya vāmaṁ tathā
dakṣorūpari paścimena vidhinā dhṛtvā karābhyāṁ dṛḍham |
aṅguṣṭhau hṛdaye nidhāya cibukaṁ nāsāgram ālokayed
etad vyādhi-vikāra-nāśana-karaṁ padmāsanaṁ procyate ||*12*||

1.12. After properly placing the right foot on top of the left thigh and the left foot on top of the right thigh, then firmly grasping the big toes by the hands [crossed] around the back and placing the chin on the chest, [the yogi] should look at the tip of the nose. This is the lotus posture or *padmāsana*, the destroyer of disease and disturbances.

After properly placing "the right foot," i.e., the outstretched base of the foot,"on top of the left thigh" (*vāmorūpari*), i.e, in the area at the base of the thigh of the left leg, and the left foot at the base of the right thigh, then by "the backwards method" (*paścimena vidhinā*), i.e., by passing both hands around the back,one should firmly grasp the big toes.

The meaning here is this: One should pass the right hand around the back to grasp the big toe of the right foot, which is placed on the left thigh, and the left hand around the back to grasp the big toe of the left foot placed on the right thigh. Then one should place the chin on the heart [i.e., the upper chest] and, as before, look at the tip of the nose. This is the *padmāsana*, the "destroyer of disease and disturbances" (*vyādhi-vikāra-nāśana-karaṁ*) for those who have restrained their passions; diseases (*vyādhi*) are the fevers and such that arise out of a disturbance in the bodily humors, and disturbances (*vikāra*) here refers to the mental distractions born of sensual desire and anger and the such. Therefore it will be said later herein, "One destroys disease by *āsana*" (2.11).

The Six Cakras

Now since without gaining control over the mind, which is riddled with inclinations towards the sense objects, one cannot come to a full understanding of one's own essential identity, and since without supporting objects [of concentration] (*avalambana*)[1] one cannot gain control over the mind, [Gorakṣa] now lists the six *cakras*, etc., which are included within the category of such supporting objects or props.

> *ṣaṭ-cakraṁ ṣoḍaśādhāraṁ dvi-lakṣyaṁ vyoma-pañcakam |*
> *sva-dehe ye na jānanti kathaṁ siddhyanti yoginaḥ ||13||*

1.13 How can those yogis succeed who do not know the six wheels (*cakras*), the sixteen containers (*ādhāra*), the two targets (*lakṣya*)[2] and the five skies (*vyoma*) in their own body.[3]

---

[1]Also *ālambana*.

[2]Several readings of this verse (such as Briggs and Feuerstein) read *tri-lakṣaṁ* and interpret it as the 300,000 nāḍis, which is clearly incorrect. Our B. manuscript also reads *tri-lakṣyaṁ*, which is most probably the correct reading as it coincides with the subject as discussed in *Siddha-siddhānta-paddhati*, 2.26-29. Our commentator, however, follows the reading that we have here. See following notes.

[3]This verse appears to be a corruption of the following, which is found in the *Siddha-siddhānta-paddhati* at 2.31. Our commentator knows this particular

The six cakras will be described further on.

The "sixteen containers" (*ṣoḍaśādhāra*)[1] are described in the *Nitya-nātha-paddhati*[2] as follows:

1. *Pādāṅguṣṭhādhāraṁ*, the seat of the vital function in the big toes. One should meditate on the luminosity there. Thus one's vision becomes steady.
2. *Mūlādhāraṁ*. [This the well-known center in the area of the anus.] One should press the heel into the *mūlādhāra* and remain in that position, which will kindle the fire [of digestion].[3]
3. *Gudādhāraṁ*. The seat of the vital function in the rectum, i.e., the sphincter. One should practice expanding and contracting it.
4. *Meḍhrādhāram*. The seat in the [male] genital organ. One should practice contracting the organ. When the life air enters the channel (*nāḍī*) known as *vajra-garbha* by the rear pathway (*paścima-mārgeṇa*) [i.e., in reverse], breaks through the three *brahma-granthis* or "knots" and then

---

tradition and follows it, but still comments on what is either a copyist's error or emendation. Other versions of *Gorakṣa-śataka* such as *Viveka-mārtaṇḍa*, have a reading closer to the original.

> *nava-cakraṁ kalādhāraṁ trilakṣyaṁ vyoma-pañcakam |*
> *samyag etan na jānāti sa yogī nāma-dhārakaḥ ||*

Nevertheless, it should be observed that our text here describes six *cakras* rather than nine, though the same nine centers are described infra in the section on *dhyāna* (Cf. 2.75). Since the *ādhāras*, *lakṣyas* and *ākāśas* are not explicitly described herein by name, one is lead to surmise that this text is earlier than SSP and that this verse is a later interpolation.

[1]"*Ādhāra* literally means "that which holds or contains." ...by the enumeration of the *ādhāras*, Gorakhnath refers to the principal seats of the vital and psychic functions, which have to be brought under voluntary control and then transcended by means of appropriate methods of yogic discipline." Akshay Kumar Banerjea, *Philosophy of Gorakhnath*, p. 182.

[2]I was not able to trace this text, though from this quotation it seems to be quite similar to the *Siddha-siddhānta-paddhati,* which covers the same subject matter with some differences at 2.10-25. Also compare *Siddha-siddhānta-saṅgraha.*

[3]This is the *mūla-bandha,* Cf. infra 1.57-59.

takes rest in the "cave of bees" (*bhramara-guhā*),[1] whereby one stops the movement of the *bindu* by drawing it upward.[2]

5. *Uḍḍīyamāṇādhāraṁ*. The seat in the entrails [lower abdomen]. By the performance of *āsanas* and *bandhas* of this *ādhāra* [i.e., *uḍḍiyāna-bandha*[3]], all infestations of the digestive tract are destroyed.
6. *Nābhi-maṇḍalādhāraṁ*. The seat in the navel area. One should there meditate on the spiritual form (*cid-rūpam*) and chant japa of the sacred syllable om, from which the mystical sounds or *nādas* arise.
7. *Hṛdayādhāraṁ*. The seat in the heart. By controlling the breath in this seat, the heart lotus blooms.
8. *Kaṇṭhādhāraṁ*. The seat in the throat. One should enter the chin deeply into this spot so that the movement of *prāṇa* in the *iḍā* and *piṅgalā nāḍis* becomes steady.[4]
9. *Ghaṇṭikādhāra*. The uvula. One should make the tip of the tongue touch here; one will thus get a portion of the nectar flowing from the moon.
10. *Talv-ādhāra*. The naso-pharynx. Through the processes of cutting and milking one should lengthen the tongue and stretch it deeply into the throat[5]; by this practice one will become inert like wood (*kāṣṭhī*).[1]

---

[1]At the upper end of the spinal column at the top of the neck.

[2]The *Siddha-siddhānta-paddhati* notes that this is known as *vajrolī*. *Vajrolī* is the *kriyā* whereby one uses the muscles in the shaft of the penis to withdraw any ejaculate that may have already descended into it, or even been spilt externally. This practice is accompanied by certain intrusive methods that are not discussed here. See *Haṭha-yoga-pradīpikā* 3.93ff for more information. Also Banerjea, op. cit., 184.

[3]Cf. infra. 1.60-61.

[4]This is otherwise known as *jālandhara-bandha*. See infra 1.62-63.

[5]This is a description of the *khecarī-mudrā*. See infra 1.64-65. *Yoga-koṣa* (p.100): "According to *Gheraṇḍa-saṁhitā* (3.26-27) first the tendon joining the tongue to the lower jaw is cut. Then the tongue is constantly moved, rubbed and pulled first with the hand after applying butter to it, and later with a pair of pincers. In this way the tongue is lengthened. This extended tongue is slowly pushed up

11. *Jihvādho-bhāgādhāra.*[2] The spot at the root of the tongue. One should rotate (churn) the tip of the tongue at the base of the tongue and this will produce ambrosia, from which one will [get the ability to compose] divine poetry.
12. *Ūrdhva-danta-mūlādhāra.* The base of the upper teeth.[3] One who holds the tip of the tongue here attains relief from all diseases.
13. *Nāsāgrādhāra.* The tip of the nose. Meditation on this point leads to steadiness of mind.
14. *Nāsikā-mūlādhāra.* The base of the nose. One should fix one's vision there and in six months one will directly see light.
15. *Bhrū-madhyādhāra.*[4] The point between the eyebrows. One will here have direct vision of a many-rayed light. By strictly practicing this [concentration], one's mind will merge into the sun-sky [see below for the five kinds of sky].
16. *Netrādhāra.*[5] The eyes. By rubbing the base of the eyes with the fingers, one will see light in the corner of the eyes. By looking constantly one will have a direct encounter with the light. Here concludes the description of the sixteen *ādhāras*.

---

into the aperture in the upper palate. With its tip turned upwards, it is pushed in until it reaches the *kapāla-kuhara* between the eyebrows from within. The gaze is also fixed on a point inside between the eyebrows."

[1]The explanation of this is given in YT commentary to verse 1.90.

[2]Our text does not give a name here. These names are taken from *Siddha-siddhānta-paddhati* and *Siddha-siddhānta-saṅgraha,* respectively. Our text more closely resembles the latter, for the former only promises freedom from diseases, the latter supremely blissful poetry. *ekādaśam rasādhāre jihvāgra-mathanāt sphuṭam | paramānanda-sandoha-kāriṇī kavitā bhavet* (2.25)

[3]Names here again differ. *SSP* has *bhrū-madhyādhāra*, i.e., the spot between the eyebrows, while *SSS* reads *ūrdhva-radādhāra,* "the upper teeth."

[4]SSP and SSS here have *lalāṭādhāra,* the forehead.

[5]SSP, *ākāśa-cakra,* SSS, *nayanādhāra.*

Next, we describe the two targets (*dvi-lakṣya*). These targets are of two kinds, external and internal. The external one refers to the tip of the nose and the point between the eyebrows. The internal refers to the *mūlādhāra*, the heart center and so on.[1]

Now "the five skies": These are described as follows in the *Nitya-nātha-paddhati*—

ākāśaṁ ca parākāśaṁ mahākāśaṁ tṛtīyakam
tattvākāśaṁ caturthaṁ syāt sūryākāśaṁ ca pañcamam
śvetaṁ raktaṁ tathā dhūmraṁ nīlaṁ vidyun-nibhaṁ punaḥ
ekaikaṁ jyotī-rūpaṁ tu sa bāhyābhyantaraṁ smaret

> The sky (*ākāśa*), the supreme sky (*parākāśa*), the great sky (*mahākāśa*) as the third, the sky of truth (*tattvākāśa*) the fourth, and the sky of the sun (*sūryākāśa*) as the fifth. These are perceived in the form of light, colored white, red, grey, blue and lightning-like, respectively. One should meditate on these skies both within and without.[2]

Moreover,

eka-stambhaṁ nava-dvāraṁ gṛhaṁ pañcādhidaivatam |
sva-dehe ye na jānanti kathaṁ siddhyanti yoginaḥ ||14||

---

[1]Both SSP and SSS refer to three *lakṣyas*, "... the objects upon which attention should temporarily be fixed for the purpose of practising the concentration of psycho-vital energy..." The third is "in between" (*madhyama*). These are inside the body, outside the body, "and some in a general way without any special reference to the body." (Banerjea, op.cit., 188-189).

[2]"...void or empty space." "*Ākāśa* is conceived as one perfectly pure (*atyanta-nirmala*) and formless (*nirākāra*) empty space pervading and unifying the outer and inner worlds. *Parākāśa* is conceived as one absolute undifferentiated darkness (*atyanta-andhakāra-nibha*) pervading the inner and outer worlds and obliterating all diversities. *Mahākāśa* is to be conceived as one infinite contentless fiery space like that in *pralaya* or total cosmic destruction (*kālānala-saṅkāśam*). *Sūryākāśa* is to be conceived as one infinite all absorbing sun shining perfectly alone with the brilliance of a crore of suns (*sūrya-koṭi-nibha*). *Tattvākāśa*, which is also known as *cid-ākāśa* or *ātmākāśa*, is to be conceived as one infinite eternal differenceless changeless self-luminous Soul or Spirit or Witness-Consciousness." (Banerjea, op.cit. 193-194).

1.14. How can those yogis who do not know the home, which has a single pillar, nine doors and five divinities (*adhidaivata*), and is present in their own body, ever attain success?

A column is what makes a house suitable for living. Being compared to it here in the body/house is the mind, due to its being the locus of all the desires or inclinations that result from previous actions (*vāsanās*). This is stated in the *Bhāgavata-purāṇa*:

cetaḥ khalv asya bandhāya muktaye cātmano matam
guṇeṣu saktaṁ bandhāya rataṁ vā puṁsi muktaye

[Kapila says to Devahūti:] "Mind alone is the cause of both the soul's bondage and of its liberation. When the mind is attached to the material qualities, one enters into bondage. When it takes pleasure in the Puruṣa, it leads to liberation." (3.25.15)

The nine doors [of the body-house] are the mouth, then the pairs of eyes, ears, and nostrils: these are the seven upper doors. The anus and urethra are the two lower doors, making nine.[1]

The five divinities are the presiding deities, namely Brahmā, Viṣṇu, Rudra, Īśvara and Sadāśiva. This is mentioned in the *Yoga-sāra*—

caturasra-dharaṇy-ādau brahmā tatrādhidevatā
ardha-candrākṛtir jalaṁ viṣṇus tatrādhidevatā
trikoṇa-maṇḍalaṁ vahnī rudras tatrādhidevatā
vāyor bījaṁ tu ṣaṭkoṇam īśas tatrādhidevatā
ākāśa-maṇḍalaṁ vṛttaṁ devatāsya sadā-śivaḥ

Brahmā is the titular deity of the earth, symbolized by the square. Viṣṇu is the deity of the water, symbolized by a half moon, Rudra that of fire, symbolized by the triangle, the seed

[1] *eka-stambhe nava-dvāre tri-sthūṇe pañca-daivate* |
īdṛśe tu śarīre vā matimān nopalakṣayet || (*Yoga-śikhopaniṣad* 1.72/73)

mantra of air is symbolized by a hexagon; its deity is Īśa. And the sky, whose *devatā* is Sadāśiva, is represented by a circle.

How, i.e., by what means, will those yogis who do not know or see these entities within their own body ever attain perfection? The meaning is they will not.

Now Gorakṣa describes the six *cakras*:

catur-dalaṁ syād ādhāraṁ svādhiṣṭhānaṁ ca ṣaṭ-dalam |
nābhau daśa-dalaṁ padmaṁ sūrya-saṅkhya-dalaṁ hṛdi ||*15*||

1.15. The *mūlādhāra* center [should be visualized as a] lotus with four petals, the *svādhiṣṭhāna* as one having six, [the center] at the navel with ten, and that in the heart having twelve petals.

Mūlādhāra-cakra. The *ādhāra-cakra* [or *mūlādhāra*] is described as a yellow-colored[1] lotus with four petals facing downwards. The petals are decorated with the four yellow letters, *va-śa-ṣa-sa*. Adorning the pericarp of the lotus, which is surrounded by eight spears, is a square-shaped foundation where the four-headed and four-armed Brahmā rides a great elephant, on the lap of the *bīja* mantra of the earth element (*laṁ*), accompanied by his consort (*śakti*) named Ḍākinī, who shines with a brilliance greater than ten million suns. Within this square figure shines the triangular-shaped throne (*pīṭha*) named Kāmākhyā.[2] In it, facing towards the rear is the great Śiva liṅga called Svayambhū around which the *kuṇḍalinī* energy, shining brilliantly like lightning, winds in three and a half coils, asleep and covering the opening of the *suṣumṇā* channel with

---

[1]Most other descriptions of this *cakra* say it is red. Cf. *Ṣaṭ-cakra-nirūpaṇaṁ* [SCN], 4. *catuḥ-śoṇa-patram*. Cf. Woodroffe, *The Serpent Power* (12th edition, Madras: Ganesh and Co., 1981), p. 330. This is probably an inadvertent mistake, as yellow letters inscribed on yellow petals seems unlikely.
[2]Further particulars are given below in verses 1.17ff. This detail about the *kuṇḍalinī* seems to be in conflict with *GŚ* 1.47.

her mouth. Her inhalations and exhalations make the movement of the *prāṇa* and *apāna* airs possible.

That is [also] stated in the *Yoga-sāra*:

yasmād utpadyate vāyur yasmād utpadyate manaḥ
yasmād utpadyate haṁso yasmād vahniḥ prajāyate
yasmād utpadyate bindur yasmān nādaḥ pravartate
tad eva kāma-rūpākhyaṁ pīṭhaṁ kāma-phala-pradam

> That place from which arises the air, from which arises the mind, from which arises the sun, from which arises fire, from which arises the *bindu*, and from which arises the subtle reverberation (*nāda*), is the throne named Kāmarūpā, which fulfills all desires.

Here ends the description of the root *cakra*, *mūlādhāra*.

Svādhiṣṭhāna-cakra. Now for the description of *svādhiṣṭhānaṁ*. At the root of the genital organ is a red-colored lotus with six petals facing upwards. The petals are decorated with the six letters from *ba* to *la* (*ba, bha, ma, ya, ra, la*). In the pericarp of this lotus is a white-colored shape like that of the half moon, the symbol of water, in which the water seed mantra (*vaṁ*) is situated. Seated on the lap[1] of that seed mantra in the company of his Śakti, Rākiṇī, is the four-armed form of Viṣṇu who has the signs of Śrīvatsa, the Kaustubha jewel and wears a yellow cloth. Here ends the description of the *svādhiṣṭhānam*.

Maṇipūra cakra. In the navel center is a blue lotus with ten petals facing upwards named *maṇipūraka*. The petals are decorated with

---

[1] According to *SCN* commentaries, "in the lap" of the various bīja mantras means within the dot (*bindu*) drawn above the letter, e.g., रं (*raṁ*), giving the nasal sound following it. See *Serpent Power*, p. 334.

the letters from *ḍa* to *pha* (*ḍa, ḍha, ṇa, ta, tha, da, dha, na, pa, pha*) which are [also] blue-colored.[1]

In the center of the pericarp is a red circle of fire around which is the four-armed fire *bīja-mantra* (*raṁ*) as bright as the sun, placed on a ram that has the shape of the *svastikā*.[2] Sitting on the lap of this seed syllable is the form of Mahārudra, who is red in color and smeared with ashes. He is accompanied by his Energy named Lākinī, who is blue in color. Here ends the description of the *maṇipūra-cakra*.

Anāhata-cakra. Above the navel in the region of the heart is a twelve-petaled lotus of red color facing upwards. The petals are adorned with the twelve letters from *ka* to *ṭha* (*ka, kha, ga, gha, ṅa, ca, cha, ja, jha, ña, ṭa, ṭha*). In the pericarp of this lotus is a hexagonal figure[3] of smoky color, which is the *maṇḍala* of the air element. Within this *maṇḍala* is the four-armed seed syllable of the air (*yaṁ*), riding a black antelope and accompanied by his energetic form named Kākinī. In its lap sits Īśvara who holds his hands inthe gestures of bestowing blessings and granting fearlessness. Within that lotus pericarp is [another] triangular figure in which a golden-colored *liṅga* shaped like an arrow (*bāṇa-liṅga*) is situated. This is called the throne of the full mountain or Pūrṇa Giri. Here ends the description of the *anāhata-cakra*.

kaṇṭhe syāt ṣoḍaśa-dalaṁ bhrū-madhye dvi-dalaṁ tathā |
sahasra-dalam ākhyātaṁ brahma-randhre mahā-pathe ||16||

1.16. At the throat is the sixteen-petaled lotus, and between the eyebrows one with two petals. In the great

[1] According to *SCN* (verse 19), the lotus is dark blue or black, like the color of heavy-laden rain clouds, while the letters are the lighter blue color of the lotus.
[2] This may be a copyist error or something got lost. According to *SCN*(19), there are three *svastika* marks outside the triangular shape of the *vahni-maṇḍalam*.
[3] Two interlacing triangles, like the Star of David.

way at the roof of the skull (*brahma-randhra*) is the lotus named the *sahasra-dala*, the thousand-petaled.

Viśuddha-cakra. Above the *anāhata-cakra* at the base of the throat is the *viśuddha-cakra* in the shape of an upward-facing sixteen-petaled lotus, clear like crystal and decorated with the sixteen vowels of the alphabet (*a, ā, i, ī, u, ū, ṛ, ṝ, ḷ, ḷḷ, e, ai, o, au, aṁ, aḥ*), which are red in color. In the pericarp of that lotus is the ethereal region (*nabho-maṇḍala*), which is circular like the full moon. There again is the spotless *maṇḍala* of the full moon. Riding a white elephant within that *maṇḍala* is the *bīja* mantra of the ether element (*ākāśa-bīja*, i.e., *haṁ*), which is of white color, with four arms, two holding the noose and goad, the other two showing the signs of blessings and fearlessness. It is accompanied by the śakti named Sākiṇī. This is the throne named *jalaṁ-dhara* ("water holding"). Here ends the description of the *viśuddha-cakra*.

Ājñā-cakra. Above that *cakra* and between the two eyebrows is the white, two-petaled, upward-facing lotus, adorned by the letters *ha* and *kṣa*, named the *ājñā-cakra*. In its pericarp, adorned by the energy named Hākinī,is the womb sphere (*yonī-maṇḍala*). In that womb stands the Śiva *liṅga* called Itara ("the Not This"). This *cakra* is said to be the locus of the mind and is the throne known as Uḍḍiyāna ("the flying, the soaring"). Here ends the description of the *ājñā-cakra* and of the Six Cakras.

Sahasrāra-cakra. In the natural sequence [of presentation, follows] the *sahasrāra* or thousand-petaled lotus, described as follows: In the great way at the roof of the skull (*brahma-randhra*), is the thousand-petaled lotus, which is white like the full moon. This lotus, which faces downwards, takes the form of the highest bliss. Its pericarp, wherein all the letters are distributed, contains a triangular shape representing a womb, with the letters *ha, la,* and *kṣa* in its three corners. In that womb is a full moon *maṇḍala* surrounded by a bursting web of light. In it [also] dances an explosion of light that is like a mass of abundant joy in the shape of flashes of lightning. There, the supreme auspicious one, Śiva, the one object of all the Vedānta, the form of spiritual bliss, reigns victorious in supreme eminence.

On his lap plays a portion (*kalā*[1]) of *nirvāṇa*, with a body curved like the half moon in the form of subtle and constant spiritual realization that is a light as bright as a thousand suns. Within this portion of *nirvāṇa*, which is like the one ten-millionth part of the hair-tip of the light of ten million suns, the opening and closing of which results in the creation and dissolution of the universe.[2] This is the play of the complete *nirvāṇa* potency.

And within that is the place of the supreme Śiva, the highest truth beyond all, who is the form of exceedingly great bliss beyond mind and speech, understandable only through yoga. From just a drop of this ecstasy, Brahmā and all the gods are themselves blissful. So ends the description of the thousand-petaled lotus.

Next [Gorakṣa] describes the throne named Kāmarūpa, in which dwell Śiva and Śakti.

ādhāraṁ prathamaṁ cakraṁ svādhiṣṭhānaṁ dvitīyakam |
yoni-sthānaṁ dvayor madhye kāma-rūpaṁ nigadyate ||17||

1.17. The first cakra is the *mūlādhāra*; the second, *svādhiṣṭhāna*. In between these two lies the *yoni-sthāna*, "the womb spot" [i.e., perineum] named *kāma-rūpa*.

The *mūlādhāra* and *svādhiṣṭhāna* have already been explained above. In between these two lies the throne (*pīṭha*) known as Kāmarūpa.

---

[1] Usually defined as a sixteenth portion, equivalent to the phases of the moon. Sir John Woodroffe, on the basis of commentaries to the Tantras, says that means *śakti*. *The Serpent Power*, p. 424.

[2] The sentence is unfortunately fragmented.

Does this then mean that between those two loci there is a third one? Answering no, [Gorakṣa] says—

ādhārākhyaṁ guda-sthānaṁ paṅkajaṁ ca catur-dalam |
tan-madhye procyate yoniḥ kāmākhyā siddha-vanditā ||18||

1.18 The four-petaled lotus called *ādhāra* is located at the anus (*guda-sthāna*). Within it is said to be the "womb" (*yoni*) named Kāmākhyā. It is praised by the accomplished.

Within the four-petaled lotus named *ādhāra* located at the anus, i.e., within the pericarp of that lotus, is the womb known by the name Kāmākhyā, which is composed of the letters of the alphabet (*mātṛkākṣaram*).[1] It is the portion within the pericarp of the *mūlādhāra* lotus that touches the downward-facing third corner of the triangle within the *suṣumṇā*. This is why it is said to be between the two *cakras*.[2] It is said to be praised or venerated by all the accomplished adepts (*siddhas*).

---

[1]The word *mātṛkā* comes from the word *mātṛ* meaning mother. In the context of the cakras, etc., this is the name given to the fifty letters of the Sanskrit alphabet or "particularized sound forms" or *bījas*, which are said to be endowed with esoteric power.

[2]The author is trying to harmonize the apparent contradiction of whether the *kāma-rūpa* triangle is within the *mūlādhāra* as stated in the commentary of verse 1.15 above, or between the two bottom *cakras* as stated here in this verse. The former opinion holds through the vast majority of texts. (See Shyamsundar Goswami, *Laya Yoga*. p. 189.) Important for understanding further discussions of the arousal of the *kuṇḍalinī*, it should be noted that *kāma* means desire, in particular sexual desire, and the *bīja-mantra* for Kāma, *klīṁ*, which is used in the worship of Kāmadeva, Kṛṣṇa and Kālī, resides in this spot. This energy is also known as *kandarpa* (another name for the god of love) and is a *vāyu,* part of the *apāna-vāyu*. This *kandarpa-vāyu* is also known as *vahni-vāyu*, the fire force, and the triangle itself as *vahni-kuṇḍa*, the "fire vessel," which is usually the term given to the seat of the sacred sacrificial fire. This energy is further identified with the *kuṇḍalinī* herself, which wrapped around the Svayambhū *liṅga* (See below). The three sides of the triangle, which is also known as *tripurā* ("the three cities"), are said to represent will, knowledge and action (*icchā, jñāna, kriyā*). See *Laya Yoga*, 189-190 and *SCM* 8 for further details.

yoni-madhye mahā-liṅgaṁ paścimābhimukhaṁ sthitam |
mastake maṇivad bimbaṁ[1] *yo jānāti sa yogavit ||19||*

1.19 In the midst of that womb is situated the great liṅga[2] [of Śiva] facing downwards.[3] He who knows the jewel-like disk in [its] head is a knower of yoga.[4]

In the middle of that womb, facing the rear, i.e., facing towards the mouth of the *suṣumṇā*, is the great *liṅga* known as Svayambhū. In the head, i.e., in the top part of the *liṅga*, is an orb (*bimba*) that glows like a jewel. As it is said in the *Yoga-sāra*—

yā mūlādhāragā śaktiḥ kuṇḍalī bindu-rūpiṇī
mastake maṇivad bimbaṁ yo jānāti sa yogavit

---

[1] *Bhinnam* in L.

[2] Goswami (p. 190) says that the *liṅga* has the form of *praṇava*, Om. See again SCM 9. "Inside the triangle is Svayambhū in *liṅga* form, beautiful like molten gold, with his head downwards. He is revealed by knowledge and meditation and is of the shape and reddish color of a leaf that has not yet unfolded, or a new twig. His spreading smile is charming like the rays of the full moon or of lightning. The god Śiva resides as happily here in a form resembling a river whirlpool as he does in Kāśī." The *liṅga* stands on the *kāma-bīja*, explaining the significance of the words *kāma-rūpa* and *kāmākhyā*.

[3] *Paścimābhimukhaṁ* would normally mean "facing the rear," but we take this meaning in keeping with the majority of Tantra-Yoga texts and commentators. Kuvalayananda and Shukla (L, page 66) propose two meanings for *paścimābhimukha* as (1) "facing downwards," or as (2) "facing the Suṣumṇā," citing HYP 1.29 and its *Jyotsnā* commentary. The former is confirmed by SCM as noted in the previous footnote.

[4] Feuerstein: "Yoni and linga represent Shakti and Shiva respectively. The sexual symbolism conceals a sweeping cosmic reality: the eternal play between feminine power and masculine consciousness, which are always united on the transcendental level, but are experienced as separate on the empirical level. The luminous disk/mirror (*bimba*) mentioned in this stanza is pictured as being fastened to the head (*mastaka*) of Śiva's symbolic phallus. Presumably it stands for the liṅga's native luminosity, which is reflected back upon itself, in evidence of Śiva's perfect autonomy." (*The Yoga Tradition*, 535)

> The energy that is present in the *mūlādhāra* is the Kuṇḍalī, which takes the form of a [reflected] point. One who knows the original form, the jewel-like orb in the head, is a knower of yoga.

One who knows them both [*bindu* and *bimba*] is a knower of yoga. The sense is that to those who are not conversant with yoga, neither of them can be known.

Next [Gorakṣa] shows that this [*yoni-sthāna*] is the locus of the fire of Time:

tapta-cāmīkarābhāsaṁ taḍil-lekheva visphurat |
trikoṇaṁ tat-puraṁ vahner adho-meḍhrāt pratiṣṭhitam ||20||

1.20. Situated below the genital is the triangular city of fire, flashing like a streak of lightning and resembling molten gold.

In the region below the base of the genital organ (*meḍhrāt*), i.e., within the pericarp of the *mūlādhāra*, between the genital and the [*kāma-rūpa*] triangle[1] resembling molten gold, or heated gold, and flashing like the streak of lightning is this "city" which is said to be the locus of fire, that is the fire of Time or universal destruction (*kālāgni*). This is confirmed by Sureśvarācārya, who says the "The fire of Time is in the root [center]" (*mūle tiṣṭhati kālāgniḥ, Mānasollāsa* 9.10). The *Yoga-sāra* also states:

[1]This is only attested in one of our three source manuscripts, the other two are unintelligible at this place. The Lonavla edition of *Gorakṣa-śataka* reads *caturasram* or four-sided figure. Descriptions of the *mūlādhāra* generally begin with a square figure inside which lies the triangle known as *kāmākhyā* or *kāma-rūpa*. The commentator seems to be saying that this three-sided figure, the place of fire, is different from that one. However, most Tantra-Yoga sources seem to confirm that the *agni-sthāna* and *kāmākhyā* are one and the same.

pātālānām adho-bhāge kālāgnir yaḥ pratiṣṭhitaḥ
sa mūlāgniḥ śarīre'smin yasmān nādaḥ pravartate [1]

> In the area at the bottom of the nether regions (*pātāla*) is situated the fire of Time (*kālāgni*). It is the root fire within the body and from it arises the *nāda* or internal sound.

Next, the author shows that this fire of Time particularly becomes the object of meditation in the moments immediately preceding the attainment of *samādhi*, when because of its all-pervasiveness, one merges the entire universe of moving and stationary beings into the conscious self:

yat samādhau paraṁ jyotir anantaṁ viśvato-mukham |
tasmin dṛṣṭe mahā-yoge yātāyātaṁ na vidyate ||21||

1.21. When in *samādhi* one sees the supreme light, infinite and facing in every direction, then in that great yoga there are no more comings and goings.[2]

In the yogi's *samādhi*, that infinite or uninterrupted, supreme light or ultimate brightness, manifests as facing in every direction or all-pervading—in the form of the fire of Time, it should here be added. If one sees this light "in the great yoga," meaning in the three limbs of yoga, *dhāraṇā, dhyāna* and *samādhi*,[3] or by the process of awakening the *śakti* in the course of one's *sādhana*, then one's comings and goings, i.e., births and deaths in this eternally turning wheel of *saṁsāra*, will come to a halt.

---

[1]This verse is also found at *Yoga-śikhopaniṣad*, 5.29. This is the first of five fires, the others being *baḍavāgni* (the subterranean fire in the bones), *pārthivāgni* (the earthly fire in the stomach where the bile duct opens); *antarikṣāgni* (the fire of the sky in the ear), and *sūryāgni* (the fire of the sun in the navel center).
[2]This verse is repeated at 2.15. It seems contextually better situated there.
[3]These are known as the internal practices of yoga according to Patañjali. Cf. *Yoga-sūtras* 3.1-7.

Next, [Gorakṣa] gives the etymology of *svādhiṣṭhāna*:

sva-śabdena bhavet prāṇaḥ svādhiṣṭhānaṁ tad-āśrayaḥ |
svādhiṣṭhānāśrayād asmān meḍhram evābhidhīyate ||22||

1.22. The word *sva* signifies the *prāṇa*, and the *svādhiṣṭhāna* is its substratum. So since it is the resting place of the *svādhiṣṭhāna*, it is called *meḍhra*, i.e. the male genital organ.

The word *sva-* signifies the *prāṇa* in the form of the swan [i.e., both the inhalation and the exhalation, *haṁ-sa*]; the word *adhiṣṭhāna* means resting place or substratum.[1] From this word (*svādhiṣṭhāna*), it is verily called or known as the *meḍhra*. The meaning is that this is the second *cakra*.[2]

Gorakṣa now speaks of the *maṇipūra-cakra*.

tantunā maṇivat proto yatra kandaḥ suṣumṇayā |
tan nābhi-maṇḍalaṁ cakraṁ procyate maṇipūrakam ||23||

1.23. The place where the "bulb" (*kanda*) is strung on the *suṣumṇā* like a jewel on a thread is the cakra of the navel region called *maṇipūraka*.

---

[1]This verse says that the *svādhiṣṭhāna* is the *cakra* where the *prāṇa* resides. This is contradicted further on in 1.34 and in YT to that verse, where it is said that the place of the *prāṇa* is the heart. The same verse states that *mūlādhāra* is the seat of the *apāna*. Since the *prāṇa* is the principal life air from which all others arise, it does not appear to be a real contradiction, as the *prāṇa* is the whole (*aṁśī*) and the other *vāyus* are its subdivisions, or *aṁśas*. The principal seat of the *prāṇa* is thus the heart, as universally accepted.

[2]The verse appears to be making an etymological argument for the word *meḍhra*, which derives from the verb root √*mih*, meaning to sprinkle, emit water, ejaculate, etc. Thus the word *megha* (cloud) is also derived from the same root. Most other derivatives (*meha, mehana,* etc.) are connected to urination. How the word *svādhiṣṭhāna* is related to this etymology is not clear to me, nor apparently to our commentator.

The word *tantu* means a thread, like *sūtra*. That place where the *kanda* is placed as if strung on the *suṣumṇā* is the navel region, and called the *maṇipūra-cakra*.[1]

Now [Gorakṣa] speaks of the *anāhata*.

dvādaśāre mahā-cakre puṇya-pāpa-vivarjite[2] |
tāvaj jīvo bhramaty eva yāvat tattvaṁ na vindati ||24||

1.24. For as long as it does not attain Reality (*tattvam*), the individual soul errs [in *saṁsāra*] within the great *cakra* (wheel) of twelve spokes, which is completely devoid of both virtuous acts and sin.[3]

---

[1]Our reading, -*maṇḍalam* is most frequently found in the verious related manuscripts. Kuvalayananda and Shukla (L, p. 69) prefer the YCU reading, -*maṇḍale*, since the *cakra* could not be the same as the entire umbilical region. The locative case makes the meaning "in the navel region." Their argument is that the *maṇipūraka-cakra* is said to be pierced by the *suṣumṇā*, so it too must be located inside the spine. The probable understanding is that the *cakra* represents a field of energy governing the entire region and thus identified with it, but having its vortex in the spine.

[2]VM, DBU here read *niyaṁtritaḥ*, "controlled by," i.e., the jīva, controlled by his own pious and sinful acts, remains bound in the heart *cakra*. YCU, the only other text with this verse, has the same as the V edition of GP, -*vivarjite*. Although all three readings can make sense, *niyantritaḥ* feels most correct since we are talking of the conditioned individual consciousness in the state of bondage.

[3]The V edition of GP translates, apparently reading the word *puṇya-pāpa-vivarjite* as *puṇya-pāpa-vivarjitaḥ*, i.e., an adjective describing the *jīva*. He then adds *saṁsāra* to fill in the meaning of *bhramati*. So, "The *jīva* who is [in reality] beyond good and evil errs [in *saṁsāra*]," etc.

Feuerstein reads the principal clause (*tāvaj jīvo bhramaty eva*) with the locative in the first line, whereas our commentary reads the subordinate clause with it. So he explains, unpersuasively: "The *jīva* or individuated consciousness is thought to restlessly move in the petals of the heart lotus, driven by its own karma and trapped by its own ignorance (*avidyā*). That nescience is the fragmented consciousness's ignorance of its true nature as the Self. When wisdom dawns, the jīva's centrifugal movement ceases, and consciousness finds its real source at the center of the heart, which is the free and blissful consciousness of the Self. For the liberated individual, there is neither merit nor demerit, which are karmic realities that pertain only to the condition of unenlightment."

In that great *cakra* of "twelve spokes," i.e., the twelve petals [of the lotus], which is free of both virtuous acts and sin, namely the *anāhata-cakra*, the jīva, who is [the entity] designated by the quintets of intelligence, the working senses and the life airs,[1] as well as the mind and intelligence, errs for so long as he does not find or attain the Reality, i.e., the truth of the Self.[2]

The Nāḍis

Now [Gorakṣa] speaks further of the "bulb" (*kanda*), which has already been mentioned above (1.23).

ūrdhvaṁ meḍhrād adho nābheḥ kanda-yoniḥ khagāṇḍavat |
tatra nāḍyaḥ samutpannāḥ sahasrāṇāṁ dvisaptatiḥ ||25||

1.25. Above the male organ and below the navel is the "bulb-womb" (*kanda-yoni*), [shaped] like a bird's egg. From it originate the 72,000 nāḍis.

Above the male organ or the area around the penis and below the navel is the bulb (*kanda*), which being like a womb and the place of origin for all the *nāḍis*, is [also] here called *yoni*. It is shaped like the egg of a bird. From it originate the 72,000 *nāḍis*, spreading here and there in every direction.

teṣu nāḍī-sahasreṣu dvisaptatir udāhṛtāḥ |
pradhānāḥ prāṇa-vāhinyo bhūyas tāsu daśa smṛtāḥ ||26||

---

[1]The first use of the word *buddhi* here must mean the *buddhīndriya*, i.e., *jñānendriya*, the five knowledge acquiring senses, namely ears, eyes, tongue, nose, and skin. The five working senses (*karmendriya*) are the hands, feet, tongue, genital and anus.
[2]The word *tattva* ("Reality") is spoken of in more detail in the section on *samādhi*, 2.92-95.

1.26. Among these thousands of channels, 72 are designated as being the principal carriers of the life-force. Again, of them, ten are said [to be primary].

Amongst these 72,000 *nāḍis*, there are 72 that are constantly carrying the life-force, always engaged in doing the business of carrying the bodily airs.[1] Therefore they are primary. Again, amongst these 72, ten are taken to be even more important.

The names and locations of the ten main *nāḍis* mentioned in the previous verse will now be elucidated over the next five verses—

iḍā ca piṅgala caiva suṣumṇā ca tṛtīyakā |
gāndhārī hastijihvā ca pūṣā caiva yaśasvinī ||27||
alambuṣā kuhūś caiva śaṅkhinī daśamī smṛtā |
etan nāḍī-mayaṁ cakraṁ jñātavyaṁ yogibhiḥ sadā ||28||

1.27-28. [These ten are known as] *iḍā* and *piṅgalā*; the third is *suṣumṇā*, then *gāndhārī*, *hastijihvā*, *pūṣā*, *yaśasvinī*, *alambuṣā*, *kuhū*, and *śaṅkhinī* as the tenth. This wheel (*cakra*)[2] composed of channels is always to be known by the yogis.

Iḍā, piṅgalā, suṣumṇā, gāndhārī, hastijihvā, pūṣā, yaśasvinī, alambuṣā, kuhū, śaṅkhinī. [The ten names are listed again so one does not take the words "third" and "tenth" as separate names]. This wheel of *nāḍis*, namely this wheel from which the *nāḍīs* spread like a web, is always to be known by the yogis. Here the channels carrying the airs and the airs themselves are both to be known, so

---

[1]I.e., since presumably all 72,000 *nāḍis* are conduits for the life force or *prāṇa*, the compound *prāṇa-vyāpāra-viśiṣṭāḥ* should perhaps be read with the emphasis on *viśiṣṭāḥ*, i.e., "special" rather than "characterized."

[2]The use of the word "circle" here carries an implication of the completeness of the *maṇḍala*. As the universe forms a complete whole, so too does the *prāṇa* body. The commentator appears to understand this as a reference to the *kanda* in accordance with the Sureśvarācārya quotation to the following pair of verses.

that one practices *prāṇāyāma* and the other kinds of yoga with no conflict between them. This is the intended meaning of both [verses].

Their locations are now given—

iḍā vāme sthitā bhāge piṅgalā dakṣiṇe sthitā |
suṣumṇnā madhya-deśe tu gāndhārī vāma-cakṣuṣi ||29||
dakṣiṇe hastijihvā ca pūṣā karṇe ca dakṣiṇe |
yaśasvinī vāma-karṇe hy ānane cāpy alambuṣā ||30||

1.29-30. *Iḍā* is located on the left side, *piṅgalā* on the right; *suṣumṇā* is in the central region, while *gāndhārī* is in the left eye. *Hastijihvā* is on the right, and *pūṣā* in the right ear, while *yaśasvinī* is in the left ear, and *alambuṣā* in the mouth.

Iḍā is situated on the left side, *piṅgalā* on the right, *suṣumṇā* is situated between these two, by which is meant that it follows the spinal column. This trio of *nāḍis* arise from the three corners of the *yoni* [triangle] in the *mūlādhāra*. The *iḍā* arises from the left corner, the *piṅgalā* from the right, and the *suṣumṇā* arises from the rear corner. The *iḍā* and *piṅgalā* embrace each other in the *suṣumṇā* and terminate in the nasal passages on their own respective sides. The *suṣumṇā* on the other hand goes all the way from the *mūlādhārā* to the *brahma-randhra*. This is the meaning. This is also stated by Sureśvarācārya:

mūlādhārāgra-koṇotthā suṣumṇā brahma-randhragā
tat-pārśva-koṇayor jāte dve iḍā-piṅgale sthite
nāḍī-cakreṇa saṁsphūrte nāsikāntam ubhe gate

The *suṣumṇā* arises from the front corner of the *mūlādhāra* and travels all the way to the *brahma-randhra*. From the two other corners come the *iḍā* and *piṅgalā*. They become fully manifested

> by [passing through] the *nādī-cakra* [i.e., the *kanda*] and then travel up to [their respective] nostrils.

Here "arising from the front corner" means from the rear corner.[1] The other *nāḍis* arise from the *kanda* in the navel center. From there, i.e., the *kanda*, *gāndhārī* travels up to the left eye. *Hastijihvā* goes as far as the right eye, *pūṣā* as far as the right ear and *yaśasvinī* up to the left ear. *Alambuṣā* goes as far as the face, meaning the mouth.

kuhūś ca liṅga-deśe tu mūla-sthāne śaṅkhinī |
evaṁ dvāraṁ samāśritya tiṣṭhanti daśa nāḍayaḥ ||*31*||

1.31. *Kuhū* is situated in the area of the penis (*liṅga*), and *śaṅkhinī* at the root [i.e., *mūlādhāra*]. Thus there are ten channels, [each of which] has recourse to a [different] gate.

Kuhū is in the area of the penis, *śaṅkhinī* at the root [the anus, *mūlādhāra*]. The idea is that these two *nāḍis* descend from the *kanda* at the navel center. Thus in this way, the ten *nāḍis* each have recourse to a different gate [i.e., bodily orifice], following these paths of the life force.

[The author] now speaks of the three principal *nāḍis*, which are more important that the others because they are [the main channels] constantly carrying the life force—

iḍā-piṅgalā-suṣumṇāḥ prāṇa-mārga-samāśritāḥ |
santataṁ prāṇa-vāhinyaḥ soma-sūryāgni-devatāḥ ||32||[1]

---

[1]Since we already know the left and right corners, there can only be one other. Still, if we look at the triangle in reverse with the point downward, then the *piṅgalā* and *iḍā* would have to be on their opposite sides, i.e., left and right respectively.

1.32. *Iḍā*, *piṅgalā* and *suṣumṇā* follow the [principal] path of the *prāṇa*. They are always carriers of the life force [and are associated with] the moon (*soma*), sun and fire gods [respectively].

Iḍā, piṅgalā and *suṣumṇā*: these *nāḍis* deal with the comings and goings of the life air (*prāṇa*) through the inward and outward breath, [so saying that] they are connected to the path of the life airs means they are its pathways. What are they like? They have Soma, Sūrya and Agni as their presiding deities. The presiding deity of *iḍā* is Soma (the moon god), Sūrya (the sun) is that of *piṅgalā*, and Agni (fire) of *suṣumṇā*.

The Life Airs and Their Functions

The author now describes the ten life airs over the next fourteen verses.[2]

prāṇo'pānaḥ samānaś codāna-vyānau vāyavaḥ |
nāgaḥ kūrmo'tha kṛkaro devadatto dhanañjayaḥ ||33||

1.33. The [ten] life airs are *prāṇa*, *apāna*, *samāna*, *udāna*, *vyāna*, *nāga*, *kūrma*, *kṛkala*, *devadatta* and *dhanañjaya*.[1]

---

[1]This verse appears in the following form in *Viveka-mārtaṇḍa* and the Lonavla edition of *Gorakṣa-śataka*:

satataṁ prāṇa-vāhinyas tisro nāḍyaḥ prakīrtitāḥ |
iḍā-piṅgalā-suṣumṇāḥ soma-sūryāgni-devatāḥ ||

"The three channels are said to constantly carry the life airs; their names are *iḍā*, *piṅgalā*, and *suṣumṇā* and their deities are the Moon, Sun and Fire [respectively]." This reading is superior because it eliminates the confusing expression *prāṇa-mārga-samāśritāḥ* ("following the path of the life force").

[2]This here appears to be where a number of verses are interpolated. The Lonavla edition skips 34-38, which are summarized in verse 37. See the verse index and concordance in the appendix.

In this list of ten airs, the first five, starting with *prāṇa* are the most important.[2] Their functions are as follows:

- Those of the *prāṇa*, inhaling and exhaling, coughing, etc., and including the digestion of food;
- of the *apāna*, the excretion of stool and urine;
- of the *vyāna*, picking up and releasing;
- of the *udāna*, bodily growth,
- nourishing the body is the work of the *samāna-vāyu*.

The functions of the other life airs will be described in the text itself.

hṛdi prāṇo vasen nityam apāno guda-maṇḍale |
samāno nābhi-deśe tu udānaḥ kaṇṭha-madhyataḥ ||34||
vyāno vyāpī śarīre tu pradhānāḥ pañca-vāyavaḥ |
prāṇādyāḥ pañca vikhyātā nāgādyāḥ pañca-vāyavaḥ ||35||

1.34-35. The *prāṇa* should always [be known to] dwell in the heart, *apāna* in the region of the anus; *samāna* is located at the navel and *udāna* in the middle of the throat. *Vyāna* pervades the [whole] body. These five beginning with *prāṇa* are the principal "winds" and are well-known as the five airs. [Now the other] five airs beginning with *nāga* [will be described].

The air known as *prāṇa* should always dwell, i.e., it does dwell, in the heart. The *apāna* is in the region of the anus, i.e., in the

---

[1]Feuerstein: "These ten names are technical terms in yoga and are not readily translatable. They stand for various aspects or functions of the life force as it manifests in the human body."

[2]The first five *prāṇas* are widely described in the older Upaniṣads, whereas the second tier of *vāyus* is sometimes given the name, *upaprāṇa* or *upavāyu*. (*Śiva-saṁhitā*, 3.8)

mūlādhāra-cakra. The *samāna* is always in the area of the navel and the *udāna* in the middle of the throat. This is an abbreviated description. In [greater detail],

- The *prāṇa* should be situated between the mouth and the nose, in the heart, in the navel area, around the *kuṇḍalī*, and in the big toes: these are [the places] of the *prāṇa* air.
- The *apāna* is in the anus, genital, thighs, knees, belly, eyes, waist and navel.
- The *vyāna* is in the ears, eyes, waist, ankles, sense of smell and throat.
- The *udāna* is in all the joints, as well as in the hands and feet.
- The *samāna-vāyu* combines with a portion of the fire of digestion and pervades the entire body. It creates a relationship with dualities such as one's happiness and distress and gives them form.[1]

Therefore these five are called the principal airs. The other five, beginning with *nāga* are situated in the skin and bones, etc.

Now the work of the secondary life airs is described:

udgāre nāga ākhyātaḥ kūrma unmīlane smṛtaḥ |
kṛkaraṁ kṣuta-kṛj jñeyo devadatto vijṛṁbhaṇe ||36||

1.36 *Nāga* is said to be present in belching, *kūrma* in the opening of the eyes; *kṛkara* should be known to cause sneezing; *devadatta* [acts in] yawning.

Belching is the work of *nāga*. "Opening of the eyes" refers to control over the eyelids, which is the work of *kūrma-vāyu*. Sneezing is the work of *kṛkara* and yawning that of *devadatta*.

[1]This last sentence is found in the A manuscript only.

na jahāti mṛtaṁ cāpi sarva-vyāpī dhanaṁjayaḥ |
ete sarvāsu nāḍīṣu bhramante jīva-rūpiṇaḥ ||37||

1.37. *Dhanañjaya* is all-pervasive and does not quit the body even when it is dead. These [ten forms of the life air] roam through all the channels, giving form to[1] the fragmented consciousness (the *jīva*).

The life air named *dhanañjaya* pervades the entire body. It does not quit or abandon one even after dying, that is to say, when the body has become a corpse.[2] These ten life airs give form to the *jīva* or fragmented consciousness; i.e., through the superimposition of identity with themselves they create in the *jīva* a relation to the dualities of happiness and distress, and thus give him form.

Then, "in the form of fragmented consciousness roaming through all the channels" means that [the life airs] so roam as the means or instruments whereby the *jīva* in its subtle body functions, experiencing dualities such as "I am happy or sad," etc. The intention of the word "roam" is to say that they never attain a situation of stability.

Here, although it is [in fact] impossible for the *jīva*, which is Consciousness that has been fragmented by ignorance, to wander in the *nāḍis*, the delimiting adjuncts of individual consciousness, namely the movements associated with the life airs that have been activated by the functions of the intelligence (*buddhi*) in the form of the *haṁsa* [the inward and outward breath] have been superimposed or projected (*āropa*) onto it, just as the movements,

---

[1]*Yoga-vāsiṣṭha* (5.78.48) states: "The vibration of breath is the action of the mind, producing the error of the existence of the world; when brought under subjection, this error is dispelled."

[2]I.e., The main function of *dhanañjaya* is nourishing and swelling of the dead body, and according to *Śiva-saṁhitā* (3.8), its function is causing phlegm and hiccup. *Kumbhaka-paddhati* (82) states "when one has control of *dhanañjaya-vāyu* the *kuṇḍalinī* absorbs all the *vāyus* in the body, in which state everything else becomes insignificant."

etc., of the moon's reflection in containers of water, i.e., its adjuncts, are then projected onto the moon itself.

The adjunct or *upādhi* of the jīva consists of the causal body or *liṅga-deha*, which is made up of mind, *buddhi*, along with the quintets of the knowledge-acquiring senses, working senses, and life airs. It is therefore designated as *cid-ābhāsa*, or the reflection of [pure] consciousness. So it is not contradictory to accept that the jīva consciousness becomes identified with the activities of the life airs, since these are an aspect of the causal body.

The three categories of *jīva* are well known. They are stated by the revered preceptor Svāmī[1]:

avacchinnaś cid-ābhāsas tṛtīyaḥ svapna-kalpitaḥ
vijñeyas trividho jīvas tatrādyaḥ pāramārthikaḥ

> There are three kinds of fragmented consciousness or jīva: one that is separated or cut off (*avacchinna*), the second that is a reflection of pure consciousness (*cid-ābhāsa*), and the third, which is imagined in dreams (*svapna-kalpita*). The first of these is transcendental (*pāramārthika*).

The separated jīva is the one conscious self who is divided into the combinations of *prāṇa* and so on [that make up the material forms] like the all-pervading space divided into small containers. The reflected consciousness (*cid-ābhāsa*) refers to the spiritual reflection of the one Consciousness like sunlight reflected into various bodies of water, which is then subject to the conditions imposed by the adjuncts (*upādhi-dharma*). This is the second kind of jīva and is the one intended here in this context. The third, which is imagined in a dream (*svapna-kalpita*), is the jīva who thinks "I am a god, I am a man" and so forth, just as if he were in a dream, identifying himself as not different from the gross material body. The first of these jīvas is transcendental, i.e., the ultimate true form of the jīva. When the

---

[1] I have not been able to trace the source of these verses nor identify the *ācārya-svāmī* in question.

causal body comes into existence, then it behaves as a fragmented individual soul or jīva. The venerable Ācārya-svāmī also states how this first jīva is transcendental or ultimately true (*pāramārthika*):

avacchedaḥ kalpitaḥ syād avicchidyaṁ tu vāstavam
tasmin jīvatvam āropāt brahmatvaṁ tu svabhāvataḥ

> Any division [of consciousness] is imagined, for in truth it is indivisible. By nature, all consciousness is Brahman, and the existence of fragmented consciousness is superimposed on that.

Now with the help of examples, over the next four verses the author shows the various conditions faced by the fragmented consciousness when it has taken form as *prāṇa* and so on in the way just described.

ākṣipto bhuja-daṇḍena yathoccalati kandukaḥ |
prāṇāpāna-samākṣiptas tathā jīvo na tiṣṭhati ||38||

> **1.38. As a ball thrown [on the ground[1]] by the hand bounces back up, so the individual consciousness when tossed around by the *prāṇa* and *apāna* cannot [ever] find rest.**

Just as a courtesan[2] throws or hits a ball, which is her toy, with "the stick of her arm," namely the palm of the hand [!], and it bounces,

---

[1]Lonavla here reads *bhuvi daṇḍena* ("on the ground with a stick") rather than *bhuja-daṇḍena* ("with the stick of the arm"), which does seem to make better sense than our commentator's reading, which is nevertheless the most popular attested reading.

[2]Playing with a ball (*kanduka-krīḍā*) is for the most part a recurring image in the context of young and unmarried noblewomen with plenty of leisure time, unlike the average dharmic housewife who would have little time for such indulgences. These are often given some erotic associations, though certainly such an image is somewhat gratuitous in this context here. Depictions of *kanduka-krīḍā* can be seen in the sculptures of Khajuraho and many other such sites. Some examples

meaning that on hitting the ground it flies upwards, and being thus repeatedly struck, first by the hand, then by the ground, can never find a single place of rest, so that its movements are a source of joy to the courtesan's mind; in the same way, when the *jīva* is under the aegis of the *prāṇa*, it is pulled away by the *apāna*, and when in the zone of the *apāna* it is pulled away by the *prāṇa*, and so being constantly pulled by *prāṇa* and *apāna* it cannot remain stable in one place.

Due to being reflected in those forms alone [i.e., due to the superimposed identification with the *upādhis*], the jīva is drawn by the *prāṇa* and *apāna* to their respective domains, and not finding stability in one place, sports in ways that are favorable to those who identify with them. Here, just as the ball is under the control of the courtesan's hands, so the *jīva* is also dependent on the life airs like *prāṇa*, which are the effects of ignorance (*avidyā-kārya*).[1]

He therefore says,

> ***prāṇāpāna-vaśo jīvo hy adhaś cordhvaṁ ca dhāvati |***
> ***vāma-dakṣiṇa-mārgeṇa cañcalatvān na dṛśyate ||39||***

1.39. Under the control of *prāṇa* and *apāna*, the fragmented consciousness runs up and down along the left and right pathways; it cannot be seen due to its febrility.

Because it is under the control or dependent on *prāṇa* and *apāna,* the jīva follows the left and right pathways by means of the *iḍā* and *piṅgalā*, running down as far as the *mūlādhāra* and then upwards to the openings in the mouth and nostrils. Therefore it cannot be

---

from literature: *Mahābhārata, Vana-parva,* chapter 110; *Bhāgavata-purāṇa* 3.22.17, 8.12.18ff, 12.8.26. Act II of *Svapna-vāsava-datta* by Bhāsa, etc.

[1]The commentary rounds out the simile by adding the courtesan who represents ignorance. Her hand and the ground represent the *prāṇa* and *apāna* respectively, and the jīva is being compared to the ball.

observed because of its febrile movement (*cañcalatvāt*), this unsteadiness arising from its being under the control of the *prāṇa* and *apāna*. The uncontrolled breath cannot be an object of meditation in the lotus of the heart and other places. The verb "to see" here is being used in the sense of knowing.

Now with the help of [another] example, [the author] shows that though Brahman becomes free from its sense of being fragmented consciousness during the state of deep sleep when the ignorance caused by identification with the body is [temporarily] obliterated, afterwards it again takes on that identification as the *jīva*:

rajju-baddho yathā śyeno gato'py ākṛṣyate punaḥ |
guṇa-baddhas tathā jīvaḥ prāṇāpānena kṛṣyate ||40||

1.40. Just as a falcon tied by a string can be pulled back even after going, so too the fragmented consciousness, tied by the knots [of material Nature] is drawn back by means of *prāṇa* and *apāna*.

Just as the falcon, a particular kind of bird, is bound by its talons with a piece of string, even after going, i.e., even after flying away from the spot to which it is bound, can be pulled back by that string and returned to its place; so similarly the *jīva* or the self as reflected consciousness (*cid-ābhāsa*), being bound by, i.e., having a strong connection with the qualities (*guṇas*), that is to say, those portions of *māyā* consisting of the proclivity to experience the remaining results of one's previous actions (*karma*), even after it goes, i.e., when the functions of the intelligence have merged [with the root nature] and it has become free of its previous material conditioning, it is still pulled back by the remaining *prāṇa* and *apāna* in order to experience the results of those aforementioned *karmas*.

The idea is that when those functions of the intelligence are again awakened, the residual life airs pull the consciousness back into its fragmented state.

An alternative interpretation is that when the *jīva* goes to the area governed by *prāṇa*, on reaching that zone it awakens, as in the example of the falcon.[1]

apānaḥ karṣati prāṇaṁ prāṇo'pānaṁ ca karṣati |
ūrdhvādhaḥ saṁsthitāv etau saṁyojayati yogavit ||41||

1.41. *Apāna* pulls on the *prāṇa* and *prāṇa* pulls on the *apāna*. [These two forms of the life force are respectively] situated above and below [the navel]. The knower of yoga joins these two.

The *apāna* is the life air which is situated in the *mūlādhāra*. It pulls on the *prāṇa* situated in the *ājñā-cakra*, taking it into its own domain. Similarly, the *prāṇa* draws the *apāna* from the *mūlādhāra* to its own domain.

Having thus described the state of the uncontrolled *prāṇa*, he then concludes the verse by indicating that someone who has controlled the *prāṇa* is never afflicted by happiness and distress in this way. The person who knows yoga by the means that will be described below joins, i.e., unites, these two, namely the *prāna* and *apāna*, which are situated in the *ājñā* and *svādhiṣṭhāna cakras*.[2] Indeed, this is verily *haṭha-yoga*. As stated in the *Yoga-cintāmaṇi*:

---

[1]The meaning of this sentence is not clear. The *Yoga-bīja* (79) reads as follows:

cittaṁ prāṇena sannaddhaṁ sarva-jīveṣu saṁsthitam |
rajjau yadvat parībaddhā pakṣī tadvad idaṁ manaḥ ||

"The mind established in every living being is bound by the *prāṇa*. Just as a bird tied by a rope is bound, so it is with the mind."

[2]This is in contradiction with the information in 1.33, where it is said that the *prāṇa* is in the heart and the *apāna* in the anus. The unification or balancing of the *prāṇa* and *apāna* is the principal purpose of the *haṁsa* mantra, about to be described below.

"The *prāṇa* and *apāna* are also known as the moon and sun. *Prāṇāyāma*, which is characterized by the unification of these two, is called *haṭha-yoga*" (*sūryākhyayoḥ prāṇāpānayor aikya-lakṣaṇaṁ prāṇāyāmo'yaṁ haṭha-yoga ity ucyate*).

What is that [*prāṇāyāma*] then? In response to this expected question, [the author] speaks of the *haṁsa-mantra* which is reflected in the inward and outward movements of the breath.

ha-kāreṇa bahir yāti sa-kāreṇa viśet punaḥ |
haṁsa-haṁsety amuṁ mantraṁ jīvo japati sarvadā ||42||

1.42. [The jīva] goes out with the sound *ha* and again enters with the sound *sa*. Thus the jīva continually recites the mantra, *haṁsa haṁsa*.

The jīva, i.e., the reflection of consciousness (*cid-ābhāsa*), having thus become identified with the *prāṇa-vāyu*, goes out with the letter *ha*, the seed [sound] of the *prāṇa*, meaning that it goes out of the *svādhiṣṭhāna-cakra.*[1] Then with the letter *sa*, the seed [of *apāna*], it enters within, i.e., it goes to the area of the *mūlādhāra*. In this way, the individual soul constantly recites the mantra, *haṁsa haṁsa*. For this reason this is known as the *jīva-mantra*. The form of the word *haṁsa* is given according to poetic license (*ārṣa*), since it should have the *visarga* added to it.

Now he gives the number of times that this mantra is repeated in any given day and night:

ṣaṭ śatāni tv aho-rātre sahasrāṇy ekaviṁśatiḥ |
etat saṁkhyānvitaṁ mantraṁ jīvo japati sarvadā ||43||

---

[1]Our B manuscript has "from the *mūlādhāra*."

1.43. The fragmented consciousness continually recites this mantra to the count of 21,600 times through one day and night.

The *jīva*, who has already been described, constantly through the day and night, repeats the mantra 21,600 times, doing japa of the mantra this number of times.[1]

[Gorakṣa] now glorifies the greatness of this mantra over the next three verses:

ajapā nāma gāyatrī yogināṁ mokṣa-dāyinī |
asyāḥ saṅkalpa-mātreṇa sarva-pāpaiḥ pramucyate ||44||

1.44. The *gāyatrī* mantra named *ajapā* is the bestower of liberation upon the yogis, and one is released from all sin merely by making the resolution to recite it.

This mantra is the *gāyatrī* named *ajapā*.[2] "Simply by making the resolution" to chant this *ajapā-gāyatrī* means even without actually reciting it. "All sin" refers to the consequences of doing what is forbidden and so on. Since one is freed from all sin, this mantra is therefore the bestower of liberation on the yogis.

---

[1]This works out to 15 breaths a minute.

[2]*Ajapā* means "unrecited" since it is equated with the breath pure and simple. As Swami Veda Bharati states, "The final stage, the highest stage, is *ajapā-japa*, the unrepeated repetition, which is the state of the highest absorption in mantra leading to the inner central point" (*Mantra and Meditation*, Honesdale: Himalayan Institute, 1981, p. 217). The potency of the mantra comes in the conscious awareness associated with the breath, when it takes on the form *so'ham*, "I am he," which is equivalent to the *mahā-vākya, ahaṁ brahmāsmi*. The word *gāyatrī* generally refers to a Vedic meter of 24-syllables, or more specifically to the *Sāvitrī-mantra*. The word itself, however, has the etymological meaning, "the mantra that protects the one who chants it." By calling it a Gāyatrī, however, the prestige of the Vedic *sūktas* is appropriated and it is equated to the *praṇava*. For more on the *haṁsa-mantra*, see *Mantra and Meditation*, pp. 51-61.

anayā sadṛśī vidyā anayā sadṛśo japaḥ |
anayā sadṛśaṁ jñānaṁ na bhūtaṁ na bhaviṣyati ||45||

1.45. There is no esoteric knowledge[1] equal to this; no other recitation equal to it; there is no wisdom equal to it [in the present]. Nor was there in the past, nor will there be in the future.

Because this *ajapā-gāyatrī* establishes the identity of the individual soul with Brahman, there is no knowledge equal to it. Similarly, there is no recitation (*japa*) that is equal to the recitation of this mantra because all other mantras only give such bounteous results after one has made a great effort. Moreover, there is no means to knowledge equal to this, for by its very form it gives birth to the experience of non-duality (*advaita*). There has never been nor will there ever be such a means to attaining this wisdom.

kuṇḍalinyāḥ samudbhūtā gāyatrī prāṇa-dhāriṇī |
prāṇa-vidyā mahā-vidyā yas tāṁ vetti sa yogavit ||46||

1.46. Having arisen from the *kuṇḍalinī*, this gāyatrī is the preserver of the *prāṇa* life force. It is the science of the *prāṇa*, the great science, and one who knows it is the knower of yoga.[2]

Since this *gāyatrī* preserves the life force and arose from the *kuṇḍalinī*, it is therefore the esoteric science of the life force, and is

---

[1]*Vidyā* can mean knowledge generally, or in the Tantric context it more often refers to a mantra with some special or esoteric purpose, like a magic spell. It can also mean a science or an art.

[2]Many texts here read "knower of the Vedas" (*vedavit*). Feuerstein comments: "Here the yogic science of breath, or life force, is presented as the quintessence of the Vedic revelation. This is not far from the truth, because breath control together with curbing the mind was the earliest form of yoga practiced even before Vedic times. It was fundamental to the Vedic ritual, especially in connection with the disciplined chanting of the sacred hymns."

therefore the "great science" (*mahā-vidyā*). One who knows it is a knower of yoga, in the sense that he knows the real purpose and meaning of yoga. Here ends the section dealing with the *ajapā mantra*.

Awakening the Śakti

Now over the next ten verses, [Gorakṣa] will introduce the subject of the awakening the power (*śakti*) by first describing the locus of the *kuṇḍalinī*:

kandordhve kuṇḍalī śaktir aṣṭadhā kuṇḍalākṛtiḥ |
brahma-dvāra-mukhaṁ nityaṁ mukhenācchādya tiṣṭhati ||47||

1.47. The *kuṇḍalinī* power remains above the "bulbous root" (*kanda*), coiled in eight rings, her mouth always covering the opening to the doorway to Brahman (*brahma-dvāra*).

The *kanda* or bulbous root is the source from which all the *nāḍis* emanate. Above it means within the pericarp of the *maṇipūra-cakra*. The *kuṇḍalinī śakti* remains there coiled eight times[1] and covering the entry to the passageway to Brahman with its mouth.

Furthermore,

yena dvāreṇa gantavyaṁ brahma-sthānam anāmayam |
mukhenācchādya tad-dvāraṁ prasuptā parameśvarī ||48||
prabuddhā vahni-yogena[2] *manasā marutā saha* |
sūcīvad guṇam ādāya vrajaty ūrdhvaṁ suṣumṇayā ||49||

---

[1]The eight coils of the serpent power are named in the *Yoga-viṣaya* (22) as follows: *praṇavā, guda-nālā, nalinī, sarpiṇī, baṅka-nālī, kṣayā, śaurī,* and *kuṇḍalī*.
[2]Some editions here read *buddhi-yogena*, but this reading is unlikely and not followed by *Yoga-taraṅgiṇī*.

1.48-49. It is through that gate that one must go to the place of Brahman, which is free of all disease. But the Supreme Goddess (*parameśvarī*) is asleep there, covering it with her mouth. [When she] is awakened by the connection with fire, she combines with the mind and the life air, and like a needle drawing a thread she moves upward through the *suṣumṇā*.

The Supreme Goddess, i.e., the *kuṇḍalinī śakti*, is sleeping and with her mouth covering that gate or pathway through which one must pass in order to attain the place of Brahman, which is the locus of unbroken bliss and free of all disease, namely all worries about misery arising from birth, death, old age and disease.[1]

Awakened or aroused from her sleep by contact with fire, i.e., by coming into contact with the flame of fire sent forth by the *prāṇa*, the *kuṇḍalinī* then joins with the mind and the life air (*prāṇa*, *marut*) and taking the way of the *suṣumṇā*, the middle channel, she moves upward towards the thousand-petaled lotus. By way of example, [the author] says, "like a needle drawing thread." Just like the needle takes a strand [of thread] and goes upward through all the individual cross-threads of a cloth, so too this *kuṇḍalinī* rises to each of the six *cakras* as conceived by the yogi, and there establishes herself. Then, gathering up the presiding deities and all the elements in these *cakras*, she continues to proceed upwards.

---

[1]Unfortunately there is no resolution of the contradiction between what is stated here in verses 1.47-48 and the earlier description based on *Ṣaṭ-cakra-nirūpaṇa* given in the commentary to 1.15, which also states that the *kuṇḍālinī* has three and a half coils rather than eight. The earlier description is by far the more frequently cited. But it would appear that there are two different traditions here. The *Siddha-siddhānta-paddhati* (2.3) places the *kuṇḍalinī*, like here, in the *nābhi-cakra*. However, it describes it as having five coils! Swami Dvārikādāsa Śāstrī attempts to resolve the difference by saying that the form of *kuṇḍalinī* in the *mūlādhāra* is the subtle form, whereas that in the *maṇipūra* is a luminous (*jyotirmaya*) transformation of that same *kuṇḍalinī*.

[Gorakṣa] further describes her form and movement:

prasphurad-bhujagākārā padma-tantu-nibhā śubhā |
prabuddhā vahni-yogena vrajaty ūrdhvaṁ suṣumṇayā ||50||[1]

1.50. When the auspicious *kuṇḍalinī* is awakened through contact with the fire, she takes the form of an aroused serpent and then, appearing like the filament of a lotus, moves upward through the *suṣumṇā*.

The *kuṇḍalinī* is awakened by contact with the flame of the fire of Time (*kālāgni*) situated in the *mūlādhāra* after it has been activated by the *apāna* air. Therefore she takes the form of an aroused serpent, which then moves vehemently with a zig-zag motion.[2] "Appearing like the filament of a lotus" means that she is very fine and luminous like the fibre of the lotus stem. She is auspicious because her essence is beneficial. She moves upward through the *suṣumṇā*, meaning that she takes the *suṣumṇā* channel.

Next, with the help of an example, [Gorakṣa] shows how one should break through the aperture of the *suṣumṇā* with the *kuṇḍalinī*:

udghāṭayet kavāṭaṁ tu yathā kuñcikayā haṭhāt |
kuṇḍalinyā tathā yogī mokṣa-dvāraṁ prabhedayet ||51||

1.51. Just as one should forcefully open a door using a key, so the yogi should penetrate the door to liberation by means of the *kuṇḍalinī*.

---

[1]This verse, which is not found in most of the related texts such as *Viveka-mārtaṇḍa* and *Yoga-cūḍāmaṇi Upaniṣad*, is likely an alternative version of the previous verse that has then been repeated. In the place of *prasphurad-*, the word *prasuptā* is found in other editions such as *Gorakṣa-paddhati*.

[2]This should be understood as an upward spiral movement.

Just as a householder can open a door that has been padlocked by forcefully using a key,[1]--the particle *tu* ("but")[2] implies that without the key he could never so open it--so the yogi should by means of the *kuṇḍalinī* cause the door to liberation, i.e., the mouth of the *suṣumṇā,* to open. Without the *kuṇḍalinī* this would never be possible. This rounds out the implications of the simile.

In the previous verse it was said that the yogi should penetrate the door to liberation by means of the *kuṇḍalinī*. This can only be done if the *kuṇḍalinī* is awakened. Therefore [Gorakṣa] now describes a particular form of the *padmāsana* that is the means for so awakening it—

kṛtvā saṁpuṭitau karau dṛḍhataraṁ baddhvā tu padmāsanaṁ
gāḍhaṁ vakṣasi sannidhāya cibukaṁ dhyātvā ca tac cepsitam |
vāraṁ vāram apānam ūrdhvam anilaṁ proccārayet pūritaṁ
muñcan prāṇam upaiti bodham atulaṁ śakti-prabodhān naraḥ ||52||

1.52. Cupping the hands and very tightly assuming the lotus posture, pressing the chin deeply on the chest and meditating on his most desired object, the yogi should repeatedly lift the *apāna* air upward, expelling the air that has been taken in. Thus he attains unequalled understanding (*bodha*) through the awakening of the [*kuṇḍalinī*] power (*śakti*).

After cupping (*saṁpuṭitau*) the hands palms upward and placing the heels of the hands against the chest, one should very firmly form the *padmāsana*, then also place the chin on the chest and meditate on the desired object.[3] Then he should repeatedly raise

---

[1]The kind of lock spoken of here would in all likelihood be large and require considerable force to open. Thus the word *haṭha* is used.
[2]Left untranslated in the English version of the verse.
[3]"Desired object" (*īpsitam*) here likely just refers to the immediate object of awakening of the *kuṇḍalinī*.

the *apāna* air, lifting it upward. The inhaled *prāṇa* should be united with the *apāna* air and held to the extent possible before releasing it. The release should come only after the preceding action has taken place. By doing all this, a man attains unequalled or immeasurable understanding, meaning knowledge. How? From the awakening of the power. The meaning is that by this practice the [*kuṇḍalinī*] energy will be awakened, and from that knowledge will be attained.[1]

Now over the next two verses [Gorakṣa] describes the rules that must be followed in this practice:

> *aṅgānāṁ mardanaṁ kuryāc chrama-jātena vāriṇā* |
> *kaṭv-amla-lavaṇa-tyāgī kṣīra-bhojanam ācaret* ||53||

1.53. He should rub his limbs with the perspiration produced by the [above] effort. Giving up bitter, sour and salty food, he should consume [only] milk.

When one begins to perspire due to the effort involved in this practice, he should massage the limbs with his sweat. Giving up forbidden foods that are bitter, sour and salty, one should consume only milk, or take a diet that is predominantly based in dairy products.[2]

---

[1]Brahmānanda's *Jyotsnā* comment on HYP 1.48: "By the union of the *prāṇa* and *apāna*, the gastric fire is aroused. The serpent *kuṇḍalinī,* which is lying in three and a half coils, blocking the opening of the *suṣumṇā* with its mouth, feels this and straightening itself begins to move upwards. Then the *prāṇa* and the *apāna* should be forced through the opening into the *suṣumṇā*. The process described in this verse is that of the *jālandhara-bandha*."

[2]Brahmopaniṣad Yogī (YCU 41) says that massaging the body with one's own perspiration makes it firm (*dṛḍha-kāya*). Just one of our MSS has "only milk," the others say "mainly milk." DBU reads *kṣīra-pāna-rataḥ*, "engaged in drinking milk [exclusively]."

Moreover,

brahmacārī mitāhārī tyāgī yoga-parāyaṇaḥ |
abdād ūrdhvaṁ bhavet siddho nātra kāryā vicāraṇā ||54||

1.54. One who is celibate (*brahmacārī*), has a measured diet (*mitāhārī*), is a renouncer (*tyāgī*) and devoted to the practice of yoga (*yoga-parāyaṇa*), will become successful [in this practice] after a year. There should be no doubt about this.

The yogi should practice *brahmacarya*,[1] which means renouncing sexual activity. That should be practiced in accordance with one's status in life. As stated in the *Yoga-cintāmaṇi*—

sarvatra maithuna-tyāgo brahmacaryaṁ pracakṣate |
brahmacaryāśrama-sthānāṁ yatīnāṁ naiṣṭhikasya ca ||
ṛtāv ṛtau sva-dāreṣu saṅgatir yā vidhānataḥ |
brahmacaryā tu saivoktā gṛhasthāśrama-vāsinām |

> Renouncing sexual activity in all respects is called *brahmacarya*. It is ordained for those who are in the first stage of life [the student], for those who are renounced monks, and for those who have taken a lifelong vow of celibacy. For those who are in the householder stage of life (*gṛhasthāśrama*), having sexual relations with one's own wife in the proper season [i.e., when she is fertile] in accordance with the scriptural injunctions is also called *brahmacarya*.

---

[1]The original meaning of the word is "engaged in the study of the Veda (*brahma*)," which was identified with the first of the four *āśramas* or stages of life, that of the student. Since the main characteristic of the student life, which would only be followed by marriage and householder life after completion of the study, was celibacy, the word itself took on the meaning of celibacy. Some nowadays break down the word etymologically as "walking in God" in order to expand the range of meaning and reduce the emphasis on sexual abstinence.

The characteristics of a measured diet will be given in the next verse. A renouncer (*tyāgī*) means one who is free of any attachment to sense objects, including any such person who does not seek personal reward from his activities.

The word *yoga-parāyaṇa* ("devoted to the practice of yoga") can be broken down as follows: One for whom yoga is the ultimate (*para*) or unexcelled place of refuge (*ayana*). This means someone who is constantly taking refuge in the practices of yoga alone and nothing else. Such a yogī will attain success after one year, meaning that he will be able to raise the *kuṇḍalinī* energy at will. If anyone wonders whether there is any possibility of doubt, the author says no, there should be none.

Now the characteristics of the "measured diet" (*mitāhāra*) are given.

susnigdhaṁ madhurāhāraṁ caturthāṁśa-vivarjitam |
bhuñjate sura-saṁprītyai mitāhāraḥ sa ucyate ||55||

1.55. A person who eats food that is very smooth and sweet, leaving aside one quarter of it, and does so for the pleasure of the gods, is called one who follows a measured diet (*mitāhārī*).

"Very smooth" means that it has sufficient oil. Sweet here means that it is free of sour and salty flavors. "Leaving aside one quarter" is in keeping with the following dictum:

dvau bhāgau pūrayed annais toyenaikaṁ prapūrayet
prāṇa-vāyoḥ pracārārthaṁ caturtham avaśeṣayet

> One should fill two parts of the stomach with food, one part with water, leaving the fourth part empty to allow for the movement of the life airs.

"For the pleasure of the gods" means that [such foodstuffs] should first be [ritually] offered to the gods. As it is said, "One should not eat food that has not been offered, and one should reject [forbidden foods like] fish and meat" (*anivedya na bhuñjīta, matsya-māṁsādikaṁ tyajet*). The food that is thus consumed by the yogi is called a measured diet.

[Gorakṣa] now states that the afore-described *kuṇḍalinī* energy, once awakened by the given process, results in liberation.

kandordhve kuṇḍalī śaktir aṣṭadhā kuṇḍalākṛtiḥ |
bandhanāya ca mūḍhānāṁ yogināṁ mokṣadā sadā ||56||

1.56. The *kuṇḍalinī śakti* [situated] in its eightfold winding form above the "bulb" (*kanda*) is always the cause of bondage for fools, but the giver of liberation to the yogis.

The first part of this verse was already explained above (1.47). The *kuṇḍalī śakti* causes bondage for the fools who are ignorant of the practices of yoga because it covers the doorway to the path to the *brahma-randhra*, i.e., the *suṣumṇā*. "Always" here means for as long as they do not take up the work of asceticism and yoga. For the yogis, however, who are well versed in the means for arousing this power (*śakti-cālana*) and so on, the *kuṇḍalinī* gives liberation because it is the means to attaining Brahman and brings an end to birth, death and the sense of separated individuality (*jīva-bhāva*).

The Five Mudrās

Now [Gorakṣa] states that the [following] five practices beginning with *mahā-mudrā* are absolutely necessary to effectuate the arousal of the [*kuṇḍalinī*] energy—

mahā-mudrāṁ nabho-mudrām uḍḍiyānaṁ[1] *jālandharam |*
mūla-bandhaṁ ca yo vetti sa yogī mukti-bhājanam ||57||

1.57. The yogī who knows the *mahā-mudrā*, *nabho-mudrā*, *uḍḍiyāna-bandha*, *jālandhara-bandha* and *mūla-bandha* is eligible for liberation.

The yogi who knows the five seals, i.e., "the great seal" (*mahā-mudrā*), "the sky seal" (*nabho-mudrā*) [otherwise known as the] "moving-in-the-sky seal" (*khecarī-mudrā*), "the flying lock" (*uḍḍiyāna*), "the net holder lock" (*jālandhara*) and the "root lock" (*mūla-bandha*) is worthy of liberation, i.e., is a worthy candidate for liberation. Thus one should learn these five *mudrās* and arouse the *śakti*, for by this alone will one become eligible for liberation and by no other means. In the *Yoga-cintāmaṇi* the following is said in response to the question of whether or not these practices lead to the arousal of the [*kuṇḍalinī*] energy:

pipīlikāyāṁ lagnāyām aṅge kaṇḍūr yathā bhavet
suṣumṇāyāṁ tathābhyāsāt satataṁ vāyunā bhavet

> When an ant bites, one feels an itch in the body. So it is that through constant practice [of the mudrās] [the energy is aroused and an itching sensation] in the *suṣumṇā* by [the movement of] the *prāṇa*.

In this way, after properly practicing to the best of one's ability day after day, at the end of [each day's] practice, one should gradually give up the *mahā-mudrā*, *khecarī* and so on and only afterward the *mūla-bandha* [but not before]. As Lord Śiva states in the *Yoga-sāra*.

---

[1]There is great variation in the spelling of this word. Our edition seems to prefer *uḍḍīyāṇa*, but is not consistent. We have chosen to follow the spelling as standardized in the *Yoga-koṣa* from Lonavla.

yadā vighaṭayen mudrāṁ khecarīṁ yoga-vittamaḥ
śaktiḥ sva-sthānam abhyeti pūrvoddiṣṭena karmaṇā

When the topmost knower of yoga accomplishes the *khecarī-mudrā*, then the [*kuṇḍalinī*] *śakti* takes to her own abode through the previously instructed practices.

Now Gorakṣa sequentially gives the characteristics of the five *mudrās* beginning with *mūla-bandha*—

pārṣṇi-bhāgena saṁpīḍya yonim ākuñcayed gudam |
apānam ūrdhvam ākṛṣya mūla-bandho vidhīyate ||58||

1.58. The "root-lock" (*mūla-bandha*) is to be performed by pressing the *yoni* with the heel portion [of the foot], contracting the anus, and pulling the *apāna* upward.

Pulling the *apāṇa* air upwards, with the heel portion of the foot pressing the *yoni*, i.e, the spot between the anus and the base of the penis, one should contract or squeeze tight the anus, i.e., the root doorway (*mūla-dvāra*). The idea is that the *apāna* should not be allowed to sink again into the lower region. This is how the root lock is to be performed.[1]

In this connection, the benefits of the root-lock [practiced alone[2]] are next described:

apāna-prāṇayor aikyaṁ kṣayo mūtra-purīṣayoḥ |
yuvā bhavati vṛddho'pi satataṁ mūla-bandhanāt ||59||

---

[1]Although the *mūla-bandha* is usually recommended along with the *siddhāsana* or *padmāsana*, sometimes it is associated with *vajrāsana*, as in *Jñāneśvarī* 6.199. See also HYP 3.114-115. This verse is also found in *Haṭha-yoga-pradīpikā* (3.61).
[2]I.e., without any other accompanying practices. This specification is not found in all texts.

1.59. Through the unification of the *apāna* and *prāṇa*, one's bodily excretions are diminished. Even an old man becomes young by constantly closing off the root.

"Constantly closing off the root" here means constant practice of the root lock (*mūla-bandha*). From such practice an old person, i.e., one who is wrinkled, whose hair has become white and who is overcome by age becomes [like] a youth of sixteen. Why is that? The reason is that by the practice of the *mūla-bandha* the *prāṇa* and *apāna* become united, i.e., perform one and the same function, as a result of which the urine and faeces are diminished, i.e, destroyed [and this then leads to renewed youthfulness].[1]

Now [Gorakṣa] explains the uḍḍiyāna-bandha.

> ***uḍḍīnaṁ kurute yasmād aviśrāntaṁ mahā-khagaḥ |***
> ***uḍḍiyānaṁ tad eva syān mṛtyu-mātaṅga-kesarī*** **||60||**

1.60. That place from which the great bird makes its tireless soaring flight would verily be the *uḍḍīyana* [-*bandha*], a lion to the elephant of death.[2]

---

[1]This verse is the same as HYP 3.65. The alternative reading in the other versions such as *Viveka-mārtaṇḍa* and *Gorakṣa-paddhati* makes the three results derive directly from the *mūla-bandha* practice, whereas YT here reads them as being sequential. The word *kṣaya* is interpreted by most translators as reduction or diminution, but here YT interprets it as the complete destruction (*nāśa*) or elimination of stool and urine, by which he appears to mean complete cessation of bodily waste production.

[2]The two verses 60 and 61 appear to have been confused, as revealed by the mixed metaphor in this verse and the awkward syntax of the next. What the original version was is somewhat difficult to ascertain, but could likely be reconstituted from a comparative reading of *Viveka-mārtaṇḍa* (43-44), *Dhyāna-bindūpaniṣat* (75b-76a), *Yoga-cūḍāmaṇi Upaniṣad* (48b-49a), and *Haṭha-yoga-pradīpikā* (3.56-57). The latter, which seems to me to be the most correct, reads as follows:

> *uḍḍīnaṁ kurute yasmād aviśrāntaṁ mahā-khagaḥ |*
> *uḍḍīyānaṁ tad eva syāt tatra bandho vidhīyate ||*

That from which (*yasmāt*), namely the "flying lock" (*uḍḍiyāna-bandha*), the great bird of the vital force (*prāṇa*) tirelessly makes its soaring flight, going up in flight to the *suṣumṇā*, is the *bandha* named *uḍḍiyāna*. Death is verily an elephant; the maned creature (*kesarī*), the lion, is able to thwart [the elephant]; and like it, this *bandha* named *uḍḍiyāna* thwarts death.[1]

Where is this lock to be performed? In expectation of such a query, [Gorakṣa] says—

> ***udarāt paścima-bhāge tv adho-nābher nigadyate |***
> ***uḍḍiyānasya bandho'yaṁ tatra bandho vidhīyate ||61||***

1.61. This lock at the back of the abdomen and below the navel is called the *bandha* of the *uddiyāna*. It is there that the lock is to be applied.

> *udare paścimaṁ tānaṁ nābher ūrdhvaṁ ca kārayet |*
> *uḍḍīyāno hy asau bandho mṛtyu-mātaṅga-kesarī ||*

"The place from which the great bird sets off on his tireless flight is [called] the *uḍḍīyāna*. It is here that one should perform the lock [known as *uḍḍīyāna-bandha*]. This lock, which is like a lion to the elephant of death, is performed by pressing the belly to the back and lifting the navel upwards."

The Lonavla *Gorakṣa-śataka* has only a single verse (35), which reads:

> *ūrdhve meḍhrād adho nābher uḍḍiyānaṁ pracakṣate |*
> *uḍḍiyāna-jayo bandho mṛtyu-mātaṅga-kesarī ||*

"Above the penis and below the navel is the region of *uḍḍīyāna*. This *bandha* controls this region and is like a lion to the elephant in the form of death."

Although Prof. Mallinson feels that the Lonavla edition does not represent the original *Gorakṣa-śataka*, a comparison of these readings indicates that the other versions may well have grown out of this rather cryptic statement. At any rate, we are bound by our commentary's reading.

[1]Feuerstein: "This colorful metaphor is based on the word play between a bird's *uḍḍīna* ("flying up") and the yogi's *uḍḍiyāna* ("soaring") which consists in pulling the stomach in and thereby forcing the air/life force upward so that the *jīva* soars like a bird. This yogic technique is said to conquer death, just as a lion can kill the much larger elephant."

That part [of the body] which is behind the belly and below the navel is called *uḍḍiyāna*; its lock is called the *uḍḍiyāna-bandha*; the phrase "by the perfected yogis (*siddhas*)" should be adduced to complete the sense. Therefore this lock is to be performed there and nowhere else.[1]

[Gorakṣa] now describes the benefits of the *jālandhara-bandha*.

badhnāti hi śirā-jālam nādho yāti[2] *nabho-jalam* |
tato jālandharo bandhaḥ kaṇṭha-duḥkhaugha-nāśanaḥ ||62||

1.62. The *jālandhara-bandha* [or throat lock] binds the network (*jāla*) of channels so that the water from the sky (*nabhas*) does not flow downward. Therefore [this practice] is the destroyer of a host of throat ailments.

The *jālandhara-bandha*, being the destroyer of a host, i.e., the totality, of ailments affecting the throat, binds or blocks the network of channels or *nāḍis* so that the water from the sky (*nabho-jala*), i.e., the nectar of the half moon (*candra-kalāmṛta*), does not flow downward, i.e., does not fall from the hollow in the skull.[3]

---

[1]This rather unhappy explanation is the result of a poor verse reading. In neither of the two verses given here is there a real description of *uḍḍiyāna* as is found in the alternate readings (see note 82). Note 83 describes how *uḍḍīyāna* should be performed. Replacing the word *-bhāga* with *-tānaṁ* would make it clearer.

[2] Our MSS have *adho-gāmi*, but the variant *nādho yāti* is attested in various other editions and is followed by the commentary, as well as being corroborated in the next verse. *Adho-gāmi* if read as a compound with *nabho-jalam* and seen as an object of *badhnāti* would convey the same meaning.

[3]The *kapāla-kuhara* is the soft palate, i.e., the depression in the roof of the mouth above the root of the tongue. *Khecarī* consists of turning the tongue backwards, letting its tip enter this center and fixing the gaze between the eyebrows. The *candra-kalāmṛta* is the secretion from the *viśuddha-cakra* in the throat and appears to be identified with this *kapāla-kuhara*. If this is not allowed to flow down to the digestive fire in the navel region, the yogi becomes immortal within a month (See 1.64 below, HYP 3.44-45). It may be said that the intricacies of meditative points and actions within the mouth are centered around the production of saliva. The throat lock increases its production, prevents its flow

He next describes the characteristics [and results] of *jālandhara-bandha*—

jālandhare kṛte bandhe kaṇṭha-saṁkoca-lakṣaṇe |
pīyūṣaṁ na pataty agnau na ca vāyuḥ prakupyati ||63||

1.63. In the practice of *jālandhara-bandha*, characterized by the constriction of the throat, the ambrosia does not fall into the fire and the air is not disturbed.

Constriction of the throat [here] means obstructing the movement of air. That action which is so characterized is the *jālandhara-bandha*, on doing which the ambrosia, namely the nectar of the half moon (*candra-kalāmṛta*), does not fall into the fire in the form of the sun and the air is not disturbed, meaning that it does not move outward.

[Gorakṣa] now describes the characteristics and benefits of the *khecarī-mudrā* over the next thirteen verses—

kapāla-kuhare jihvā praviṣṭā viparītagā |
bhruvor antar-gatā dṛṣṭiḥ mudrā bhavati khecarī ||64||

1.64. When the tongue is reversed and placed in the hollow of the skull [i.e., the soft palate] and the gaze is fixed between the eyebrows, then that is called the *khecarī-mudrā*.

The tongue is reversed and enters the hollow of the skull, by which is meant the recess just above the uvula. The gaze should be

---

into the esophagus and results in its absorption within the mouth itself. This process will be elaborated in the discussion of *viparīta-karaṇī* in the second half of this work (Cf. 2.30-49).

directed, fixed and motionless, to the spot between the eyebrows. This is the *khecarī-mudrā.*

The benefits of performing *khecarī-mudrā* are described over the next six verses.

na rogo maraṇaṁ tasya na nidrā na kṣudhā tṛṣā |
na ca mūrcchā bhavet tasya yo mudrāṁ vetti khecarīm ||65||

1.65. He who knows the *khecarī-mudrā* does not experience disease, death, nor sleep, hunger, thirst, or fainting.

The yogi who knows the *khecarī-mudrā,* whose characteristics have been given above, is one who has long practiced it. Such a yogi does not experience disease from a disturbance of the humors, nor death, i.e., the particular situation produced from the life airs leaving the body. Sleep and fainting, hunger and thirst are other particular conditions, none of which are possible for him.

pīḍyate na sa śokena lipyate na sa karmaṇā |
bādhyate na sa kālena yo mudrāṁ vetti khecarīm ||66||

1.66. He who knows the *khecarī-mudrā* is not troubled by grief, tainted by actions [or karma], or bound by time.

The yogi who knows the *khecarī-mudrā*, the characteristics of which have been given above, who performs it according to the instructions given him by his preceptor, is not troubled by grief. Being above the creation of the illusory energy Māyā, he is not tainted by his actions or by their resulting happiness and distress. He is not touched even by time, which puts an end to this universe.

Now [the author] breaks down the word *khecarī* into its constituent parts [to explain its meaning]—

cittaṁ carati khe yasmāt jihvā carati khe gatā |
tenaiva khecarī-mudrā sarva-siddhair namaskṛtā ||67||

1.67. Because the mind (*citta*) roams in space (*khe*), and the tongue roams in space, for this reason alone this *mudrā* is known as "the sky roamer" (*khe-carī*) and is venerated by the perfected beings (*siddhas*).

Because, i.e., due to this cause, the mind or inner organ that is absorbed and fixed in Brahman, roams in space, i.e., in the void; [and] the tongue roams in the space, meaning in the sky.[1] Or the verb *carati* can here have the sense "to drink" as well as "to go," so by drinking the moon-nectar, one's inner organ (*antaḥ-karaṇa*) terminates any relationship it had with the sense objects. For these reasons, the *khecarī-mudrā* is revered or worshiped even by all the *siddhas*.

bindu-mūlaṁ śarīraṁ tu śirās tatra pratiṣṭhitāḥ |
bhāvayanti śarīraṁ yā hy āpāda-tala-mastakam ||68||

1.68. The *bindu* (semen) is the root of the body, in which are established the channels [nerves] that enliven the body from the soles of the feet to the top of the head.

In the body, the *bindu* is the root, meaning its cause; thus the body is said to have the *bindu* as its root, meaning that it is preserved by the *bindu* alone. What does that mean? In answer to this [Gorakṣa]

[1]The word *kha* ("space") means aperture or cavity. The explanation in the commentary, as *ākāśa*, does not seem to be sufficiently clear, since the aperture meant is clearly the *kapāla-kuhara*, which is somewhat ambiguous and potentially refering to several vital locations.

says that it is because the nerve-channels (*śirāḥ*) enliven the body from the soles of the feet to the top of the head, that is, they give life to the body by sprinkling the *bindu* throughout it. [In this way] those nerve conduits are established in the *bindu*, so for that reason the *bindu* is the root or basis of the body.[1]

khecaryā mudritaṁ yena vivaraṁ lambikordhvataḥ |
na tasya kṣarate binduḥ kāminyāliṅgitasya ca ||69||

1.69. The *bindu* of one who has sealed the cavity above the uvula by means of the *khecarī-mudrā* does not flow out, even though he may be embraced by a desirable woman.

And so, that yogi who seals or blocks off the cavity or hole in the throat pipe above the uvula, i.e., in the throat above the uvula, by means of the *khecarī-mudrā*, such a yogi's semen (*bindu*) does not flow out, is not spilled, even if he is embraced by a desirable woman.

It was said that the semen does not flow out. Should someone query, "What is the point of that?" [Gorakṣa] answers:

yāvad binduḥ sthito dehe tāvan mṛtyu-bhayaṁ kutaḥ |
yāvad baddhā nabho-mudrā tāvad bindur na gacchati ||70||

1.70. Where is the fear of death while the *bindu* remains within the body? And for as long as one maintains the sky seal (*nabho-mudrā*), the *bindu* is not lost.

[1]The word *tatra* ("there") is somewhat vague here and could refer to either the body or to the *bindu*.

For the duration of time that the *bindu* remains situated in the body, for that duration of time, where is there any fear of death? The meaning is that there is none. The place of the *bindu* is above the *vyoma-cakra.*[1] The intent is that time does not reach that spot. For how long will the *bindu* remain stable? The answer is given in the second line of the verse: For the duration of time that the "sky seal" (*nabho-mudrā*) or *khecarī-mudrā* is held, for that duration the *bindu* will not go, i.e., it will not flow out.

***calito'pi yadā binduḥ saṁprāptaś ca hutāśanam*[2] |**
***vrajaty ūrdhvaṁ hataḥ śaktyā niruddho yoni-mudrayā* ||71||**

1.71. Even when the *bindu* moves and reaches the fire, being impeded by the *śakti* and restrained by the *yoni-mudrā*, it turns back up again.

When, i.e., at any time, even if the *bindu* moves and reaches the fire, namely the *sūrya-maṇḍala*, in that very instant it is impeded by the *śakti,* which has been raised from its own place and is moving upward. Then it is restrained and held firmly in place by the *yoni-mudrā.*[3] This is the meaning.

---

[1] Or *ākāśa-cakra.* In the classification of nine cakras found in the *Siddha-siddhānta-paddhati*, it is located at the highest point in the *sahasrāra.* (See SSP 2.9, Banerjea, 180-181.) In HYP 3.35 and 4.45, the *vyoma-cakra* is specifically connected to *khecarī*. However, 2.73 here makes clear that this is the *ājñā-cakra.*

[2]The HYP 3.43 reading here is *yoni-maṇḍalam,* which Brahmānanda glosses as *yoni-sthānam.* Gharote and Devnath explain *hutāśanam* ("fire") as the pelvic region, obviously intending the genital itself. (*Haṭha-pradīpikā*, 5.66, page 107). If by the *bindu* the gross physical ejaculate is meant, the fire is doubtless the *kālāgni* in the *yoni.* If it is the nectar flowing from the *viśuddha-cakra*, then it is likely the fire of digestion. It seems to me the context here clearly intends the former interpretation, but a further elaboration of the relation of the two *bindus* will be given in the next few verses.

[3] Our commentator does not elaborate on *yoni-mudrā* here. Brahmānanda glosses *yoni-mudrā* in this verse (as found in HYP 3.43) .as being synonymous with *vajroli* (*yoni-mudrayā meḍhrākuñcana-rūpayā. etena vajrolī mudrā sūcitā*). A full description of what later texts call *yoni-mudrā* can be found in *Gheraṇḍa-saṁhitā*, 3.38-48, according to which the particular practice described in 2.16 below can

The subdivisions of the *bindu* are now given.

sa punar dvividho binduḥ pāṇḍuro lohitas tathā |
pāṇḍuraṁ śukram ity āhur lohitākhyaṁ mahā-rajaḥ ||72||

1.72. Again, the *bindu* is of two kinds: one white, the other red. The white one is called semen (*śukra*), while the one named red is "the great dust" [particle, powder] (*mahā-rajas*).[1]

That *bindu* is of two kinds, one being white, the other red. Of the two, the white one is called semen (*śukra*); the [other] is named the "great dust," which means it has the appearance of a woman's menstrual fluid.

[Gorakṣa] now shows the location of the two *bindus*.

sindūra-drava-saṁkāśaṁ ravi-sthāne sthitaṁ rajaḥ |
śaśi-sthāne sthito binduḥ tayor aikyaṁ sudurlabham ||73||

---

be identified as the same. Though *vajrolī* may be the intent here, it seems more likely that simply the *mūla-bandha* or *bandha-traya* is intended here, where *yoni* refers to the *yoni-sthāna* and the *śakti-cālana* exercises. This *yoni-mudrā* is described in *Śiva-saṁhitā* 4.42, where it is clear that if one can unite the *prāṇa* and *apāna vāyus* while performing the *mūla-bandha*, then that is *yoni-mudrā: apāna-prāṇayor aikyaṁ prakaroty adhikalpitam | bandhenānena sutarāṁ yoni-mudrā prasiddhyati* ||.

[1]Feuerstein: "White *śukra* is the male semen and the red *mahā-rajas* refers to the female vaginal secretion, which is sometimes misunderstood as menstrual blood or ova." Although this may be true, 1.73-74 clearly indicate that the two kinds of *bindu* are both present in the same, presumably male, body. Since one basic principle of the *haṭha-yoga* system outlined here and in works like *Siddha-siddhānta-paddhati* is that the individual body is a self-contained unit where correspondences to all phenomena in the universe can be found, it is necessary to understand *śukra* and *rajas* in another way. See Feuerstein's own comment to 1.73, given below.

1.73. The *rajas* is situated in the place of the sun and resembles liquid vermilion.[1] The [*śukra*] *bindu* is located at the place of the moon. The union of the two is extremely rare.[2]

Liquid vermilion comes of mixing red lead with oil, etc. Resembling it in having the same color is the *bindu* in the form of *rajas*. It is situated in the place of the sun, namely in the region of the navel.[3] The *śukra-bindu* is situated in the region of the moon, i.e., the sixteen-spoked wheel [of the *viśuddha-cakra*]. The unification of these two is possible by the means that will be described further on, but is nevertheless very rarely achieved. The benefits of doing so will also be spoken of further on.

Now [Gorakṣa] gives evidence that the statement by which the world is simply the combination of Śiva and Śakti is true:

binduḥ śivo rajaḥ śaktir bindur indū rajo raviḥ |
ubhayoḥ saṅgamād eva prāpyate paramaṁ padam ||74||

1.74. The *bindu* is Śiva, *rajas* Śakti. The *bindu* is the moon, *rajas* the sun. Only through the union of both [*bindu* and *rajas*] is the supreme state attained.

The *bindu*, here meaning the white *bindu* as previously described, is Śiva. The *rajas* is a portion of Śakti. Moreover, that *bindu* is the

---

[1] *Sindūra*, which is the red unguent placed by married women in the part of their hair to indicate that they are married and the husband is alive.

[2] Feuerstein. "It is clear from this stanza that, from a yogic perspective, the *bindu* represents more than the sperm produced in the testicles, just as the *rajas* stands for more than the female genital secretion. Both have their energetic aspects as well. Thus the *rajas* is associated with the solar element in the abdomen and the *bindu* with the lunar element in the head."

[3] See Verses 2.32 and 2.40. YK: "Here it stands for something in the navel region, presumably heat, which dries up the nectar flowing from the center above called *śaśi* (moon)."

moon, while *rajas* is the sun [*ravi* or *sūrya*]. By this it is also being indicated that the moon and sun are Śiva and Śakti respectively.[1] Therefore, in the discussion of the basic definition of *haṭha-yoga*, where it is said that the union of sun and moon, of the *prāṇa* and *apāna*, or of the individual soul and the Supreme Soul (*jīvātma-paramātmanoḥ*), it should be taken that these are all intended as synonyms for one another.[2] Through the unification of these the supreme state is attained.

The means (*upaprāpakaṁ*) and benefits of the union of *bindu* and *rajas* will now be stated:

vāyunā śakti-cāreṇa preritaṁ tu yadā rajaḥ |
yāti bindoḥ sahaikatvaṁ bhaved divyaṁ vapus tadā ||75||[3]

---

[1]There is some confusion here, as *piṅgalā* and *iḍā* are invariably identified with the sun and moon, respectively, the opposite of what is stated here. Swami Satyananda Saraswati writes, " *Piṅgalā* can be defined as the dynamic, active, masculine, positive, yang energy within our personality. It has a physical and mental side. Its material qualities are light, heat, solar, energy accumulating, creative, organizing, focused (centripetal) and contractive. The positive, dynamic mental side within Freud's system is Eros, the pleasure principle, and in Jung's system, it is the conscious personality, the rational, discriminating side. We can say that *piṅgalā* is psychosomatic energy, outwardly directed, mind acting on body to motivate the organs of action, the *karmendriyas*. It is the basic energy of life." *Kundalini Tantra* (Bihar: Yoga Publications Trust, 2007), 333.

[2] See infra 2.85-86, HYP 4.7. Interestingly, YT's use of the expression *haṭha-yoga-prakaraṇe*, implicitly identifies *haṭha-yoga* with *samādhi*, rather than as a means to *rāja-yoga*, as found in HYP 1.1-2, 1.67, 2.76, 4.79, etc. *ha-kāraḥ kīrtitaḥ sūryaṣ ṭha-kāraś candra ucyate | sūrya-candramasor yogād haṭha-yogo nigadyate ||* [SSP 1.69]; *yo'pāna-prāṇayor aikyaṁ sva-rajo-retasos tathā | sūryācandramasor yogo jīvātma-paramātmanoḥ || evaṁ tu dvandva-jālasya saṁyogo yoga ucyate |* [*Yoga-śikhopaniṣad* 68]

[3] Other readings of this verse:

vāyunā śakti-cālena preritaṁ khe yathā rajaḥ |
raviṇaikatvam āyāti bhaved divyaṁ vapus tadā | [*Dhyāna-bindūpaniṣad* 89]

This reading seems contrary to the principles described.

vāyunā śakti-cālena preritaṁ khe yadā rajaḥ |
bindor ekatvam āyāti yo jānāti sa yogavit || [*Viveka-mārtaṇḍa* 57]

1.75. When the *rajas* is impelled through the activation of the [*kuṇḍalinī*] *śakti* by means of the *prāṇa*, it then achieves oneness with the *bindu*. At that time, the body becomes divine.

Śakti-cāra should here be understood as synonymous with *śakti-cālana*. That which causes the *śakti* to be activated is called *śakti-cāra*. By that wind (*vāyu*) which activates the *śakti*, the *rajaḥ*, that is to say the menstrual blood, is impelled or raised upward whereby it enters into permanent union with the *bindu*. In other words, the two achieve a state of equilibrium.[1] At that time, the body becomes divine, meaning that it cannot be burned or cut, and it is free from [the signs of old age like] wrinkles or graying hair.[2]

Moreover,

śukraṁ candreṇa saṁyuktaṁ rajaḥ sūryeṇa saṁyutam |
tayoḥ sama-rasaikatvaṁ yo jānāti sa yogavit ||76||

1.76. The śukra is joined with the moon, the rajas linked with the sun. He who knows their union in equilibrium[3] is a knower of yoga.

---

[1] Which is synonymous with *samādhi*. Cf. 2.86 = HYP 4.6.

yadā saṁkṣīyate prāṇo mānasaṁ ca pralīyate |
tadā samarasatvaṁ ca samādhir abhidhīyate ||

[2]Feuerstein: "The creation of a divine body (*divya-deha*), which is endowed with all the great paranormal powers, is the avowed goal of *haṭha-yoga*. This stanza briefly mentions the esoteric process by which this is accomplished." This statement is not borne out by the rest of the text, which though glorifying the health benefits of its various practices is concerned primarily with the goal of liberation. The sacralized body is only the means to that goal.

[3]I have come across the following translations: harmony, equality, balance, etc. *Yoga-koṣa* has, in reference to this verse: "the all-merged-into-one-state." YK goes on: "In the state of *samadhi*, according to this text, neither is *prāṇa* active in any sense, nor is there any *citta-vṛtti* (consciousness). Ātmā and ātmā alone is there. Everything has disappeared in the ātmā." Feuerstein."The phrase *samarasa-*

The semen (*śukra*) in the form of the *bindu* is joined with the moon, i.e., it is situated together with it; and the *rajaḥ* is joined with the sun, situated together with it. One who knows the oneness in equilibrium of *bindu* and *rajaḥ*, which are situated in the forms of the moon and sun respectively, is a knower of yoga, since the union of these two is the very definition of yoga.

This is the end of the section on *khecarī-mudrā*.

[The author] now begins the section on *mahā-mudrā*, starting by describing its benefits:

śodhanaṁ nāḍi-jālasya cālanaṁ candra-sūryayoḥ |
rasānāṁ śoṣaṇaṁ caiva mahā-mudrābhidhīyate ||77||

1.77. The purification of the net of channels, the arousing of the sun and moon, as well as the drying up of the juices, is called *mahā-mudrā*.

The purification of the net of channels, i.e., the expansion of all the channels or *nāḍis*, means the removal of all the humors such as wind and bile.[1] The arousal of sun and moon here means their unification. The drying up of the juices refers to the destruction of those juices that result from the food and drink one is digesting [i.e., chyle]. That *mudrā* by which all these results pertain is called *mahā-mudrā*.

---

ekatva, here translated as "coessential unity," refers to the mingling of the energetic aspects of the two types of semen, male and female. *Sama-rasa* is an important notion in Tantrism and *haṭha-yoga*. It stands for the realization of the fundamental identity of all differentiated things, that is, non-duality in duality."

[1]Since the practice of this *mudrā* causes the body to twist, it favors either the left or right nostril, i.e., the one opposite to the outstretched leg. Thus the posture is naturally accompanied by *nāḍi-śodhana* breathing. See next note.

[Gorakṣa] now describes the features of this *mahā-mudrā*:

vakṣo-nyasta-hanuḥ prapīḍya suciraṁ yoniṁ ca vāmāṅghriṇā
hastābhyām anudhārayan prasaritaṁ pādaṁ tathā dakṣiṇam |
āpūrya śvasanena kukṣi-yugalaṁ baddhvā śanai recayed
eṣā vyādhi-vināśinī sumahatī mudrā nṛṇāṁ kathyate ||78||

1.78. Placing the chin on the chest, pressing intently the perineum with the left foot, and taking hold of the extended right foot with both hands, one should fill both sides of the abdomen,[1] hold the position and then exhale. This disease-destroying seal is called the "great seal" or *mahā-mudrā.*

The yogi places his chin on the chest, with his left foot, i.e., the heel of the left foot, he presses firmly against the *yoni* (the perineum) as previously noted. Then taking hold of the extended right foot with both hands, he fills both sides of the abdomen with the breath, i.e., with the *prāṇa*. He should then hold the position, i.e., hold the breath, and then slowly exhale. This position is the most glorious *mudrā* which destroys all the diseases of mankind.

The procedure for conducting this practice is further described:

candrāṁśena samabhyasya sūryāṁśenābhyaset punaḥ |
yāvat tulyā bhavet saṅkhyā tato mudrāṁ visarjayet ||79||

---

[1]In practicing this *mudrā*, the breath naturally fills one side of the chest and abdomen more than the other. In general, all yoga positions that are practiced on two sides are accompanied by a breath awareness that is dominated by one or the other nostril. This is the import of the words *candra* and *sūrya* in this description. In general, it may be stated that whatever locks or seals, breathing practices, etc., can be practiced with a particular bodily posture, should be. So this *mudrā* includes within it a kind of *nāḍi-śodhana* exercise. Thus the instruction to equalize the two sides.

1.79. After practicing with the lunar part, one should again practice it with the solar part. He should discontinue [practice of] this seal when the count is equal.

One should first practice this *mahā-mudrā* on the moon part and when completed, then practice on the sun side. The lunar part means on the left and solar part the right side. One should continue this practice as long as the measure of time is equal, i.e., on both the left and right sides. After this one should give up the practice of the *mudrā,* meaning it is no longer necessary to practice on a daily basis.[1]

The benefits of the *mahā-mudrā* are explained over the next three verses:

na hi pathyam apathyaṁ vā rasāḥ sarve'pi nīrasāḥ |
api bhuktaṁ viṣaṁ ghoraṁ pīyūṣam iva jīryati ||80||

1.80. There is no prescribed or forbidden diet. All tastes are indeed without taste. Even deadly poison, if consumed, is digested as though it were ambrosia.

When this *mahā-mudrā* is practised, there is no need to consider whether foods are wholesome or unwholesome. All the tastes such as bitter, sour, salty, etc., are without taste, meaning that they are unable to affect the eater with their respective virtues and flaws. Even if deadly poison or other things are consumed, they will be digested; that is, they will be unable to produce madness or other

[1]In later *haṭha-yoga* texts it becomes clear that once a particular technique has been mastered, it can be discontinued as a regular practice, since its benefits will be more or less permanent and can be accessed quickly by a lesser effort when needed. This is what is meant when it is said that after one or two months of cultivating a particular technique one should attain mastery of it, after which one can proceed to other practices or combining techniques.

ill effects, but like ambrosia will be assimilated and become favorable to the health of the body. What to speak, then, of other, beneficial foods?

Therefore, since the digestive fluids become favorable, diseases like tuberculosis and leprosy are cured [by performing *mahā-mudrā*]:

kṣaya-kuṣṭha-gudāvarta-gulmājīrṇa-purogamāḥ |
rogās tasya kṣayaṁ yānti mahā-mudrāṁ ca yo'bhyaset ||*81*||

1.81. For one who practices the *mahā-mudrā*, all diseases are eliminated, notably tuberculosis, leprosy, constipation, enlargement of the spleen and improper digestion.

For the yogī who practices *mahā-mudrā*, all diseases such as tuberculosis, leprosy, constipation, enlargement of the spleen, and indigestion are eliminated or destroyed.

[The author] now concludes [the section on *mahā-mudrā*],

kathiteyaṁ mahā-mudrā mahā-siddhi-karī nṛṇām |
gopanīyā prayatnena na deyā yasya kasyacit ||82||

1.82. The *mahā-mudrā*, which has been described herein, is the cause of great success[1] for humanity. It should carefully be kept secret and not revealed to all and sundry.

Humanity here means those who are followers of the path (*upāsaka*). This *mahā-mudrā*, which brings humankind great success, has been described by me. It should be carefully kept

[1]The phrase *mahā-siddhi*, here rendered as "great success" should be understood to mean the great accomplishment of liberation and not, in this case, the paranormal powers traditionally associated with the yogis.

secret or protected, and not revealed to all and sundry, for it is agreed by all that "[*Haṭha-yoga*] is potent when kept secret and impotent when revealed" (*Haṭha-yoga-pradīpikā* 1.11). In other words, it should only be taught to those who are practitioners.

The Practice of Oṁkāra

Now for the next seven verses, [Gorakṣa] explains how one should practice chanting Om (*praṇava*) in order to destroy one's desires.

padmāsanaṁ samāruhya sama-kāya-śiro-dharaḥ |
nāsāgra-dṛṣṭir ekānte japed oṁkāram avyayam ||83||

1.83. One should recite the imperishable syllable Om in a secluded place, sitting in the lotus posture, holding the body and head balanced while gazing at the tip of the nose.[1]

In a secluded place, in a place where there are no people, one should properly enter the lotus posture as earlier described, and holding the body and head balanced, i.e., keeping the body and neck straight, and with the eyes fixed on the tip of the nose, chant *japa* of *praṇava*, the syllable Om.

What is the nature of the syllable Om that one should chant? In answer, [Gorakṣa] says—

bhūr bhuvaḥ svar ime lokāḥ soma-sūryāgni-devatāḥ |
yasya mātrāsu tiṣṭhanti tat paraṁ jyotir om iti ||84||

1.84. The supreme light in whose constituent parts abide these upper, middle and lower realms [*bhūḥ*,

[1]Compare 2.63, *dhyāna-mudrā*. Meditation with the eyes open and focusing on the tip of the nose is one of the features of the Nātha-yoga path.

bhuvaḥ, svaḥ] and the moon, sun and fire deities reside, is known as Om.

In the constituent parts of this *omkara*, namely the letters *a, u,* and *m*, the worlds known as *bhūr-loka*, *bhuvar-loka*, and *svar-loka*, as well as the moon, sun and fire deities respectively reside. Om is the supreme light, namely that resplendant light of consciousness that is the supreme cause, that is to say, its seed form.

trayaḥ kālās trayo vedāḥ trayo lokās trayaḥ svarāḥ |
trayo devāḥ sthitā yatra tat paraṁ jyotir om iti ||85||

1.85. That supreme light in which are situated the three times, the three Vedas, the three worlds (*lokas*), the three intonations (*svara*), and the three gods is known as Om.

How further is that Om-syllable described? The three times are past, present and future; the three Vedas are the Ṛk, Yajur and Sāma-vedas; "the three *lokas*" refers either to the three kinds of creatures, namely those born of perspiration, those born of eggs and those born from a womb, [in which case] the fourth category, namely those growing from seeds like plants and trees are included within the womb-born category.[1] Or alternatively the three lokas are *svarga* (heaven), *martya* (the world of death, i.e, the world of humans), and *pātāla* (the lower regions). The three intonations (*svara*) [three ways of accenting Vedic mantras] are *udātta, anudātta* and *svarita*. And the three deities are Brahmā, Viṣṇu and Rudra. These sets of three are present respectively in the component sounds of the omkāra—*a*, *u*, and *m*. Om is the form of

[1]There are usually four kinds of creature categorized according to their method of taking birth, not three: *catur-vidhā jarāyujāṇḍaja-svedajodbhijja-rūpeṇa* (Śrīdhara to *Bhāgavata-purāṇa* 2.10.39). Cf. *Manu-smṛti* 1.43-46.

supreme light, the seed mantra. The conclusion is that one should chant Om.

kriyā icchā tathā jñānaṁ brāhmī raudrī ca vaiṣṇavī |
tridhā śakti sthitā yatra tat paraṁ jyotir om iti ||86||

1.86. That supreme light, wherein is situated the threefold power (*śakti*) as action, will and wisdom, associated with Brahmā, Rudra, and Viṣṇu [respectively], is Om.

Again, how is that Om-syllable to be described? It is the *praṇava* in which the threefold *śakti*, namely the Brāhmī, Vaiṣṇavī and Raudrī, differentiated according to the division of action, will and wisdom,[1] are situated in its component parts *a-u-m*, respectively. That Om is the supreme light.[2]

a-kāraś ca u-kāraś ca ma-kāro bindu-saṁjñakaḥ |
tridhā mātrā sthitā yatra tat paraṁ jyotir om iti ||87||

1.87. That supreme light, wherein abide the three *mātrās*, namely the component sounds *a, u*, and *ma*, which is known as the *bindu*, is Om.

Again, how is that Om-syllable to be described? That light in which reside the three types of *mātrā*, the syllables *a, u*, and *ma*, which is also called the *bindu*, is the seed syllable Om, which has the form of supreme light.

---

[1]See *Śvetāśvatara Upaniṣad* 6.8: *parāsya śaktir vividhaiva śrūyate svābhāvikī jñāna-bala-kriyā ca ||*

[2]Feuerstein. "The feminine aspect of the Divine, epitomized in the term *śakti* is thought to comprise the three functions of creative action (*kriyā*), creative will (*icchā*) and creative wisdom (*jñāna*). These are also refered to by the adjectival forms of the three great deities, Brahmā, Rudra and Viṣṇu."

Furthermore,

vacasā taj japed bījaṁ vapuṣā tat samabhyaset |
manasā tat smaren nityaṁ tat paraṁ jyotir om iti ||88||

1.88. With one's voice, one should always do *japa* of that supreme light Om, the seed (*bīja*); one should practice it with the body and remember it with the mind.

With one's voice one should do japa of that *praṇava* alone, meditating on it as the seed (*bīja*), i.e., the cause of the entire universal manifestation. Its being the cause [is explained as follows]: From *praṇava* come the seven utterances[1] [i.e., the names of the seven regions, *bhūḥ, bhuvaḥ, svaḥ, mahaḥ, janaḥ, tapaḥ, satyam*]; from the seven utterances arises the Gāyatrī, from Gāyatrī comes Sāvitrī and from Sāvitrī comes Sarasvatī.[2] From Sarasvatī arise the Vedas. From the Vedas Brahmā arises, and from Brahmā the worlds. This is stated in the Śruti (*tato lokāḥ pravartante*).

One should practice the *praṇava* with one's body. One should think of the *praṇava* as Brahman with attributes and endowed with the power of action (*kriyā*). Then in a way that is conducive to this understanding of the mantra, one should remain with the body positioned in the *siddhāsana* or some other *āsana*. Action, will and wisdom were mentioned in the previous verse, so *kriyā* or action

[1]The *sapta vyāhṛti* refers to utterance of the names of the seven lokas of which *bhūḥ, bhuvaḥ,* and *svaḥ* are the first three. In general, when chanting the Gāyatrī mantra one only recites the first three, but in more elaborate practices, especially where *prāṇāyāma* is prescribed, the full seven *vyāhṛtis* and another sacred phrase, the *Gāyatrī-śiraḥ* (*om āpo jyotī raso'mṛtaṁ brahma bhūr bhuvaḥ suvarom*), are added to the basic mantra. Cf. *Encyclopedia of Hinduism* by Swami Harshananda, Vol. I, p. 633-634.

[2]From *Devī-bhāgavata* 12.3: The goddess Gāyatrī has three aspects: As Gāyatrī she is the feminine counterpart of Brahmā and associated with the morning sun; Sāvitrī is associated with Viṣṇu and the midday sun; Sarasvatī with Rudra and the evening sun. They are also associated with the Ṛk, Sāma and Yajur Vedas respectively. *Encyclopedia of Hinduism* by Swami Harshananda, Vol. 1, p. 632.

has been accepted as a component of the *praṇava*. Thus it is clear that any actions or practices that are favorable to the chanting of Om are also considered a part of the practice of Om.

With the mind, one should always remember that very light in the form of the Supreme Brahman, that self-effulgent consciousness that is the resting place (*adhiṣṭhāna*) of the three worlds, the three times, the moon, sun and fire deities, the three Vedas, the three gods Brahmā, Viṣṇu and Rudra, and the three energies of action, will and wisdom, and not to allow any other desires to enter the mind, but whenever encountering any object from the phenomenal universe, whether gross or subtle, should remember the self-revealed and all-pervading consciousness that is indicated by the *praṇava* syllable. This is the purport of this entire section.

[Gorakṣa] now explains the benefits of the *japa* of *praṇava*.

śucir vāpy aśucir vā'pi yo japet praṇavaṁ sadā |
na sa lipyate pāpena padma-patram ivāṁbhasā ||89||

1.89. Whether pure or impure, one who always does the *japa* of *praṇava* is not affected by sin, any more than a lotus leaf [is made wet] by water.

Pure means one who is cleansed both internally and externally; impure is one who has not undergone such purifications. Any such person who constantly chants the *praṇava* seed mantra as described earlier, while also meditating on its significations, meaning that he repeatedly establishes the *praṇava* in consciousness, for as Patañjali says, "[*Praṇava*] should be recited and its meaning contemplated" (YS 1.28).

Such a yogi is not affected by sins, meaning that he does not have any relation to the destiny resulting from engaging in acts that are either forbidden or not forbidden [by scripture or by society]. How does that happen, and to what can it be compared? Just as the lotus leaf floating on the water is not affected or touched by the water, it is like that.

In this verse, the word "sin" is indicative of both sin and piety, since by practice of *praṇava*, whose brilliant light is immediately reflected on the practitioner, the sin that is a product of ignorance is destroyed. In the same way, since piety is also a product of ignorance, it is only appropriate that it too should be destroyed by practice of the *praṇava-japa*. This is the intended meaning.

In Praise of Prāṇāyāma

In the next four verses, [Gorakṣa] praises the control of the breath.

cale vāte caled bindur niścale niścalo bhavet |
yogī sthāṇutvam āpnoti tato vāyuṁ nirodhayet ||*90*||

1.90. When the air moves, the *bindu*[1] moves; when it is still, [the *bindu* will also be] still. A yogi attains pillar-like motionlessness (*sthāṇutva*), [therefore] he should restrain the air.

When the air, namely the life air, moves, that is to say when the action of inhalation and exhalation are going on, then the *bindu*, which was described earlier as the semen, also becomes activated. When the life air is motionless, i.e., when it is inactive or still, then the *bindu* also becomes motionless or steady. When that happens, the person restraining the breath attains pillar-like motionlessness, meaning that he is able to tolerate opposites like heat and cold and sustain his yoga practice over a long period of time. For that reason the yogi should restrain the life-air.

---

[1]Alternative readings of this verse found in other sources include *sarvam* ("everything" VM 71) and *cittam* ("mind" HYP 2.2).

Moreover,

yāvad vāyuḥ sthito dehe tāvaj jīvanam ucyate |
maraṇaṁ tasya niṣkrāntis tato vāyuṁ nirodhayet ||91||

1.91. One remains alive for as long as the air remains in the body.[1] Death is the departure [of the breath]. Therefore one should control the air.

For the duration of time that the air or life air (*prāṇa*) is present within the body, either in the form of attachment to the activity of inhaling and exhaling, or by being held within the body in *kumbhaka*, for that duration one is said to be alive.[2] When the life air departs or goes out of the body, that is called death. Thus life and death are dependent on the life air, and so one should definitely control it.

Moreover,

yāvad baddho marud dehe yāvac cittaṁ nirāmayam |
yāvad dṛṣṭir bhruvor madhye tāvat kālād bhayaṁ kutaḥ ||92||

1.92.For as long as the wind is captured within the body, for as long as the mind is free of ills, and for as long as the gaze [is held] between the eyebrows, whence [will arise] the fear of time?

---

[1]A variant here: *tāvaj jīvaṁ na muñcati* "it does not release the fragmented consciousness " (GP). Feuerstein's translation suits the version of YCU 90: *tāvaj jīvo na mucyate.* The GP vaṛiant does not have a significant difference of meaning from our YT version.

[2]Likely a reference to the yoga tradition that each person has a fixed number of breaths allocated to him or her. Thus, one lives longer the more slowly one breathes. The restless monkey breathes at the rate of 32 times a minute, in contrast to man's average of 15 times. Elephant, tortoises, snakes, and some creatures that have a slower respiratory rate than humans have greater longevity. The giant tortoise, for instance, breathes only four times a minute but is said to live three hundred years.

For as long as the wind, i.e., the life air, is captured within the body, either engaged in the activity of breathing in and out as explained in the previous verse or being held in *kumbhaka*, and for as long as the mind is free of ills, ills here being the mental absorption in any functions other than those connected to one's own spiritual purpose, and the mind being free of ills or free from such [unwholesome] proclivities, and for as long as the gaze is held fixed between the eyebrows, for that duration, where is there any fear of Time in the form of death? What it means is that there is none whatsoever.

Here, it seems that the second quarter of the verse is superfluous, since the movements of the breath are the external manifestations of the mind, and both mind and breath follow the same rhythm. Nevertheless, it should be known that this [understanding] only truly applies if the mind does not seek out other objects. Even in cases where the mind does seek out other objects, if one performs *prāṇāyāma* then there is no obstacle to the mind's following the same rhythm [as the breath] and then the two become one. If this is done, the yogi is not bound by time.

[Gorakṣa] now gives evidence of this:

ataḥ kāla-bhayād brahmā prāṇāyāma-parāyaṇaḥ |
yogino munayaś caiva tato vāyuṁ niruddhayet ||93||

1.93. Thus, out of a fear of death, Brahmā is intent on breath control, as are the yogis and sages. Therefore one should restrain the wind.

Thus, for this reason, namely since both life and death are under the aegis of the breath, out of a fear of death, Lord Brahmā, yogis like Sanaka, and sages like Kaśyapa, as well as others fearful of death, all became intent on *prāṇāyāma*, i.e., they are all engaged in the practice of *prāṇāyāma*. Therefore, any other person who is fearful of death should also control the breath, i.e., engage in the practice of *prāṇāyāma*, in order to become free of old age and death.

Now he shows that the life air has the same form as the swan (*haṁsa*)—

> *ṣaṭtriṁśad-aṅgulo haṁsaḥ prayāṇaṁ kurute bahiḥ |*
> *vāma-dakṣiṇa-mārgeṇa tataḥ prāṇo'bhidhīyate ||94||*

1.94. The *haṁsa* departs (*prayāṇa*) thirty-six fingers outside through the left and right pathways. It is therefore called *prāṇa*.

Thirty-six fingers here means a distance of thirty-six fingers (approx. 64 cm.).[1] *Haṁ-sa* refers to the breath including both inhalation and exhalation (*prāṇa* and *apāna*). The left and right pathways refers to the *iḍā* and *piṅgalā* channels. "Departs outside" means the exhalation. Because it engages in the activity of going out it [expiration] is given the name *prāṇa*.[2] In this way, the *prāṇa* and *apāna* together take the form of the *haṁsa*. The intent is that one should not fall into error and think that the *haṁsa* is something else.[3]

---

[1]The breath is measured by the distance from the nostrils that it can be perceived by the touch. Whether this is what is meant here is not clear. Generally speaking, when one engages in vigorous activity the breath becomes more forceful and when meditative, especially when one attains the stage *kevala-kumbhaka*, it becomes completely imperceptible. Even if we think of this as a measure of time/distance, the normal breath indicated by *haṁsa* (i.e., 15 times in a minute) would certainly not be of this duration. Unfortunately our commentary is not helpful here.

[2]A more usual etymological definition understands the prefix *pra* a meaning "[going] forth" and the verb root *an*, "to breath"; i.e., "breathing forth."

[3]Since the word *prāṇa* is here being defined as "that which goes out," whereas previously we have known it only as the inhalation, the clarification is being made that here both the inhalation and exhalation are being included.

śuddhim eti yadā sarvaṁ nāḍi-cakraṁ malākulam |
tadaiva jāyate yogī prāṇa-saṅgrahaṇe kṣamaḥ ||95||

1.95. As soon as the entire circle of channels, afflicted by impurities, becomes cleansed, the yogi becomes capable of controlling (*saṁgrahaṇa*) the life force.

When the entire circle of channels (*nāḍi*), afflicted or permeated by impurities, is purified by means of the previously described methods of *nāḍi-śodhana*, they become cleansed and give up that web of impurities, at that very time, the yogī becomes capable of controlling or stilling the life breath. The meaning is that otherwise he will not be capable of preserving the *prāṇa*.

After glorifying *prāṇāyāma*, the author now describes its method [over the next twenty-two verses][1]:

baddha-padmāsano yogī prāṇaṁ candreṇa pūrayet |
dhārayitvā yathā-śaktir bhūyaḥ sūryeṇa recayet ||96||

1.96. The yogi should sit in the bound lotus posture and breathe in the life force through the moon and after holding it to his capacity, expel it again through the sun.

---

[1]This reference to 22 verses is found in the A MS only. It does not concur with the summary of contents found at the end of the commentary, nor with the actual contents themselves. The 22 verses also straddle the division of the work into two *śatakas*. The first verse of the second *śataka* is also introduced as being the first in a series of 21 verses describing *prāṇāyāma*. It would make more sense to understand this first version of *prāṇāyāma* to in fact be *nāḍi-śodhanam* in accordance with verse 1.95 and the header preceding it up to the concluding verse of the section, 1.101, which also glorifies *nāḍi-śodhanam*. *Nāḍi-śodhanam* is of course a kind of *prāṇāyāma*, and according to the account given here, the two processes are almost indistinguishable.

Out of fear of expanding the volume of the text, the proper seating cover has not been described, even though it is necessary [information]. The following verse from the *Nāradīya-purāṇa*[1] explains:

kuśaiś ca sumṛdubhiś chinnaiḥ pavitreṇātha carmaṇā |
tatropaviṣṭaḥ satataṁ yogāṅgāni samabhyaset ||

> One should sit on the ground covered with soft cut *kuśa* grass and a pure deerskin, one should constantly engage in the practice of the different limbs of yoga.

The *Yoga-sāra* also says that one should sit on a seat made of *kuśa* grass, a cloth and a [usually deer or tiger] skin.[2] Thus one should first spread the grass, the deerskin over it, and the cloth on top of that, then placing oneself on this seat one should sit in the bound lotus posture as earlier described, and then fill the lungs with air through the moon, namely the *iḍā* channel [the left nostril]. Then slowly, without forcing, after drawing the air in one should hold it in *kumbhaka* for as long as one can, then exhale through the sun or *piṅgalā* channel, i.e., the right nostril.

He now describes the meditation [the yogi should engage in] while practicing the *prāṇāyāma* through the *candra* path,

amṛtaṁ dadhi-saṁkāśaṁ go-kṣīra-dhavalopamam |
dhyātvā candramaso bimbaṁ prāṇāyāmī sukhī bhavet ||97||

[1]Not found in the extant edition.
[2]See also *Bhagavad-gītā* 6.11, *celājina-kuśottaram*. The tiger or deerskin is placed over the *kuśa* grass, and the cloth over that.

1.97. The practitioner of [this] *prāṇāyāma* becomes happy meditating on the disk of the moon, immortal, resembling yogurt, white like the milk of a cow.[1]

The person practicing *prāṇāyāma*, meditating on the circle of the moon, the form of immortal nectar, resembling yogurt, i.e., having the [white] color of yogurt, or [white] like the milk of a cow, should be happy, meaning that the transformation of his mental processes into the shapes of happiness will result in the constant experience of happiness.

Having described the practice on the lunar side, [Gorakṣa] now explains the practice on the solar side:

dakṣiṇe śvāsam ākṛṣya pūrayed udaraṁ śanaiḥ |
kuṁbhayitvā vidhānena punaś candreṇa recayet ||98||

1.98. Drawing in the breath (*śvāsa*) through the right [nostril], he gradually should fill the abdomen. Then retaining it in accordance with the rules, he should expel it again via the path of the moon.

The word "right" is in the locative case ("in the right [nostril]") and should be taken as an instrumental ("by [means of] the right [nostril]"). This reading will [then] follow the same syntax as *candreṇa* later in the verse. The right channel is called *piṅgalā* and through it one should slowly draw the air into the abdomen, without rushing. "According to the rules" (*vidhānena*) means the rules of measuring the length of the *kumbhaka*. One should hold the breath and then release the held breath through the moon, i.e., the left, channel named *iḍā*.

---

[1]The unnecessary repetition seems to indicate a deviation from the original reading. *Viveka-mārtaṇḍa* here has *amṛtodadhi-madhya-stham,* "Situated in an ocean of ambrosia," while the GP reads in the second quarter, *go-kṣīra-rajatopamam,*"white as cow's milk or silver."

He now explains the meditation that should accompany the *prāṇāyāma* of the solar portion—

prajvala-jvalana-jvālā-puñjam āditya-maṇḍalam |
dhyātvā nābhi-sthitaṁ yogī prāṇāyāmī sukhī bhavet ||99||

1.99. The yogi who is a practitioner of [this] *prāṇāyāma* becomes happy meditating on the *maṇḍala* of the sun, a mass of brightly burning flames located in the navel.

The yogi practicing this *prāṇāyāma* yogī should become happy by meditating on the orb or the sun (*āditya*) which is situated in the navel lotus like a mass of flames in a brightly burning fire, in other words, like a great fire.

[To summarize] These two verses are thus saying the following: First one should inhale the outside air through the *iḍā* channel for the length of time it takes to repeat the *praṇava* twelve times, according to any one of the basic (*adhama*), middle (*madhyama*) or advanced (*uttama*) durations,[1] then for sixteen *praṇava*s one should hold the breath in *kumbhaka*, and then fully empty the lungs in ten *praṇavas*. When doing this, one should meditate on the orb of the moon in the navel center as stated earlier. In the same way, one should then fill the lungs through the *piṅgalā* for the length of twelve *praṇavas*, hold for sixteen and then exhale for ten. And again, while holding the *kumbhaka* one should meditate on the sun-disk in the navel area.

Now [Gorakṣa] summarizes the contents of the four previous verses in one:

[1]See verse 2.5.

prāṇaṁ ced iḍayā pibet parimitaṁ bhūyo'nyayā recayet
pītvā piṅgalayā samīraṇam atho baddhvā tyajed vāmayā |
sūryācandramasor anena vidhinā bimba-dvayaṁ dhyāyatāṁ
śuddhā nāḍi-gaṇā bhavanti yamināṁ māsa-trayād ūrdhvataḥ ||100||

1.100. If one should drink in a measured amount of *prāṇa* through the *iḍā*, exhale it again through the other [nostril], then drinking the air in through the *piṅgalā*, he should, after holding it, release it again through the left. According to this rule, those who are self-controlled and meditate on the two disks of the sun and moon, will have purified [all] their channels after three months.

If one drinks in the life air (*prāṇa* or *samīraṇa* in this verse) in a measured amount, i.e., according to the measures of time that were described above, through the *iḍā* channel or left nostril, he should then hold it in *kumbhaka* for the requisite measure of time, and then slowly exhale through the other nostril, i.e., the *piṅgalā*, according to the correct measure. In other words, not through the same *iḍā* channel. Furthermore, when one drinks in the air according to the proper measure through the *piṅgalā*, he should similarly hold it in *kumbhaka* and then exhale through the left nostril. So, performing the *prāṇāyāma* according to this rule, after filling the lungs through the left channel when holding the breath in *kumbhaka*, one should meditate on the moon disk, and when holding it after the filling through right nostril on the sun disk; in this way meditating on the two orbs of the sun and moon, the channels of those those who are self-controlled yogis will become purified after three months.

The intent then is that there is no special necessity to go to the trouble of engaging in the six purificatory tasks (*ṣaṭ karma*)[1] for the

[1]Not discussed in this book. These six purificatory processes (*dhauti, basti, neti, nauli, trāṭaka* and *kapālabhāti*) are described in *Gheraṇḍa-saṁhitā* 1.12 and

sake of purifying the channels (*nāḍi-śodhana*), and when the three humors [*kapha* or phlegm, *pitta* or bile, and *vāta* or wind] are in balance, there is no necessity even for the *nāḍi-śodhana* exercises.

According to the Pāṇini *sūtra devatā-dvandve ca* [6.3.26], which follows on the *sūtra, ānaṅ-ṛto dvandve* [6.3.25], the term *dvandva* is carried over, [indicating that the same rule is being applied in both *sūtras*. The rule is that] when two words that are customarily related [such as mother-father, *mātā-pitarau*] are joined together in a *dvandva* compound, the final vowel in the first word is changed to *ā* [instead of remaining a short vowel, e.g., the *ṛ* in *mātṛ-pitarau*]. In the case of the gods, this rule is to apply only when the two gods in question are simultaneous recipients [of oblations] in a sacrifice, such as is the case of Mitra and Varuṇa (*mitrāvaruṇau*). However, in the case of the Sun and Moon, this does not apply, as they are never simultaneous recipients of any sacrificial offering. Therefore some people say that the compound *sūryācandramasoḥ*, as found in this verse, is a "usage of the seers" (*ārṣa-prayoga*). This is not the case, however, since the Sun and Moon are indeed customarily combined when speaking of establishing the time of the Darśapaurṇamāsī sacrifice [the fortnightly sacrifice performed on the new and full-moon days]; moreover, since the two are customarily combined in the minds of people throughout the world, there is really no obstacle to this usage. As stated in the *Gobhila-gṛhya-sūtra* (1.5.7), "When the distance of sun and moon (*sūryācandramasoḥ*) is at its greatest, that is called the full moon (*paurṇamāsī*), and when they are closest, that is called the new moon (*amāvāsyā*)." For more information on this subject one can consult the *Nirṇayāmṛta* where the question arises about the compound *āditya-candrau* and whether the word *āditya*, meaning "son of Aditi" and therefore synonymous with Indra, Upendra and

---

Hāṭha-yoga-pradīpikā 2.21ff. The latter verse (HYP 2.21) also states that there is no need for the six karmas for one whose humors are in equilibrium: *meda-śleṣmādhikaḥ pūrvaṁ ṣaṭ-karmāṇi samācaret | anyas tu nācaret tāni doṣāṇāṁ sama-bhāvataḥ ||*.

Aditi's other sons, cannot be used to establish the *tithi* of the full moon, etc., and is refuted. Let us now be done with these childish distractions.

[Gorakṣa] now shows the benefits of purifying the channels:

yatheṣṭaṁ dhāraṇam vāyor analasya pradīpanam |
nādābhivyaktir ārogyaṁ jāyate nāḍi-śodhanāt ||101||

1.101. [The benefits arising from] purifying the channels are the ability to hold the breath according to desire, the flaming up of the fire [of digestion], the manifestation of the subtle inner vibration (*nāda*), and freedom from disease.

After the purification of the channels one can retain the breath according to desire, i.e., for the length of time one wishes, meaning that there is beautification in the inner channel.[1]

"Flaming up of the fire" means that the fire of digestion is kindled. "The manifestation of the *nāda*" means that one hears the subtle inner vibration clearly. "Freedom from disease" means that the body is free from the obstacles created by the humors. All this results from the purification of the channels whereby one becomes qualified to take up the more advanced practices.

[1]I find the reading *antar-nāḍyāṁ śobhanam* doubtful, but no variants are given. I would expect *antar-nāḍyāḥ śodhanam*, "purification of the inner channel."

Gorakṣa-śatake dvitīya-śatakam

Prāṇāyāma

śrī-gaṇeśāya namaḥ |

maheśaṁ rameśaṁ dineśaṁ gaṇeśaṁ
pareśīṁ girīśāṁ guruṁ jñāna-mūrtim |
jhaṣendrādi-siddhān munīn kaśyapādīn
purīḥ satya-gaṅgādi-tīrthāni naumi ||

I bow down to Maheśa (Śiva), to Rameśa (Viṣṇu), to Dineśa (the Sun), to Gaṇeśa, to the Mother Goddess (Pareśī), to Girīśā (Pārvatī) and to my spiritual master, the embodiment of knowledge, to Matsyendranātha and all the Siddhas, to the sages like Kaśyapa, to the holy towns [like Haridvāra] and to the holy rivers like the Gaṅgā.

Thus, when the yogi has purified his breathing passages [through *nāḍi-śodhana*], has practiced the first three limbs of yoga, namely *yama, niyama* and *āsana*, has come to know the six *cakras*, the 16 *ādhāras* and so on, and is acquainted with all the *nāḍis* and the life airs that pass through them, then on an auspicious moment when the moon and stars are in a favorable alignment, he should have *pūjā* of the Guru,[1] Ganeśa and so on performed, along with auspicious chanting and blessings and so on, and then worship the guru and take his permission to begin the practice of *prāṇāyāma*.

---

[1] i.e. Gorakṣanātha, according to Mahīdhara Śāstrī, the translator of the Hindi GP.

[Gorakṣa] will now describe *prāṇāyāma* in twenty-one verses, beginning with a discussion of the different measures as well as of its characteristic signs and benefits—

prāṇo dehe sthito vāyur apānasya nirodhanāt ||
eka-śvasana-mātreṇodghāṭayed gagane gatim ||1||

2.1. The life force (*prāṇa*) remains in the body through the restraint of the *apāna*. By but a single breath, one may open the way into the sky.[1]

The air named *prāṇa* is situated in the body, it remains within the body through the restraint of the *apāna* air situated in the *mūlādhāra*. Restraint here means raising it upward. By such raising through only a single breath, or a single unit consisting of both inhalation and exhalation, one opens the way into the sky, i.e., the spiritual sky (*cid-ākāśa*) that is within the *suṣumṇā*. The meaning is that by opening the entrance to the *suṣumṇā*, which has been blocked by the *kuṇḍalinī*, one attains the pathway in the sky. This is possible in the state of *kumbhaka* when one has practiced *prāṇāyāma*.

[Gorakṣa now] begins the description of *prāṇāyāma*, as previously alluded to, by listing its subdivisions:

---

[1]There are important variants to this verse. Those found in *Viveka-mārtaṇḍa* (82) and the Lonavla edition (42) seem most appropriate if we consider this to be the beginning of a second century and of a new subject matter, that of *prāṇāyāma*, for both give an etymological definition of *prāṇāyāma*: "The *prāṇa* is the air in the body, and *āyāma* means its restraint. [Where] a measure is equivalent to a single breath, that yoga becomes [infinite] like the sky." (*prāṇo deha-sthito vāyur āyāmas tan-nibandhanam | eka-śvāsamayī mātrā tad yogo gaganāyate* ||) VM has the same first three quarters as L, but its last quarter is the same as the version given above. The word *mātrā* in these variants is problematic, however, since the breath itself is being measured and cannot be the measure itself. See next verse and note.

recakaḥ pūrakaś caiva kuṁbhakaḥ praṇavātmakaḥ |
prāṇāyāmo bhavet tredhā mātrā-dvādaśa-saṁyutaḥ ||2||

2.2. The threefold breath control [consists of] exhalation (*recaka*), inhalation (*pūraka*) and retention (*kumbhaka*), is of one essence with the *praṇava* (*om*), and possesses twelve measures (*mātrā*).[1]

That *prāṇāyāma* is threefold, meaning that it is of three kinds, the distinction being made in the division of exhalation (*recaka*), inhalation (*pūraka*) and retention (*kumbhaka*). *Pūraka* consists in bringing the external air into the body, *kumbhaka* in holding the inhaled air within, and *recaka* is the external movement of the withheld air.

What is the nature of this *prāṇāyāma*? It "possesses twelve measures" (*mātrā-dvādaśa-saṁyutaḥ*). A measure is the time it takes to chant the *praṇava* once. So one should inhale for the length of time it takes to repeat the *praṇava* twelve times. *Japa* here means deep reflection in the mind of the mantra, which for brāhmaṇas will take the form of the Gāyatrī[2] preceded by *praṇava* and the seven *vyāhṛtis* (*bhūr bhuvaḥ svaḥ jano maho tapo satyaṁ*) and followed by *gāyatrī-śiras*,[3] or simply *praṇava* alone. Others [i.e.,

---

[1]A *mātrā* or measure is a unit of time, which is defined in various ways. In the *Bṛhad-yogi-yājñavalkya Smṛti* (8.112) it is explained as the time it takes to snap one's fingers three times, circle the knee with the hand once and then clap three times. In the present text it is equated with the duration of the *om* sound, lasting a couple of seconds.

[2]The Gāyatrī proper reads: *tat savitur vareṇyaṁ / bhargo devasya dhīmahi / dhiyo yo naḥ pracodayāt*. "We meditate upon that effulgence of God, the creator. May He guide our intellect."

[3]*oṁ āpo jyotī raso'mṛtaṁ brahma bhūr bhuvaḥ suvarom*. "Om. He is water, light, flavor, ambrosia and also the three worlds." The *vyāhṛtis* and *Gāyatrī-śiras* are only used in the process of *prāṇāyāma* and not as a regular part of *japa*.

non-brāhmaṇas] will chant the mantra given according to their respective sect, Śaiva, Vaiṣṇava or other.[1]

Also within the repetition of the *praṇava*, one should remember *a* [the first letter of omkara] in the *pūraka*, *u* in the *kumbhaka*, and *ma* in the *recaka*. Therefore in answer to the question what is the nature of this *prāṇāyāma*, [Gorakṣa] says it is "of one essence with *praṇava*" (*praṇavātmaka*), meaning that it is a form of *praṇava*.

Now, the author reminds us that if impurities should appear in the *nāḍis* of one engaged in the practice of *prāṇāyāma*, for whatever reason, then he should practice the prescribed *prāṇāyāma* only after engaging in repeatedly purifying the *nāḍis* (*nāḍī-śuddhi*):

mātrā-dvādaśa-saṁyuktau niśākara-divākarau |
***doṣa-jālam apaghnantau jñātavyau yogibhiḥ sadā* ||3||**

2.3. The yogis should learn of the day- and night-makers [the sun and moon] connected with the twelve measures, which remove the network of defects (*doṣa*).

"Connected with the twelve measures"; the twelve measures refers to the [time it takes for] twelve repetitions of the *praṇava*, whereby one progressively completes the *praṇāyāma* exercise through the

---

[1]Though *Gorakṣa-śataka* is the text of a particular sect that expresses itself primarily in symbols, etc., appropriate to Śaivism, yoga itself is non-sectarian, as *described in Ṣaṭ-cakra-nirūpaṇaṁ (44):*

śiva-sthānaṁ śaivāḥ parama-puruṣaṁ vaiṣṇava-gaṇāḥ
lapantīti prāyo harihara-padaṁ kecid apare |
padaṁ devyā devī-caraṇa-yugalāmbhoja-rasikā
munīndrā apy anye prakṛti-puruṣa-sthānam amalam ||

"The Śaivas see [the *brahma-randhra*] as the abode of Śiva, the Vaiṣṇavas as that of the Supreme Person. Some others often name it the place of Hari-Hara [the combined form of Śiva and Viṣṇu]. Those who take delight in the taste of the Goddess's lotus feet take it to be her abode, while other sages call it the pure spot where Prakṛti and Puruṣa unite."

left and right channels beginning with the *pūraka*;[1] "connected" means along with the addition of meditation [engaged in assiduously] during the time of performing one's personal practices. These meditations are of "the maker of the night" (the moon) and "the maker of day" (i.e., the sun) [respectively], which destroy the network of defects [or darkness], i.e., the impurities that are affecting the *nāḍis*.[2]

Now he describes the three divisions of *prāṇāyāma*—

pūrake dvādaśīṁ kuryāt kuṁbhake ṣoḍaśī bhavet |
recake daśa oṁkārān prāṇāyāmaḥ sa ucyate ||4||

2.4. It is called *prāṇāyāma* when one counts twelve omkāras during *pūraka*, sixteen during *kumbhaka*, and ten during the *recaka*.[3]

One should count a measure of twelve oṁkāras on the *pūraka*, a count of sixteen on the kumbhaka and ten during the *recaka*. The sense is completed by adding "one should do *japa*."[4] Though these are three [in number], they are taken together to form a single *prāṇāyāma*.

---

[1]And presumably with the concomitant counts for *kumbhaka* and *recaka*, which are 16 and 10 respectively, as per the next verse.

[2]In his commentary to *Yoga-cūḍāmaṇi Upaniṣad* (102) on this same verse, Brahmopaniṣad Yogī gives a quite different interpretation, which refers to the natural transfer of breath from one dominant nostril (i.e., the sun or moon) to another over the course of a day. Twelve refers to the number of times that the dominant nostril changes over the course of one day and one night, each period lasting five *ghaṭikās* or two hours. The yogi should be aware of the dominant nostril and compensate for it by inhaling through the clearer channel and exhaling through the other, a process that should be continued until balance is achieved. This will facilitate the proper practice of *prāṇāyāma*.

[3]In other words, the counting is what makes it *prāṇāyāma*, otherwise it is just breathing.

[4]Grammatically this doesn't make sense, at least *iti śeṣaḥ* is usually about completing the grammatical sense, supplying some missing word (*adhyāhāra*) or an *anuvṛtti*, etc.

With the intent of showing that this *prāṇāyāma* has a threefold division according to the relative superiority or inferiority of the practice, namely low, middle and superior. He now shows the different measures that are the basis for making such a differentiation,

adhame dvādaśī mātrā madhyame dviguṇā matā |
uttame triguṇā proktā prāṇāyāmasya nirṇayaḥ ||5||

2.5. [Three levels of] *prāṇāyāma* are distinguished in the following way: on the lowest level it consists of twelve measures, in the median [stage] twice that; in the advanced [stage] three times that.

The *prāṇāyāma* of twelve *mātrās*, etc., described in the previous verse is the lowest state. The middle variety doubles that amount, and in the same way in the highest stage one triples it. Thus the counts are 12-16-10 *omkaras* for the *pūraka*, *kumbhaka* and *recaka* in the lowest stage, 24-32-20 in the middle, and 36-48-30 in the most advanced stage. This establishes the number of the count for each of these three levels of *prāṇāyāma*.

Now [Gorakṣa] describes the indicators of these three levels of *prāṇāyāma*—

adhame pracuro gharmaḥ kampo bhavati madhyame |
uttiṣṭhaty uttame yogī tato vāyuṁ nirundhayet ||6||

2.6. In the lower [stage], there is a great amount of perspiration; in the middle [stage] there is trembling;

in the superior [stage] the yogi rises up.[1] Hence he should [carefully] restrain the air (*vāyu*).

In the lowest stage, namely in a practice that has only recently been begun, one counts to twelve measures; when such a practice is underway, then because one is unable to rise from his seated position,[2] there is a great deal of perspiring. In the middle stage of

---

[1]This verse in the third quarter has a wide variety of readings and interpretations. Readings here include "In the superior stage of advancement, the yogi attains 'his place'." (*uttame sthānam āpnoti*, YCU 102, HYP 2.12); "He attains a pillar [-like state of stillness and tolerance]." (*sthāṇum āpnoti*, NW). These verses end with the exhortation to engage in the practice of *prāṇāyāma*. VM here reads: "The yogi in the highest stage rises while sitting in the bound lotus posture." (*uttiṣṭhaty uttamo deho baddha-padmāsano muhuḥ*, VM 87) [Note that YT is apparently reading at least partially the same as VM]. The Lonavla edition (49) also gives the variant reading: "The life airs rise constantly in the person in the highest stage as he sits in the *padmāsana*." (*uttiṣṭhanty uttame prāṇā baddha-padmāsane muhuḥ*). HP 4.18 has more or less the same thing (*uttiṣṭhaty uttame prāṇo baddhe padmāsane dṛḍhe*), and in both cases, as with other Lonavla publications such as the *Yoga-koṣa*, understands this idea of the *prāṇa* rising as "levitation." The Lonavla *Yoga-kośa* (p.72) tones it down a little: "a feeling of elevation... the *sādhaka* attains the state of *kevala-kumbhaka* which gives a feeling of elevation of the body." In *Yogi-yājñavalkya* 6.25 and *Vasiṣṭha-saṁhitā* 4.22, *utthāna* is given as the fruit of the *uttama* practice. This is translated by Desikachar "as a feeling of lightness." Brahmānanda in the *Jyotsnā* commentary to HYP 2.12 quotes *Liṅga-purāṇa* (1.8.46) which similarly describes the result of the *uttama* practice as simply *utthāna*, "rising." The word *utthānaṁ* does not seem to appear as a technical term in any yoga context other than this specific description of the three levels of *prāṇāyāma* practice. The *Liṅga-purāṇa* commentator is disappointingly silent on the term, as is Brahmopaniṣad Yogī in the Yoga Upaniṣads. But Yogi's comment on *sthānam āpnoti* (YCU 102) is *uttame prāṇāyāme sthānam brahma-randhram āpnoti; sthana-prāpty-anumeya uttamaḥ*. "He attains the highest place, namely the *brahma-randhra*." The Hindi translator interprets, perhaps according to another commentary, "The *ādhāra* of the *yoni* rises." See next note.

[2]I am reading as *āsanotthānāsambhavāt* rather than the *āsanotthāna-sambhavāt* which is our only reading, but conflicts with the definition of the *uttama-prāṇāyāma* later in the commentary. But this also sheds light on the meaning of the verse as YT interprets it. Being able or unable to rise from the *āsana* is a consequence of the completion or incompletion of the task; i.e., whether one is finished or not. For example, *utthā* as a verb is seen in *Pañcatantra* 4.14/15, *anaśanād uttiṣṭhati*, "to rise up from or complete a fast." Though this is not a particularly satisfying interpretation, since the mere completion of a task is rarely

prāṇāyāma, there will be trembling or movement of the body's limbs. In the highest stage, the yogi in the bound lotus posture gets up, i.e., he is able to rise from his seated position. For that reason one should control the breath, i.e., one should practice *prāṇāyāma*.

Now [Gorakṣa] shows *prāṇāyāma* as an aspect of yoga practice—

> ***baddha-padmāsano yogī namaskṛtya guruṁ śivam |***
> ***nāsāgra-dṛṣṭir ekākī praṇāyāmaṁ samabhyaset ||7||***

2.7. Seated in the bound lotus posture in solitude,the yogi should salute his teacher and Lord Shiva, and then practice breath control, his gaze fixed on the tip of the nose.

[The compound word] *baddha-padmāsanaḥ* ("bound lotus posture") here is an adjective describing the yogī, meaning one who is seated in that position. He should be alone, in a secluded place like a *maṭha*[1] on a seat as previously described made of a grass mat

---

given as the symptom of its completion; levitation nevertheless seems to be going a bit too far, as it is a completely unattested meaning. Moreover, it does not fit our commentator's remarks, which seem to be straightforward. The most logical reading to me is *sthānaṁ* or stability, i.e., that of HYP, since that opposes the two previous symptoms clearly. The idea that the life air or *prāṇa* rises is also a possibility. Since the next verse seems to separate these exercises from the procedures that follow, it likely does just mean "to graduate." However, the later (17th-18th century) text, *Śiva-saṁhitā* (3.40-41) without using the word (*utthāna*) confirms that in the early stages sweating and trembling are symptomatic, while in the higher stages "jumping like a frog" (*dārdurī*) and "moving in the sky" (*gaganecara*). "One can know that a yogi has perfected *prāṇāyāma*, when even while sitting in the *padmāsana* he can rise above the ground and remain there." (*Śiva-saṁhitā* 3.42: *yogī padmāsana-stho'pi bhuvam utsṛjya vartate | vāyu-siddhis tadā jñeyā saṁsāra-dhvānta-nāśinī* ||) Here *utsṛjya vartate* could be looked on as a gloss of *uttiṣṭhati*.

[1]Most yoga texts include a description of the ideal location for *haṭha-yoga* practice, e.g., HYP 1.12-13. "A yogi should practise *haṭha-yoga* in a small room, situated in a solitary place, measuring four cubits square and free from stones, fire, water, disturbances of all kinds, and in a country where justice is properly administered, where good people live and food can be obtained easily and

covered by a [deer or tiger] skin and a cloth, on a nice flat surface, sitting in the *padmāsana*. In this position he should salute his guru and Lord Śiva, fixing his gaze at the tip of the nose, which according to the statement "the orb of the moon is between the brows" (*bhrū-madhye śaśabhṛd-bimbam*) means one should gaze at this point where the orb of the moon is dripping nectar.

If one is initiated as a twice-born, he should practice *prāṇāyāma* while chanting the *praṇava* or Gāyatrī as previously described, while others should chant their Śaiva or Vaiṣṇava mantras. The meaning is that one should do so without interruption.[1]

ūrdhvam ākṛṣya cāpāna-vāyuṁ prāṇe niyojayet |
ūrdhvam ānīyate śaktyā sarva-pāpaiḥ pramucyate ||8||

2.8. Drawing up the *apāna* air, one should place it in the *prāṇa*. When led upward by the [*kuṇḍalinī*] power, one is liberated from all sins.

By contracting the *ādhāra* [i.e., the anal sphincter in *mūla-bandha*] one should draw the *apāna* air upward and place it in the *prāṇa*, make it one with the *prāṇa*. Then when the *prāṇa* is joined together with the *apāna*, if it is led upwards by the *śakti*, i.e., the *kuṇḍalinī* power, then one is liberated from all sins.

---

plentifully. The room should have a small door, be free from holes, hollows, neither too high nor too low, well plastered with cowdung and free from dirt, filth and insects. On its outside there should be bowers, a raised platform, a well, and a compound." Translation by Srisa Chandra Basu (Allahabad: Panini Office, 1914).

[1]HYP 2.11: "*Kumbhaka* should be performed four times: in the morning, midday, evening and at midnight, gradually [increasing the count to] up to eighty [each time]."

Now he explains the *kumbhaka*—

dvārāṇāṁ navakaṁ nirudhya marutaṁ pītvā dṛḍhaṁ dhāritaṁ
nītvākāśam apāna-vahni-sahitaṁ śaktyā samuccālitaṁ |
ātma-dhyāna-yutas tv anena vidhinā vinyasya murdhni dhruvaṁ
yāvat tiṣṭhati tāvad eva mahatāṁ saṅghena saṁstūyate ||9||

2.9. Having closed the nine gates (*dvāra*), [the yogi] should drink in the air, and then conduct that firmly-held air to the sky (*ākāśa*) together with the *apāna* air and the fire (*vahni*), after it has been activated by the [*kuṇḍalinī*] power. Then meditating on the Self, he should by this method place [the *prāṇa*] firmly in the [*brahma-randhra* in the] head. As long as one remains thus, he will be praised by the community of great souls.

The nine gates were described earlier (Cf. 1.14). Blocking off these gates by the method to be described [in 2.16], one should drink in the air, filling the abdomen with it. Along with the fire and the *apāna* air that are there, one should hold firmly the *prāṇa* in the *mūlādhāra-cakra*, in other words, one should stabilize it there. Then one should activate this *prāṇa*, raising it upwards to the sky, namely the area above the *ājñā-cakra*, and steadily hold it there. Then one places the *prāṇa* in the head, namely in the thousand-petaled-lotus. Having done so, the yogi, who is meditating on the Self, should focus his attention on his own true spiritual identity in that very place. As long as he goes on following this procedure, i.e., for as long a period of time as he steadily meditates on the Self in this way, for that duration, he will be praised by the community of great souls, i.e., those who are engaged in meditation on the Self. This is because such a person is eminently worthy of reverence.

prāṇāyāmo bhavaty evaṁ pātakendhana-pāvakaḥ |
bhavodadhi-mahā-setuḥ procyate yogibhiḥ sadā ||10||

2.10. In this way, breath control becomes the fire whose fuel is sin. [Therefore] the yogis always call it "the great bridge over the ocean of existence."

Thus, by this method, when *prāṇāyāma* is regularly being practiced, it becomes the fire for which sins, of which the murder of a brāhmaṇa is the worst, become the fuel, just like cotton or grass, which quickly burn to ashes. Such *prāṇāyāma* is said by the yogis to be the great bridge that takes one across [material] existence (*bhava*) or repeated birth and death (*saṁsāra*), which is [vast] as the ocean.

[Gorakṣa] now confirms the power of *prāṇāyāma* to destroy sin:

āsanena rujo hanti prāṇāyāmena pātakam |
vikāraṁ mānasaṁ yogī pratyāhāreṇa muñcati ||11||

2.11. The yogī destroys diseases through *āsana*, sin through *prāṇāyāma*, and becomes free from the modifications (*vikāra*) of the mind through *pratyāhāra*.

The yogi kills or destroys diseases, namely the obstacles arising from the body, by means of the physical postures like *mayūrāsana* or *matsyendrāsana*, which pacify the bodily humors. As already stated above, by *prāṇāyāma* he destroys sin [*pātaka*, lit. "that which causes one to fall"], by the purification of their basis (*adhiṣṭhāna*). By means of *pratyāhāra* or breaking the [mind's] connection to the sense objects, one gives up or becomes free of mental disturbances.

dhāraṇābhir mano-dhairyaṁ dhyānāc caitanyam adbhutam |
samādhau mokṣam āpnoti tyaktvā karma śubhāśubham ||12||

2.12. Through *dhāraṇā* [the yogi] attains steadiness of mind, from *dhyāna* a supernatural consciousness, and

in *samādhi* he attains liberation, having cast off all auspicious and inauspicious karmas.

By the *dhāraṇā*s, which will be described further down, one improves one's steadiness of mind. The word "improves" or "increases" (*vardhayati*) needs to be supplied as it is not in the text.[1] From *dhyāna* he attains a "marvelous consciousness" by which is meant the highest wisdom. In *samādhi* he gives up auspicious and inauspicious actions and the results [that arise from them] through a sense of identification with the body. This leads to liberation, which takes the form of *kaivalya* or complete spiritual individuation.

Now [Gorakṣa] shows that through *prāṇāyāma* alone one attains the results of practising *pratyāhāra*:[2]

prāṇāyāma-dviṣaṭkena pratyāhāraḥ prakīrtitaḥ |
pratyāhāra-dviṣaṭkena jāyate dhāraṇā śubhā ||13||

2.13. [That which is produced] by twice-six *prāṇāyāmas* is known as *pratyāhāra*; auspicious concentration (*dhāraṇā*) comes about from twice-six *pratyāhāras*.

By twice-six *prāṇāyāmas*, i.e., through practicing *prāṇāyāma* twelve times, [it] is known as *pratyāhāra*; in other words, it is said that the results of *pratyāhāra* manifest. Similarly, from twice-six *pratyāhāras*, that is to say, from twelve times twelve or 144

[1]In this translation we have simply taken the only verb in the verse, *āpnoti*, "attains," as also applying to this portion of the verse.
[2]The D MS here reads: "He now indicates the times of *pratyāhāra*, etc." Throughout the commentary to this and the next verse he reads it as the length of time, i.e., the length of time it takes to do twelve *prāṇāyāmas* equals one *pratyāhāra*, the time of twelve *pratyāhāras* equals one *dhāraṇā*, etc.

prāṇāyāmas, *dhāraṇā* comes about, that is, one gets the benefits of *dhāraṇā*.

Next is explained the lengths of time one is to remain in the [last] three parts of yoga, namely *dhāraṇā, dhyāna* and *samādhi*—

dhāraṇā dvādaśa proktaṁ dhyānaṁ dhyāna-viśāradaiḥ |
dhyāna-dvādaśakenaiva samādhir abhidhīyate ||14||

2.14. Experts in meditation say that twelve concentrations (*dhāraṇā*) are equal to meditation. *Samādhi* is said [to come about] with twelve meditations.

Experts in meditation (*dhyāna-viśārada*), i.e., those who are well-versed in the six kinds of meditation[1] say that *dhyāna* is equivalent to twelve times *dhāraṇā,* which is equivalent to twelve times *pratyāhāra*, etc., which then again multiplied by twelve comes to equal *prāṇāyāma* multiplied 1728 times. This *dhyāna* in turn multiplied by twelve is the equivalent of *samādhi,* i.e. *prāṇāyāma* times 20,736. This is the same as saying that *samādhi* is attained by twelve days and nights of *dhyāna*.

The author now describes the nature of *samādhi*[2]—

yat samādhau paraṁ jyotir anantaṁ viśvato-mukham |
tasmin dṛṣṭe kriyā-karma-yātāyātaṁ na vidyate ||15||

2.15. When in *samādhi* one sees the supreme light, infinite and [shining] in all directions, then in that

[1]This appears to be a reference to the six-fold meditation of *Vasiṣṭha-saṁhitā* (4.20): five kinds of *saguṇa* meditation and one *nirguṇa*. *saguṇaṁ pañcadhā proktam ekam eva hi nirguṇam.*

[2]According to YT, this and the next verse are about *samādhi*. This verse, which is a repetition of 1.21, appears superfluous here.

great yoga there are no comings and goings, nor actions and their results.

This verse was already expounded on earlier (Cf. 1.21).

The next verse shows the method of *samādhi*[1]—

sambaddhāsana-meḍhram aṅghri-yugalaṁ karṇākṣi-nāsā-puṭa-
dvārāṇy aṅgulibhir niyamya pavanaṁ vaktreṇa saṁpūritam |
dhṛtvā vakṣasi vahny-apāna-sahitaṁ mūrdhni sthitaṁ dhārayed
evaṁ yāti viśeṣa-tattva-samatāṁ yogīśvaras tan-mayaḥ ||16||

2.16. The master of yogis should assume a posture with the genital held tightly between the two heels, and controlling the gates of the ears, eyes, and nostrils with the fingers, inhaling the air through the mouth, holding it in the chest, then holding it steady in the head together with the fire and *apāna*. Thus, the lord of yogis, absorbed in that (*tan-maya*), reaches sameness (*samatā*) with the special Truth (*viśeṣa-tattva*).

When the *āsana* and the genital organ have been properly placed, and [the practitioner] has placed his feet properly,[2] he has seated himself in the *siddhāsana*. This can be deduced from the earlier description of this *āsana* which says that the feet should be pressed against the *yoni-sthāna* (Cf. 1.11). [Seated in this position] he should control, i.e., block the gates of the ears, eyes and nostrils with his fingers. The idea here is that he should block both ears

[1]In the context of the two previous verses, *samādhi* comes as a final consequence of *prāṇāyāma* itself. The definition of *samādhi* as "sameness with the special Truth" is in keeping with the description of *samādhi* given in verses 2.85-97.

[2]The construction given here is grammatically awkward. Reading the past participle *sambaddha-* as the gerund *sambadhya* etc. would resolve the issue without any pain, and is in fact the only way one can make sense of it. The VM reading *sambaddhāsanam eka-buddhir acalaṁ* also makes clear sense grammatically.

with the two thumbs, the eyes with the forefingers, the nostrils with the middle fingers, and the remaining fingers should be used to cover the mouth.[1] First one fills up with air taken in through the mouth, and then according to the method earlier described one should mix it with the *apāna* air and fire situated in the *mūlādhāra*, lift it to the chest, i.e., hold it in the heart lotus, and then lift it further to the head, where it should be stabilized in the thousand-petaled lotus. By practising in this way, the lord of the yogis becomes "absorbed in that," i.e., absorbed in or fully identified with the *prāṇa* combined with the *apāna* and fire [of Time], and then attains sameness or equality with "the special Truth," that is he becomes non-different from the all-seeing witness, the indwelling Self.

gaganaṁ pavane prāpte dhvanir utpadyate mahān |
ghaṇṭādīnāṁ pravādyānāṁ tadā siddhir adūrataḥ ||17||

2.17. When the air reaches the "space" (*gagana*),[2] there arises a great sound of musical instruments such as a bell and so on. Then [it can be understood that] success (*siddhi*) is not far off.

By following the above process, the air reaches the space or sky. When this happens a loud noise such as that made by musical instruments such as bells, bugles and drums is produced. When one encounters such a sign, then success is not far off, indeed, it is very close by.

So one should practice *prāṇāyāma* in this way without interruption:

---

[1]This is a description of the *yoni-mudrā* or *ṣaṇmukhī-karaṇa* (Cf. *Maṇḍala-brāhmaṇopaniṣad* 2.2). See note 91 to verse 1.71 above.
[2]The *ājñā-cakra*. See verse 2.73 below.

prāṇāyāmena yuktena sarva-roga-kṣayo bhavet |
ayuktābhyāsa-yogena sarva-rogasya saṁbhavam ||18||

2.18. Through proper breath control, all illnesses will be terminated. All illnesses are possible where the practice of yoga is done incorrectly.

By proper *prāṇāyāma*, that is breath control practiced in the proper manner, all diseases whether chronic or recently acquired will be destroyed. Where the practice of *prāṇāyāma* is done incorrectly or irregularly, then all diseases are possible.

What diseases are possible when one's practice is improperly done? [Gorakṣa] says:

hikkākāśas tathā śvāsaḥ śiraḥ-karṇākṣi-vedanāḥ |
bhavanti vividhā rogāḥ pavanasya vyatikramāt ||19||

2.19. From a disruption in the flow of the air come about various illnesses [such as] hiccups, cough, asthma, headache, earache and pain in the eyes.

From disruption or irregularity (*vyatikrama*) in the air caused by improper practice [of breath control], various illnesses such as hiccup, cough, asthma, headache, earache and pain in the eyes, etc., in other words, particular aches and pains in those parts, as well as other [problems] such as loss of speech, swelling, etc.

Therefore, the author advises that one should take up the *prāṇāyāma* practices gradually, by way of an example—

yathā siṁho gajo vyāghro bhaved vaśyaḥ śanaiḥ śanaiḥ |
anyathā hanti yoktāraṁ tathā vāyur asevitaḥ ||20||

2.20. Just as a lion, elephant, or tiger should be tamed gradually, for otherwise they will kill the trainer, so it is with the air [which will kill the yogi] when it is not properly employed.

The tiger, lion, elephant and other wild creatures are gradually tamed or made useful for one's own purposes if one gently engages them with favorable treatment. But if one treats them in an unbefitting way, they will kill the trainer. So it is with the *prāṇa*. If one follows according to the given rules, one will be able to bring it under control. On the other hand, if one neglects the rules as they have been given and continues to practice, then it will kill the person engaged in these practices through the aforementioned diseases.

At first one should practice to a lower time count:

yuktaṁ yuktaṁ tyajed vāyuṁ yuktaṁ yuktaṁ ca pūrayet |
yuktaṁ yuktaṁ ca bandhīyād evaṁ siddhim avāpnuyāt ||21||

2.21 One should release the air in a very controlled manner. One should inhale in a very controlled manner. One should retain it in a very controlled manner. In this way one will attain success.

In a very controlled manner means without excessive force, i.e., such that only a small particle of ground barley meal held in the hand directly before the nostrils would stir when one exhales. Similarly, when one holds the breath or inhales, it should also be done in the same way. The repetition of the word *yuktam* ("appropriately, controlled") should be taken to infer that even a yogi capable of the middle level of practice [as described above in verse 2.5] should still continue [at the beginning of his daily practice] to spend some time following the measures of the beginner, and one capable of the advanced practice should still spend some time practicing *prāṇāyāma* at the intermediate level.[1]

Pratyāhāra

Now Gorakṣa takes up the subject of *pratyāhāra* over the next thirty verses:

caratāṁ cakṣur-ādīnāṁ viṣayeṣu yathā-kramam |
yat pratyāharaṇaṁ teṣāṁ pratyāhāraḥ sa ucyate ||22||

2.22. To sequentially withdraw the senses, such as the eyes, from the objects with which they are engaged, is called *pratyāhāra* ("sense withdrawal").

The sense objects (*viṣayeṣu*) refers to the specific sense objects of each particular sense, form, taste, odor, touch and sound. The senses beginning with the sense of sight single-pointedly engage with these objects. Sequentially here means in the proper order or not in the wrong sequence, that is to say, after the two limbs of *āsana* and *prāṇāyāma* have been completed. Refraining from engagement with these sense objects, i.e., not presenting them to awareness (*anabhimukhī-karaṇam*), is called *pratyāhāra*. Alternatively, withdrawal from engagement with the sense objects, which are situated at a distance and are greatly inferior, is called *pratyāhāra*.[2]

---

[1]In other words one should warm up at a lower level of difficulty before going on to the more challenging practices.

[2]Something appears to have gone missing from the last part of the commentary, as the portion following *yad vā* ("alternatively") does not agree syntactically with the preceding.

[Gorakṣa] further illustrates this very matter with the help of an example:

yathā tṛtīya-kāla-stho raviḥ pratyāharet prabhām |
tṛtīyāṅga-sthito yogī vikāraṁ mānasaṁ tathā ||23||

2.23. Just as the sun withdraws its luster when in the third time-period, so the yogi situated in the third limb [of yoga] [withdraws] the mental modifications (*vikāra*).

The third time[1] means at the end of the day, at which time the sun withdraws its luster or light, so similarly, the yogi engaged in the third limb of yoga, i.e., the practice of *pratyāhāra*, withdraws the mental modifications in the form of tendencies to sense enjoyment. In other words, he breaks the connection to the sense objects.[2]

[Gorakṣa] gives another example:

aṅga-madhye yathāṅgāni kūrmaḥ saṁkocayed dhruvam |
yogī pratyāharaty evam indriyāṇi tathātmani ||24||

2.24. Just as a tortoise contracts its limbs into the middle of its body, so does the yogi firmly withdraw the senses into the Self.

The tortoise shrinks its limbs, i.e., its head and feet, into its own body, so in the same way, a yogi withdraws his senses, such as his eyes and tongue, etc., into himself. The word *dhruvam* ("firmly")

---

[1]Likely the third juncture or *sandhyā*, i.e., dawn, noon and evening.
[2]After faithfully following *Gorakṣa-śataka* to this point, *Yoga-cūḍāmaṇi Upaniṣad* ends abruptly with this verse. Brahmopaniṣad Yogī unconvincingly interprets *tṛtīyāṅga* as youth (of infancy, childhood and youth), or the causal body (of *sthūla-sūkṣma-kāraṇa* bodies), the *sattva-guṇa* (of *tamas, rajas* and *sattva*), or the *vānaprastha* (of *brahmacārī, gṛhī* and *vānaprastha*), adding that in all cases the yogi should be detached from these external categories.

here means that he does so in a steady or composed manner, without alarm or perturbation. [1]

yaṁ yaṁ śṛṇoti karṇābhyām apriyaṁ priyam eva vā |
taṁ tam ātmeti vijñāya pratyāharati yogavit ||25||

2.25. The knower of yoga withdraws [into the Self], knowing that whatever sound he hears with the ears, whether pleasant or unpleasant, is the Self.

Whatever sounds are heard by the ear, i.e., encountered directly through the sense of hearing, whether they are pleasant, i.e., producing meanings that are agreeable to one, or whether they are unpleasant, expressing something that is contrarian, one should know them to be the Self, the *ātmā*, i.e., one should recognize that they are part of oneself, the substratum of consciousness onto which the illusion of non-self (*vivarta*) is superimposed.

Vivarta means the thought that something not different from its substratum is [in reality] different from it, such as when one thinks a rope is a snake, or a pillar is a man. In the same way, one thinks of one's body or the world itself as separate or different from the conscious self, which is essentially pure bliss. When one is established in recognition of the truth, one withdraws [from the illusory reality].

This means that the function of the intelligence to accept the [sense objects] as separate [from the self, i.e., for the sake of enjoyment] is rejected as an error and, one therefore arrests the functions of the sense of hearing that follow in the wake of this erroneous understanding. In this way, since the illusion (*vivarta*) is not different from the substratum on which it is superimposed, and since it is clear that the created universe of five elements is one

[1] This verse, of course, brings to mind *Bhagavad-gītā* 2.58.

with the Self, so too one should consider the sense objects such as sound to be one's own self.

As Śrī Krishna said to [his father] Nanda,

> *vivarto brahmaṇaḥ prokto dehādī rajju-sarpavat*
> *na bhinno rajjutaḥ sarpo brahmaṇo na jagat tathā*

> The body and so on are said to be illusory appearances (*vivarta*) [superimposed] on Brahman, like that of a snake on a rope. The snake is not something separate from the rope, nor is the universe separate from Brahman.

Śrīpāda Śaṅkarācārya has also said,

> *sṛṣṭir nāma brahma-rūpe sac-cid-ānanda-vastuni*
> *ambu-phenādivat sarvaṁ nāma-rūpa-prasāraṇam*

> Like foam that appears on the surface of water, that which is called the creation is nothing more than the expansion of names and forms [superimposed on] the true substance, which is eternity, consciousness and bliss in the form of Brahman.

agandham athavā gandhaṁ*[1] *yaṁ yaṁ jighrati nāsikā |
taṁ tam ātmeti vijñāya pratyāharati yogavit ||26||

2.26. The knower of yoga withdraws [into the Self], knowing that whatever his nose smells, whether it has an odor or no odor, is the Self.

amedhyam athavā medhyaṁ yaṁ yaṁ paśyati cakṣuṣā |
taṁ tam ātmeti vijñāya pratyāharati yogavit ||27||

---

[1] *sugandhaṁ vā vigandhaṁ vā* is the superior VM reading.

2.27. The knower of yoga withdraws [into the Self], knowing that whatever he sees with the eyes, whether pure or impure, is the Self.

aspṛśyam athavā spṛśyaṁ yaṁ yaṁ spṛśati carmaṇā |
taṁ tam ātmeti vijñāya pratyāharati yogavit ||28||

2.28. The knower of yoga withdraws [into the Self], knowing that whatever he touches with the skin, whether touchable or untouchable, is the Self.

lavaṇyam alavaṇyaṁ vā yaṁ yaṁ rasati jihvayā |
taṁ tam ātmeti vijñāya pratyāharati yogavit ||29||

2.29. The knower of yoga withdraws [into the Self], knowing that whatever he tastes with the tongue, whether savory or unsavory, is the Self.

In the same way, whatever one smells with the nose, whether it is favorable or unfavorable, whatever one sees with the eye, whether it is pure or impure, such as a mountain or a dog, whatever one contacts with the skin or sense of touch, whether touchable like a cow or Brāhmaṇa, or untouchable like a dead body, and whatever one tastes with the tongue, whether savory, i.e., tasty due to the addition of salt and spices, or unsavory, without such additions, in all such cases the person who knows yoga, i.e., who knows the meaning of yoga, should recognize [both] the senses and the sense-objects as being non different from the Self and withdraw, that is to say, he gathers up the functions of the senses after they have been turned away from their respective objects and moves them in the reverse direction, bringing them into the orbit of the Self, i.e., he prevents them from going outwards towards the sense objects.[1]

---

[1]In *Tantrāloka* (4.92): *Pratyāhāra* means "withdrawing the awareness of the senses from their objects. A definite nailing down of the unbound bound in the

Having given a definition of *pratyāhāra* that applies in general to all yoga [systems],[1] [Gorakṣa] now shows in various ways the *pratyāhāra* that is the goal of *haṭha-yoga* [specifically], namely the gathering up of the stream of nectar flowing from the Moon Orb:

candrāmṛta-mayīṁ dhārāṁ pratyāharati[2] *bhāskaraḥ* |
yat pratyāharaṇaṁ tasyāḥ pratyāhāraḥ sa ucyate ||30||

2.30. The sun consumes the stream of lunar ambrosia (*amṛta*). The withdrawal of this torrent is called *pratyāhāra*.[3]

The lunar ambrosia is the nectar that drips from the moon situated in the throat. The sun situated in the navel region consumes the stream of lunar ambrosia. *Pratyāhāra* means to recover this ambrosia by taking it on the tongue in the way that will be described below.

---

interior." Commentary by Jayaratha: "...the cognitions of the senses such as the eyes being withdrawn from their objects such as the forms, imitating the state of the *citta* [mind-field] and thereby attaining the reassimilation into one's self. As is stated when the senses cease conjunction with the objects in their realm, they thereby become assimilate, as it were, with the mind-field's nature. That is called *pratyāhāra*, withdrawal." (See Swami Veda Bhāratī, *The Yoga Sūtras of Patañjali*, Vol. II, p. 744.

[1]Cf. *Yoga-sūtra* 2.54: "When the mind is withdrawn from sense-objects, the sense-organs also withdraw themselves from their respective objects and thus are said to imitate the mind. This is known as *pratyāhāra*." (*sva-viṣayāsamprayoge cittasya svarūpānukāra ivendriyāṇāṁ pratyāhāraḥ*).

[2]The reading attested [only] in VM is *āhārayati*, which means to consume, devour, or eat. This is clearly the intended meaning in the context and probably the original reading also, though not followed by our commentator. The verb *praty-ā√hṛ* has the less frequent meaning "destroy" in the first instance of the word's usage in this verse. To me it seems that the GŚ author's intent is to play on the word *ā√hṛ*, meaning to consume, the prefix *prati* indicating a reversal of that process. The word *viparīta-karaṇī* thus can be understood as meaning "that which reverses," i.e., facilitates the *pratyāhāra* as is being described here.

[3]Lonavla translation: "The Sun [at the navel] draws [to itself] the stream of nectar flowing from the Moon [situated at the base of the palate]. The withholding of this nectar [from the sun] is called *pratyāhāra*."

ekā strī bhujyate dvābhyām āgatā candra-maṇḍalāt |
tṛtīyo yaḥ punas tābhyāṁ sa bhaved ajarāmaraḥ ||31||

2.31. A woman[1] come from the orb of the moon is enjoyed by two. Again, a third, [i.e., one other] than those two, should become free of old age and death.

One woman who has come from the moon orb, which is situated in the sixteen-petaled lotus [of the *viśuddha-cakra*], i.e., the flow of nectar arising there. She is enjoyed by two, namely the moon and the sun. But a third should become her enjoyer and [thereby become] free of old age and death.

The meaning is this: The nectar of immortality flows from the moon orb in the throat, whence it falls into the orb of the sun situated in the navel area. One who retains this nectar in the mouth by means of *viparīta-karaṇī* ("the process of reversal"),[2] which is [next] to be described, is freed from old age and death.

Now explaining who the two that enjoy this woman are, [Gorakṣa] discusses the *viparīta-karaṇī* over the next three verses:

nābhi-deśe vasaty eko bhāskaro dahanātmakaḥ |
amṛtātmā sthito nityaṁ tālu-mūle ca candramāḥ ||32||

2.32. One, the sun, dwells in the navel region, made of the power to burn. And the moon, made of nectar, is always situated at the base of the palate.

---

[1]The word *dhārā* ("flow") is feminine.

[2]Neither the original text nor the commentary refer to *viparīta-karaṇī* as a *mudrā*, the word *karaṇī* ("process") itself appearing to be the category of discipline to which this position belongs. This is true in later texts like HYP. In *Gheraṇḍa-saṁhitā,* which like *Gorakṣa-śataka* does not distinguish between *bandhas* ("locks") and *mudrās* ("seals"), *viparīta-karaṇī* is included among the 25 *mudrās* (3.2).

One [of the two] is the sun, which is made of the power to burn, i.e., is dominated by the fire element, and dwells in the navel region. The other is the moon, which is made of nectar, i.e., is the embodiment of the nectar of immortality, who is always situated at the base of the palate in the *viśuddha-cakra*.

varṣaty adho-mukhaś candro grasaty ūrdhva-mukho raviḥ |
jñātavyā karaṇī tatra yayā pīyūṣam āpyate ||33||

2.33. The moon, with its face downward, showers [the nectar]; the sun, facing upward, swallows it. This being the case, one should know the means [or posture] by which this ambrosia can be intercepted.

The moon with its face down showers or releases the flow of nectar. The sun, with its mouth upturned, swallows it, i.e., drinks the nectar that spills from the moon. That [posture or method] by which this nectar can be intercepted, i.e., the *viparīta-karaṇī*, must be known, i.e., should be learned from the verbal teachings of a guru.

What is that process (*karaṇī*)?

ūrdhvaṁ nābhir adhas tālur ūrdhvaṁ bhānur adhaḥ śaśī |
karaṇī viparītākhyā guru-vākyena labhyate ||34||

2.34. The navel above, the palate below; the sun above and moon below. That is the pose called "the reversed,"which should be learned through the words of the preceptor.

"The navel above" means the navel area is raised upwards, "the palate below" means that the base of the palate, namely the *viśuddha-cakra*, is lowered. In the same way, the sun in the navel region is lifted above, and the moon in the palate is lowered. So as these positions are reversed, the name of this action or position is called "the reversed" (*viparīta*). Further characteristics of the posture should be taken from a preceptor's direct instructions.

Now in order to elucidate the *khecarī-mudrā*,[1] [Gorakṣa] speaks of the *anāhata-cakra*—

tridhā baddho vṛṣo yatra roravīti mahā-svanaḥ |
anāhataṁ ca tac cakraṁ hṛdaye yogino viduḥ ||35||

2.35. The yogins know the *anāhata-cakra*, in which the bull bound threefold repeatedly roars a mighty roar, to be situated at the heart.

Where, in which *cakra*, the bull is bound threefold or in three ways; this is a reference to the individual soul, which is reflected in the material nature with its three qualities (*guṇas* or ropes), due to inexperience or knowledge, and who making a loud sound, i.e., roars, or makes a sound repeatedly and with great intensity. This sound (*svana*) is that sound vibration associated with the middle power (*madhyamā*)[2] [of the word]. For as it is said in *Yoga-sāra*:

hṛdaye vādyate ghoṣo garjat-parjanya-sannibhaḥ
tatra sthitā mahā-devī madhyamety abhidhīyate

---

[1]Though the same subject was broached with respect to the *khecarī-mudrā* earlier in verses 1.64-76, the context here is of the *viparīta-karaṇī*. No doubt, *khecarī* should be performed in tandem with *viparīta-karaṇī*.

[2]The word principle in Sanskrit linguistic and Tantric tradition has four phases: *parā*, its transcendent state; *paśyantī*, "the seeing," i.e., the word prior to articulation; *madhyamā*, "the middle" or transitional state where the sound is formulated in the mind; and *vaikharī*, the manifest sound. According to Swami Veda Bhārati, these phases of sound are manifest in *asamprajñāta-samādhi*, *samprajñāta-samādhi*, in mental concentration and in communication respectively. For a more complete discussion, see his *Mantra and Meditation*, pp. 94-102.

> In the heart plays a sound like the roar of thunder, in which is present the great goddess named Madhyamā.

That *cakra* is in the heart and is named "the unstruck" (*anāhata*). The yogis, those who are absorbed in instrospective meditation, know this.

[Gorakṣa] now instructs [the yogi] to drink this nectar in the *khecarī-mudrā* in two verses.

anāhatam atikramya cākramya maṇipūrakam |
prāpte prāṇe mahā-padmaṁ yogitvam amṛtāyate ||36||

2.36. Once the *prāṇa* has passed through the *maṇipūra-cakra*, crossed the *anāhata* center and reached the great lotus, the yogi's yoginess[1] becomes immortalized.

By the earlier described method, when one has lifted the *apāna* air and united it with the *prāṇa*, lifting it to the *maṇipūra*, and then afterwards crossing or leaping over the *anāhata* center. Here the word "and" (*ca*) implies the inclusion of the unmentioned *viśuddha* and *ājñā*, i.e., after crossing the *viśuddha* and *ājñā-cakras*. The "great lotus" means the thousand-petaled lotus. Here the abstract noun suffix *-tva* is not intended, rather it simply means that the yogi [himself] becomes immortal, i.e., free from the cycle of birth and death.

mūrdhnaḥ ṣoḍaśa-patra-padma-galitaṁ prāṇād avāptaṁ haṭhād
ūrdhvāsyo rasanāṁ nidhāya vidhivat śaktiṁ parāṁ cintayan |
utkallola-kalā-jalaṁ suvimalaṁ jihvākulaṁ yaḥ piben
nirdoṣaḥ sa mṛṇāla-komala-tanur yogī ciraṁ jīvati ||37||

---

[1]*Yogitvam*, i.e., the qualities or characteristics of an accomplished yogi. The commentator does not like this use of the abstract noun ("yogi-ness") and rejects it, saying that only "yogi" is meant.

2.37. The yogi who while meditating on the Supreme Śakti according to the prescribed method turns his face upward and places his tongue [in the cavity[1]] and drinks the drops from the exceedingly clear stream of moon liquor as it trickles down from the head to the sixteen-petaled lotus, and which has then been acquired forcefully (*haṭhāt*) from the *prāṇa* and taken on the tongue after being stirred by it develops a body that is as soft as the stem of a lotus and lives a very long time.

Thus [as described in the previous verse] once the *prāṇa* of the yogi has reached the great lotus (*mahā-padma*); then he should drink the drops from the great waves of absolutely pure nectarean juice that have been agitated by the tongue, i.e., extracted by the churning movements of the tongue after it has been placed or entered into the cavity above the nose (*nāsikordhva-vivare*). This nectar after trickling or falling from the head, namely the thousand-petaled lotus, into the sixteen-petaled lotus, namely the *viśuddha-cakra*, has been brought to the cavity above the nose on account of the *prāṇa* that has been forced upwards.[2] [The yogi] drinks this nectar by

---

[1]Here the verse is ambiguous. The word *vidhivat*, here translated "according to the prescribed method," and read with "meditating," etc., is replaced by *vivare*, "in the cavity," read with "places his tongue" in many versions of the verse (e.g., VM 118, HYP 3.51, HP 5.74). Our commentator's gloss *nāsikordhva-vivare*, "the cavity above the nostrils," is a reference to the fully extended *khecarī mudrā*, whereby the tongue has been stretched and turns upward at the throat. This then feels to the meditator as though the tongue is touching and connected to the root of the nose, not from below but from behind, i.e., it has entered the sinus cavities. Something analogous can be experienced through mental concentration on the relevant areas of the gross and subtle bodies, though the actual physical touch is no doubt a stronger stimulus for triggering the intended psychosomatic response. Brahmānanda in *Jyotsnā* (HYP 3.51) gives the synonym *kapāla-kuhare*. *Nāsānta-suṣira* is mentioned in 2.42-43 below.

[2]*Haṭhāt*. The word in the ablative is used commonly as an adverb "forcefully." It seems that YT is reading it as an adjective, since it appears to be in apposition with *prāṇāt*. Nevertheless, the meaning is practically the same, since the sudden or forceful movement of the *prāṇa* is mentally directed and active in both the subtle and gross bodies. Cf. 1.51 above.

turning the face or mouth upwards according to the prescribed method, while thinking of or meditating on the Supreme Śakti, i.e., the *kuṇḍalinī-śakti* that had [also] been lifted into the thousand petaled lotus along with the *prāṇa*. His body then becomes soft like a lotus stem; he is faultless, devoid of all the defects of the body, from ringworm to leprosy, and of the mind, from attachment to aversion, and goes on to live for a very long time.

Here [Gorakṣa] explains some of the techniques (*kriyā*), principally the *śītalī* breath,[1] that are used to overcome old age, disease and death:

kāka-cañcūvad-āsyena śītalaṁ salilaṁ pibet |
prāṇāpāna-vidhānena yogī bhavati nirjaraḥ ||38||

2.38. That yogi does not age who [along with] the process [for uniting] the *prāṇa* and *apāna* airs drinks the cool flow [of air] with the mouth [shaped] like a crow's beak.

Making the mouth into the form of a crow's beak (*kāka-cañcū*)[2] the yogi should inhale and exhale according to the method previously described for uniting the two airs (*prāṇāpāna-vidhānena*). Then he

---

[1] *Śītalī* is usually described as a curling the length of the tongue into a tube and then channeling the inhaled breath through it, exhaling through the nostrils (See HYP 2.57). Nothing is stated about the tongue here, and from other accounts in yoga texts, the *kāka-cañcū mudrā* and *śītalī* are distinct. Moreover, if we read this verse together with the next, it would seem that *khecarī* is to be maintained here even while breathing through the mouth. See next notes also.

[2]Mallinson writes: "During the practice, fluid gathers in the mouth. By pushing out the lips into the shape of a bird's beak, there is more room for the fluid to collect. In the *haṭhayogic* practice of *jālandhara-bandha* the throat is constricted by letting the head hang forward. The fluid dripping from the moon is thus diverted into the mouth and prevented from falling into the solar region in the stomach [hence the suitability of the name of the practice, *jālandhara,* 'holding water'). *Khecarī-vidyā,* p. 211, note 267. This differs somewhat from the description given in the preceding and following notes, which connects this practice with the *śītalī* breath.

should drink in the cool flow (*salila*) or outside air (*bāhya-vāyu*),[1] i.e., fill the lungs. By so doing, he becomes free of old age.

rasanā-tālu-mūlena yaḥ prāṇam anilaṁ pibet |
abdārdhena bhavet tasya sarva-rogasya saṁkṣayaḥ ||39||

2.39. For one who drinks the *prāṇa* [at the] base of the palate and the tongue, all illnesses will be destroyed in half a year. [2]

The compound *rasanā-tālu-mūlena* ("by the tongue [and] base of palate") should be resolved as follows: *rasanā* means tongue; there is a cavity formed by the root of the palate with the help (*sahāya*) of the tongue.[3] For the yogi who drinks in or fills the lungs with the

---

[1]The most common meaning for *salilaṁ* is water, but its etymological origins are in the idea of flowing, etc. The meaning of *salila* as a special kind of air has one attestation in Monier-Williams' dictionary, but it is nowhere else found with this meaning in either yoga or other literature. In the *Yoga-prakāśikā* commentary to this same verses as found in the ten-chapter version of *Haṭha-pradīpikā* (5.54), Bālakṛṣṇa has taken it to mean water: *...jala-pānaṁ kartavyaṁ ity āha—kāketi. jala-pāna-prāṇāyāmābhyāsābhyāṁ nirjaro bhavatīti bhāvaḥ*. The VM reading here is *śītalaṁ śītalaṁ*. *śītalaṁ* is also attested in some lexicons as a synonym for air (*Trikāṇḍa-śeṣa* 3.409, *Medinī*). Our commentary has *śītalaṁ śītalaṁ salilaṁ*, i.e. repeating the word *śītalam* as in the VM, so perhaps this was the original intent that resulted in confusion. Here, "flow" adequately conveys the intended sense. *Gheraṇḍa-saṁhitā* (3.66) describes *kākī-mudrā*, "One should slowly take in air through the mouth formed like the beak of a crow." In an interpolated verse it is added that "by performing this *mudrā* one becomes free of disease like a crow." However, to identify this with the *śītalī* breath does not seem immediately probable. In that practice, one sucks in the air via the curled tongue, holds it briefly and then exhales through the nostrils.(*Gheraṇḍa-saṁhitā* 5.68-69). Only the *Kumbhaka-paddhati* (141-151) of Raghuvīra explicitly combines the two as *śītalī-kāka-cañcuka,* though *śītalī* itself is described separately (136-143).

[2]This appears to be a description of the *ujjāyī* breath. See *HYP* 2.51-53: "[It] consists of closing the mouth and slowly inhaling through both nostrils so that the inspired air touches the lining membrane from the throat down to the chest and a low sound is thus produced." (*Yoga-kośa*, p. 69).

[3]This likely means nothing more than "between the root of the tongue and the base of the palate." See next note also.

prāṇa air through this cavity,[1] all diseases will be destroyed in half a year, i.e., six months.

[Gorakṣa] further describes how to drink the moon-nectar without allowing it to fall into the mouth of the sun:

viśuddhe pañcame cakre dhyātvā soma-kalāmṛtam |
unmārgeṇāhṛtaṁ yāti vañcayitvā mukhaṁ raveḥ ||40||

2.40. After contemplating[2] the nectar of the moon in the *viśuddha-cakra*, the fifth center, it is then drawn by the upward path, having escaped the mouth of the sun.

In the *viśuddha-cakra*, which is the fifth center in the throat, one should meditate on the nectar of the moon. Then when this nectar is pulled along by the upward path, it escapes the mouth of the sun and goes to one's own stomach.[3] The meaning is that being digested there it destroys the aging process and all kinds of diseases.

[Gorakṣa] now explains the meaning of the word *viśuddha*:

vi-śabdena smṛto haṁso nairmalyaṁ śuddhir ucyate |
ataḥ kaṇṭhe viśuddhākhyaṁ cakraṁ cakra-vido viduḥ ||41||

2.41. The prefix *vi*-means "the swan" (*haṁsa*); spotless purity is called *śuddhi*. Thus the knowers of the cakras call the center in the throat by the name *viśuddha*.

---

[1]This rather convoluted explanation is again likely the result of a faulty reading. The HP (4.47) has the somewhat clearer *rasanā-tālu-yogena*, "by the combination of tongue and palate."
[2]Though the variants on this verse are widely diverging, *dhṛtvā* ("after holding") in the place of *dhyātvā* ("after meditating") seems to be the correct verb here.
[3]*Svasyodaram*. The idea seems to be that this subtle nectar is destroyed by the inner fire and only by being intercepted by the tongue is it made to descend into the regular digestive tract. See YT 2.42.

The word *vi* denotes a bird, by which is intended the swan (*haṁsa*).[1] Purity is indicated by the word *śuddhi*. For this reason, as the bird [i.e., the breath] becomes spotless or purified in the region of the neck, it is called *viśuddha* by the yogis who are knowers of the meaning of the *cakras*.

amṛtaṁ kandare kṛtvā nāsānta-suṣire kramāt |
svayam uccālitaṁ yāti varjayitvā mukhaṁ raveḥ ||42||

2.42. [The life force] after escaping the jaws of the [inner] sun, rises of its own accord into the hollow at the end of the nose [after the yogi] has placed the nectar into that cavern.

The nectar that is situated in the *viśuddha-cakra* is as described previously made to rise upwards by the *prāṇa* that has been so stirred up to the cavern, i.e., the hollow above the uvula, and from there gradually leading it to the hollow at the end of the nose. Thus it bypasses the mouth of the sun and goes to the stomach like any other food or drink that has been swallowed and is there consumed by the digestive fires.

Moreover,

baddhaṁ soma-kalā-jalaṁ suvimalaṁ kaṇṭha-sthalād ūrdhvato
nāsānte suṣire nayec ca gagana-dvāraṁ tataḥ sarvataḥ |
ūrdhvāsyo bhuvi sannipatya nitarām uttāna-pādaḥ pibed
evaṁ yaḥ kurute jitendriya-gaṇo naivāsti tasya kṣayaḥ ||43||

---

[1]This verse remains something of a mystery. The *Yoga-koṣa* (p. 321) explains: "*Haṁsa*, a bird, particularly a swan. The center for meditation in the throat is named *viśuddha* because it resembles a clean, pure bird." GP following his commentary simply says, "*Viśuddha* means superior to all (*sarvotkṛṣṭa*)." Feuerstein glosses *haṁsa* as "the spontaneous breath," in a reference to the natural breath described as the *haṁsa-mantra* in 1.42-46. This seems to be the intention.

2.43. One should draw the exceedingly pure water of the moon portion from the region of the throat upwards to the hollow at the end of the nose and then completely conduct it to the "gate to the sky." Lying on the ground face upwards with the legs stretched up, one should drink it. One who has conquered his senses and does as here described will never know decay or diminution.

One should take the exceedingly pure water of the moon portion (*soma-kalā-jalam*), i.e., moon nectar, from the neck and hold it in the higher region and then bring it to the hollow at the end of the nose. And, again, one should bring it to the place above all these, the gate to the sky, namely the area of the *ājñā-cakra*. Then, lying on the ground facing upwards with the legs stretched upwards,[1] one should drink that nectar. The yogi who has controlled all his senses and goes on doing this practice will never know decay or diminution, i.e., death. The meaning is that he will not die.

Furthermore,

ūrdhva-jihvāṁ sthirāṁ kṛtvā soma-pānaṁ karoti yaḥ |
māsārdhena na sandeho mṛtyuṁ jayati yogavit ||44||

2.44. The knower of yoga who drinks the ambrosia (*soma*) by holding the tongue firmly upward undoubtedly conquers death within half a month.

One who holds the tongue firmly in the cavity above the uvula and drinks the *soma* or *amṛta*, such a knower of yoga, i.e., one who is

[1]Although the word *uttāna-pāda-* is currently used primarily to mean simply outstretched or stretched, it is also used specifically to indicate the *āsana* in which the legs are lifted upwards at a 45° angle. Since the context here is still the *viparīta-karaṇī*, one would assume that the intention here is that the legs are stretched straight upwards as in *śīrṣāsana, sarvāṅgāsana* or *viparīta-karaṇī mudrā*, all of which fit this description.

expert in the techniques of yoga, in half a month, i.e., in just a fortnight of following this practice, will conquer over death, i.e., even if Death himself should arrive before him, he would be unable to do anything. In this matter one should have no doubt whatsoever.

baddhaṁ mūla-bilaṁ yena tena vighno vidāritaḥ |
ajarāmaram āpnoti yathā pañca-mukho haraḥ ||45||

2.45. He who closes off the root cavity[1] overcomes [every] obstacle and reaches [the state] beyond old age and death, like the five faced Hara.

That yogi who closes off or blocks the root hole, namely the root gate [i.e., the anus], completely destroys all obstacles in the form of old age and death, etc. Along with old age and death, he casts off his illusion that the body is the self and attains the nature of the pure Self, which is always free from old age and death. In doing so he is like the five-faced Śiva who has neither bodily consciousness nor susceptibility to old age and death.

Furthermore,

saṁpīḍya rasanāgreṇa rāja-danta-bilaṁ mahat |
dhyātvā'mṛta-mayīṁ devīṁ ṣaṇ-māsena kavir bhavet ||46||

2.46. Pressing the tip of the tongue against the great cavity at the uvula[2] and meditating on the ambrosia-

---

[1]Nowotny's edition here reads *ūrdhva-bilam* ("the upper hole"), which would likely be synonymous with the *kapāla-kuhara*.

[2]*Rāja-danta* is usually translated as the front upper teeth, and the *rāja-danta-bila* as the cavity formed at the front of the mouth where the palate meets these teeth. (Cf. *Yoga-kośa*, 244-245). Mallinson, however, identifies it as the uvula, which hangs like a single great tooth in the throat (*Khecarī-vidyā*, p. 209, note 258).

laden goddess, he becomes a poet (*kavi*) within six months.

After pressing the cavity at the uvula (*rāja-danta*) with the tip of the tongue, meditating on the goddess of speech (*vāg-īśvarī*), after six months of practice he will become a poet, and take pleasure in composing wonderful poetic works.

The author next tells of the methods followed by the yogi who practices the five kinds of *dhāraṇā* that are to be described [starting with 2.52]:

sarva-dvārāṇi badhnāti tad-ūrdhvaṁ dhāritaṁ mahat |
na muñcaty amṛtaṁ kvāpi sa panthāḥ pañca-dhāraṇāḥ ||47||

2.47. He blocks all the gates and above that the great (*mahat*), being held, never lets go the flow of nectar. That is the path of the five concentrations (*dhāraṇās*).[1]

The yogi blocks that "great" recess in the roof of the mouth behind the upper teeth, pressing his tongue against it; in this way he blocks all the gates, i.e., the openings to the channels (*nāḍis*). He does not ever let go the ambrosia that flows[2] above that. This is the path that is followed by the yogi who practices the process of *dhāraṇā* as will be described. Just as gathering up and consuming the nectar that flows from the moon has been called *pratyāhāra*,

---

[1]This verse seems to be out of place, as the topic of *dhāraṇā* is only begun from 2.52. The five *dhāraṇās* are described from 2.54-58. Since the rest of the verse is in line with the topic under discussion, however, it seems more likely that the reading is incorrect. *Viveka-mārtaṇḍa* here reads *ṣaṭ yathā candramā-kalāḥ*.

[2]The commentary seems a bit confused here. Indeed, the verse does present something of a problem, which is perhaps one reason that it is not found in any of our parallel works on *yoga*. The commentator splits the syntax of the verse here, reading *dhāritaṁ* as "flowing" (*dhārākāraṁ*) with *amṛtam*, rather than as "held" with *mahat*, but the last sentence of the commentary clarifies the intent of the word *dhāritaṁ* as related to *dhāraṇā*.

similarly holding the nectar in the cavity above the uvula is called *dhāraṇā*.

Moreover,

cumbantī yadi lambikāgram aniśaṁ jihvā rasa-syandinī[1]
sa-kṣāraṁ kaṭukāmla-dugdha-sadṛśaṁ madhv-ājya-tulyaṁ tathā |
vyādhīnāṁ haraṇaṁ jarāntaḥ-karaṇaṁ[2] *śāstrāgamodgīraṇaṁ*
tasya syād amaratvam aṣṭa-guṇitaṁ siddhāṅganākarṣaṇam ||48||

2.48. If one's tongue, flowing with juice, constantly kisses the tip of the uvula, which tastes [alternatively] salty, or is pungent, sour or like milk, honey and ghee, and which removes all diseases, puts and end to old age and death, and which gives the ability to utter the various branches of learning, then he will attain immortality and the eight qualities, as well as attracting *siddha* women.

One whose tongue constantly kisses the tip of the uvula which sometimes tastes salty, sometimes has a bitter taste, sometimes sour, sometimes has the taste of milk, sometimes is like honey and sometimes like ghee, i.e., has all these various flavors, and causes its rasa to flow, thus flowing with juice, i.e., takes on all these flavors itself, then all the diseases of such a person, such as those previously described, will be destroyed; even if he is old or in the last stage of life, still he will be able to use his mind clearly (*jarāntaḥ-karaṇaṁ*), and will be able to recite the scriptures and the

---

[1]This verse becomes awkard because of this adjective, which no doubt should have read *-syandinaṁ* and been an adjective of *lambikāgram*. Other readings of the verse put the adjectives in the second line in the feminine to make them agree with *jihva* ("tongue"), but this is less desirable.
[2]Most readings here have *jarānta-karaṇaṁ*, which seems much more natural and does not force the kind of interpretation to which our commentator has recourse.

āgamas,[1] meaning that he will be able to explain the conclusions [taught in the scriptures (*śāstras*)] and the *yantras* and *mantras* [taught in the *āgamas*], even without previously having studied them. Furthermore, the eight mystic powers will appear in him; he will become one of the immortals or shining ones (*devas*) who possess these eight powers; and simply through thinking of them he will be able to attract the *siddha*[2] women.

Concluding this section, [Gorakṣa] now describes the benefits of *pratyāhāra* over the next three verses:

amṛtāpūrṇa-dehasya yogino dvi-tri-vatsarāt |
ūrdhvaṁ pravartate reto'py aṇimādi-guṇodayaḥ ||49||

2.49. After two or three years, the semen (*retas*) of the yogi whose body has thus been filled completely with nectar will move upward and the qualities like miniaturization (*aṇimā*) will appear.

Thus by following the method outlined, when the yogi's body has been completely filled with nectar, then after two or three years his semen will move upward. And when the semen rises, then the various mystic powers will appear in him.[3]

---

[1]The *āgamas* are generally understood to be the sacred texts of the Tantra. *Śāstra* is a broader category that includes both sacred and secular texts, but not including purely poetic or literary works.
[2]Although the word *siddha* is used for any adept or accomplished practitioner of yoga, especially one who has attained the mystic *siddhis*, it also applies to a category of semi-divine beings who have their own realm. This latter meaning is most likely intended here, but the yogini adept is also being hinted at.
[3]Feuerstein."The upward-streaming of the subtle aspect of the male semen is the yogic counterpart to what in psychological language is known as 'sublimation.' More precisely, it is a form of superlimination, since the process involves going beyond the threshold (Lat. *limen*) of the ordinary psychophysical condition. This rare state is technically known as *ūrdhva-retas*."

indhanāni yathā vahnis taila-vartī ca dīpakaḥ |
tathā soma-kalā-pūrṇaṁ dehaṁ dehī na muñcati ||50||

2.50. The embodied being does not leave the body when it is filled with the [nectarean] portion (*kalā*) of the moon, any more than fire leaves fuel, or a lamp [flame] an oil-drenched wick.

Just as fire does not abandon fuel, i.e., dried wood, or a lamp [flame] does not leave a wick that is soaked in oil, so the embodied being, the fragmented self, does not leave the body that has been filled with the portions of the moon [i.e., the nectar] by the method previously outlined.

nityaṁ soma-kalā-pūrṇaṁ śarīraṁ yasya yoginaḥ |
takṣakenāpi daṣṭasya viṣaṁ tasya na sarpati ||51||

2.51. When a yogi's body is constantly being filled with the lunar nectar, then even if bitten by the serpent king Takṣaka himself, the poison will not spread.

In the body of the yogi which is constantly being filled with the moon nectar, even if it should be bitten by Takṣaka, the great serpent, the poison that it releases will not spread through his body.

Dhāraṇā

The yogi who has practised the first three limbs of yoga should now take up the practice of *dhāraṇā,* which will be explained over the next nine verses.

āsanena samāyuktaḥ prāṇāyāmena saṁyutaḥ |
pratyāhāreṇa sampanno dhāraṇāṁ ca samabhyaset ||52||

2.52. One who has mastered posture, breath control and sense-withdrawal should practice concentration (*dhāraṇā*).

One who has fully mastered *āsana*, meaning that he has mastered the ability to remain undisturbed in any one of the previously described *āsanas* through practice; in the same way, to have mastered *prāṇāyāma* means to have gone through all the stages characterized as the beginning, intermediate and advanced (Cf. 2.5), and mastery of *pratyāhāra* means that he has properly withdrawn all his sense functions; such a yogi should now apply himself to the practice of *dhāraṇā* or concentration.

hṛdaye pañca-bhūtānāṁ dhāraṇaṁ ca pṛthak pṛthak |
manaso niścalatvena dhāraṇā sābhidhīyate ||53||

2.53. Holding the five elements within the heart, each one separately, with complete immobility of the mind, is called *dhāraṇā*.

In the heart means in the region of the heart.[1] The word *ca* indicates that not only the mind, but also the *prāṇa* is to be included when there is talk of immobility. So along with the stability of mind and *prāṇa*, separately holding the five elements is called *dhāraṇā* or concentration.

[Gorakṣa] begins by describing the concentration on the earth element (*pṛthivī-dhāraṇā*):

---

[1]This is unusual in that these elements are usually associated with the five lower *cakras*, but here all of the elements are to be separately visualized along with their *bīja*-mantras, etc., in the heart region. Kuvalayananda and Shukla gloss "in the heart" as "inside the body" and "separately" (*pṛthak pṛthak*) as "in different places." This is justifiable as some of the following verses do indicate other locations for these visualizations, even though they do not follow the customary sequence such as that found in *Ṣaṭ-cakra-nirūpaṇam*. For those descriptions, see the *Yoga-taraṅgiṇī* commentary to verses 1.15-16.

yā pṛthvī haritāla-hema-rucirā pītā la-kārānvitā
saṁyuktā kamalāsanena hi catuṣkoṇā hṛdi sthāyinī |
prāṇaṁ tatra vilīya pañca-ghaṭikaṁ cittānvitaṁ dhārayed
eṣā staṁbhakarī sadā kṣiti-jayaṁ kuryād bhuvo dhāraṇā ||54||

2.54. That earth [element] [is visualized as] a square established in the heart, beautiful like orpiment or gold, adorned with the letter *la*, and combined with the lotus-seated [Brahmā]. Merging [oneself] there, one should hold the *prāṇa* along with the mind for five *ghaṭikās* [two hours], for this concentration on the earth is the stabilizer that will bring victory over the earth.

The earth, which is beautiful like *haritāla* (yellow orpiment) or gold, adorned with the yellow letter *la*[1] as its seed mantra, combined with the lotus-seated Lord Brahmā who is its presiding deity, having a square shape established in the heart, i.e., it is there that it should be made the object of meditation. There in that *maṇḍala* [square] of the earth element, one should also merge oneself, i.e., one should become one with the earth element, and hold the *prāṇa* there along with the mind for a period of five *ghaṭikās*. This *dhāraṇā* of the earth is stabilizing (*stambha-karī*), which means that it arrests [any possibility] of falldown even from the most serious causes (*guru-hetuka-patana-staṁbhikā*). If constantly carried out, it will lead to victory over the earth. The process of *staṁbhana*[2] should be learned directly from the guru.

[1]The adjective *pītā* would not ordinarily be read with the compound *la-kārānvitā*, but visualizations of the earth element in the *svādhiṣṭhāna* do usually describe the square as one yellow, the letters as also being yellow. It is likely just a result of metrical considerations. Many manuscripts here have *tattvaṁ* in the place of *pītā*, but this does not scan any better, even though the word *tattva* appears in three of the subsequent *dhāraṇās*.

[2]*Stambhana.* The word means to stiffen, rigidify, paralyze. It would appear to be related to the concepts of *sthāṇutva* and *kāṣṭhī*, Cf. 1.90. The insertion in our A. MS. (*guru-hetuka-patana-staṁbhikā*) defines it as preventing the propensity to

Next is the concentration on water (*vāruṇī-dhāraṇā*):

ardhendu-pratimaṁ ca kunda-dhavalaṁ kaṇṭhe'mbu-tattvaṁ sthitaṁ
yat pīyūṣa-va-kāra-bīja-sahitaṁ yuktaṁ sadā viṣṇunā |
prāṇaṁ tatra vilīya pañca-ghaṭikaṁ cittānvitaṁ dhārayed
eṣā duḥsaha-kāla-kūṭa-dahanī syād vāruṇī dhāraṇā ||55||

2.55. The water [element] (*ambu-tattva*) resembling a half moon, [white] like a *kunda* flower is located at the throat;it is endowed with the nectar seed syllable *va* and always associated with Viṣṇu. Merging [oneself] there [in the throat], one should hold the *prāṇa* along with the mind for five *ghaṭikās* [two hours], for this concentration on the water element will burn up the *kālakūṭa* poison of intolerable suffering.

The water *tattva* has the image of the half moon, i.e., taking that form, meaning that it has the curved shape of a half moon. Like the *kunda* flower means that it is white in color. The *bīja*-syllable *va* is formed of ambrosia. The deity Viṣṇu accompanies the element as he is identified with it. It is situated in the neck region, i.e., in the *viśuddha-cakra*. In that water element, one should also merge oneself, and then merging the *prāṇa* there along with the mind, one should hold it there for a period of five *ghaṭikās*. This *dhāraṇā* of

---

sinful action, which in the hierarchy of the five *dhāraṇās* appears to be in its legitimate place, as it is followed progressively by higher states of yogic achievement. *Stambhana* is also a kind of magical act meant to paralyze or stop the movements of others (*niśceṣṭīkaraṇam*). In this respect, it is also one of the arrows of Cupid. In the *Indrajāla-śāstram*, there are several types: *mukha-stambhanaṁ, naukā-stambhanaṁ, nidrā-stambhanaṁ, śastra-stambhanaṁ,* etc. *Indrajāla-vidyā-saṅgraha,* Kalikātā: Vācaspatya Press, 1915, p.14. The five elements here can be correlated to various other groups of five, especially as viewed by the Tantra literature, both Hindu and Buddhist. Cf. Alex Wayman, *The Buddhist Tantras: Light on Indo-Tibetan Esoterism.* New York: Samuel Weisman, 1973. See chapter 15, "The five-fold ritual symbolism of passion", pp. 202-210.

the water element burns up,[1] i.e., reduces to ashes, the intolerable *kālakūṭa* poison, i.e., it destroys any power that such poison has to disturb one.

The *dhāraṇā* of fire is now described:

yat tālu-sthitam indragopa-sadṛśaṁ tattvaṁ trikoṇānalaṁ[2]
tejo repha-yutaṁ pravāla-ruciraṁ rudreṇa yat saṅgatam |
prāṇaṁ tatra vilīya pañca-ghaṭikaṁ cittānvitaṁ dhārayed
eṣā vahni-jayaṁ sadā vitanute vaiśvānarī dhāraṇā ||56||

2.56. The fire [element] is situated in the palate; it is [crimson] like the *indragopa* insect [cochineal]; triangular in shape, it is associated with *repha* [i.e., the syllable *ra*], bright like coral, and is in the company of Rudra. Merging [oneself] there [in the palate], one should hold the *prāṇa* along with the mind for five *ghaṭikās* [two hours], for this concentration on the fire element (*vaiśvānarī dhāraṇā*) will lead to victory over fire.

Having a triangular shape, similar to the *indragopa* [insect], bright like coral, associated with the *repha* seed letter, accompanied by Rudra, who is the deity who identifies with this element, situated in the palate, is the element or *tattva* of fire. Merging [oneself] there [in the palate], one should hold the *prāṇa* along with the mind for five *ghaṭikās*. This *vaiśvānarī dhāraṇā* if constantly practised will lead to or expand one's victory over fire, i.e., one will not be affected by burns.

---

[1]Technically, one would here expect the word *drāviṇī* in accordance with the character of the *tattva* itself, "washing away, melting, liquifying" as in verse 2.74. However, the five verses do not in fact seem to follow any such plan.
[2]The variant *-ojjvalaṁ* is probably correct, since *analaṁ* and *tejaḥ* are synonyms and thus unnecessarily repetitive.

He next speaks of the *dhāraṇā* of the air (*vāyavī dhāraṇā*):

yad bhinnāñjana-puñja-sannibham idaṁ vṛttaṁ bhruvor antare
tattvaṁ vāyu-mayaṁ ya-kāra-sahitaṁ tatreśvaro devatā |
prāṇaṁ tatra vilīya pañca-ghaṭikaṁ cittānvitaṁ dhārayed
eṣā khe gamanaṁ karoti yamināṁ syād vāyavī dhāraṇā ||57||

2.57. The *tattva* of the air resembles crushed collyrium, is round in shape, and located between the eyebrows; it is associated with the letter *ya* and has Īśvara as its presiding deity. Merging [oneself] there [between the eyebrows], one should hold the *prāṇa* along with the mind for five *ghaṭikās*, for this concentration on the air element (*vāyavī dhāraṇā*) will make it possible for the yogis to travel in the sky.

Vṛttaṁ here means circular in shape. It is like a heap of crushed collyrium, meaning that it is black in color; it is accompanied by the seed mantra *ya* and the deity Īśvara, who identifies with this element. It is situated between the eyebrows. Merging [oneself] in the air *tattva*, one should as before hold the *prāṇa* there along with the mind for five *ghaṭikās*, for this concentration on the air element (*vāyavī dhāraṇā*) will result in the ability to move or travel in the sky.

He now speaks of the *dhāraṇā* of the sky element (*ākāśa*)—

ākāśaṁ suviśuddha-vāri-sadṛśaṁ yat brahma-randhre sthitaṁ
tan-nādena sadā-śivena sahitaṁ tattvaṁ ha-kārānvitam |
prāṇaṁ tatra vilīya pañca-ghaṭikaṁ cittānvitaṁ dhārayed
eṣā mokṣa-kapāṭa-pāṭana-paṭuḥ proktā nabho-dhāraṇā ||58||

2.58. The ether (*ākāśa*) element, which is [clear] like extremely pure water, is located at the *brahma-randhra*; it is associated with Sadā Śiva, the [inner]

sound (*nāda*) and the syllable *ha*. Merging [oneself] there [in the *brahma-randhra*], one should hold the *prāṇa* along with the mind for five *ghaṭikās*, for this concentration on the sky element (*nabho-dhāraṇā*) is said to expertly break open the door to liberation.

"Extremely pure" means without any pollution, so this *tattva* is clear like such water. In it the unmanifest sound becomes manifest. It is associated with Sadā Śiva, who identifies himself with this *tattva*, and is accompanied by the seed syllable *ha*. It is situated in the *brahma-randhra*. As before, one should merge oneself there into the *ākāśa-tattva* and there hold the *prāṇa* along with the mind for five *ghaṭikas*, for it is said that this concentration on the sky element is expert or capable of breaking or knocking down the doorway to liberation, meaing that the yogi who does such concentration will have the result of becoming liberated.

[Gorakṣa] now summarizes by listing the results of each of the five concentrations:

stambhinī draviṇī caiva dahanī bhrāmiṇī tathā |
śoṣiṇī ca bhavanty etā bhūtānāṁ pañca dhāraṇāḥ ||59||

2.59. Stopping (*stambhinī*), liquifying (*draviṇī*), burning (*dahanī*), whirling (*bhrāmiṇī*) and desiccating (*śoṣiṇī*) result from the five *dhāraṇās* or concentrations on the elements.

These are the respective results of performing the five *dhāraṇās*.[1]

karmaṇā manasā vācā dhāraṇāḥ pañca durlabhāḥ |
vijñāya satataṁ yogī sarva-duḥkhaiḥ pramucyate ||60||

[1]In other words, by concentrating on the earth element, as in verse 2.54, one becomes capable of stopping or stabilizing things, and so on. These are to be defined as in the commentaries to the preceding verses.

2.60. The five concentrations are rarely attained through deeds, mind, or speech. The yogi who has realized them is freed from all suffering.

Deeds (*karma*) means rituals; mind means by thought; "by speech" means indicatory statements like "It is thus."[1] The yogis who has realized these five rare concentrations is liberated from all pains.

Dhyāna

Now as [Gorakṣa] introduces the section on meditation, which will continue over the next 24 verses, he first explains the meaning of the word *cintā* or thought.

> *smṛ ity eva sarva-cintāyāṁ dhātur ekaḥ prapadyate |*
> *yac citte nirmalā cintā tad dhi dhyānaṁ pracakṣate ||61||*

2.61. The verb root √*smṛ* (to remember) is used to mean all thought. That thought which is pure in the mind is certainly known as meditation (*dhyāna*).[2]

---

[1]Through the intellectual process of definition.

[2]This verse (unsurprisingly) takes on quite different forms in other texts. The Lonavla edition of *Gorakṣa-śatakam* reads:

> *sarva-cintā-samāvarti yogino hṛdi vartate |*
> *yat tattve niścitaṁ cetas tat tu dhyānaṁ pracakṣate* || (76)

"All kinds of thoughts reside in the heart of the yogi, but when the mind is fixed on the Principle [*tattva*] (i.e., the ātman), that is called *dhyāna*." [Their translation.]

The ten-chapter edition of *Haṭha-pradīpikā* (6.19) reads:

> *dhyānaṁ ca sarva-cintānāṁ nivṛttir vai nigadyate |*
> *yā tattve niścalā cintā saiva dhyānaṁ prakīrtitam ||*

"Meditation is said to be the end of all thoughts. That thought which is fixed on the Principle is called *dhyāna*." Their translation: "*Dhyāna* is said to be the technique which sets the mind free from all thoughts. The practice of unswerving concentration of the thoughts on any of the elements (*tattva*) is

The verb root √*smṛ* is used for all thought; in other words, it is a general term that includes all kinds of thinking processes. It should be understood that this is according to the grammarians. That pure thought process that is not concealed by any material sense object is the *smaraṇa* or "remembering" that is taught in the scriptures. The word *hi* ("certainly") is meant to convey certitude. This most certainly is known as *dhyāna*.

This *dhyāna* has two divisions, with attributes (*saguṇa*) and without attributes (*nirguṇa*), so he says:

dvividhaṁ bhavati dhyānaṁ sakalaṁ niṣkalaṁ tathā |
sakalaṁ varṇa-bhedena niṣkalaṁ nirguṇaṁ bhavet ||62||

2.62. Meditation is twofold, with parts (*sa-kala*) and without parts (*niṣ-kala*). That which has parts is differentiated according to *varṇa*, and that without parts is without attributes (*nirguṇa*).

There are two kinds of the afore-described *dhyāna*. One "with parts" meaning that in accordance with the material qualities (*guṇas*)[1] of *sattva, rajas* and *tamas,* it takes the form of various shapes, colors, symbols and forms, etc. This is thus known as *saguṇa* meditation, i.e., on [forms of the gods] such as those having four arms or five heads. The meditation that is without all these is called *nirguṇa*, without attributes. That is to say, it takes the form of light.

---

defined as *dhyāna*." It seems more likely that *tattva* refers to "the Reality" of the Self (the *ātmā*), as the great elements (which are subsequently called the *upādhis* in verse) have already been covered in the section on *dhāraṇā*. Indeed this fits in with the following verses.

[1]The word color (*varṇa*) is directly connected to the three *guṇas*, which color everything in the world. Black or blue represents *tamas,* red is associated with *rajas*, and white or yellow with *sattva*. Everything in the world is a mixture of the three *guṇas*, just as all colors come out of the mixture of the three primary colors.

[Gorakṣa] now describes the way one should situate oneself while meditating:

antaś-ceto bahiś-cakṣur adhaḥ sthāpya sukhāsanam |
samatvaṁ ca śarīrasya dhyāna-mudreti kathyate ||63||

2.63. Keeping the lower [part of the body] firmly established in a comfortable posture (*sukhāsana*),[1] the mind fixed inward and the gaze outward, and the [upper] body straight—this is called the meditative position (*dhyāna-mudrā*).[2]

The mind inward means that the inner organ (*antaḥ-karaṇa*) should be fixed on the *cakras* beginning with *mūlādhāra*, as will be described in the upcoming verses. The eyes should be fixed on the tip of the nose. "Below" here means on an even surface; one should take a comfortable position to sit in as was described earlier [Cf. 1.83]. In this way establishing the evenness of the body, i.e., sitting with the trunk, head and neck in a straight line, one should engage in one's meditation practice. This is called the meditative position (*dhyāna-mudrā*).

Now over the next few verses, [Gorakṣa] will describe the different loci of meditation, beginning with the *mūlādhāra-cakra*:

---

[1]Though *adhaḥ sthāpya* is the widely accepted reading of this verse, the *Viveka-mārtaṇḍa* has the better *adhiṣṭhāya*. The expression in this verse is not only grammatically incorrect, but the meaning is obscure in the context of the verse.

[2]We have been translating *mudrā* as "seal," especially where the *mahā-mudrā*, etc., are concerned. Here the word is being used in a more general sense, as *dhyāna-mudrā* is nowhere included in the listing of *mudrās*, of which there are 24 by the time we get to the *Gheraṇḍa-saṁhitā*. It simply means the position or attitude one takes for the purpose of meditation. *Sukhāsana* here does not refer to the specific *āsana* of that name, which is sometimes called "the tailor's pose" in English. It simply means, as the *Yoga-sūtra* describes it, a sitting position that is "comfortable and steady."(*sthiraṁ sukham āsanam*, 2.46).

ādhāraṁ prathamaṁ cakraṁ svarṇābhaṁ ca caturdalam[1] |
kuṇḍalinyā samāyuktaṁ dhyātvā mucyeta kilbiṣaiḥ ||64||

2.64. Meditating on the first center, the *ādhāra* which is the color of gold, has four petals and is combined with the *kuṇḍalinī*, one is released from stains.

The *ādhāra* is the first *cakra*, known as the *mūlādhāra.* It is gold and has four petals. The yogi who meditates on it along with the *kuṇḍalinī* is liberated from stains, i.e., sins. In other words, he is completely purified. One should on hearing the word *ādhāra*, include with it the presence of the Svayambhū-liṅga [and other features].

svādhiṣṭhāne ca ṣaṭ-patre san-māṇikya-sama-prabhe |
nāsāgra-dṛṣṭir ātmānaṁ dhyātvā yogī sukhī bhavet ||65||

2.65. That yogi becomes joyful who keeps his gaze fixed on the tip of the nose and contemplates the Self in the six-petaled *svādhiṣṭhāna* center, which resembles a perfect ruby.

The *svādhiṣṭhāna* is a six-petaled lotus that has the color of a perfect ruby, meaning a brilliant red color. The yogi who keeps his gaze fixed on the tip of the nose and meditates on the Self, either in the form with attributes as his chosen worshipable deity (*iṣṭa*), or in the attributeless form as light, will become happy.

Furthermore,

taruṇāditya-saṅkāśe candre ca maṇipūrake |
nāsāgra-dṛṣṭir ātmānaṁ dhyātvā saṅkṣobhayej jagat ||66||

---

[1]In some readings *tapta-kāñcana-sannibhaṁ*, matching more closely 1.20 above. See L.

2.66. That yogi sets the world trembling who keeps his gaze fixed on the tip of the nose and contemplates the Self in the *maṇipūra* center, the moon that shines like the youthful sun.

Again, the "youthful" sun means the sun which is newly arisen, being a reddish orb. The *maṇipūra-cakra* shines like the newly risen sun, lighting up the world. That yogi who keeps his gaze fixed on the tip of the nose and meditates on the Self sets the entire world a-trembling.

hṛd-ākāśe sthitaṁ śambhuṁ pracaṇḍa-ravi-tejasam |
nāsāgre dṛṣṭim ādhāya dhyātvā brahma-mayo bhavet ||67||

2.67. Fixing the gaze at the tip of the nose and meditating on Śambhu, who is situated in the heart space and is as brilliant as the summer sun, he becomes one with Brahman.

In the "heart space" (*hṛd-ākāśa*), i.e., in the hollow of the heart lotus or *cakra* named *anāhata.* There, with the brilliance of the fierce-rayed intense summer sun is Śambhu, i.e., Śiva in the form of the Bāṇa-liṅga. Fixing the gaze on the tip of the nose and meditating on him, one becomes non-different from Brahman, in other words all one's limiting adjuncts are completely removed [and one realizes one's true identity as Brahman].

vidyut-prabhe ca hṛt-padme prāṇāyāma-vibhedataḥ |
nāsāgra-dṛṣṭir ātmānaṁ dhyātvā brahma-mayo bhavet ||68||

2.68. That yogi becomes one with Brahman who keeps his gaze fixed on the tip of the nose and through the divisions of breath control meditates on the Self in the heart lotus, which is lustrous like lightning.

In the aforementioned heart lotus, which is lustrous like lightning, having the bright effulgence of a flash of lightning, through the divisions of breath control, i.e., by the practice of breath control as described earlier, meditates on the Self in the manner spoken of before, keeping his gaze on the tip of the nose, becomes one with Brahman.

satataṁ ghaṇṭikā-madhye viśuddhe dīpaka-prabhe |
nāsāgra-dṛṣṭir ātmānaṁ dhyātvā mṛtyuṁ pramuñcati ||69||

2.69. That yogi becomes free from death who keeps his gaze fixed on the tip of the nose and constantly contemplates the Self in the *viśuddha* center, in the midst of the uvula, which shines like a lamp.[1]

In the midst of the *ghaṇṭikā* in the region of the neck, i.e., in the *viśuddha-cakra,* which shines with the light of a lamp, the yogi who keeps his gaze fixed on the tip of the nose and constantly, without cessation, contemplates the Self, becomes free from death, i.e., he becomes immortal.

[1]There is much confusion about the term *ghaṇṭikā*. Feuerstein comments on this verse that it means "small bell" and "may here refer to the thyroid or thyroidal cartilage, or possibly the epiglottis. Since verse 2.75 lists this separately from the *lambikā*, it cannot be the same as the uvula." The *Yoga-koṣa* has tried to draw a distinction between *lampikā* and *lambikā*, one meaning the uvula and thereby synonymous with *ghaṇṭikā*, and the other meaning the tongue (p. 249). We are not able to make a conclusive statement and have here translated *ghaṇṭikā* as uvula, following the dictionaries. Interestingly, the *Viveka-mārtaṇḍa* here has two verses (148-149) which seem to have been conflated in our version. In that reading the word *lambikā* is found, but *ghaṇṭikā* is not.

satataṁ kaṇṭha-madhye tu viśuddhaṁ dīpaka-prabhaṁ |
nāsāgradṛṣṭir ātmānaṁ dhyātvā duḥkhaṁ vimuñcati ||
sravat-pīyūṣa-saṁpūrṇe lambikā-candra-maṇḍale |
nāsāgra-dṛṣṭir ātmānaṁ dhyātvānandam avāpnuyāt ||

Moreover,

bhruvor antar-gataṁ devaṁ san-māṇikya-śikhopamam |
nāsāgra-dṛṣṭir ātmānaṁ dhyātvā"nanda-mayo bhavet ||70||

2.70. That yogi becomes filled with bliss who keeps his gaze fixed on the tip of the nose and meditates on the Self as a divine being in the space between the eyebrows, which is like the flame from a spotless ruby.

In the space between the eyebrows, i.e., in the *ājñā-cakra*. Meditating on the Self[1] that is situated there, who is of a reddish color like that of a flame from a spotless ruby. Keeping his gaze fixed on the tip of the nose, [the yogi] becomes filled with bliss, i.e., all the suffering that arises from the perception of duality melts away.

dhyāyen nīla-nibhaṁ nityaṁ bhrū-madhye parameśvaram |
ātmānaṁ vijita-prāṇo yogī yogam avāpnuyāt ||71||

2.71. That yogi attains *yoga* who has conquered the life air (*prāṇa*) and contemplates the Self as the Supreme Lord (*parameśvara*) of blue appearance in the space between the eyebrows.

Between the eyebrows in the *ājñā-cakra* is the Supreme Lord Śiva, of a blue color. He is the Self, or the Supreme Self (the Paramātmā). One who has conquered over the life air and constantly meditates on him attains yoga, namely the union of the individual self with the Supreme Self.

nirguṇaṁ ca śivaṁ śāntaṁ gagane viśvato mukham |
nāsāgra-dṛṣṭir ekākī dhyātvā brahma-samo bhavet ||72||

---

[1]Our commentator has not glossed the word *devaṁ*.

2.72. One who, being alone, keeping his gaze on the tip of the nose, meditates on Śiva in the sky as the unqualified, tranquil, and all-facing, becomes the same as Brahman.

In the sky (*gagane*), i.e., in the place of the *ājñā-cakra*; [Meditating on Śiva,] the unqualified, i.e., who is free of even the sixteenth part of a self-conception as the agent or enjoyer of the fruits, etc. [of action], and [who is] therefore peaceful. "All-facing" here means omnipresent in the universe. The yogi who meditates on Śiva, his gaze fixed on the tip of his nose, alone, i.e., remaining in a place where he is completely free from contact with any other person, becomes the same as Brahman, i.e., he is completely devoid of any of the qualities or attributes that would bestow on him the sense of being a fragmented separate entity or *jīva*, even in the state of empirical reality or practical worldly dealings (*vyavahāra-daśā*).

ākāśe yatra śabdaṁ syāt tad ājñā-cakram ucyate |
tatrātmānaṁ śivaṁ dhyātvā yogī yogam avāpnuyāt ||73||

2.73. In the sky (*ākāśa*) where sound would be, that is called the *ājñā-cakra*. The yogi who there meditates on the Self as Śiva attains *yoga*.

"In the sky," in the locus of the *ākāśa* element or *tattva*, which is where sound would be, i.e., the place where the unmanifest sound vibration (*nāda*) becomes manifest, that is called the *ājñā-cakra*, which is situated between the eyebrows. There, in that *cakra*, is the Self as Śiva, i.e., taking the form of Śiva. Meditating on this Self in the way aforementioned, the yogi attains liberation in the form of unicity (*kaivalya*). This is the sphere of the *ākāśa* element, so it is appropriate that the *nāda* would manifest here, as the ether is the element that has sound as its quality. This is stated in the *Yoga-sāra*:

ākāśa-maṇḍalaṁ vṛttaṁ devatāsya sadā-śivaḥ
nāda-rūpaṁ bhruvor madhye manaso maṇḍalaṁ viduḥ

> The *maṇḍala* of the sky is round. Its deity is Sadāśiva. It has the form of inchoate sound (*nāda*) and is situated between the eyebrows. It is also known as the *maṇḍala* of the mind.

Now [Gorakṣa] speaks of the common meditation in the empty space that is above the *ājñā-cakra*:

nirmalaṁ gaganākāraṁ marīci-jala-sannibham |
ātmānaṁ sarvagaṁ dhyātvā yogī muktim avāpnuyāt ||74||

2.74. That yogi attains liberation who contemplates the all-pervading Self, which is pure like the sky, appearing like the water in a mirage.

"Pure" here means free of any connection to such impurities as would cause its essence to be concealed. Therefore it is like the sky, clear and free from clouds. The comparison to the sky means that it is all-pervading, being the same everywhere, since it can have no interruption causing segmentation. Therefore it spreads everywhere. Is it then devoid of all form? He says, "It appears like the water in a mirage." The idea is that just like the water in an apparition appears like shimmering light, so too does the ātmā. The yogi who meditates on the ātmā in this way will attain liberation.

[Gorakṣa] now speaks of the locations for such meditation [on the ātmā] in two verses:

gudaṁ meḍhraś ca nābhiś ca hṛt-padmaṁ ca tad-ūrdhvataḥ |
ghaṇṭikā lambikā-sthānaṁ bhrū-madhyaṁ ca nabho-bilam ||75||
kathitāni navaitāni dhyāna-sthānāni yogibhiḥ |
upādhi-tattva-yuktāni kurvanty aṣṭa-guṇodayam ||76||

2.75-76. Yogis tell of nine loci (*sthāna*) for meditation. These are the anus, genital organ, navel, heart lotus, the one above that, the uvula, the palate, the spot between the eyebrows, and the sky cavity (*brahma-randhra*). When associated with the adjuncts and the substance, these bring about the appearance of the eight virtues.

The nine loci: The anus refers to the *mūlādhāra*, the genital is the *svādhiṣṭhāna*, the navel is the *maṇipūraka*, the heart lotus refers to the *anāhata*, the locus above that is the *viśuddha-cakra*, the root of the *ghaṇṭikā (uvula)*, and the place of the *lambikā*;[1] the spot between the eyebrows is the *ājñā-cakra*, the sky cavity is the place of the void above the *ājñā*.[2] The word *upādhi-tattva* ("adjuncts and the substance")[3] should be understand to mean first the *upādhis*, which are the great elements of earth, water, fire, air, and ether, [and are associated with each of these loci], while *tattva* or "substantive truth" refers to the Self. So the yogis describe these loci in association with these elements and the Self. By the word "tell" (*kathitāni*) it should be understand that these yogis engage with these loci through the yoga of meditation and by so doing

---

[1]There is some confusion about the words *lambikā* and *ghaṇṭikā*, which both mean uvula. Our commentator has not clarified, but it seems from the text that the two are meant to be synonymous. The Lonavla *Yoga-koṣa* attempts to solve the problem by distinguishing between *lampikā* and *lambikā*, which are simply orthographical variants. For *lampikā* (which is the way they read this verse): "...one of the nine *dhyāna-sthānas* (spots on the body for meditating upon). It is probably the highest of the three parts of the throat, below which there are the *ghaṇṭikā* and *candra*. The yogi, however, does not meditate on the uvula, but on the spot somewhere near or inside it in the mouth; although *ghaṇṭikā* is the uvula." *Yoga-koṣa* (p.249) takes *lambikā* to mean the tongue itself, refering to the extending or lengthening process (*lambī-karaṇam*) that the yogi engages in for perfecting the *khecarī-mudrā*.

[2]These nine correspond exactly neither with the nine *cakras* nor the sixteen *ādhāras* as given in *Siddha-siddhānta-paddhati*, which calls the entire palate from the uvula to the teeth the *tālu-cakra*. There the eighth cakra is the *brahma-randhra* or *nirvāṇa-cakra*, and the *ākāśa-cakra* ("the sky cakra") is the complex of meditation points visualized outside and above the head. For more details see *Yoga-taraṅgiṇī* 1.13 and footnotes.

[3]See below, 2.81-82.

bring about the appearance of the eight qualities, i.e., the mystical accomplishments or *siddhis*, such as making oneself very small, etc.

nābhau saṁyamya cittaṁ pavana-gatim
adho rodhayet saṁprayatnād
ākuñcyāpāna-mūlaṁ hutavaha-sadṛśaṁ
tantuvat sūkṣma-rūpam |
tad viddhvā hṛt-saroje tad anu caraṇake
tāluke brahma-randhre
bhittvānte yāti śūnyaṁ praviśati gagane
yatra devo maheśaḥ ||77||[1]

2.77. By controlling (*saṁyama*[2]) the mind in the navel and carefully blocking the movement of the *prāṇa* below it, contracting the *apāna* root, which is like fire and of subtle form like a thread, as well as by piercing the heart lotus and then the *viśuddha-cakra*, and breaking through the palate and the *brahma-randhra*, one finally enters the emptiness in the sky, where abides the god Maheśa.

By controlling or stabilizing the *citta* or inner organ within the navel, i.e., the *maṇipūra-cakra*, then carefully, i.e., with great care, contracting the *apāna* root, i.e., the rectal sphincter, one should block or hold the movement of the air, namely the *apāna*, below, i.e, in the rectal gateway. Then one should raise it upwards, by uniting it with the mind and the *prāṇa*. It is called fire here because it is like fire, having the form of enflamed brilliance. One should

[1]This verse is not numbered, nor is it included in the *Viveka-mārtaṇḍa*. The commentator himself says that it and the one following are interpolated, but has commented on them in spite of this. So we have just incorporated the two verses and given them each a number. The concordance given in the Appendix will help orient the interested reader.

[2]*Saṁyama* is a technical term in the *Yoga-sūtra* (3.4), refering to the three last *aṅgas* of yoga, namely *dhāraṇā*, *dhyāna* and *samādhi*, when all three are focused on the same object. In YS, *saṁyama* on various objects leads to particular *siddhis*.

think of it as having the subtle form of a thread, i.e., appearing like a very thin filament. After this, one should pierce through the navel center and go on to the heart center, then to the *caraṇaka*,[1] which is the *viśuddha-cakra* in the throat, then to the palate center and finally the *brahma-randhra*, in that order. In the end, at the time of leaving the body, one should pierce through the *brahma-randhra*, where the supreme form of the god Śiva abides. There alone does [the yogi] enter into the emptiness of the sky of consciousness (*cid-ākāśa*) and dissolve.

nābhau śubhrāravindaṁ tad upari vimalaṁ
maṇḍalaṁ caṇḍa-raśmeḥ
saṁsārasyaika-rūpāṁ tribhuvana-jananīṁ
dharma-dātrīṁ narāṇām |
tasmin madhye tri-mārge tritaya-tanu-dharāṁ
chinna-mastāṁ praśastāṁ
tāṁ vande jñāna-rūpāṁ maraṇa-bhaya-harāṁ
yoginīṁ jñāna-mudrām ||78||

2.78. There is a white lotus in the navel; above it, in the pure region of the fierce-rayed sun, in the threefold subtle flow at the center of the triple path, resides the auspicious goddess Chinnamastā. I venerate her, the *yoginī*, the single form of the entire phenomenal world (*saṁsāra*), the mother of the three worlds, the bestower of the duties of humankind, who possesses a body that is threefold, who is the form of knowledge, the remover of the fear of death, and the wisdom seal (*jñāna-mudrā*).

[First] meditating on the white lotus in the navel center or *maṇipūra-cakra*. Above it, i.e., in that lotus is the spotless terrain

---

[1]This word and the variant reading *dalanaka* are elsewhere unattested, but seem to clearly indicate the *viśuddha-cakra*, as per our commentator.

(*maṇḍala*) of the fierce-rayed (*caṇḍa-raśmi*) sun. Within that region in the "triple path" (*trimārga*), i.e., in the opening to the Suṣumṇā, which is threefold due to the adjuncts of the three qualities of material nature (*sattva, rajas* and *tamas*), is the Goddess, possessing a body that is threefold (*tritaya-tanu*) because of having the form of knowledge (*jñāna-rūpā*), thus she is the auspicious *yoginī*, meaning that she can only be known through yoga; she is the wisdom seal (*jñāna-mudrā*),[1] meaning that she is only cut off [from the Absolute] by the adjunct of wisdom; therefore she removes the fear of death. I worship or revere that Goddess who has chopped off her own head, Chinnamastā Devī.

Though the last two verses are interpolations, they have been explained due to the excellence of their meaning.

eṣu*[2] *brahmātmakaṁ tejaḥ śiva-jyotir anuttamam |
dhyātvā jñātvā vimuktaḥ syād iti gorakṣa-bhāṣitam ||79||

2.79. One who in these contemplates and realizes the unequalled light of Śiva, the luster that is identical with Brahman, will be liberated. So it has been stated by Gorakṣa.

"In these" means in the nine loci of meditation [described in 2.75]. The word *anuttama*, means something that has nothing greater than it, that which is unsurpassed or the best of all. The light of Śiva is the light (*jyotiḥ*) that has the nature of Śiva, identified [particularly] with the heart lotus and *ājñā-cakras*, i.e., as having the form of Lord Śiva. "The luster that is identical with Brahman" (*brahmātmakaṁ tejaḥ*) is the formless and attributeless Brahman.

---

[1] I would take this as a *bahuvrīhi* compound: "She keeps her hands in the position of the *jñāna-mudrā*, whereby her forefinger and thumb are held in contact while the other fingers are extended."

[2] The word *eṣu* refers back to the nine loci of meditation listed in 2.75-76, clear evidence that verses 2.77-78 are interpolated.

According to this method, one should meditate on both these kinds of forms [*saguṇa* and *nirguṇa*] in each of these loci and realize them there. When one does so one becomes liberated, i.e., free from the continued repetitions of the cycle of birth and death. "So it has been stated by Gorakṣa" means that this is his promise and so one should have no doubts on the matter.[1]

He now concludes:

aśvamedha-sahasrāṇi vājapeya-śatāni ca |
ekasya dhyāna-yogasya kalāṁ nārhanti ṣoḍaśīm ||80||

2.80. A thousand horse sacrifices or a hundred vājapeya sacrifices are not worth even one-sixteenth part of a single yogic meditation.

Thousands of horse sacrifices (*aśvamedha*) and hundreds of *vājapeya* sacrifices—all are full of the slaughter of animals. Therefore they are not worth even one-sixteenth of a single yogic meditation, i.e., they are not capable of bestowing even the sixteenth part of the benefits that accrue to a meditator.

Samādhi

Over the next fifteen verses [the author] describes *samādhi*, beginning with four verses demonstrating the factual situation (*vastu-sthiti*)—

upādhiś ca tathā tattvaṁ dvayam etad udāhṛtam |
upādhiḥ procyate varṇas tattvam ātmābhidhīyate ||81||

---

[1]As the word of the realized master is the final authority.

2.81. The adjuncts (*upādhi*) and the substance are explained [as follows]: the adjuncts are said to be the letters [or colors], and the substance is called the Self.

The term *upādhi*[1] is derived from the prefix *upa* meaning "nearby" and *ādhīyate*, "placed upon," meaning that in which the Self is held by all parts (*sarvāvayayena*); it is the locus within which the Self is revealed. And the substance (*tattva*) is the conscious self. These two have been spoken of [as follows]: The *upādhis* take the form of the letters or that of the *praṇava*, whereas the substance [or Reality] is called the Self.

He now clarifies this statement—

upādher anyathā jñānaṁ tattva-saṁsthitir anyathā |
samastopādhi-vidhvaṁsī sadābhyāsena jāyate ||82||

2.82. On account of the adjuncts, one's knowledge is of one kind; the actual state of reality is other [than that]. The actual state of reality that destroys all the adjuncts manifests through constant practice (*abhyāsa*).

The word *upādheḥ* is taken as being as an ablative of cause; "due to the *upādhis*" one's knowledge rather than being a genuine reflection of reality informs one of the opposite.[2] For example, next to a hibiscus flower, a crystal takes on the red color.[3] Or, the reflected consciousness [due to the *upādhis*] thinks, "I am happy, I am sad" and so on. The actual state of reality (*tattva-saṁsthiti*) is something quite different. Just like the crystal appears red, but is in fact white and not red, so the *jīva*, who is dispersed by the influence of the

[1]A superimposed condition, not an inherent attribute or state; a condition external to the intrinsic nature of an object or entity. The "names and forms."
[2]*Viparyaya* or false cognition.
[3]The word *varṇa* has numerous meanings, one of which is "color." This then becomes the classification of four classes of man, the *varṇas*.

senses that give the experience of happiness or distress, is in fact formed of knowledge and bliss and has no connection to any [externally produced] happiness or distress. By constant application of the yoga practices that have been taught [in this book] the yogi becomes the destroyer of all the *upādhis*.

[Gorakṣa] now describes the characteristics of *samādhi*:

śabdādīnāṁ ca tan-mātraṁ yāvat karṇādiṣu sthitam |
tāvad eva smṛtaṁ dhyānaṁ samādhiḥ syād ataḥ param ||83||

2.83. As long as the sense objects [*tanmātras* or subtle elements] such as sound are present to the ears and other senses, that is called meditation. *Samādhi* only comes after that.

For the yogi engaged in meditation, as long as the *tanmātras* of the sense objects such as sound are present to the senses such as the ears, i.e., perceived by them, that is said to be meditation. When the senses have been submerged in the Self and one is in the state where there is only the flash of meaning,[1] then the word *samādhi* can [appropriately] be employed.

In this connection [Gorakṣa] gives the measure of *dhāraṇā* and so on:

dhāraṇā pañca-nāḍībhiḥ dhyānaṁ ca ṣaṣṭi-nāḍibhiḥ |
dina-dvādaśakena syāt samādhiḥ prāṇa-saṁyamāt ||84||

---

[1]*Artha-mātrāvabhāsa*. This is taken from Patañjaḷi's *Yoga-sūtra* 1.43, which defines the *nirvitarkā samāpatti*. "When there has occurred complete and all-round purification of memory and the mind-field is, as it were, devoid of its own form and illuminative of only the object signified, it is called *samādhi* without gross thought." (Translation by Swami Veda Bharati, *The Yoga-sūtras of Patañjali*, Vol I, p. 387).

2.84. *Dhāraṇā* by two hours of control over the breath; *dhyāna* by twenty-four hours; *samādhi* by twelve days.

When one has attained full control of the breath for five *nāḍis*[1] then that is *ḍhāraṇā*. By the same token, sixty *nāḍis* of *prāṇāyāma* is *dhyāna*. And twelve days, by which is meant a full day [or 24-hour period] including both day and night, of such breath control results in *samādhi*.

Now he defines *samādhi*:

yat sarva-dvandvayor aikyaṁ jīvātma-paramātmanoḥ[2] |
samasta-naṣṭa-saṅkalpaḥ samādhiḥ so'bhidhīyate ||85||

2.85. *Samādhi* is defined as the [state wherein there is] complete unification of all dualities [and] of the individual self with the supreme Self, and all desire-ideation (*saṅkalpa*) has been completely banished.

That unification of all dualities or pairs of opposities such as happiness and distress or heat and cold, meaning that due to the emptiness of the world that arises from such dualities, one experiences it as the causal form alone (*kāraṇa-mātra-rūpatvam*). In exactly the same way, that which is the oneness of the individual and Supreme selves is alone called the *samādhi* that is free of all desire-ideation.

He now gives an example of how the individual self and Supreme Self are one:

---

[1]*Nāḍī*, like *ghaṭikā*,is a unit of time equal to half a *muhūrta*, i.e., 24 minutes.
[2]*Viveka-mārtaṇḍa* (164) and *Haṭha-yoga-pradīpikā* (4.7) here both read *yat samatvaṁ dvayor atra jīvātma-paramātmanoḥ*, "That state of equilibrium, which is the union of the individual self and the Supreme Self." Mahadeva Shastri points out that this is *asamprajñāta-samādhi*.

ambu-saindhavayor aikyaṁ yathā bhavati yogataḥ |
tathātma-manasor aikyaṁ samādhir abhidhīyate ||86||

2.86. Just as the oneness of salt and water comes from their combination (*yoga*), so too the oneness of Self and mind is called *samādhi*.

When one throws salt into water, then from their *yoga*, i.e., their combination, they become one, i.e., non different; so too in the same way, through turning inward (*antar-mukhatayā*) [i.e., yoga], the functions of the mind take the shape of the Self, and thus oneness or union of the mind and the self is achieved. This state is called *samādhi*.

Now he describes the *nirvikalpa-samādhi*:

yadā saṅkṣīyate prāṇo mānasaṁ ca pralīyate |
tadā samarasatvaṁ ca samādhiḥ so'bhidhīyate ||87||

2.87. When the *prāṇa* is dissolved and the mind merges, then the complete equilibrium (*samarasatva*) [that results] is called *samādhi*.

The yogi stops the activities of mind and breath together and contemplates the Self. "When his breath is dissolved," i.e., even without applying the *jālandhara-bandha* and other techniques he is unable to observe any movement of exhalation, in other words the breath becomes merged into the Self. Furthermore, when the mind or inner instrument merges or attains a formless state, there is no fluctuation (*vṛtti*) at all. Up to this point, these characteristics can also be found in the *sa-vikalpa-samādhi*. The special characteristics of the *nirvikalpa* state is explained as follows: When the oneness of the individual soul and the Supreme Soul has reached the same kind of non-difference of identity (*samarasatvaṁ*) that is seen in the dissolution of salt in water, then that is called *samādhi*.

Now [Gorakṣa] describes the situation of the yogi in that state:

na gandhaṁ na rasaṁ rūpaṁ na ca sparśaṁ na niḥsvanam |
nātmānaṁ na paraṁ vetti yogī yuktaḥ samādhinā ||88||

2.88. The yogi who is fixed in *samādhi* knows neither himself nor another, nor smell, taste, form, touch or sound.

The yogi fixed in *samādhi*, i.e., having attained the state of oneness, since all the senses have merged with the mind alone, does not know the objects of the senses such as smell and so on. In the same way, he does not know himself as the meditator, nor the Supreme Self as the object of meditation, and the word *ca* ("and") here implies that he does not know or is not aware of the activity of meditating either. The idea is that knowledge of the sense objects arises through sense perception, but the Self is not an object (*aviṣaya*) in this way.

abhedyaḥ sarva-śastrāṇām avadhyaḥ sarva-dehinām |
agrāhyo mantra-tantrāṇāṁ yogī yuktaḥ samādhinā ||89||

2.89. The yogi who is fixed in *samādhi* cannot be pierced by any weapon, killed by any embodied being, nor be controlled by any spell (*mantra*) or occult diagram (*tantra*).

The yogi who is fixed in *samādhi* cannot be pierced by any weapon; it is not possible for him to be cleft by them. Similarly, embodied beings like lions and elephants cannot kill him. Spells and occult diagrams used in black magic cannot affect him, for he is beyond death and delusion and matters connected thereto.

bādhyate na sa kālena lipyate na sa karmaṇā |
sādhyate na ca kenāpi yogī yuktaḥ samādhinā ||90||

2.90. The yogi who is fixed in *samādhi* is not bound by time, tainted by action, nor can he be influenced by anyone or anything.

That yogi who is fixed in *samādhi* is not bound by time, meaning that the conditions that give rise to old age and death do not affect him. He is not tainted by actions, which are a cause of good and bad results. In other words, he does not harbor the kinds of pious or sinful actions that give rise to consequences like old age and death. Therefore no one, not even [the creator god] Brahmā himself can influence him, i.e., he cannot be won over by [promises of the] fulfilment of any material desire.

How can such [*samādhi-*] *yoga* be attained? In answer [the author] says—

yuktāhāra-vihārasya yukta-ceṣṭasya karmasu |
yukta-svapnāvabodhasya yogo bhavati duḥkhahā ||91||

2.91. Yoga ends the suffering of one who is balanced in eating and leisure activity, who is balanced in his efforts in karmas, and balanced in sleeping and waking.

The compound *yuktāhāra-vihāra* means one whose eating and leisure activities are balanced.[1] Balance in eating has already been

[1]The passive participle *yukta*, with the meanings "regulated, restrained, moderate, appropriate, or disciplined" is here being translated as "balanced," though the idea of discipline to achieve such balance is also applicable, the former as the result, the latter as the means. According to the *Gītā* (6.3), the

spoken of earlier with regards to a measured diet (Cf. 1.54). Balance in leisure activities (*vihāra*) refers to mundane dealings and so on. *Karma* here refers to regular and irregular religious rituals that are to be performed. One should be balanced, i.e., free from too much attachment, in one's efforts to perform them. Balance in sleeping and waking means that one is measured in both sleeping and staying awake. The yoga practice of a yogi who is balanced in these ways will end his suffering; it will bring an end to the illusion of birth and death, etc.

In the next two verses [Gorakṣa] explains what this state of yoga is:

nirādy-antaṁ nirālambaṁ niṣprapañcaṁ nirāśrayam |
nirāmayaṁ nirākāraṁ tattvaṁ tattva-vido viduḥ ||92||

2.92. The knowers of Reality know that Reality to be without beginning or end, without any support, undevolved, without any substratum, without any ills, and formless.

Nirādy-antam means that It is devoid of either beginning or end. It has no support and no substratum, meaning that It is not like the material world which is situated within the illusory energy (*māyā*). It is "undevolved" (*niṣprapañca*) meaning that It is devoid of the material elements that are the product of the [mis]conception of duality. "Free of all ills" (*nirāmaya*): free from the suffering that arises from falling or dying, etc. "Formless" (*nirākāra*): It is without form (*ākāra*); this refers to particular transformations such as hands and feet. The Reality (*tattva*) means the unity of the separated consciousness (the *jīva*) and the Self (*ātmā*), i.e., the

---

earlier stage of yoga is characterized by effort, the latter by pacification of the mind. This word is also formed from the same root as the word *yoga*, shedding light on the meaning of the latter word. Cf. Gītā 2.48, *samatvaṁ yoga ucyate*. This verse (2.91), the only external quote from a known text in GŚ, is taken from the *Bhagavad-gītā*, 6.17.

essential being of the Self, which is the meaning intended by the word *yoga*. Those who are knowers of that Reality, i.e., the yogis, know It thus.

Moreover,

nirmalaṁ niścalaṁ nityaṁ niṣkriyaṁ nirguṇaṁ mahat |
vyoma vijñānam ānandaṁ brahma brahma-vido viduḥ ||93||

2.93. The knowers of Brahman know Brahman to be pure, motionless, eternal, inactive, without attributes, and great. It is space, direct knowledge and bliss.[1]

Pure (*nirmala*) means devoid of impurities such as the desire for the fruits of action. Motionless (*niścala*)means free from any effort intending union [with the favorable] or distance [from the unfavorable]. Inactive (*niṣkriya*) means that there is nothing in Brahman resembling purposeful engagement. "Without attributes" (*nirguṇa*) means that It has no connection or contact with the material qualities, namely *sattva, rajas* and *tamas*. Great (*mahat*) means that It is not divided by time and space. "It is space (*vyoma*)" means that It has the form of the space of consciousness (*cid-ākāśa*); *vijñāna* means spiritual realization, of which It is the essence. Those who know Brahman, i.e., the yogis, recognize Brahman as the non-dual form of bliss.

Who knows Brahman, and what is It like?

nirātaṅke nirālambe nirādhāre nirāmaye |
yogī yoga-vidhānena pare brahmaṇi līyate ||94||

---

[1]Feuerstein."Vedānta metaphysics typically characterizes the Absolute (*brahman*) as pure being (*sat*), pure consciousness (*cit*), and pure bliss (*ānanda*). Here infinite space (*vyoman*) is substituted for pure being."

2.94. The yogi through the process of yoga merges into the transcendent Brahman, which is free from fear, without support, without any substratum, and beyond ill.

Through the methods of the six-limbed yoga system and by practising according to the proper method, the yogi merges into the Supreme Brahman, which is devoid of fear, any support, substratum or impurity. Merging means to attain these same characteristics.

hetu-dṛṣṭānta-nirmuktaṁ mano-buddhyor agocaram |
vyoma vijñānam ānandaṁ tattvaṁ tattva-vido viduḥ ||95||

2.95. The knowers of Reality know It has neither cause (*hetu*) nor comparison (*dṛṣṭānta*); It cannot be perceived by the mind or intelligence. It is void (*vyoma*), direct knowledge and bliss (*ānanda*).

The Supreme Reality is liberated, i.e., devoid of any cause[1] by which one can directly perceive It, as well as of any comparison. It cannot be perceived by the mind or intelligence because It is not a sense-object. Those who are knowers of the Reality know It to be space, direct knowledge and bliss.

It was said above (2.94) that the yogi merges. Does this mean that he just disappears like a stone thrown into the water, all the while keeping his distinct form? In answer, [Gorakṣa] says, no,

---

[1]Since *hetu* is followed by *dṛṣṭānta*, it appears that the original intent was to state that Brahman is beyond logical argument, i.e., rational proof, as well as impossible to understand by way of example (*dṛṣṭānta*). These are two essential elements in the five-fold syllogism of Nyāya argumentation. *pratijñā-hetūdāharaṇopanaya-nigamanāni pañcāvayavāḥ* (*Tarka-saṅgraha,* 60)

yathā ghṛtaṁ ghṛte kṣiptaṁ ghṛtam eva hi jāyate |
kṣīre kṣīraṁ tathā yogī tattvam eva hi jāyate ||96||

2.96. Just as ghee poured into ghee becomes only ghee and nothing else, as it is with milk [poured] into milk, so does the yogi become the Reality and nothing else.

Just as the ghee poured into ghee is ghee and does not become something else, or as milk poured into milk similarly remains milk, so the yogi who merges into Brahman, which is the form of the Supreme Reality, becomes that Reality, this is because both the individual soul and Brahman are consciousness itself, without any distinction.

In order to support the idea that the individual soul and Brahman are different in name only, [Gorakṣa] now gives an example of how a single thing can have different names—

dugdhe kṣīraṁ ghṛte sarpir agnau vahnir ivārpitaḥ |
tanmayatvaṁ vrajaty eva yogī līnaḥ pare pade ||97||

2.97 Just as the secretion from a cow's udder when offered into milk, or clarified butter into ghee, or flames into fire, attain the same properties, so it is with a yogi who merges into the Supreme Truth.[1]

Just as the milk one offers into milk, the ghee [poured] into ghee, or the fire [placed] in a fire, all have the same properties, or like the light of two lamps which when lit one next to the other take on the same single identity, so it is with the yogi. The rest is clear.

[1]The verse here deliberately uses synonyms, i.e., different names for the same object, in order to illustrate that it is the name alone that is different, the essence is always the same, since pure consciousness is the true identity both of the individualized self and the Supreme Soul.

Conclusion

Now directly addressing the audience, the author brings his work to a conclusion by announcing the benefits that come from studying it:

bhava-bhaya-haraṁ nṝṇāṁ mukti-sopāna-saṁjñakam |
guhyād guhyataraṁ guhyaṁ gorakṣeṇa prakāśitam ||98||

2.98. The secret (*guhya*) revealed by Gorakṣa, which was more hidden than any other secret, is called the ladder to liberation and the remover of the fear of existence for all humans.

[This yoga] is the remover of the fear of existence for all people in the world, that is, the fear arising from repeated births and deaths. Moreover, it is the ladder to liberation, i.e., the rapid means for attaining liberation. It is more secret than all other secrets, but [even so] it has been revealed or spoken by Gorakṣa. This verse should be read together with the following [i.e., the Sanskrit is syntactically meant to be read as one sentence].

iti gorakṣa-śatakaṁ yoga-śāstraṁ janaḥ paṭhet |
sarva-papa-vinirmukto yoga-siddhiṁ labhed dhruvam ||99||

2.99. Any person who would study this science of yoga, *Gorakṣa-śataka*, will be released from all sins and will surely attain success in yoga.

The person who would study the foregoing scripture of yoga named the *Gorakṣa-śataka*, after being released from all sins, will most certainly without any doubt attain the perfection of yoga.

Now [Gorakṣa] says that since all other scriptures only bestow trivial fruits, one should reject them and study this one alone:

yoga-śāstraṁ paṭhen nityaṁ kim anyaiḥ śāstra-vistaraiḥ |
yat svayaṁ cādināthasya nirgataṁ vadanāmbujāt ||100||

2.100. One should regularly study this yoga scripture, which issued from the lotus mouth of the original Lord himself. What then is the need of so many other scriptures?[1]

The yogi should regularly study this authoritative text on yoga. What will be gained from studying other scriptures? For this yoga scripture came out of the lotus mouth of Ādinātha [Śiva] himself. In other words, it was composed by him.

One who has studied this *Gorakṣa-śataka*, which directly teaches about liberation, has covered everything [that needs to be done or known]. To indicate this, [the author] speaks the following verse:

snātaṁ tena samasta-tīrtha-salile dattā dvijebhyo dharā
yajñānāṁ ca hutaṁ sahasram ayutaṁ devāś ca saṁpūjitāḥ |
satyaṁ tena sutarpitāś ca pitaro svargaṁ ca nītāḥ punar
yasya brahma-vicāraṇe kṣaṇam api prāpnoti dhairyaṁ manaḥ ||

2.101. One whose mind has attained even a moment's stillness while deliberating on Brahman has bathed in the water of all the places of pilgrimage, has given the [entire] earth in charity to the Brāhmaṇas, has performed thousands of millions of sacrifices and worshiped all the gods. Truly, he has properly pleased the forefathers and led them to heaven.

[1]This verse is clearly calqued on the famous *Gītā-māhātmya* verse: *gītā sugītā kartavyā kim anyaiḥ śāstra-vistaraiḥ | yā svayaṁ padmanābhasya mukha-padmād viniḥsṛtā ||*

That person has bathed in the waters of all the *tīrthas*, from the Gaṅgā on. Moreover, he has given the entire world in charity to the brāhmaṇas. He has performed hundreds of thousands of scrifices. He has perfectly worshiped the gods and brāhmaṇas. All the forefathers have been propitiated and led to heaven by him. All this is true. Who is that person? It is he whose mind has attained or adopted even a moment's calm or stillness in deliberating on Brahman, i.e., in meditating on his actual true spiritual identity. In other words, whatever benefits bathing in the Ganges and other holy places and engaging in these other religious and pious acts bestow will be attained by even just a moment of yoga, which takes the form of meditating on the Self.

In order to understand the nature of the Self one should examine what has been established by the *Tattva-saṅgraha*.[1]

The contents of the text summarized

- The first five verses describe the four *anubandhas*.
- In one verse, the benefits of yoga are described,
- and in one verse the six limbs of yoga are given.
- The next five verses describe the *āsanas*
- followed by twelve verses describing the *cakras*.
- The ten *nāḍis* are described over the next eight verses
- The next fourteen verses describe the life-airs and their functions.
- The following ten describe the glorious process of arousing the *śakti*.
- In 26 verses are told the five *mudrās* beginning with *mahā-mudrā*.
- In the next seven verses, the practice of *praṇava* is discussed and *prāṇāyāma* is praised.

[1] I have not been able to trace this verse to any known text of the name *Tattva-saṅgraha*.

- Then four verses talk about mastering the breath and [the next] eight of purifying the *nāḍis*.
- The next 21 verses further describe *prāṇāyāma*.
- Thirty verses for *pratyāhāra* and nine for *dhāraṇā*.
- 24 for *dhyāna* and thirteen for *samādhi*.
- And finally the benefit of studying the *Gorakṣa-śataka* is spoken of in four verses.

I have commented on the *Śataka* according to this sequence of subjects; if I have done anything foolish, may the saintly please forgive me for it, for how could one's mind not become agitated on hearing the great words of the master of yoga?

One should definitely not share this secretmost knowledge with anyone who is dishonest, devoid of devotion or attached to the belly and genitals.

Here ends the *Gorakṣa-śataka*.

Bibliography

Primary Sources – editions and translations

Amanaska-yoga (Tāraka-amanaska Yoga).

(ed. Brahmamitra Avasthī), Eng. trans. Bajraṁga Siṁha. Dillī: Svāmī Keśavānanda Yoga Saṁsthāna Prakāśana, 1987.

Ātma-bodha of Śaṅkarācārya Bhagavatpāda.

Trans. Swami Nikhilananda. Madras: Sri Ramakrishna Matha, 1947.

Bhagavad-gītā.

With commentary of Śaṅkara. Delhi: Motilal Banarsidass, 1987.

Bhāgavata-purāṇa.

With the commentary of Śrīdhara Svāmī. (ed.) Ram Tej Pandeya. Varanasi: Chowkhamba, 1987.

Dakṣiṇa-mūrti-stotram.

N. S. Venkatanathacharya(ed.): *Śaṅkarācārya's Śrī Dakṣiṇamūrti-stotram with Mānasollāsa of Sureśvarācārya.* Mysore: Oriental Research Institute, University of Mysore, 1972.

Devī-bhāgavata-purāṇa.

(ed.) Ram Tej Pandeya. Varanasi: Chowkhamba, 1986.

Gautamīya-tantra.

(ed.) Bhagirath Jha. Varanasi: Chowkhamba Sanskrit Series Office, Saṁ. 2033 (1977).

Gheraṇḍa Saṁhitā.

Swami Digambarji and Dr. M.L.Gharote (ed.): Lonavla, Kaivalyadhama S.M.Y.M. Samiti, 1997 (1st ed. 1978)

Gobhila Gṛhyasūtram

With the Sanskrit commentary *Mṛdulā* of M.M.Shri Mukund Jha Bakshi on First & Second *Prapāṭhaka* and *Saralā* Sanskrit Commentary on Third & Fourth *Prapāṭhakā* with *Anākulā* Hindi Translation. (ed.) Sudhākara Mālavīya. The Kashi Sanskrit Series 118. Varanasi, Chaukhambha Sanskrit Sansthan, 1997 (2nd ed.)

Gorakṣa-śataka.

Nowotny, Fausta: *Das Gorakṣaśataka*, Dokumente der Geistesgeschichte; 3. Koln: K. A. Nowotny, 1976.

Swāmi Kuvalayānanda & S. A. Shukla (ed.): *Gorakṣaśatakam* (With Introduction, Text, English Translation, Notes etc.). Lonavla, Kaivalyadhama S.M.Y.M. Samiti, 2006.

Gorakṣa-paddhati (GP or V)

Paṇḍita Mahīdharaśarma (transl.): *Gorakṣapaddhati*, Hindi translation. Mumbai, Khemaraj Shrikrishnadass, 1996.

Gorakṣa-siddhānta-saṅgrahaḥ.

(ed.) Śrī Janārdana-Śāstrī Pāṇḍeya. Sarasvatī Bhavana Grantha Mālā, Vol. 110. Vārāṇāsī : Vārāṇaseya-saṁskṛta-viśvavidyālayaḥ, 1973.

Gorakṣa-vacana-saṅgraha (see Banarjee, Akshaya Kumar)

Haṭha-pradīpikā (HP).

M. L. Gharote and Parimal Devnath (ed.): *Haṭha-pradīpikā* of Svātmārāma, with *Yogaprakāśikā* commentary by Bālakṛṣṇa. Lonavla, The Lonavla Yoga Institute (India), 2001.

Indrajāla-vidyā-saṅgraha.

Kalikātā: Vācaspatya Press, 1915

Jñāneśvarī Gūḍhārtha-dīpikā.

(*Vivaraṇakāra*) Śrī Bābājī Mahārāja Paṇḍita. Gorakhpur: Gita Press. 2nd edn. Saṁ 2055 (CE 1999).

Haṭha-yoga-pradīpikā (HYP) of Svātmārāma, with the commentary Jyotsnā of Brahmānanda and English Translation. Madras, The Adyar Library and Research Centre, 1972.

Haṭha-yoga-pradīpikā (HYP)

(Trans.) Srisa Chandra Basu (Allahabad: Panini Office, 1914.

Kumbhaka-paddhati.

M. L. Gharote and Parimal Devnath (Ed.): *Kumbhakapaddhati of Raghuvīra Science of Prāṇāyāma.* Lonavla, The Lonavla Yoga Institute (India), 2000.

Kuṇḍalinī Tantra.

(ed.) Swami Satyananda Saraswati. Bihar: Yoga Publications Trust, 2007

Khecarī-vidyā of Ādinātha.

Trans. and Ed. James Mallinson. Varanasi: Indica Books, 2007 (2010).

Liṅga Pūrāṇa

J.L. Shastri (ed.): *Liṅga-purāṇa.* Delhi: Motilal Banarsidass, 1980.

Manu-smṛti with commentary *Manvartha-muktāvalī* of Kullūka Bhaṭṭa.

(ed.) J.L. Shastri, (Eng. trans.) S. C. Banerji. Delhi: Motilal Banarsidass, 1990 (1983).

Sarva-darśana-saṅgraha of Mādhavācārya.

(ed.) Umāśaṅkara Sharma "Rishi." Varanasi: Chowkhamba, 1984.

Ṣaṭ-Cakra-Nirūpaṇa (SCN).

in Woodroffe, Sir John. *The Serpent Power, being the Ṣaṭ-Cakra-Nirūpaṇa and Pādukā-Pañcaka*. Two works on Laya-Yoga, Trans. from the Sanskrit, with Introduction and Commentary. Madras, Ganesh & Co., Twelth Edition 1981.

Siddha-siddhānta-paddhati (SSP)

ed, Hindi trans. Swami Dvārikādāsa Śāstrī: Vārāṇasī: Chaukhambā Vidyābhavana, 2006

Siddha-siddhānta-saṅgraha (SSS)

Surendra Kumār Vermā (transl.): *Balabhadra-viracitaḥ Siddha-siddhānta-saṅgraha*. Dehli, Eastern Book Linkers, 1986.

Śiva-saṁhitā.

(trans.) Rai Bahadur Srisā Chandra Vasu. Delhi: Munshiram Manoharlal, 1990 (original 1914).

Tantrāloka of Abhinava Gupta.

With the commentary *Viveka* by Jayadratha. In 8 volumes. (ed.) R.C. Dwivedi and Navjivan Rastogi. Delhi: Motilal Banarsidass, 1987. (First edition 1918-1938).

Vasiṣṭha-saṁhitā.

Swami Digambarji, Pitambar Jha, Gyan Shankar Sahay (ed.): *Vasiṣṭha-saṁhitā*. Lonavla: Kaivalya Dham, 1984.

Yoga-bīja.

Ed. Rāmalāla Śrīvāstava. Gorakhpur: Gorakhnath Mandir, 2039 saṁ (=1983)

Yoga-karṇikā of Nath Aghorānanda.

Ed. Narendra Nath Sharma. Delhi: Eastern Book Linkers. 1981.

Yoga Upaniṣads.

Pandit A. Mahadeva Sastri (ed.): *The Yoga Upaniṣad-s*, with the commentary of Śrī Upaniṣad Brahmayogin). Madras, The Adyar Library and Research Centre, Vol.6, 1968 (1st ed. 1920).

Yoga-sūtra.

Salvatore Zambito, (Ed.): *The Unadorned Thread of Yoga: The Yoga-Sūtras of Patañjali in English*, A Compilation of English Translations of Śri Patanjali's Exposition on the Yoga Darśana. With a foreword by Swami Veda Bharati. Washington, The Yoga-Sūtras Institute Press, 1992.

Swāmī Veda Bhāratī (transl., comm.): *Yoga Sutras of Patañjali With The Exposition of Vyās*, Vol.I Samādhi-Pāda. Honesdale, Pennsylvania, The Himalayan International Institute of Yoga Science and Philosophy of the U.S.A., 1986.

Swāmī Veda Bhāratī (transl., comm.): *Yoga Sutras of Patañjali With The Exposition of Vyās*, Vol.II Sādhanā-Pāda. Delhi, Motilal Banarsdiass, 2001 (reprint 2004).

Yoga-Vāsiṣṭha.

English translation by Vihari Lal Mitra, edited by Ravi Prakash Arya. (Delhi: Parimal Publications, 2005).

Yogayājñavalkya Samhitā.

T.K.V. Desikachar (transl.): *Yogayājñavalkya Samhitā The Yoga Treatise of Yājñavalkya.* Krishnamacharya Granthamala Series 4. Chennai, Krishnamacharya Yoga Mandiram, 2004.

Secondary Sources

Banerjea, Akshaya Kumar: *Philosophy of Gorakhnath.* With *Gorakṣa-vacana-saṅgraha.* Delhi: Motilal Banarsidass, 1988 (reprint).

Bernard, Theos. *Haṭha-yoga*. London: Rider and Company, 1950.

Briggs, George Weston: *Gorakhnāth and the Kānphaṭa Yogīs*. Delhi: Motilal Banarsidass, 1989 [1st ed. 1938].

Dvivedī, Hajārī Prasāda: *Nāthasampradāya*. Ilāhābāda: tritīya saṁskaraṇa 1981.

Dvivedī, Hājārī Prasāda. *Kabīra*. Delhi: Rājakamala Prakāśana. (13th printing), 2006.

Eliade, Mircea (ed.) : Encyclopedia of Religions., NY: Simon and Schuster Macmillan, 1995.

Feuerstein, Georg: *The Yoga Tradition*: Its History, Literature, Philosophy and Practice. Prescott (Arizona): Hohm Press, 1998.

Feuerstein, Georg: *The Encyclopedia of Yoga And Tantra*. Boston: Shambhala Publications, 2011 (Revised and expanded edition of The Shambhala Encyclopedia of Yoga, 1997).

Goswami, Shyam Sundar: *Layayoga*. Delhi: Motilal Banarsidass Publishers Private Limited, 2011.

Harshananda Swami: *Encyclopedia of Hinduism*. Bangalore: Ramkrishna Math, 2008.

Kwak, Seung Hyun: *A Study of Prāṇāyāma Based on the Yogic and Tantric Texts*, Ph.D. Thesis. Haridwar: Gurukul Kangri Universtiy, 2008.

Mallinson, James. "*The Original Gorakṣa-śataka*" in *Yoga in Practice*, David Gordon White(ed.). Princeton: Princeton University Press, 2011.

Maṁgalagiri Kṛṣṇāgiri: *Navanātha Caritra*. Delhi: Garga and Company (no publishing date)

Naṁjuṇḍana, Ke. Āra. *Mahāyogī Gorakṣanātha*. Madarāsa: Vidyā Bhāratī Prakāśana, reprint, 1992 (1921).

Swami Veda Bharati (Pandit Usharbudha Arya): *Mantra & Meditation Superconscious Meditation*, Vol.2.. Honesdale, Pennsylvania: The Himalayan International Institute of Yoga Science and Philosophy of the U.S.A., 1981.

Swami Veda Bharati. *Philosophy of Hatha Yoga*. Honesdale: 1988.

Wayman, Alex. *The Buddhist Tantras: Light on Indo-Tibetan Esoterism*. New York: Samuel Weisman, 1973.

Yogī Yatīndranātha Jī Mahārāja. *Gorakha Vāṇī aur Gorakha Yoga*. Haridvāra: Raṇadhīra Prakāśana, 2005.

Zambito, Salvatore: *The Yoga-Sūtra Sanskrit-English Dictionary*, Chandramani Shastri and Jagadānanda Das (Jan Brzezinski) (Editors-in-Chief). USA: The Yoga-Sūtras Institute Press, 2010.

Recommended Bibliography on Kuṇḍalinī

Swami Veda Bharati. *Mantra & Meditation: Superconscious Meditation*, vol. II. Honesdale, PA: The Himalayan International Institute of Yoga Science and Philosophy, 1981.

———, *Subtler than the Subtle: The Upanishad of the White Horse*. Saint Paul, MN: Yes International Publishers, 2002.

———, *Kuṇḍalinī: Stilled or Stirred?*. New Delhi: D. K. Printworld (P) Ltd., 2013.

"Energy of Consciousness in Human Personality" in Ronald S. Valle and Rolf von Eckartsberg (eds.), *Metaphors of Consciousness*. New York and London: Plenum Press, 1981, 1989.

Silburn, Lillian (tr.) *Kundalini: Energy of the Depths*. Albany, NY: State University of New York (SUNY) Press, 1988.

Swami Rama, *Sacred Journey: Living Purposefully and Dying Gracefully*, Dehradun: The Himalayan International Hospital Trust, distributed by Lotus Press. Twin Lakes, WI, 2002.

———, *Wisdom of the Ancient Sages: Mundaka Upanishad*. Honesdale, PA: The Himalayan International Institute of Yoga Science and Philosophy, 1990, pp. 28, 56, 60, 163.

———, *Path of Fire and Light, vol II: A Practical Companion to Volume I*. Honesdale, PA: The Himalayan International Institute of Yoga Science and Philosophy, 1988, pp. 83, 91, 151-78, 211.

———, *Path of Fire and Light, vol I: Advanced Practices in Yoga*. Honesdale, PA: The Himalayan International Institute of Yoga Science and Philosophy, 1986, pp. 7, 9, 33, 42, 50-51, 54, 60-61, 76, 92, 110, 122, 129-39, 143-60.

———, *Perennial Psychology of the Bhagavad Gita*. Honesdale, PA: The Himalayan International Institute of Yoga Science and Philosophy, 1985, pp. 339.

———, *Inspired Thoughts*. Honesdale, PA: The Himalayan International Institute of Yoga Science and Philosophy, 1983, pp. 211-30.

———, *Life Here and Hereafter*. Honesdale, PA: The Himalayan International Institute of Yoga Science and Philosophy, 1976.

Swami Rama, Rudolph Ballentine and Alan Hymes, *Science of Breath: A Practical Guide*. Honesdale, PA: The Himalayan International Institute of Yoga Science and Philosophy, 1979.

Swami Rama, Rudolph Ballentine and Swami Ajaya, *Yoga and Psychotherapy: The Evolution of Consciousness*. Honesdale, PA: Himalayan Publisher, 1976.

White, John (ed.), *Kundalini: Evolution and Enlightenment*. New York: Paragon House, 1990.

Woodroffe, Sir John and Sir John Arthur Avalon, *The Serpent Power* (repr.). Chennai: Ganesha & Co., 2003.

Manuscripts

A. Sayaji Rao Gaekwad Central Library, Banaras Hindu University, CN 4927.Devanagari script. d. 1930. This was our only complete manuscript containing both *śatakas*. Ostensibly a copy of MS. IX. F. 48 of the Adyar Library, Adyar Madras. (MS. no. in doubt. The photocopy of the original manuscript in Brahmi script as per their catalogue contained a text other than the *Yoga-taraṅgiṇī*.

B. MS. P3746/3 Serial. no 35103, Oriental Research Institute, University of Mysore. First *śataka* only.

C. MS. G-9094 Serial. no. 6616, Asiatic Society, Kolkata. First śataka only. Contains 98 verses, of which 1-92 are equivalent to our 1.1-1.92. Then the text switches to the second śataka. Verses 93 to 98 = our 2.96-100. These verses include the YT commentary. The text is quite incorrect and has many gaps due to damage.

D. MS. 4-85 National Archives, Kathmandu, Nepal.22 leaves.Missing 3,7,22. No date. Riddled with scribal errors. Contains only 1.92-101 of the first śataka, second śataka is complete.

E. The text included in George Weston Briggs, *Gorakhnath and the Kanphaṭa Yogis*, MLBD Reprint 1989 (1938).

VM. *Viveka-mārtaṇḍa* of Gorakṣa. MSS Central Library, Baroda Acc. No. 4110, Transcribed by James Mallinson, 2009.

Gorakṣa-śatakam. MS R No. 7874 Government Oriental Manuscripts Library (Madras), copied from R.No.2831(P). Transcribed by James Mallinson 2009.

Verse Index and Concordance

The *Gorakṣa-paddhati* has not been included as with a few exceptions, most notably the mixup of verses 58-81, the numbers follow our edition quite closely. L = Lonavla edition of *Gorakṣa-śataka*, VM = *Viveka-mārtaṇda*, HP = *Haṭha-pradīpikā*, HYP = *Haṭha-yoga-pradīpikā*, YCU = *Yoga-cūḍāmaṇi Upaniṣad*, DBU = *Dhyāna-bindu Upaniṣad*, YKU = *Yoga-kaivalya Upaniṣad*, YŚU = *Yoga-śikhā Upaniṣad.*

Variant readings have not been catalogued. In some cases fairly different readings have been accepted as equivalents.

[a]

YOGA-TARAṄGIṆĪ

YOGA-TARAṄGIṆĪ

[ka]

kaṭv-amla-lavaṇa-tyāgī kṣīra-bhojanam ācaret... 1.53b (L 50, VM 36, YCU 41, DBU 71)

kaṇṭhe syāt ṣoḍaśa-dalaṁ bhrū-madhye dvi-dalaṁ tathā... 1.16a (VM 9, YCU 6)

kathitāni navaitāni dhyāna-sthānāni yogibhiḥ... 2.76a (VM 155, HP 6.56)

kathiteyaṁ mahā-mudrā mahā-siddhi-karī nṛṇām... 1.82a (VM 62, HYP 3.18, HP 5.22, YCU 70)

kandordhve kuṇḍalī śaktir aṣṭadhā kuṇḍalākṛtiḥ... 1.47a (L 30, VM 32, HP 5.142, YCU 36)

kandordhve kuṇḍalī śaktir aṣṭadhā kuṇḍalākṛtiḥ... 1.56a (VM 39, HYP 3.107, HP 1.146, YCU 44, YŚU 6.55)

kapāla-kuhare jihvā praviṣṭā viparītagā... 1.64a (L 34, VM 47, HYP 3.32, HP 5.37. YCU 52, DBU 79)

karaṇī viparītākhyā guru-vākyena labhyate... 2.34b (L 59, VM 115, HYP 3.79, HP 5.111)

karmaṇā manasā vācā dhāraṇāḥ pañca durlabhāḥ... 2.60a (L 75, VM 140, HP 6.18)

kāka-cañcūvad-āsyena śītalaṁ salilaṁ pibet... 2.38a (VM 119, HP 5.54)

kṛkaraṁ kṣutakṛt jñeyo devadatto vijṛṁbhaṇe... 1.36b (VM 23, YCU 25)

kṛtvā saṁpuṭitau karau dṛḍhataraṁ baddhvā tu padmāsanaṁ... 1.52a (VM 35, HYP 1.48, HP 5.145, YCU 40, DBU 69)

kuṇḍalinyā samāyuktaṁ dhyātvā mucyeta kilbiṣaiḥ... 2.64b (L 78, VM 144, HP 6.29)

kuṇḍalinyā tathā yogī mokṣa-dvāraṁ prabhedayet... 1.51b (HYP 3.105, HP 5.144, YCU 39, DBU 68)

kuṇḍalinyāḥ samudbhūtā gāyatrī prāṇa-dhāriṇī... 1.46a (VM 31, HP 5.163, YCU 35)

kuṁbhayitvā vidhānena punaś candreṇa recayet... 1.98b (L 45, VM 79, HYP 2.8)

kuhūś ca liṅgadeśe tu mūla-sthāne tu śaṅkhinī... 1.31a (L 22, YCU 21)

kriyā icchā tathā jñānaṁ brāhmī raudrī ca vaiṣṇavī... 1.86a (VM 67, HP 10.10, YCU 86)

kṣaya-kuṣṭha-gudāvarta-gulmājīrṇa-purogamāḥ... 1.81a (VM 62, HYP 3.17, HP 5.20, YCU 69)

kṣīre kṣīraṁ tathā yogī tattvam eva hi jāyate... 2.96b (L 100, VM 172)

khecaryā mudritaṁ yena vivaraṁ laṁbikordhvataḥ... 1.69a (VM 51, HP 5.64. YCU 57, DBU 83)

[ga]

gaganaṁ pavane prāpte dhvanir utpadyate mahān... 2.17a (VM 98, YCU 115)

Word Index

In this index, the letter s is subdivided into three, following the order ś-ṣ-s.

Jan Brzezinski

Jan Brzezinski was born in Sheffield, England, in 1950 and emigrated to Canada in 1957.

In 1970 he became a member of the International Society for Krishna Consciousness (ISKCON), which introduced him to Sanskrit and the Indian religious tradition. He became involved in ISKCON's educational division, serving four years as the headmaster of the Gurukul at Mayapur Chandrodaya Mandir in West Bengal.

In 1979, he took sannyas in ISKCON, with the name Hiranyagarbha Swami, but left that organization soon thereafter to be initiated by Sri Lalita Prasad Thakur, son and disciple of Bhaktivinoda Thakur, in a more traditional branch of Gaudiya Vaishnavism. His guru gave him the name Jagadananda Das and told him to "bring joy to the world." This is the name by which he is most generally known. For the following six years he followed an intense regimen in the renounced tradition of *bhakti-yoga*, living mainly in Nabadwip and Vrindavan, India.

Jagadananda Das returned to Canada in 1985 and plunged into the study of comparative religion at McGill University, and then completed his Ph.D. dissertation on Jiva Goswami's *Gopāla-campū* at the School of Oriental and African Studies (University of London) in 1992.

Subsequently, he taught at the University of Manitoba and at McGill University in Montreal, but also worked as a freelance translator and editor for various clients.

In 1999, he published a scholarly translation of Rupa Goswami's *Haṁsadūta* and *Uddhava-sandeśa*. He has also published numerous articles, primarily on Vaishnava history, literature and theology.

In 2007, Jagadananda returned to India, staying at Swami Rama Sadhaka Grama in Rishikesh where he taught Sanskrit and also received training in yoga and meditation from Swami Veda Bharati, the founder and acharya of AHYMSIN and an unparalleled scholar and *sādhaka* in the Himalayan yoga tradition. He has also assisted Swami Veda in the publication of several books.

He has also been collaborating with Satya Narayan Das Babaji of the Jiva Institute in Vrindavan as an editor of a major project, namely the translation and commentary on the six *Sandarbhas* of Jiva Goswami.

Other projects that he has undertaken include the Gaudiya Grantha Mandir, an online repository of Sanskrit texts in digital format, and Vrindavan Today, an online news site for Vrindavan, the principal holy town connected to Lord Krishna, which is facing numerous crises related to development, environment and heritage preservation. He currently resides in Vrindavan, with visits to Swami Rama Sadhaka Grama.

Besides his native English, he is a fluent speaker of French, Hindi, Bangla and Sanskrit.

YOGA-TARAṄGIṆĪ

Mahamandaleshwara Dr. Swami Veda Bharati

Swami Veda Bharati was born in 1933 in a Sanskrit speaking family and given the name Usharbudh Arya. A child prodigy, he began publicly teaching the *Yoga-sūtras* of Patañjali in 1942, at the age of 9.

In 1946, a number of articles appeared in the Hindi press proclaiming his exceptional knowledge of the scriptures, especially his ability to instantly give threefold translation of any of the 20,000 mantras of the four Vedas. After this, Pandit Usharbudh Arya began to be invited to address crowds of thousands as well as colleges and universities throughout North India.

Between 1965 and 1967-68 he also obtained all his degrees: B.A. (Honours) and M.A.(London), D.Litt.(Holland). He is also a Fellow of the Royal Asiatic Society (FRAS).

In 1969 he met his yoga guru Swami Rama of Himalayas (author of *Living with Himalayan Masters*) who initiated him into the highest paths of *dhyāna-yoga*.

From 1946 to the beginning of 2013, Swami Veda spent much of his time travelling worldwide, lecturing, participating in conferences related to spirituality and giving guidance to 60 meditation groups on all continents. These groups are united under the banner of the Association of Himalayan Yoga Meditation Societies International (AHYMSIN).

Swami Veda has recorded 5000 hours of lectures on the history, philosophy and practices of meditation. These include several hundred hours of recordings of guided meditations, into which one must be initiated and need to be learnt in gradual steps, methodically.

These recordings are currently being transcribed and preserved in the form of 45,000 pages of transcripts, most of which are yet to be edited and published.

He has written 20 books including a 1500 page commentary (so far in two volumes) on the first two *pāda*s of the *Yoga-sūtras* which has been proclaimed by scholars as a highly scholarly and meticulous work. Work on the third *pāda* is now in progress.

Having varying degrees of access to 17 languages, Swami Veda teaches meditation from within the religious, spiritual and literary traditions of different world cultures from China to Africa to different parts of Europe. In each culture he teaches meditation from within that culture, for example in Italy he teaches Dante's *Il Paradiso* as a text of the experience of divine light in meditation. He is visited by masters of the Sufi orders and has 45 hours of recordings of lectures on Christian traditions of meditation.

Taking sannyas in 1992, Swami Veda holds the prestigious title of Mahamandaleshwara in the community of the Swami order of monks and is chancellor and spiritual guide of the Himalayan Institute Hospital Trust (HIHT) established by Swami Rama in Dehradun.

He is spiritual guide to two ashrams in Rishikesh: his own guru's ashram, Sadhana Mandir, and Swami Rama Sadhaka Grama (SRSG), of which is the founder, where seekers from 25 countries come to learn meditation and undergo varying periods of guided silence.

Swami Rama Sadhaka Grama, with numerous highly trained and qualified teachers, guides, sannyasis and sanyasinis, is dedicated entirely to teaching the path of meditation.

Having a keen interest in the relationship of science and meditation, Swami Veda established the Meditation Research Institute, research laboratory at SRSG where psycho-neuro-physiological responses to the different practices of meditation can be measured.

At the Meditation Research Institute the state of brain waves and other psycho-neuro-physiological parameters during (a) meditation and (b) prolonged periods of *mauna-vrata* (silence) are being recorded and analysed in data collected from those practising meditation and periods of silence.

His own brainwaves in meditation show rare phenomena not previously recorded by neurologists : 0.5 htz delta (epsilon) brain wave and 101 htz high gamma (lambda), normally associated with highest measurable stages of meditation. Those familiar with these terms will understand what a unique state Swami Veda achieves in meditation from which he guides his initiates.

In the same context, he has been the subject of several experiments in the neurology of meditation in institutions like the Institute of Noetic Sciences, California (established by astronaut Edgar Mitchell). In a unique experiment, sitting outside a Faraday Chamber, he blocked the photon beams in an interferometer, which was inside the chamber, nine times in a row, proving the power of the volition of consciousness over material energies. The results of this experiment have been published in the scientific press.

On Shivaratri, March 10, 2013, at the age of 81, Swami Veda entered a five year vow of silence (*mauna-vrata*).

For further information please inquire from Association Of Himalayan Yoga Meditation Societies International (AHYMSIN) at http://www.ahymsin.org.

Among Swamiji's academic publications, see:

(1) "Consciousness: Measurable or Immeasurable?" in *Spirituality and Science of Consciousness: Papers read at an International Seminar held at the Ramakrishna Mission Institute of Culture,* Kolkatta, 2010. Published by Ramakrishna Mission Institute of Culture, Kolkatta. January 2011, pp. 116-141 and 411-414.

(2) "Shanti: An Indian Perspective" in *The Palgrave International Handbook of Peace Studies: A Cultural Perspective*, edited by Wolfgang Dietrich and others. Published by UNESCO Chair of Peace studies (University of Innsbruck, Austria) and Palgrave Macmillan, London and New York, 2011. 191-228.

(3) *Commentary on Yoga-sūtras of Patañjali*, First Two Padas. Volume 1 first published in 1986, a revised edition awaiting publication; and Volume 2, New Delhi: MLBD Publishers, 2000.

(4) *Song of the Lord: Bhagavad-gītā in Yoga-vāsiṣṭha.* Delhi: D.K. Printworld, 2013. This contains the dialogue of Krishna and Arjuna as found in *Yoga-vāsiṣṭha*.

A list of his inspirational and spiritual works maybe obtained from

ahymsinpublishers@gmail.com
www.ahymsin.org
www.swamiveda.org
www.swamivedablog.org

Books of related interest :

Gorakhnath and the Kanphata Yogis — GEORGE W. BRIGGS

Philosophy of Gorakhnath : With Goraksha-Vachana-Sangraha — AKSHAYA KUMAR BANERJEA

The Yoga Sutras of Patanajali
(A Study Guide for Book I Samadhi Pada)
— Translation & Commentary by BABA HARI DASS, Edited with an Introduction by DAYANAND DIFFENBAUGH

The Yoga Sutras of Patanjali — SWAMI VENKATESANAND

The Yoga Sutras of Patanjali or Concentration of Mind —FERNANDO TOLA & CARMEN DRAGONETTI, Translated by K.D PRITHIPAUL

Yogasutra of Patanjali : With the Commentary of Vyasa — Translated from Sanskrit into English with Notes by BANGALI BABA

Yoga-System of Patanjali or the Ancient Hindu Doctrine of Concentration of Mind
— Translated by J.H. WOODS

Yoga Stura of Patanjali with the Exposition of Vyasa
(Vol. II : Sadhana-Pada)
— Translation & Commentary by VEDA BHARATI

HINDU TRADITION SERIES

The Hindu Tradition Series aims to bring together books of the highest academic standard that critically interrogate Hindu tradition in the widest sense. Its focus is on cultural and religious history, including relevant political and social developments. The interaction with other traditions, whether originally from inside or outside the Indian subcontinent, will figure prominently among its volumes.

1. **The Mahābhārata and Greek Mythology** — FERNANDO WULFF ALONSO [978-81-208-3791-1]

2. **Viraha-Bhakti :** The Early History of Kṛṣṇa Devotion — FRIEDHELM HARDY [978-81-208-3616-1]

3. **Classical Hindu Mythology :** A Reader in the Sanskrit Purāṇas — Ed. and Tr. by CORNELLA DIMMITT and J.A.B. VAN BUTTENAN [978-81-208-3972-4]

4. **Mythology of Brahma** — GREG BAILEY

ANCIENT INDIAN TRADITION AND MYTHOLOGY

Mahapuranas

Translated into English

General Editor

DR. G.C. TRIPATHI

Founder Editors

Late J.L. SHASTRI and G.P. BHATT

PUBLISHED VOLUMES

Vols. 1-4 SIVA PURANA Tr. *J.L. Shastri*

Vols. 5-6 LINGA PURANA Tr. *J.L. Shastri*

Vols. 7-11 BHAGAVATA PURANA Tr. *G.V. Tagare*

Vols. 12-14 GARUDA PURANA Tr. *J.L. Shastri*

Vols. 15-19 NARADA PURANA Tr. *G.V. Tagare*

Vols. 20-21 KURMA PURANA Tr. *G.V. Tagare*

Vols. 22-26 BRAHMANDA PURANA Tr. *G.V. Tagare*

Vols. 27-30 AGNI PURANA Tr. *N. Gangadharan*

Vols. 31-32 VARAHA PURANA Tr. *S. Venkitasubramonia Iyer*

Vols. 33-36 BRAHMA PURANA Tr. *J.L. Shastri*

Vols. 37-38 VAYU PURANA Tr. *G.V. Tagare*

Vols. 39-48 PADMA PURANA Tr. *N.A. Deshpande*

Vols. 49-71 SKANDA PURANA Ed. *G.P. Bhatt*, Tr. & Annot *Shridhar Balooni & Pratosh Panda*

Vol. 72-73 VAMANA PURANA (Pt. I) Tr. & Annot. *R.S. Shiva Ganesha Murthy*

Vol. 74-75 GANESA PURANA (Pt. I : Upasana-Khanda) Tr. & Annot. *Greg Bailey*